böhlau

exil.arte-**Schriften** Band 3

Für exil.arte

herausgegeben von Gerold Gruber

The Impact of Nazism on Twentieth-Century Music

Edited by Erik Levi

2014

BÖHLAU VERLAG WIEN KÖLN WEIMAR

Gedruckt mit freundlicher Unterstützung durch
Jewish Music Institute SOAS University of London
Kulturamt der Stadt Wien – MA 7
Nationalfonds der Republik Österreich
Zukunftsfonds der Republik Österreich
International Centre for Suppressed Music

Bibliografische Information der Deutschen Nationalbibliothek:
Die Deutsche Nationalbibliothek verzeichnet diese Publikation in der
Deutschen Nationalbibliografie; detaillierte bibliografische Daten
sind im Internet über http://dnb.d-nb.de abrufbar.

Coverabbildung: *Composition 26* © Joanne Levi

© 2014 by Böhlau Verlag Ges.m.b.H & Co. KG, Wien Köln Weimar
Wiesingerstraße 1, A-1010 Wien, www.boehlau-verlag.com

Umschlaggestaltung: Michael Haderer, Wien
Satz: Bettina Waringer
Druck und Bindung: General Nyomda Kft., Szeged
Gedruckt auf chlor- und säurefreiem Papier
Printed in Hungaria

ISBN 978-3-205-79543-8

Inhalt

Erik Levi

Introduction

The International Conference entitled 'The Impact of Nazism on Twentieth-Century Music' took place in April 2008 at the University of London's Senate House. It was organised by the International Centre for Suppressed Music (ICSM), which operates under the auspices of the Jewish Music Institute (JMI) at the School of Oriental and African Studies, University of London, and was arranged in partnership with the Institute for Musical Research at London University's School of Advanced Study. The Conference also featured some marvellous concerts given by the outstanding ARC chamber ensemble from the Royal Conservatoire of Music, Toronto.

When I was asked by the ICSM to convene this Conference, alongside my distinguished colleague Michael Haas, I did not anticipate the avalanche of proposals from all corners of the globe that followed our call for papers. Both Michael and I were absolutely overwhelmed by the wealth of fascinating topics that emerged from this process. Indeed, although we had set aside four days for the Conference, it was agonisingly difficult to make decisions as to which papers best suited our purposes. In the end, we opted for as diverse a programme as possible, and it's this diversity which is fully represented here in the selection of papers that are featured in the current publication.

Normally an introduction of this nature attempts to draw threads, continuities and connections between the various chapters. It seems pointless to embark on such a task here since this puts an artificial straitjacket on the book where one is not required. Rather, I would prefer to draw your attention to contemplating how interest in the topic of Nazism and music has mushroomed since the pioneering books by Joseph Wulff (1963) and Fred Prieberg (1982) were published. The range of enquiry featured here is huge and highlights many areas, such as the relationship between music in Franco's Spain and Nazi Germany, which to my knowledge has not attracted scholarly attention to the same extent in other publications.

There are many people that warrant acknowledgement for generously helping me to put together this book. In particular, I should like to thank Geraldine Auerbach, former director of the Jewish Music Institute, and Simon Wynberg, Artistic Director of the Royal Conservatoire of Music Toronto, for having the foresight to set up the Conference to coincide with a visit from the Canadians to perform at London's Cadogan Hall. I am also grateful to JMI for providing funds which have facilitated the publication of this book. Special thanks are due to my colleagues on the Conference Committee of ICSM, Michael Haas, Peter Tregear and

Malcolm Miller, for having helped to choose the papers, to run the conference, scrutinise the papers for publication and offer many constructive comments along the way. Likewise, I want to thank all contributors for their patience in enabling me to edit their chapters and especially to Eva Hagan and Alyssa Rodriguez for their sterling work in proofreading the typescript. Finally, I am especially indebted to Professor Gerold Gruber, director of our European Partner organisation ExilArte at the University of Vienna, who generously suggested that this book could form one of the first publications to be issued in their prestigious ExilArte series.

Albrecht Dümling

What is Internal Exile in Music?

The Cases of Walter Braunfels, Heinz Tiessen, Eduard Erdmann and Philipp Jarnach

Historians tend to contrast the immensely rich musical life of the Weimar Republic with a much more restricted and reduced landscape that existed under the Nazis. They describe the gaping hole in European culture created by the loss of a great number of talented musicians that had to leave their country.[1] Yet despite these losses, the majority of German musicians had a rather different experience. For them, Hitler's coming to power offered new opportunities and fulfilled some of their old dreams. The idea of a central organization of all German musicians, a music chamber, was one such dream. Men like Richard Strauss, Max von Schillings and Fritz Stein had mentioned it again and again in the meetings of the Allgemeiner Deutscher Musikverein over a number of years.[2] After Hitler's appointment as German chancellor, it took only a few months before a Reich's Music Chamber was established in November 1933. Richard Strauss was named its president, and Wilhelm Furtwängler his deputy. These experienced men soon discovered that music would receive much more state support than under any former German government.[3]

---

1 See, for example, Joseph W. Bendersky, *A History of Nazi Germany* (Lanham: Rowman & Littlefield, 2000), 144.

2 Already in 1912, the ADMV had published a brochure dedicated to that topic entitled *Materialien zur Gründung einer Zentralstelle für die Wahrnehmung der gemeinsamen Interessen aller Musiker (Musikerkammer). Stenographische Aufzeichnung über die am 27. September 1912 im Architektenhause zu Berlin abgehaltene Konferenz von Delegierten musikalischer Fachverbände* (Berlin: Allgemeiner Deutscher Musikverein, 1912). Also see Wilhelm Klatte, 'Allgemeiner Deutscher Musikverein: zur Frage der "Musikerkammer"', *Der Reichsbote*, Berlin 1915. Several lectures were given on the need for a *Musikkammer* also during the *Tonkünstlerversammlungen* of 1926 in Chemnitz and 1929 in Duisburg. See Nina Okrassa, *Peter Raabe: Dirigent, Musikschriftsteller und Präsident der Reichsmusikkammer (1872–1945)* (Köln – Weimar – Wien: Böhlau, 2004), 190–95, and Thomas Radecke, 'Von der Musikerkammer zur Reichsmusikkammer: der ADMV und das historische Mißverständnis des Peter Raabe', in *Musik–Politik–Ästhetik: Detlef Altenburg zum 65. Geburtstag*, ed. Axel Schröter and Daniel Ortuño-Stühring (Sinzig: StudioVerlag, 2012), 321–43.

3 Until 1933, all culture had been the concern of the single German *Laender* rather than the State.

One flagship institution that particularly benefited from the increased state subsidy for music after 1933 was the Berlin Philharmonic Orchestra. In the early 1930s, it had been in a desperate situation, with financial problems becoming more acute every year. Yet neither the German state nor the city of Berlin was able to provide the orchestra with the necessary finances to ensure its future stability. After the Nazis came to power, the orchestra's principal conductor, Wilhelm Furtwängler, sought to alleviate this situation in April 1933 by establishing direct contact with Joseph Goebbels in the hope of enlisting the support of the Minister for Popular Enlightenment and Propaganda for a financial rescue plan. Fortunately, Goebbels realised how important it was for the new regime not to allow such a venerable musical institution to flounder. So he seized the opportunity to sponsor the orchestra—a tactic which fully accorded with Hitler's promise that his coming to power would coincide with a cultural revolution in which music was to be regarded as the most German of the arts. Thus supported by the Third Reich, the Berlin Philharmonic Orchestra became a Reich's Orchestra, and at least economically was in a safe haven.[4]

One could also mention the situation of the Performing Rights organisations, which had been deeply divided before 1933. There had been ongoing disputes between the societies representing the so-called serious composers on one side (Genossenschaft Deutscher Tonsetzer, or GDT), and those representing the entertainment industry (Gesellschaft für musikalische Aufführungsrechte, or GEMA) on the other. Goebbels decided that the rival organisations had to be united. Serious composers like Richard Strauss, in the newly established STAGMA (Staatlich genehmigte Gesellschaft zur Verwertung musikalischer Urheberrechte), now regained the executive power, which they had lost in the years before.[5] It is therefore hardly surprising that Strauss welcomed the new government with open arms.

A majority of the German musicians in those years shared similar experiences to those of Strauss, Furtwängler, and the Berlin Philharmonic Orchestra.[6] This explains why so many voluntarily joined the Nazi Party. In fact the evidence presented in Fred K. Prieberg's monumental database *Handbuch Deutsche Musiker 1933–1945* suggests that party membership then was rather normal among musicians.[7] Yet after 1945, the commissions responsible for de-

---

4   Misha Aster, *Das Reichsorchester. Die Berliner Philharmoniker und der Nationalsozialismus* (Berlin: Siedler 2007), 43–47.

5   Albrecht Dümling, *Musik hat ihren Wert. 100 Jahre musikalische Verwertungsgesellschaft in Deutschland* (Regensburg: Con Brio, 2003), 178.

6   For example, see the rising number of contracts in German theatres mentioned in Erik Levi, *Music in the Third Reich* (New York: Macmillan, 1994), 181.

7   Fred K. Prieberg, 'NSDAP Musiker; Parteinummern und Daten', in *Handbuch Deutsche Musiker 1933–1945*, CD-ROM 9941-9987. Also http://www.fred-prieberg.de/mediapool/21/215679/data/Handbuch-Gratis.pdf. Prieberg's list includes 2174 musicians who joined the Party.

Nazification soon realized that party membership alone would not qualify someone as being regarded as a card-carrying Nazi supporter.[8]

On the other hand, far too many Germans claimed to have been victims or even members of the resistance. Inevitably it proved extremely difficult for them to substantiate such arguments in the aftermath of the Second World War. Furthermore, there was a bitter dispute between artists who had fled Germany and those who had remained in the country, between refugees on the one side and non-refugees on the other. The first group tended to regard members of the second – like Furtwängler or Strauss – as supporters of the regime. Researchers who work on refugees often share this critical view. A good example is the Weill scholar, Kim Kowalke, who presents a rather negative attitude towards Weill's teacher and colleague, Philipp Jarnach, presumably as a result of his decision to remain in Germany after 1933.[9]

At the same time, a number of artists that had chosen not to leave their home-country quite frequently suggested that they had actually suffered more under the dictatorship, not least from being under constant threat of bombardment during the war. They believed this to be a far more bitter fate than that of the refugees whom they regarded, however misleadingly, as having enjoyed the good fortune to lead a secure existence on a distant shore. Furthermore, they claimed to have surveyed Hitler and his cultural policies from a critical distance whilst living in Germany in a state of *Innere Emigration* (internal exile). The writers Werner Bergengruen, Ricarda Huch, Erich Kästner, Reinhold Schneider and Ernst Wiechert, or the artists Ernst Barlach, Otto Dix and Oskar Schlemmer could justifiably present themselves in this way. Such figures discovered at quite an early stage that the generous state support for the arts offered by the Nazis came with a heavy price and was inevitably connected with restrictions and growing control.[10]

At this juncture, one should note that the English- and German-speaking worlds hold somewhat different notions of *Innere Emigration*. In English articles, this label mostly describes forced special settlement.[11] However, in German-speaking countries, the terms 'In-

---

8   Toby Thacker, *Music after Hitler, 1945–55* (Aldershot: Ashgate, 2007), 39–74.

9   Kim H. Kowalke, 'Hin und zurück: Kurt Weill heute', in *Vom Kurfürstendamm zum Broadway. Kurt Weill (1900–1950)*, ed. Bernd. Kortländer, Winrich Meiszies and David Farneth (Düsseldorf: Droste Verlag, 1990), 17.

10   Other figures associated with Internal Exile, such as the writers Gottfried Benn and Ernst Jünger, at least initially supported Hitler and his government.

11   For example, the Wikipedia entry entitled 'Exiles' states: 'It is common to distinguish between *internal exile*, i.e., forced resettlement within the country of residence, and *external exile*, deportation outside the country of residence.' A more sophisticated exploration of this topic with specific reference to music can be found in Lydia Goehr, 'Music and Musicians in Exile. The Romantic Legacy of a Double Life', in *Driven into Paradise. The musical migration from Nazi Germany to the United States*, ed. Reinhold Brinkmann and Christoph Wolff (Berkeley: University of California Press 1999), 69–85.

ternal Exile' or 'Inner Migration' are understood as a self-imposed isolation of an artist who otherwise remained in his home country. In this sense, such a concept is widely accepted in studies of German literature.[12] In music history, however, it still remains a rather unexplored category—with one notable exception: Karl Amadeus Hartmann.[13] Already in 1933, Hartmann, a socialist non-Jew, had quoted a Jewish folksong in his first string quartet.[14] The composer explained this citation as a manifestation of his personal protest against the anti-Semitism of the time. An orchestral work entitled *Miserae*, also composed during the same period, focussed on the persecution of social democrats and communists, as Hartmann dedicated this composition to the victims of the Dachau concentration camp.

Yet despite Hartmann's defiant position, the Nazis never imposed an official ban on his music. It was the composer who refused to allow any of his works to be performed in his home country.[15] His boycott of German concert halls was possible since only one of his compositions had been published. All the other works existed only as manuscripts, thus enabling the composer to exert complete control over their dissemination. Furthermore, unlike Hindemith, Nazi officials did not regard Hartmann as an important enough figure to be proscribed. Although he was asked not to leave Germany without official permission from the Reichs Chamber of Music, he simply ignored this advice. In fact, he travelled abroad quite frequently assisting performances of his works in Switzerland, Prague or London. It was Hartmann himself who drove his music into exile.

In his biography of Hartmann, Andrew McCredie used the term 'Internal Exile' in connection with the composer. Yet he failed to explain his reasoning for this definition. One may well speculate as to whether this term, already used by Thomas Mann in 1933, is only valid for the first years after Hitler's coming to power, as Ludwig Holtmeier suggests.[16] Indeed, can it also be applied to Paul Hindemith, who until 1937 remained a professor at the Berlin State Academy of Music (Hochschule für Musik), while his works were not allowed to be

12   Reinhold Grimm, 'Innere Emigration als Lebensform', in *Exil und Innere Emigration: Third Wisconsin Workshop,* ed. Reinhold Grimm and Jost Hermand (Frankfurt: Athenaum Verlag, 1972), 31–74; see also Ralf Schnell, *Literarische Innere Emigration 1933–1945* (Stuttgart: Metzler, 1976).

13   Andrew McCredie, *Karl Amadeus Hartmann. Sein Leben und Werk* (Wilhelmshaven: Heinrichshofen, 1980), 53–64.

14   McCredie, 34.

15   A single exception was his music for *Macbeth*, written in 1942 for the Residenztheater München. See. Prieberg, 2682. See Marie-Therese Hommes, *Verkettungen und Querstände. Weberns Schüler Karl Amadeus Hartmann und Ludwig Zenk und die politischen Implikationen ihres kompositorischen Handelns vor und nach 1945* (Schliengen: Argus, 2010), 21–84.

16   Ludwig Holtmeier, 'Peter Schacht und das Projekt der "Inneren Emigration"', in *Arnold Schönbergs „Berliner Schule",* ed. Heinz-Klaus Metzger and Rainer Riehn (Munich: Edition Text u. Kritik, 2002), 88.

performed in Germany? This argument seems problematic, particularly since Hindemith, unlike Hartmann, tried very hard to secure German performances of his works, but with little success.

Hartmann was perhaps a unique case since the majority of his works had not yet been published. At the same time, there are other slightly older composers who were similarly distanced from the Nazi regime that could be regarded as representatives of a kind of 'Inner Emigration'. I am thinking here particularly of such figures as Walter Braunfels, Heinz Tiessen, Eduard Erdmann and Philipp Jarnach. These composers are rarely ever mentioned in music histories of the Thirties, and still today seem to be rather overlooked. Yet before 1933, they had been key figures in the musical life of the country.

Walter Braunfels, the son of a Jewish father and a Christian mother, studied in his home-town of Frankfurt, as well as in Vienna and in Munich. He enjoyed great success with or-chestral works and with operas like *Die Vögel* (The Birds, 1919). During the First World War, he served in the German Army and was wounded in February 1918. The horrors of war had a profound impact on his outlook, causing him to experience some kind of religious awak-ening. As a consequence, he converted to Catholicism and composed sacred works like a *Te Deum*, which created a sensation when in 1922 it was performed in Cologne. In 1925, a State Academy of Music was founded in that city—the second State Academy of Music after Berlin. Braunfels was chosen by Leo Kestenberg, advisor for music policy in the Prussian Ministry for Science, Art and Education,[17] and Konrad Adenauer, the young mayor of the city of Cologne that until 1945 belonged to Prussia, as one of its two directors, along with the conductor Hermann Abendroth, a friend from his early years. This appointment proved propitious since Braunfels was already well known in Cologne, following the success of his *Te Deum,* and was also equally admired as a fine pianist. As a composer, he was not a modernist, but *'zeitlos unzeitgemäß'*, as Alfred Einstein in September 1931 famously characterized him.

More courageous than Braunfels were Heinz Tiessen and his pupil, Eduard Erdmann. Born in 1887 in the East Prussian city of Königsberg (now part of Russia), Tiessen in 1905 had settled in the German capital to study law and music. In his early compositions he was influ-enced by Richard Strauss, as can be recognized from such works as his 1914 Septet in which the melodic figures are derived from bird songs, especially those of blackbirds. As an open-minded artist, Tiessen soon discovered the new works of Arnold Schoenberg, Igor Stravinsky and Paul Hindemith, and supported their musical innovations. As a result of the exposure given to his symphonies and theatre music, Tiessen became one of the leading composers

---

17 Leo Kestenberg, *Bewegte Zeiten* (Wolfenbüttel: Möseler, 1961), 54. For more information on Kesten-berg see *Leo Kestenberg. Musikpädagoge und Musikpolitiker in Berlin, Prag und Tel Aviv*, ed. Susanne Fontaine, Ulrich Mahlert, Dietmar Schenk and Theda Weber-Lucks (Freiburg: Rombach, 2008).

of the German musical expressionism—a position emphasised by the critic H.H. Stuckenschmidt:

> Tiessen's work mirrors the development of German music from the turn of the century to the Expressionism of the inter-war years. […] He came to epitomize the tonality crisis in a highly individual way while also exemplifying a harmonically free linear polyphony.[18]

When in 1922 the German Section of the International Society for Contemporary Music was founded in Berlin, Tiessen belonged to its first board of directors. One of the main aims of that society was to overcome the former nationalism that had blighted Europe. Another was to bring composers and musicians from different countries together.[19] Tiessen shared these ideals with Leo Kestenberg, who in turn was influenced by his teacher, Ferruccio Busoni. The Tiessen Archives at the Academy of the Arts Berlin house a letter written by Kestenberg in September 1916 reflecting his deep admiration for Tiessen's music, and which he regarded as among the most interesting and progressive of the time. In the same letter, Kestenberg mentioned the war as the terrible enemy of all goodwill.[20]

In 1925, Tiessen was appointed a professor for composition at the Berlin State Academy of Music where he taught an international group of students including Josef Tal, Erik Bergman from Finland and Sergiu Celebidache from Romania. Tiessen was especially proud of Eduard Erdmann, whom he praised as his most universal and original student.[21] Erdmann, born in 1896 into a Baltic German family, had moved to Berlin in 1914, where Tiessen became his teacher. Since Walter Braunfels also appreciated Erdmann's qualities as well, he appointed him professor of piano at his new State Academy in Cologne in 1925.[22]

Philipp Jarnach, the second well-known musician who also moved from Berlin to Cologne, was a cosmopolitan, like Busoni and Kestenberg. This son of a Spanish father and a Flemish mother started his musical studies in Paris, where he met Debussy and Ravel. About the same time, Jarnach discovered his love for German culture and married a German musician. As a Spaniard with a German wife, he decided to go to Zurich during the First World War. The

18   H. H. Stuckenschmidt, 'Heinz Tiessen – der Freund', in *Für Heinz Tiessen 1887–1971, Aufsätze – Analysen – Briefe – Erinnerungen – Dokumente – Werkverzeichnis – Bibliographie,* ed. Manfred Schlösser (Berlin: Akademie der Künste 1979), 10.

19   Christof Bitter and Manfred Schlösser, *Begegnungen mit Eduard Erdmann* (Darmstadt: Agora, 1968), 47.

20   Letter of 21 September 1916. Tiessen Archives, No. 831.

21   Bitter and Schlösser, 26.

22   Ernst Krenek, *Im Atem der Zeit. Erinnerungen an die Moderne* (Hamburg: Hoffmann und Campe, 1998), 598.

young musician regarded this Swiss city to be the spiritual capital of Europe at that time. It was there that he met James Joyce, Jakob Wassermann, Hermann Hesse and the composers, Braunfels and Stravinsky. But the greatest influence on him was Ferruccio Busoni, Jarnach's venerated colleague, who became a friend. When the Prussian Academy in Berlin appointed Busoni as director of a master class for composition, Jarnach followed him to the German capital in 1921. Like Busoni, Jarnach was also sought after as a teacher; Kurt Weill, Wilhelm Maler and Nikos Skalkottas were among his pupils. His compositions achieved considerable success at avant-garde festivals during this period. Together with Tiessen, Jarnach directed the innovative Melos concerts, belonged to the revolutionary Novembergruppe, and was a co-founder of the German section of the ISCM.[23] When Busoni died in 1924, Jarnach supported Kestenberg's idea of choosing Arnold Schoenberg as his successor at the Prussian Academy.

In 1927, Jarnach was appointed professor at the State Academy of Music in Cologne. At just 35 years of age, he was, together with Paul Hindemith, Germany's youngest professor of composition. As head of one of the two classes for composition—the other one directed by Braunfels—Jarnach proved to be a very successful teacher. Among his pupils in Cologne were the conductor Günter Wand and the composers Jürg Baur and Bernd Alois Zimmermann. In 1931, Jarnach applied for German citizenship on the basis that having lived long enough in the country, he believed himself not to be a foreigner any more. One year later, he received the necessary documents—about the same time as his colleague Eduard Erdmann also became a German citizen. For both musicians, taking such a step in 1933, with the Nazis' rise to power, would have been rather unlikely.

Becoming a member of the Prussian Academy of the Arts was one significant way of dem-onstrating a musician's prominence. Braunfels had been granted this honour already in 1921, whilst Tiessen became a member in 1930. But also Jarnach and Erdmann—though not Acad-emy members—were among the best-known composers of the Weimar Republic. Whilst Jarnach later avoided mentioning his membership of the Novembergruppe, no other com-poser secured more performances in their concerts than him.[24] Also Jarnach ranked promi-nently in other concerts. According to Martin Thrun, who researched German concert life between 1918 and 1933, Jarnach was in the fifth place among the most-performed contem-porary composers, directly behind Busoni, Béla Bartók, Arnold Schoenberg and Paul Hin-demith.[25] Thrun demonstrates that his work was featured more prominently than that of Krenek, Berg, Webern, Milhaud, Ravel and Stravinsky.

---

23   Stefan Weiss, *Die Musik Philipp Jarnachs* (Cologne: Dohr, 1996), 143.
24   Weiss, 144.
25   Martin Thrun, *Neue Musik im deutschen Musikleben bis 1933* (Bonn: Orpheus, 1995), 580. Cited in Weiss, 9.

In 1932, the situation for many musicians changed. Leo Kestenberg, for example, lost his influential position, forced out by the Papen government. One year later, Tiessen also faced increasing difficulties, as he later recalled in his autobiography: 'The year 1933 brought for me not only a provisional end of my creative work; it also meant a crisis in my life.'[26] Although not Jewish, Tiessen abhorred National Socialism. Since he had been closely linked with Kestenberg and the Social Democratic Party, his position at the State Academy of Music was in danger. Fritz Stein, the new director charged with rooting out politically and racially undesirable teaching staff, asked his colleagues what to do with Tiessen. However, because Hindemith spoke powerfully in his defence, Stein decided to leave Tiessen in his position, but with a rather small salary.[27] Yet at the same time, Tiessen's music was no longer performed. As a consequence, the composer's income from his performing rights went down to almost nothing. Already in 1933, he received only 1 per cent of his earlier income.[28] As he commented in 1962, 'these setbacks brought financial problems, but were of no importance compared to the negative effect of the political events of the day on my soul. In the first place, I suffered hearing about the fate of so many Jews, who were close to me.'[29]

Because of his Jewish father, Walter Braunfels now was labelled a 'half-Jew' and in 1934– like Schoenberg and Schreker—lost his membership of the Prussian Academy.[30] Despite laws that supposedly protected war veterans, Braunfels' military service as a German soldier in the First World War did not help his case.[31] In March 1934, Braunfels also was dismissed as professor of composition and as co-director of the State Academy of Music in Cologne. Furthermore, despite the conservative nature of his music, the atmosphere in Germany, mixed with a mood of terror and anxiety, was such that no musician or concert organiser dared to put a work of a Jew or even a so-called 'half-Jew' like Braunfels on a concert programme.[32]

Although neither Jewish nor politically active, Eduard Erdmann was not dismissed. Yet as a modernist like Tiessen, he felt deeply isolated and his compositions were no longer performed. In 1934, Erdmann lost a potentially powerful ally when his colleague Hermann Abendroth was forced out of the State Academy of Music by the local leader of the Nazi party,

26 Heinz Tiessen, *Wege eines Komponisten* (Berlin: Akademie der Künste, 1962), 56.
27 Bitter and Schlösser, 55.
28 Tiessen, 56.
29 Tiessen, 57.
30 *Lexikon der Juden in der Musik*, ed. Herbert Gerigk and Theophil Stengel (Berlin: Hahnefeld, 1940), 39.
31 Joseph Wulf, *Musik im Dritten Reich. Eine Dokumentation* (Gütersloh: Mohn, 1963), 52.
32 Okrassa, 208. One of the earliest manifestations of the ban on Braunfels's music took place in June 1933 at the 63rd ADMV Festival in Dortmund where his recently completed orchestral composition was removed from the programme, as happened also to works by Webern and Peter Schacht.

after being condemned in particular for his close collaboration with Braunfels and other Jewish artists.[33] Abendroth's students and colleagues at the Academy protested, among them two professors. When those professors were beaten up by Nazi Storm troopers, Erdmann decided to give up his secure position.[34] In 1935, he left Cologne and settled permanently in his summer house next to the Baltic Sea. Given the importance of composing for Erdmann, it is all the more remarkable that during the Third Reich, he stopped creating new works (with one single exception, his String Quartet op. 17). Instead, he earned a living by touring as a pianist throughout Europe. In spring 1938, Erdmann appeared in Amsterdam, where his friend Ernst Krenek stayed at the same hotel. Since Krenek, the composer of *Jonny spielt auf*, had been attacked by the Nazis as a 'degenerate' composer, it was dangerous for Erdmann to meet him. They decided, as Krenek wrote, not to meet in public, but secretly in a hotel room.[35]

Philipp Jarnach, as a non-Jewish German citizen—but labelled a Cultural Bolshevist—was in a comparable situation. He lost all his former honorary positions in the Allgemeiner Deutscher Musikverein and the ISCM, but not his position as a professor at the Cologne Academy. Like Tiessen and Hartmann, his music was no longer performed—at least not in the first years of the Third Reich—and he was also deprived of teaching any Jewish pupils like Werner Wolf Glaser who emigrated to Sweden

One might ask why Walter Braunfels, Eduard Erdmann, Philipp Jarnach and Heinz Tiessen did not follow Glaser's example and emigrate? But it was an enormous undertaking to leave a country where one had spent almost all of one's life. Huge taxes also had to be paid before leaving the country. Besides, many countries only accepted refugees with enough financial securities. Karl Amadeus Hartmann, as his wife explained, could not have made a living, for example, in France. As a composer, he was too young and unknown to get performances there. In addition, Hartmann had to support his brother who had been placed under constant surveillance by the Gestapo, and was then forced to flee to Switzerland. So he decided to stay in Germany where his wealthy father-in-law supported him.

For a while, Walter Braunfels had also considered leaving Germany. He later explained why he remained, and defended his decision to remain there with views similar to those of Wilhelm Furtwängler:

First of all, I believed that through my existence, I was a stone in the dam that had to be reinforced against the evil spirit that threatened to destroy everything; but also I had the feeling that by leaving my home country, I would lose the most important root of my

---

33   Prieberg, 40.
34   Bitter and Schlösser, 56.
35   Bitter and Schlösser, 83.

creativity […] This decision was truly rewarded; I had years of lucky concentration. My creativity was reborn.[36]

Being married to a wife recognized as 'Aryan', a so-called 'privileged mixed marriage', also gave him some protection at least until autumn 1944. The family first moved from Cologne to the small city of Bad Godesberg, and later to a village at Lake Constance. In 1938, Braunfels lost his membership of the Reich Chamber of Music, thus making it legally impossible for him to perform in public. He lived a quiet and secluded life next to the Swiss border. But the defamation of his personality continued. In 1941, for example, his former colleague Hermann Unger singled out Braunfels for particular condemnation in an article entitled 'Jews in the Musical Life of Cologne'. At issue was the fact that after his appointment as Director of the Cologne Academy, Braunfels 'had hired quite an army of Jewish teachers and, supported by Jewish spies, had fought an ardent campaign against all those people he thought would belong to the movement of Adolf Hitler.'[37]

Heinz Tiessen, like Paul Hindemith, retained his position as a professor at the Berlin State Academy of Music. Thanks to the support of Max von Schillings and Georg Schumann, he also retained his membership at the Prussian Academy.[38] But his works, like those of Hindemith, were no longer performed. The authorities remembered that during the Weimar Republic, Tiessen had conducted socialist choirs and was a leading member of the Novembergruppe.[39] Not surprisingly, in 1935, Tiessen's name figured on a list of so-called Cultural Bolshevists compiled by the NS Kulturgemeinde.[40] Reflecting on his situation during the Third Reich, the composer in 1963 explained: 'In order to stay alive, I had to simulate being dead.'[41] He was forced to appear as unobtrusive as possible. Anneliese Schier, who at the time studied at the Berlin State Academy with him, recalled that:

> Tiessen was assigned to room 43, a tiny room with a bad piano. He would sit in front of the piano, absorbed, intensive and silent, and demonstrate the wonders of chordal modulation in the great masterworks, especially those by Schubert. I was very surprised when later I learned that this refined and silent man once had written revolutionary, dissonant and even brutal music […] The students at the Academy did not know about this creative output since from

36   Ute Jung, *Walter Braunfels (1882–1954)* (Regensburg; Bosse, 1980), 289.
37   Hermann Unger, 'Judentum im Musikleben Kölns', *Westdeutscher Beobachter*, 30 May 1941.
38   Correspondence with Fritz Stein. Letter of 17.December, 1954. Tiessen Archives No. 1147.
39   Okrassa, 284. Also see Nils Grosch, *Musik der Neuen Sachlichkeit* (Stuttgart: Metzler, 1999), 21.
40   Eckhard John, *Musikbolschewismus. Die Politisierung der Musik in Deutschland 1918–1938* (Stuttgart – Weimar: Metzler, 1993), 358.
41   Prieberg, 7194.

1933 onwards, Tiessen was totally forgotten as a composer. Our lessons at the Academy then normally ended with Brahms or perhaps Reger. Surrounded by bombs and military personnel, we lived in an island of music, guided by Tiessen, our universally educated mentor. Only after the war, when I married him, did I discover that Tiessen was a composer.[42]

Because of his poor financial circumstances, Tiessen had to take out a loan and even use his piano as collateral.[43] This problem was slightly ameliorated when his former pupil Heinz Drewes became head of music in the Ministry of Propaganda. For instance, Drewes invited Tiessen to become a member of the jury for the Reichsmusiktage 1939 at Düsseldorf where, as a rare event, one of his compositions was played.[44] But still his income from concerts was extremely low. In the season 1942/43, it was limited to 236 RM. Yet with the help of Drewes, the composer finally got some state support.[45] Fritz Stein followed suit in 1943 by supporting his advancement to become a fully salaried professor.

Like Tiessen, Philipp Jarnach also chose the strategy of remaining unobtrusive, as his biographer Stefan Weiss described it.[46] Yet this position was not always fully appreciated, as is evident from the article on the composer by Hans Ferdinand Redlich, which appeared in the fifth edition of *Grove's Dictionary of Music and Musicians*, published in 1954:

> The strange fact should be recorded that this French-born half-Spaniard decided to stay on in a Germany which many of the finest native artists and scholars were only too anxious to leave. Jarnach remained at his post in Cologne, apparently unmolested, during that country's political upheaval right up to 1949.[47]

Likewise, in her book on Busoni's composition class in Berlin, Tamara Levitz alluded to a rather obtuse relationship between Jarnach and the new regime: 'Characteristically, Jarnach left no trace of his activities between 1933 and 1945 [...] his *Nachlaß* is strikingly incomplete in this respect.'[48] One gets the impression here of potentially dark points in Jarnach's life

---

42 Quoted from Christoph Schlüren, 'Einheit von Gehalt und Gestalt', Bavarian Radio, 1 April 2004.

43 Prieberg, 7195.

44 *Passacaglia und Fuge für Orgel*. See Okrassa, 289 and 304. This composition had originally been on the programme of the ADMV Tonkünstlerfest, in Weimar, 1936.

45 Prieberg, 7193.

46 Weiss, 263.

47 Hans Ferdinand Redlich, 'Jarnach, Philipp', *Grove's Dictionary of Music and Musicians*, vol. 4, ed. Eric Blom (London: Macmillan, 1954), 595.

48 Weiss, 266. See also Tamara Levitz, *Teaching New Classicality. Ferruccio Busoni's Master Class in Composition* (Frankfurt: Peter Lang, 1996), 433.

which the composer tried to suppress. This negative evaluation of Jarnach's behaviour during the Third Reich must have circulated among other refugees as well. When in 1951, Jarnach invited Arnold Schoenberg to lecture at the Hamburg Academy, he got the following answer: 'My dear Mr. Jarnach: I have been told that you have been an active supporter of the Nazi regime. Without any further explanation, I cannot believe it. But please tell me more.' Jarnach wrote back, expressing great sadness that such a statement came from a man like Schoenberg. 'How could you only for a moment believe', he asked, 'that I had in any way and at any point showed sympathy with the terrible regime of the Third Reich?'[49]

Although there is no evidence for the regime mounting official sanctions against his works, it is remarkable that in the 25 months between January 1933 and March 1935, there was only one single performance of Jarnach's music. Despite the fact that during the Weimar Republic he was one of the most-performed contemporary composers, Jarnach now was equally invisible as composer and pianist. This changed in March 1935 when Hermann Abendroth conducted the first performance of a new orchestral work by Jarnach, entitled *Musik mit Mozart* (Music with Mozart), which achieved considerable success and was performed many times over the next few seasons. Just a few months after having been expelled from Cologne, the conductor showed his sympathy for his former colleague, as he did at the same time for the composer Günter Raphael, who – like Braunfels – was lambasted as a half-Jew.[50]

At the Cologne Academy, Jarnach, like Tiessen, tried to behave in as correct and un-political a manner as possible. The conductor Günter Wand, who studied during this time with Jarnach, remembered that in rare moments, he was courageous enough to show one of his pupils scores of Schoenberg and Hindemith.[51] But when in the summer of 1936, his former pupil Otto Luening came from the United States and invited him to settle at his college in Vermont, Jarnach 'explained that his wife and son were German citizens, and it would be too much of an adjustment to move to the United States.'[52]

Jarnach felt particular sympathy for his colleague Eduard Erdmann who in 1935 had left Cologne for Northern Germany, and now was completely forgotten as a composer. Writing about him in 1954, Jarnach explained:

It is difficult to imagine what such an experience meant for a creative personality. No artist can in the long run live without ever having the chance to be heard. Every creative person-

---

49   Weiss, 267.
50   Prieberg, 42.
51   Josef Müller-Marein and Hannes Reinhardt, *Das musikalische Selbstporträt von Komponisten, Dirigenten, Instrumentalisten, Sängerinnen und Sängern unserer Zeit* (Hamburg: Nannen, 1963), 247.
52   Weiss, 288.

ality needs in any case contacts with the world around him; for only this communication with the outside world produces a balance between subjective and objective ideas and thus gives him new impulses.[53]

This confession also explains why Jarnach now composed a more traditional work like his *Musik mit Mozart*: he simply could not face the prospect of his work being permanently suppressed.

Eduard Erdmann, like Jarnach, was helped by his former colleague Hermann Abendroth, who in 1937 recommended him as a soloist with the Berlin Philharmonic Orchestra. At the same time, it is surprising that Abendroth, a highly courageous man, joined the Nazi party on 1 May 1937. One can only speculate as to his motives, but perhaps the conductor thought this step would give him more possibilities to help his colleagues.[54] Indeed, the new party member had not in fact become a Nazi. Abendroth made this very clear in June 1938, when he refused to become a member of the honorary committee of the anti-Semitic Vortragsbühne des Westens in Berlin, on the grounds that for him the Jews were human beings like the Aryans.[55] Writing such a letter to an anti-Semitic Nazi organisation then was surely a risky act of resistance. Erdmann undoubtedly adopted a similar stance to Abendroth. In all likelihood, he must also have shared the conductor's justification for party membership, since on the same day he also joined their ranks. This information again demonstrates that there were varying reasons for those agreeing to accept party membership.

Indeed Abendroth and Erdmann were not the only liberal artists who joined the party at that particular time. Among hundreds of musicians, I discovered such figures as the conductors Karl Elmendorff, Otto Jochum, Peter Raabe, Johannes Schüler (who had performed Alban Berg's *Wozzeck* in Oldenburg) and Hans Weisbach, the composers Wilhelm Maler (a pupil of Jarnach) and Hans Vogt, the Jazz experts Alfred Baresel and Dietrich Schulz-Köhn and the socialist music educator Arnold Ebel.[56] It would be wrong to suggest that all of these

---

53   Weiss, 284.

54   One reason for entering the Nazi party might also have been that his wife was not able to prove her Aryan ancestry. See Irina Lucke-Kaminiarz, *Hermann Abendroth – Ein Musiker im Wechselspiel der Zeitgeschichte* (Weimar: Weimarer Taschenbuch Verlag, 2007), 87.

55   Prieberg, 44.

56   The inclusion of Peter Raabe in this list warrants more detailed comment. Although accepting the Presidency of the Reichsmusikkammer in succession to Richard Strauss in 1935, and authoring books such as *Die Musik im dritten Reich. Kulturpolitische Reden und Aufsätze* (1935) and *Kulturwille im deutschen Musikleben* (1936), Raabe had also conducted Mahler and Schoenberg before 1933, and in 1938 was a vociferous opponent of the Entartete Musik Exhibition. See Nina Okrassa's biographical study of Raabe for a more detailed consideration of his controversial career.

were ardent Nazis. Party membership in itself cannot be a sufficient qualification. One must remember that, for instance, Heinrich Müller, the head of the Gestapo, never took the formal step of joining the Nazi party.

For Walter Braunfels, the period 1933–45 became the most productive period of his life. He had enough funds to survive and even to support another composer of the internal exile, namely Heinrich Kaminski. At Lake Constance, he did not attend concerts. But he was eager to hear new works on the radio and from time to time at places outside Germany. In November 1938, he visited Zurich, where Hindemith's new opera *Mathis der Maler* was performed, and this work inspired him to create another opera, *Szenen aus dem Leben der heiligen Johanna* (The life of the holy Joan) which was completed in 1943.[57] 'We live here like on a safe island, surrounded by very stormy weather,' Braunfels wrote during the war.[58] Having frequently attended evenings in which chamber music was being performed in private homes, he now turned again to writing for that genre. After completing two string quartets (in A minor and F major) in 1944, he finally in December of the same year began his String Quintet opus 63, a rarely-heard masterpiece, which in its expressive chromaticism reflects the bitter feelings of the time.

In stark contrast to Braunfels, who now composed more works than ever before, Heinz Tiessen experienced a deep artistic crisis during the Nazi era. Among his very limited output of those years were some compositions for the Berliner Singegemeinschaft, a choir consisting of former members of the workers' singing movement.[59] As with the Social Democratic and Communist parties, the huge workers' singing organisation had been forbidden and was dissolved. But a few choirs secretly survived under a new name. The members of the Singegemeinschaft, conducted by Tiessen, were anti-Nazis. However, in their concert programmes, they could show this only in a very covert way, for example by singing love songs with a concealed political message, songs from the Thirty Years War, or songs based on texts by Schiller which had assumed a revolutionary meaning in the Workers' Movement.

The creative output of Eduard Erdmann during his internal exile was even more limited. The String Quartet op. 17 was the only work that he composed in that period. Erdmann began sketching it in 1932, but the work occupied him until June 1937. It was dedicated to the painter Emil Nolde, an old friend, who experienced a serious crisis during that summer. As an early member of the Nazi party, he had initially believed that his art would be acceptable

---

57   Jung, 292.
58   Jung, 295.
59   Dorothea Kolland, '… in keiner Not uns trennen… Arbeitermusikbewegung im Widerstand', in *Musik und Musikpolitik im faschistischen Deutschland*, ed. Hanns Werner Heister and Hans-Günter Klein (Frankfurt: Fischer, 1984), 207. Among the few compositions Tiessen created during this period was his opus 48, entitled *Drei Liebeslieder im Volkston* (Three Love Songs in Popular Style).

to the Third Reich. But the Degenerate Art Exhibition of July 1937 included no less than twenty-seven of his paintings, which now were defamed. Indeed, a total of 1052 of Nolde's works were confiscated from German museums.[60] Nolde was so distraught by these events that he cancelled the celebration of his seventieth birthday. Since Erdmann finished his String Quartet in June 1937, two months before his friend's 70th birthday, it is very likely that his dedication was intended not merely as a birthday present, but also as a sign of solidarity with another artist who was not falling into line with the regime, and who was now effectively forbidden from producing art.[61] Unlike the artists, the banned composers were not prohibited to compose. But Erdmann's String Quartet was never performed during the Third Reich. It had to wait thirty years before it was premiered in January 1967. In this strictly modern five-movement work, we feel the power and courage of a composer who was not willing to adjust to the restrictions of the regime.[62]

While Erdmann had left the State Academy of Cologne, Philipp Jarnach remained there as a professor. After having composed his *Musik mit Mozart*, he also made arrangements of Mozart's compositions, performing the solo part in some of his piano concertos.[63] As was already the case for Busoni, this composer symbolised for Jarnach a pure art unharmed by the conflicts of the time. In January 1939, the composer divorced his wife and married shortly afterwards a former piano student. The following summer, the couple spent their honeymoon on the island of Amrum in the North Sea. Jarnach's *Amrumer Tagebuch* (Amrum Diary) for piano solo refers to this place, but was not composed there. Jarnach created his composition during the years 1941–42 in his flat in Bad Godesberg. It might be that, with the small island in the title, he wanted to hint at his own isolated situation, effectively a manifestation of his internal exile. It was a personal confession, first performed by the composer himself in 1942 in a concert at the Cologne State Academy of Music dedicated to his 50th birthday. The first of the three movements is titled 'Hymnus' (Hymn). But the falling chromatic figures sound rather melancholic, like sighs that presage the 'Elegie', the second movement. Listening to this music, one does not get the impression that it illustrates the happiness of a honeymoon or celebrates glorious victories of the German army. These dark sounds rather show us the composer Philipp Jarnach, as his colleagues and students of that period remember him: shy, reserved and with his head cast down.[64] This was not the type of artist that the Third Reich needed for its propagandistic aims. Such music was not composed to demonstrate the superiority of the Aryan race. Rather it was music of the internal exile.

---

60   Stephanie Barron, *"Degenerate Art". The Fate of the Avantgarde in Nazi-Germany* (Los Angeles: Abrams, 1991), 319.
61   Secretly he produced small-sized watercolours, which he called 'unpainted paintings'.
62   Volker Scherliess, 'Zum Streichquartett op. 17', in Bitter and Schlösser, 156–61.
63   Weiss, 287.
64   Weiss, 290.

It should also be remembered that refugees did not always have a clear picture about what had happened inside Germany during the Third Reich. So their predominantly critical views must be checked carefully. All the more, it seems significant that Leo Kestenberg, one of the most heavily attacked musicians during that period, continued his friendship with Heinz Tiessen. In January 1952, he wrote to him from Israel: 'You belong to those characters that affirm my belief in mankind, with whom I can feel connected through the moral laws within us and in the cosmos.'[65] And in November 1954: 'Dear heartily admired Mr. Tiessen, a letter from you is for me a joyous, uplifting event.' Tiessen also resumed his friendship with Erdmann and Jarnach, as can be seen from the large number of letters they exchanged. In his last years, he had been elected president of the music section of the Berlin Academy of Arts. In a letter written on 27 November 1957, he asked Jarnach to be his successor. He pointed out that the date was the day of the 75th birthday of Leo Kestenberg, their common friend in Israel.

I have tried to demonstrate how wrong it is to declare as Nazis all artists who had remained in Germany during the Third Reich. There were many musicians who did not want to support a regime that perhaps at first seemed very attractive for their professional group. Since active resistance was highly dangerous, only very few of them—like the conductor Leo Borchard or the pianist Helmut Roloff—belonged to resistance groups like the Rote Kapelle, Europäische Union or Weiße Rose. But a larger number of musicians tried to evade official engagements, and they hoped not to be used in the huge propaganda machine installed and directed by Joseph Goebbels.

All cases were different, as we have seen. There were those, like Walter Braunfels, who after suffering persecution on both racial and political grounds, survived in a small place, far away from the big cities. Although Braunfels had no chance to be publicly performed, he was more active as a composer than ever before. Heinz Tiessen, on the brink of being dismissed from his positions as a so-called Cultural Bolshevist, tried to be as invisible as possible, and nearly stopped composing. Like him, both Erdmann and Jarnach, equally prominent in the avant-garde of the Weimar Republic, miraculously kept their teaching positions. While their creativity reached a low-point, they remained active as pianists, and concentrated their attention on performing the classic repertoire.

It is evident that there is no clear-cut catalogue of criteria for assessing internal exiles. To formulate such a catalogue would be problematic. If all public servants would have to be regarded as supporters of the Third Reich, then indeed Tiessen and Jarnach could not figure as members of the Internal Exile. More telling is perhaps the number of public performances they enjoyed. Unlike the unique case of Hartmann, who was able to boycott the Third Reich, since he still possessed the performing rights for most of his works, Erdmann, Jarnach and

---

65   Letter from Leo Kestenberg to Heinz Tiessen, January 1952. Tiessen Archives.

Tiessen were suppressed by the regime. The individual cases have to be checked carefully. As the fate of Eduard Erdmann showed, even party membership must not necessarily qualify a person as a Nazi. If a musician was not financially independent, like Braunfels or Hartmann, a compromise had to be found to survive. Even if Erdmann continued to perform as a pianist, even if Tiessen remained a teacher at the Academy, and even if Jarnach got some performances, not one of those artists gave up their political and aesthetical views, which all differed significantly from the cultural policy pursued by the Third Reich.

Yet Braunfels, Tiessen, Erdmann and Jarnach are not the only composers whose careers during the Nazi era require reappraisal. Others that warrant consideration include Max Butting, Wolfgang Jacobi, Karl Klingler, Walter Kollo, Heinz Schubert and Felix Woyrsch.[66] Some research has already been done on Ernst Pepping[67], Günter Raphael[68], Peter Schacht[69], Heinrich Kaminski[70], Siegfried Borris[71] and Hanning Schröder[72]. Music-history can never be described in black and white terms. There are different colours, transition areas and grey zones as well. Instead of generalizing, one should take each individual case on its own merits. After the war composers like Heinz Tiessen, Eduard Erdmann, Walter Braunfels and Philipp Jarnach suffered from the fact that they had remained in Germany during the Third Reich. Their continuing neglect was partly due to that. For a long period, artists of the internal exile had either not been recognized or were overlooked. We will surely discover that their music, too, is worthwhile playing and should be heard again.

66　For example, the Pfohl-Felix Woyrsch—Gesellschaft claims that the composer and conductor Felix Woyrsch (1860–1944), who in 1936 received the Goethe medal from Hitler, spent his last years in inner exile. See http://www.p-w-g.de/woyrc_e.html

67　Burkhard Meischein, 'Anpassung, Verweigerung, innere Emigration? Ernst Pepping im Nationalsozialismus,' in *"Für die Zeit—gegen den Tag". Die Beiträge des Berliner Ernst-Pepping-Symposions 2001*, ed. Michael Heinemann (Cologne: Dohr, 2002), 179–200.

68　Thomas Schinköth, *Musik—das Ende aller Illusionen? Günter Raphael im NS-Staat* (Hamburg: von Bockel, 1996)

69　Holtmeier, 84–102.

70　Manfred Peters, 'Heinrich Kaminski im Nationalsozialismus', in: *mr-Mitteilungen* Nr. 72 (August 2010), 8–16.

71　Albrecht Dümling, 'Waldidyll inmitten einer Schreckenswelt. Zum 100. Geburtstag von Siegfried Borris', in: *mr-Mitteilungen* Nr. 60 (November 2006), 11–20.

72　Nico Schüler, *Hanning Schröder* (Hamburg: von Bockel, 1996) Also see Gottfried Eberle, 'Als Verfemte überwintern'—zwei Musiker im Dritten Reich: Ein Gespräch mit Cornelia und Hanning Schröder', in Heister and Klein, 253.

Lily E. Hirsch

Defining 'Jewish Music' in Nazi Germany

Handel and the Berlin Jewish Culture League

The Berlin Jüdischer Kulturbund, or Jewish Culture League, was a closed cultural organization created by German Jewish luminaries in cooperation with the Nazi government. From
1933 until 1941, only Jews—defined generally at that time as any person descended from a
Jewish parent or grandparent—were allowed and encouraged to participate in this organization both as performers and as audience members.[1] However, Hans Hinkel, the Nazi in
charge of the organization who by July 1935 exercised control over the cultural activity of non-
Aryan citizens living in the Reich, insisted on certain operational terms.[2] He expected the
League's musical and theatrical performances to be Jewish, segregating Germany's cultural life
with German performing arts for Germans and Jewish ones for Jews. But this requirement
was difficult to honour. After all, what was 'Jewish' in Nazi Germany?

The Berlin League inspired subsequent branches; by 1935, there were forty-six local chapters in other towns and cities. However, in this chapter, I focus on the musical performances
of the Berlin League as the principal—as well as first and last—site of League activity. First
and foremost, I will describe the Berlin branch's debate on 'Jewish music,' and its culmina-
tion, represented by the Jewish Culture League Conference. This conference, convened under
Nazi and Zionist duress in September 1936, yielded no definitive solution to the problem of
a Jewish repertoire, but hinted at practical criteria of Jewish music that governed programme
selection in the League. In the second part of this chapter, I examine the League's repertoire

---

Sections of this article previously appeared in chapters 2 and 5 of *A Jewish Orchestra in Nazi Germany:
Musical Politics and the Berlin Jewish Culture League,* published by the University of Michigan Press. I
am grateful to the University of Michigan Press for permission to reuse this material.

1   The only exception to this rule was the presence of Nazi officials at each event, including concerts at
    synagogues.
2   See Michael Kater, *The Twisted Muse: Musicians and their Music in the Third Reich* (Oxford: Oxford
    University Press, 1997), 97; Erik Levi, *Music in the Third Reich* (New York: St. Martin's Press, 1994), 51;
    and Horst J.P. Bergmeier, Ejal Jakob Eisler, and Rainer E. Lotz, *Vorbei... Beyond Recall: Dokumentation
    jüdischen Musiklebens in Berlin 1933–1938.... A Record of Jewish musical life in Nazi Berlin 1933–1938*
    (Hambergen: Bear Family Records, 2001), 55.

in order to access these criteria. However, the repertoire may in fact further complicate our enquiry. As I will show, George Frideric Handel, of German origin, was quite popular in the League, in part, because his music was considered to be Jewish. Despite or maybe because of such contradictions, this chapter is perhaps able to shed light on the complicated process of defining Jewish music in Nazi Germany. It also offers a glimpse into the inner workings of this unique organization, the Jewish Culture League, a product of collaboration between Jews and Nazis, and, for many, a place of both salvation and damnation.

Before discussing the League Conference, I must cover some preliminaries about the creation of this organization. One of the Nazi regime's primary objectives was to eradicate the Jewish presence in Germany's cultural life. To achieve this goal, regime officials had instituted the Gesetz zur Wiederherstellung des Berufsbeamtentums (Law for the Reconstitution of the Civil Service (7 April, 1933), which effectively barred non-Aryans from positions at state-run cultural institutions, including opera houses and concert halls. [3] Why then would Nazi leaders support the Jewish Culture League, let alone require the cultivation of 'Jewish music' within it? Some insisted that the initial leader and co-originator of the League, Kurt Singer, a conductor, musicologist, and psychiatrist, must have hypnotized the Nazi administrator Hans Hinkel in order to gain official acceptance.[4] But there are several less fantastical explanations that account for Hinkel's acceptance of the organization. First, the League operated within the Nazi propaganda machine. That is to say, by pointing to their support of the League, the Nazis could claim that Jews were not oppressed but encouraged to find their own forum for cultural expression. [5] Second, the League functioned as a mechanism of local social control,

---

3   The Law for the Restitution of the Civil Service of 7 April originated with Wilhelm Frick who submitted the decree to the cabinet on 24 March 1933. At first, upon Reich President Paul von Hindenburg's insistence, Jewish combat veterans and employees, who had begun their employment in the civil service by August 1914, were exempt. These exemptions were nullified with Hindenburg's death in August 1934. Alan E. Steinweis, *Art, Ideology, and Economics in Nazi Germany* (Chapel Hill & London: University of North Carolina Press, 1993), 106. See also Saul Friedländer, *Nazi Germany and the Jews, Vol. I: The Years of Persecution, 1933–1939* (New York: Harper Collins Publishers, 1997), 28; and Erik Levi, 'Music and National Socialism: The Politicization of Criticism', in *The Nazification of Art: Art, Design, Music, Architecture & Film in the Third Reich*, ed. Brandon Taylor and Wilfried von der Will (Hampshire: The Winchester Press, 1990), 168.

4   Ken (Kurt) Baumann, 'Memoiren', Leo Baeck Institute, New York, 42. For more information on Singer, see Sophie Fetthauer, 'Kurt Singer', *Lexikon verfolgter Musiker und Musikerinnen der NS-Zeit*, ed. Claudia Maurer Zenck and Peter Petersen (University of Hamburg), http://www.lexm.unihamburg.de/object/lexm_lexmperson_00001059.

5   See Martin Goldsmith, *The Inextinguishable Symphony: A True Story of Music and Love in Nazi Germany* (New York: John Wiley & Sons, Inc., 2000), 298; Kater, 98; Levi, 51; Michael Meyer, *The Politics of Music in the Third Reich* (New York: Peter Lang, 1991), 75; Bernd Sponheuer, 'Musik auf einer kulturellen und physischen Insel: Musik als Überlebensmittel im Jüdischen Kulturbund 1933–1941', in

where Nazi leaders hoped to quell any potential resistance by providing the many recently displaced Jews, following the April laws, with a new source of income. And third, with the censorship of Richard Wagner and Richard Strauss, and, in subsequent years, Ludwig van Beethoven, Handel, and Wolfgang Amadeus Mozart (see figure 1), the League offered a way for the Nazis to stop Jewish cultural appropriation and perceived degradation of the German masterworks.[6] In this way, the creation and maintenance of the League was consistent with the Nazi ideal of musical authenticity, an allusive and multivalent concept, which, based on the authoritative aspect of the term,[7] upheld Jewish music as simply a more appropriate enterprise for a Jewish organization.[8]

Figure 1. Composers Banned from the League's Programmes

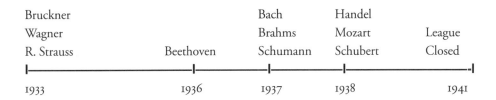

The assimilated League leaders, however, hoped simply to offer unemployed Jewish musicians a means of income and a place of solace, and did not initially focus on Jewish repertoire.[9] To some, such a repertoire was, in fact, at odds with their sense of German-ness and threatened to turn their Jewish organization into a ghetto. In November 1933, League official Julius Bab explained:

Musik in der Emigration 1933–1945. Verfolgung, Vertreibung, Rückwirkung, ed. Horst Weber (Stuttgart/ Weimar: Metzler, 1993), 111; and Herbert Freeden, *Jüdisches Theater in Nazideutschland* (Tubingen: J.C.B. Mohr, 1964), 51.

6   These bans were ordered by both Hinkel's office, which reviewed each programme before performance, as well as an internal League 'reader' or self-censor in Berlin, who read programmes with 'National Socialist eyes.' Baumann, 63.

7   See Peter Kivy, *Authenticities: Philosophical Reflections on Musical Performance* (Ithaca: Cornell University Press, 1995), 3.

8   See the explanation of this use of the League in chapter 1, in Lily E. Hirsch, *A Jewish Orchestra in Nazi Germany: Musical Politics and the Berlin Jewish Culture League* (Ann Arbor, MI: University of Michigan Press, 2010).

9   'Es ist uns spaeter vorgeworfen worden, dass wir den Kulturbund nur gegruendet haben um ein paar juedischen Kuenstlern Arbeit und Brot zu geben; das ist nur halb-richtig. Natuerlich waren wir darauf bedacht, den hunderten von juedischen Kuenstlern, die gerade fristlos entlassen waren, zu ermoeglichen, bis zu ihrer Auswanderung ein bescheidenes Einkommen zu haben, aber viel wichtiger war er uns damals, dem juedischen Publikum in Deutschland, das in der Vorfront des deutschen Kulturlebens gestanden hatte, eine Heimat zu bieten, so lange es noch moeglich war.' Baumann, 38.

What we German Jews seek and find in this cultural movement is maintenance and care of that two-fold root of life from which our being has grown up to this point. If we are ready even now, as people of Jewish tradition and German culture, to take all the consequences of the isolation and self-sufficiency imposed on us by Germany's political situation, we do not want to create an illusory nothing for ourselves-but Jewish culture, a ghetto culture, within these limitations. We want to remain in active connection with the great cultural goods of Germany and the world.[10]

From the very start, the *Jüdische Rundschau*, a newspaper serving the Zionist movement, challenged this German mindset and demanded that the League confront the changing situation of Jews in Germany and the need for a repertoire connected to Jewishness. Indeed, following the League's theatrical premiere on October 1, 1933—a performance of Lessing's *Nathan the Wise* that many viewed as a show of support for assimilation rather than a distinct Jewish identity,[11] an article in the *Jüdische Rundschau* insisted that League organizers lacked direction and must elucidate their 'spiritual foundations.'[12] Despite clear ideological distinctions, the Zionist movement was better equipped at this early date to fulfil Nazi repertoire expectations for the League.

The conflict here, which the heterogeneous Jewish public only compounded, in part, explains why League leaders did not follow the example of other organizations dedicated to the question of 'Jewish music.' One such organization was the Society for Jewish Folk Music, founded in St. Petersburg in 1908, which was devoted to the collection of Jewish folk tunes and synagogue music and the creation of modern national Jewish music based on this material. Their trajectory corresponded to the thinking of a host of nationally-oriented scholars and composers, who maintained that the study of a country's indigenous music was a fundamental first step toward the creation of its art music. Though the tools and methodological

---

10   'Was wir deutschen Juden in dieser Kulturbewegung suchen und finden, das ist Erhaltung und Pflege jener zweifachen Lebenswurzel, aus der bisher unser Dasein wuchs. Wenn wir als Menschen jüdischer Tradition und deutscher Kultur auch heute bereit sind, alle Folgerungen aus jener Abgeschlossenheit, aus jenem Auf-sich-selbst-gestellt-sein zu ziehen, die die politische Situation Deutschlands uns auferlegt, so wollen wir uns doch innerhalb dieser Schranke keineswegs eine illusorische nichts-als-jüdische Kultur, eine Ghettokultur bereiten. Wir wollen im lebendigen Zusammenhang bleiben mit den großen Kulturgütern Deutschlands und der Welt.' Julius Bab, 'Kulturarbeit der deutscher Juden', *Der Morgen* (November 1933), 326.

11   Zionists also viewed the play as a distraction from the realities of the Jews' situation in Germany. See Barbara Müller-Wesemann, *Theater als geistiger Widerstand: Der Jüdische Kulturbund im Hamburg 1934–1941* (Stuttgart: M & P Verlag für Wissenschaft und Forschung, 1996), 339.

12   'Nathan der Weise: Die Premiere des 'Kulturbundes'', *Jüdische Rundschau*, 4 October 1933, 18.

theory to support such a project were already in Berlin at the Phonogramm-Archiv,[13] the League lacked both support for such a mission as well as the time (the organization was never envisioned as a long term venture). For these reasons, the League leaders had to find 'Jewish music' already in existence that would suit the concerns and tastes of their varied constituency while simultaneously appeasing the Nazi authorities. After three years of debate about their repertoire and Jewish music, with no solution in sight, Singer convened the Jewish Culture League Conference.

The conference, officially designated 'Die Kulturtagung des Reichsverbandes der Jüdischen Kulturbünde in Deutschland,' opened on the evening of 5 September 1936 in the auditorium of the Joseph Lehmann-School in Berlin. On the following day, prominent Jewish scholars of theatre and music advised League representatives how best to satisfy all those involved in the League through a Jewish repertoire. The musical reports included: Arno Nadel, a musicologist and the choir director of the Jüdische Gemeinde in Berlin,[14] on Jewish liturgical music and Jewish folk song; Karl Adler, a leader in the artistic community in Stuttgart,[15] on Jewish choral music; Anneliese Landau, a musicologist by training and the only woman involved in the founding of the League, on Jewish art song[16]; and Hans Nathan, a professor of musicology and music critic for the *Jüdische Rundschau*,[17] on Jewish orchestral and chamber music.

---

13 The Berlin Phonogramm-Archiv was under the direction of Carl Stumpf (1841-1936) originally and Erich Moritz von Hornbostel (1877-1935) from 1905 until his emigration two months after the Nazi takeover. The archive, later known as the 'Berlin School of Comparative Musicology,' had been working to collect music from all the peoples of the world since its inception in 1900 and could have helped the League with their own collection of Jewish folk song and synagogue music. See Artur Simon, ed. *Das Berliner Phonogramm-Archiv 1900-2000: Sammlungen der traditionallen Musik der Welt* (Berlin: Verlag für Wissenschaft und Bildung, 2000); Dieter Christensen, 'Erich M. von Hornbostel, Carl Stumpf, and the Institutionalization of Comparative Musicology', in *Comparative Musicology and Anthropology of Music: Essays on the History of Ethnomusicology*, ed. Bruno Nettl and Philip V. Bohlman (Chicago and London: The University of Chicago Press, 1991), 201–09; and Erich Stockmann, 'Ethnomusicology in Berlin: Aspects and Perspectives', in *European Studies in Ethnomusicology: Historical Developments and Recent Trends,* ed. Max Peter Baumann, Artur Simon, and Ulrich Wegner (Wilhelmshaven: Florian Noetzel Verlag, 1992), 13–25.

14 In 1943, Arno Nadel died in Auschwitz. See Stephen Stompor, *Jüdisches Musik- und Theaterleben unter dem NS-Staat* (Hannover: Europäisches Zentrum für Jüdische Musik, 2001), 43.

15 Adler assumed the leadership of the *Stuttgarter Jüdische Kunstgemeinschaft* after he was dismissed from his post at the Stuttgart Conservatory of Music in March 1933. See Hannah Caplan and Belinda Rosenblatt, ed. *International Biographical Dictionary of Central European Emigrés 1933–1945,* Vol. I (Munich: K.G. Sauer, 1983), 11.

16 Lily Hirsch, 'Introduction to Anneliese Landau and the Kulturbund: In her Own Words', *Musical Quarterly 90,* 3–4 (2007), 508–20.

17 Caplan and Rosenblatt, 845.

During the course of the speeches, these scholars advanced several conflicting views of 'Jewish music' that, for the most part, only complicated the League's programme selection.

In his speech, Arno Nadel gave the most concrete definition of 'Jewish music.' He insisted that 'authentic Jewish music' was Jewish folk song and music for the synagogue,[18] a conclusion Richard Wagner also advanced in his notorious article 'Judaism in Music,' 1850.[19] In his closing remarks on September 7, Kurt Singer, who was primarily responsible for the League's musical choices, agreed with Nadel. However, he concluded that Jewish folk song and synagogue music were not appropriate for the concert hall.[20] They could be performed in the synagogue. However, in the League's orientation report of February 1934, Singer admitted these concerts did not appeal to League audiences.[21]

Compounding the confusion, Karl Adler offered a standard for Jewish music useful in theory, but unclear in practice. He argued that the only logical criteria for Jewish choral music were 'the religious [tradition], the language, the land.'[22] This emphasis on land, a cornerstone of Nazi thinking and their paradigm of *Blut und Boden*, indexed a Zionist position that Jewish music could not exist outside Palestine.[23] Joachim Prinz, a Zionist rabbi, had explained this position during his speech at the conference on Jewish theatre. He contended that without a common land, the League could only have a 'national-pedagogical' function—building 'a bridge from a denationalized Jewry, living remote from Jewish prime sources, to Jewish life.'[24] In other words, the League could not perform authentic 'Jewish art,' but could encourage a Jewish awareness, which could foster future Jewish cultural activities in Palestine.

Anneliese Landau's speech represents a microcosm of the various positions on the issue of Jewish music at the time. Initially, she reiterated this Zionist position that 'Jewish music' did

---

18   *Geschlossene Vorstellung: Der Jüdische Kulturbund in Deutschland 1933–1941*, ed. Akademie der Künste (Berlin: Akademie der Künste, 1992), 285.

19   Wagner wrote that 'the synagogue is the solitary foundation whence the Jew can draw art motives at once popular and intelligible to himself', Richard Wagner, 'Judaism in Music', in *Richard Wagner's Prose Works: The Theatre,* vol. III, trans. William Ashton Ellis (London: Kegan Paul, Trench, Trübner & Co. Ltd., 1894), 90.

20   'Das jüdische Volkslied und die liturgische Musik muss nicht in den Konzertsälen, sondern in den Synogogen gebracht werden.' *Geschlossene Vorstellung*, 294.

21   'Der Besuch der Konzerte lässt im Allgemein nach sehr zu wünschen übrig, besonders, da die Veranstaltung von Konzerte in Synagogen sowohl aus religiösen als auch aus akustischen Gründen sich im Publikum nicht einbürgert.' The Jewish Culture League's *Orientierungs–Bericht*, dated February 1934, Fritz-Wisten-Archiv, Akademie der Künste, Berlin, 2.

22   *Geschlossene Vorstellung,* 289.

23   This idea had already appeared in discussions of the League's repertoire and had been the subject of a recent quarrel waged in the *Mitteilungsblätter des jüdischen Kulturbundes Rhein-Ruhr.*

24   Quoted in Herbert Freeden, 'A Jewish Theatre under the Swastika', *Year Book of the Leo Baeck Institute* (1956), 149.

not yet exist.[25] At the same time, she offered a practical solution to the League's immediate performance needs by accepting all art songs created by composers with Jewish roots as Jewish music. She then betrayed both of these positions by presenting something of a gradation of Jewishness, if you will, as she discussed the songs of Mendelssohn, Meyerbeer, and Offenbach. She explained, 'These songs have nothing to do with the Jewishness of their composers. They grow from the atmosphere of the country in which they were written.'[26] In contrast, she listed composers such as Joel Engel, Heinrich Schalit, Darius Milhaud, and Ernest Bloch, and explained that, within the twentieth-century art-song tradition, these composers created Jewish *Lieder* 'in complete consciousness by Jews for Jews.'[27]

Hans Nathan also distinguished between the music of various Jewish composers through the organization of his speech in two parts: 'Jewish orchestral and chamber music' and 'general literature.' Under the category of 'Jewish orchestral and chamber music,' he again recognized composers Ernest Bloch and Heinrich Schalit. Under 'general literature,' he discussed composers of Jewish origin such as Mendelssohn and Offenbach, who he did not believe displayed Jewish musical inclinations.[28] Of Mendelssohn, he stated simply that the composer was the 'purest German classicist.'[29]

Both Landau and Nathan did not explain the grounds for their separate categorization of Jewish composers—why for example the music of Mendelssohn, the grandson of the great Jewish philosopher Moses Mendelssohn, was not seen as Jewish at the time—and the Jewish Culture League Conference ended with no definitive criteria of Jewish music. Indeed, these speeches show that the idea of Jewish music was still very much contested. Yet the Nazis were

---

25 'For the time being, there is still no Jewish art song in the stylistic sense; the generation born in Palestine will hopefully give it to us one day' ('Ein jüdisches Kunstlied gibt es vorläufig bei uns stilistisch gesehen noch nicht; die in Palästina geborene Generation wird es uns hoffentlich einmal geben'). 'Anneliese Landau, Das jüdische Kunstlied', transcribed in *Geschlossene Vorstellung*, 291. Ten years later, Landau reiterated a similar sentiment: 'A national Jewish music can only be created by a free Jewish nation, living on Jewish soil, a nation which daily imbibes the breath, smell, light, and the hidden melody of its own country, a nation, which has revived its Hebrew mother tongue, which reads daily Hebrew papers, and Hebrew books, and attends Jewish schools, theaters and movies – in other words by a Jewish nation that enjoys its own distinctive social and cultural life. The Palestine-born generation will be called upon to give us our national secular music. The upsurge of musical activities in Israel during the last years shows that Israel is fully aware of this mission.' See Anneliese Landau, *The Contribution of Jewish Composers to the Music of the Modern World* (Cincinatti, Ohio: National Federation of Temple Sisterhoods, 1946), 54.

26 'Diese Lieder haben gar nichts mit dem Judentum ihres Komponisten zu tun. Sie wachsen aus der Atmosphäre ihres Land, in dem sie geschrieben werden.' *Geschlossene Vorstellung*, 291–92.

27 Ibid., 292.

28 Ibid., 286.

29 'reinster deutscher Klassizist.' *Geschlossene Vorstellung*, 288.

at least satisfied with the League's new devotion to the question of Jewishness in music. An article of September 11, 1936 explained, 'The reports were so completely in accordance with the mind and hearts of the Nazis that the overseer Hinkel explained that 'from the German side nothing [was] to be added nor to be cut' [...][30] The Zionist Association, for different reasons, was also pleased with the conference reports, and, in the following month, exhorted its members to embrace the League at last. It stated:

> The programme formation of the first months, however, seemed to show that the Culture League was not yet seized by any such Jewish cultural desire. Thus, it happened that our people participated in the work of the Kulturbund only in very small measure.
> Three years of development among Jews have fundamentally changed the circumstances. The Culture League has become conscious of its responsibility for Jewish tasks. Its artistic leadership is making a serious effort to shape the work of the Culture League in a Jewish way. Zionists are playing a decisive role in the leadership of the Association of Jewish Culture Leagues.
> [...] Thus we call today on the Zionists to join the Culture Leagues.[31]

Of course this attention was of little practical help. But the show had to go on and, despite theoretical conflict, in practice the League regularly performed and accepted certain works as Jewish. With no consensus at the conference, how do we find out what idea of Jewish music governed programme formation on the ground? The next sight of investigation must be the repertoire, as a record of music reception.

There are many composers in the repertoire that inspire immediate hypothesizing. To avoid gross generalizations that undermine the complexities of the League, I focus, in the remainder of this chapter, on Handel. Given his German origins, Handel might seem an

---

30   'Die Referate waren so ganz nach dem Sinn und dem Herzen der Nazis, dass der Aufpasser Hinkel erklaerte [...] 'von deutscher Seite her weder etwas hinzufügen noch abzustreichen.' Unter Hinkels Aufsicht: Eine Tagung des 'Reichsverbandes juedischer Kulturbuende in Deutschland' Den Referaten 'von deutscher Seite nichts hinzufügen [...]' *Pariser Tageszeitung,* 11 September 1936, Wiener Library Archives, Leo Baeck Institute, New York.

31   'Die Programmgestaltung der ersten Monate schien uns aber zu zeigen, daß der Kulturbund von einen solchen jüdischen Kulturwillen noch nicht erfaßt war. So kam es, daß unsere Menschen nur in sehr geringem Umfange sich an der Arbeit des Kulturbundes beteiligten.
     Drei Jahre innerjüdischer Entwicklung haben die Verhältnisse grundlegend geändert. Der Kulturbund ist sich seiner verantwortlichen jüdischen Aufgabe bewußt geworden. Seine künstlerische Leitung ist ernsthaft um jüdische Gestaltung der Kulturbund-Arbeit bemüht, an der Verwaltung des Reichsverbandes Jüdischer Kulturbünde sind Zionisten maßgeblich beteiligt [...] Daher rufen wir heute die Zionisten auf, sich dem Kulturbunde anzuschließen.' 'Zionistische Vereinigung in Deutschland, "Für den jüdischen Kulturbund"', *Jüdischer Rundschau,* 16 October 1936, 3.

unlikely candidate for the next phase of our discussion, but it will soon be evident as to his bearing on the issue of Jewish music.

Handel's music was included in 37 League concerts. The performance of his music was also consistently celebrated and applauded by all factions involved in the League. One might ask why it achieved such popularity within a Jewish organization? Of course a composer of German origins would have corresponded to the German self-identification of many League members. For Bab and others, such as Hans Samter, who wrote for the German-oriented *Der Schild,* the presentation of German culture was *the* means of opposition to forced ghettoization.[32] This orientation was clearly reflected and displayed in the League repertoire from 1933 to 1936, before the organization gained prominent Zionist representation and Hinkel's office increasingly restricted musical selections by composers of German origin. Yet Handel was also in part performed as often as he was because the Nazis allowed the League to perform Handel until 1938, longer than any other German composer. Yet why did the Nazis protect Bach and Beethoven from Jewish appropriation and only reclaim Handel at this late date? For the Nazis, Handel was a problem. Former League member Herbert Freeden explains Handel 'was compromised in the eyes of the Nazis by his love for England and by his Biblical themes.'[33] Indeed, Handel had spent most of his life outside of Germany, in Italy, but mainly in England. There he developed a distinguished reputation as a composer of *opera seria* and oratorios based on Jewish themes. Moreover, these oratorios portrayed the Hebrew nation in a positive light, and, in some works, as heroic—totally at odds with Nazi ideologies of Aryan heroic supremacy. Of course, Handel was still German and to completely disown him would have challenged the very basis of Nazi musical ideology. And so, throughout Hitler's reign, Nazi personnel attempted to sanitize Handel—make him worthy of his Aryan heritage.

First, to rationalize Handel's abandonment of Germany and eventual relocation to England, some scholars cited his 'German character'—a term that has romantic 'elements of struggle, heroism, masculinity, intellectual depth, passion, and didacticism.'[34] These writers explained that in England, Handel struggled, and although he could have returned to Germany and gained fame and fortune, he could not abandon this noble fight.[35] In this form of contorted logic, Handel's time in England was exploited to prove his Germanness. Writers sympathetic to the Nazi cause also explained away his ties to Jewish themes in Nazi musicological writings and speeches. In an address commemorating Handel's birth, Alfred Rosenberg, a

---

32   Hans Samter, 'Der Kulturbund – ein Träger unserer Zukunft?', *Der Schild,* 26 January 1934, Fritz-Wisten-Archiv, Akademie der Künste, Berlin.

33   Herbert Freeden, 'A Jewish Theatre under the Swastika', *Year Book of the Leo Baeck Institute* (1956), 155.

34   Pamela M. Potter, *Most German of the Arts: Musicology and Society from the Weimar Republic to the End of Hitler's Reich* (New Haven: Yale University Press, 1998), 224.

35   Ibid.

one-time rival of the president of the Propaganda Ministry Joseph Goebbels,[36] stated, 'Handel eventually in the absence of great subjects chose stories from the Old Testament. It must have been hard on this shaper of sounds to have to receive texts out of second-rate hands, and to have a message called by names which little harmonized with the ways of his soul.'[37] To circumvent this problem, any evidence of Jewish references was eliminated by reworking and rewriting his oratorios, changing the text and story altogether. *Judas Maccabeus* was subject to the most reworking—a testament to the relative worth the Nazis placed on the work. The NS-Kulturgemeinde commissioned Hermann Burte to recast *Judas Maccabeus* as the *Held und Friedenswerk* (Hero and Work of Peace), an ode to Adolf Hitler. Other revisions of the work were produced by Hermann Stephani,[38] Ernst Wollong, and Johannes Klöcking and C.G. Harke (*Der Feldherr, Freiheitsoratorium,* and *Wilhelmus von Nassauen,* respectively).[39]

Although not all Germans supported this activity,[40] the government's 'Aryanization' of Handel continued into war time. The *Manchester Guardian,* a remarkably clear-sighted newspaper at the time, sarcastically reported on this latter activity in the article 'Making Handel and Bach Safe for Nazi Ears' of 1942: 'The expurgation of the masterpieces of German art from Jewish contamination is reported to be making rapid progress, all the more remarkable in a country at present engaged in a life-and-death struggle, where concentration of a nation's entire strength on essentials is imperative.'[41] The article's caustic tone continued as it described the 'shameless non-Aryanism' of Handel's oratorios, including the oratorio *Joseph* which the article mused might remain untouched by order of the Propaganda Ministry, under the control of Joseph Goebbels.[42]

---

36 For information on the rivalry between Goebbels and Rosenberg, see Kater, 14–17.

37 Alfred Rosenberg, Address on Handel's 250th birthday, reprinted in Alfred Rosenberg, *Gestaltung der Idee* (Munich: Verlag Eher, 1936), 281.

38 Stephani had actually already produced a revision of *Judas Maccabeus* in 1914. This was the first adaptation of a Handelian oratorio. See Pamela M. Potter, 'The Politicization of Handel and His Oratorios in the Weimar Republic, the Third Reich, and the Early Years of the German Democratic Republic', *Musical Quarterly* 85, no. 2 (Summer 2001), 324.

39 Ibid., 323–24. See also Isabelle Müntzenberger, 'Händel-Renaissance(n): Aspekte der Händel-Rezeption der 1920er Jahre und der Zeit des Nationalsozialismus', *Musik-Konzepte* (January 2006): 83, and Katja Roters, *Bearbeitungen von Händel-Oratorien im Dritten Reich* (Halle: Händel Haus, 1999).

40 In a 1937 edition of the periodical *Das Wort,* edited by Lion Feuchtwanger, Bertolt Brecht, and Willi Bredel, an article appeared which challenged the rewriting of Handel's oratorios. In the article, the author Hans Behrend, writing under the pseudonym Albert Norden, called the Handel activity an example of 'the arrogance and irreverence' (*die Arroganz und Ehrfurchtlosigkeit*), with which German creations are treated in service to the state. Quoted in Müntzenberger, 83.

41 'Making Handel and Bach Safe for Nazi Ears', *Manchester Guardian,* 17 February 1942, 6.

42 Ibid.

Table 1. Oratorio performances in the Jewish Culture League, Berlin

1933/1934	1934/1935	1935/1936	1936/1937	1937/1938
Mendelssohn's *Elijah* (performed at the Synagoguc on Oranienburgerstr.)	Hugo Adler's *Balak und Bilam* (Synagogue on Oranienburgerstr.)	Ferdinand Hiller's *Die Zertstörung Jerusalems* (?)	Jacob Weinberg's *Freitagabend-Liturgie* (Synagogue on Oranienburgerstr.)	Oskar Guttmann's *Schöpfungshymnus B'reschith* (Synagogue on Oranienburgerstr.)
Handel's *Judas Maccabeus* (Philharmonie on Bernburgerstr.)	Handel's *Samson* (Synagogue on Oranienburgerstr.)	Max Ettinger's *Das Lied von Moses* (Bach-Saal)	Handel's *Israel in Egypt* (Bach-Saal, Synagogue on Oranienburgerstr.)	Leo Kopf's *Freitag-Abend-Liturgie* (Synagogue Prinzregentenstr.)
Heinrich Schalit's *Eine Freitagabend-Liturgie* (Synagogue on Oranienburgerstr.) Ernest Bloch's *Avodas Hakodesh* (Synagogue on Oranienburgerstr.)	Handel's *Belshazzar* (Philharmonie)		Mendelssohn's *Elijah* (Synagogue on Oranienburgerstr.)	Handel's *Joshua* (Synagogue on Oranienburgerstr.)
	Zoltán Kodály's *Psalmus Hungaricus* (Synagogue on Oranienburgerstr.) Enrico Bossi's *Schir haschirim* (Synagogue on Oranienburgerstr.)			Handel's *Saul* (Synagogue on Oranienburgerstr.)

The Ministry's specific attention to Handel's oratorios and their Aryanization grew out of the belief that the oratorio was particularly German, a perception reflected in nineteenth-century discussions of the oratorio, in works, for example, by Carl Hermann Bitter and Otto Wangemann.[43] This belief in the oratorio as a national genre had to do with its portrayal of historical figures, connecting the audience to a common past, and inclusion of chorales. Indeed, choral singing represented the feelings of the group, not the individual, and was thus thought to have powers of unification. [44]

The leaders of the Jewish Culture League, forced in many ways by the regime to generate a cohesive Jewish community, recognized and harnessed the unique powers of the oratorio, regularly programming, above all, the oratorios of Handel. Not only that, in a tug of war with the regime, they exercised their own appropriation of Handel and his oratorios for Jewish nationalistic ends. Handel's oratorios dominated the League's regular presentation of oratorio (see table 1). The intense engagement with each of these Handelian works is noteworthy. However, the League's performance of *Judas Maccabeus*, celebrated as one of the season's high points, received great attention within the Jewish press and offers the most critical insight into the League's appropriation of Handel. The performance, which was directed by Kurt Singer, took place on 7 and 8 May, 1934, in honour of Handel's 250th birthday.[45] Critics and audiences were enthusiastic about the work. They responded to the oratorio's themes of freedom of worship, national unity, and religious identity as well as the work's promise of hope as the Jewish nation triumphs over adversity in the end. This response was evident during the League performance when the popular chorus: 'See, the conqu'ring hero comes!' (*Seht, er kommt*) was encored after thunderous applause. [46] This chorus, borrowed from Handel's oratorio *Joshua,* celebrates the victory of Judas, the Israelite leader, over Antiochus, the Syrian leader. The simple homophonic style made the message especially accessible and effective, allowing the League audience as whole to participate in the festive mood the chorus creates (see example 1).

---

43   Quoted and translated in Howard E. Smither, *A History of the Oratorio,* vol. 4 (Chapel Hill: University of North Carolina Press, 2000), 13.

44   See Conrad L. Donakowski, *A Muse for the Masses: Ritual and Music in an Age of Democratic Revolution 1770-1870* (Chicago: University of Chicago Press, 1977), 122.

45   Herbert Freeden, *Jüdisches Theater in Nazideutschland* (Tübingen: J.C.B. Mohr, 1964), 101.

46   See Kai, 'Dr. Kurt Singer über Judas Makkabäus', *CV- Zeitung,* 3 May 1934, 6.

Example 1. Bars 1–4 of the Full Chorus 'See, the conqu'ring hero comes!'

Example 1. Bars 1-4 of the Full Chorus "See, the conqu'ring hero comes!"

The most significant factor, however, in the success of *Judas Maccabeus* was its basis in the Old Testament. Though this source was hardly uncommon during Handel's lifetime,[47] the League community viewed it in a new light.[48] Singer, himself, at the close of the Jewish Culture

---

47   See Ruth Smith, *Handel's Oratorios and Eighteenth-Century Thought* (Cambridge: Cambridge University Press, 1995), 94 and 141–45.

48   Handel's reliance on the Old Testament was consistently highlighted in the Jewish press during the period. Gerhard Goldschlag wrote, '*Judas Maccabeus* belongs to that main group of Handelian oratorios, whose content like *Saul, Israel, Joshua, Messiah* and *Deborah* to name only a few others, is drawn from the Old Testament' (Der Judas Maccabäus gehört zu jener hauptgruppe Händelscher Oratorien, deren Stoffe wie Saul, Israel, Josua, Messias und Deborah, um nur einige andere zu nennen, dem Alten Testament entnommen sind). Gerhard Goldschlag, 'Zweimal Kulturbund: Haendel: 'Judas Maccabäus'/ Shakespeare: 'Was ihr wollt!'—Das Oratorim in der Philharmonie', 17 May 1934, Juedischer Kulturbund Collection, Leo Baeck Institute, 14. Charles Jennens (1700–1773) created the Messiah's text based on selections from both the Old and New Testaments.

League Conference, called attention to the biblical foundations of Handel's oratorios and explained that the composer 'dedicated half of his life to Jewish history.'[49] Hans Nathan, writing in the *Jüdische Rundschau,* portrayed this dedication as a symbolic gesture of tolerance, citing Handel's oratorios as proof that this 'German master,' looked on by all with respect, had 'a fondness for the history of the Jewish people.'[50] In the programme notes, accompanying the League performance, Rudolph Kastner tied this fondness directly to the situation of Jews at the time. He wrote:

> The fact that he [Handel] reaches again and again to the themes and figures of the Old Testament and glorifies them is among the most eternal, inextinguishable honours, which a great spirit in world history, as well as a German man and a German heart, could ever show to the Jewish people. To keep this honour in mind today, to refer to it with pride and modesty at the same time, appears a special necessity on the occasion of the present performance [...][51]

In this way, these Jewish leaders tailored Handel's oratorios to meet their nationalistic goals, just as Nazi leaders did based on their own ideology outside the Jewish organization. I point out this similarity not to accuse these writers of wrongdoing or equate them with the evils of the Nazis: they simply responded to the radically altered conditions the Nazi regime had created for them, and fought, with the Nazis' own techniques, to assert their national worth through music.

Given all that was at stake in this fight, it may come as no surprise that the League also challenged the Nazi appropriation of Handel's works as Aryan with their own treatment of his music as Jewish. In a letter of July 11, 1938, Singer identified and categorized Handel's oratorios as Jewish music:

> [...] there were about fifty concerts in the Jüdischer Kulturbund of Berlin by the Sand-

---

49 'der sein halbes Leben der jüdischen Geschichte gewidmet,' *Geschlossene Vorstellung,* 294.
50 'eine Vorliebe für die Geschichte des jüdischen Volkes.' Hans Nathan, '"Judas Maccabäus" in the Kulturbund', *Jüdische Rundschau,* 10 May 1934, 13.
51 'Daß er dabei immer wieder zu Vorwürfen und Gestalten des alten Testaments greift und sie glorifiziert, gehört zu den ewigen, unausrottbaren Ehren, die jemals ein großer Geist im Weltgeschehen, dazu ein deutscher Mann, ein deutsches Herz dem jüdischen Volk erweisen konnte. Dieser Ehre heute eingedenk zu sein, auf sie mit Stolz und Bescheidung zugleich hinzuweisen, scheint ein besonderes Gebot anläßlich der gegenwärtigen Aufführung [...]' Rudolf Kastner, 'Haendel und sein Werk', in the programme from the Jewish Culture League performance of Monday 7 May and Tuesday 8 May, 1934 of Handel's *Judas Maccabeus* directed by Kurt Singer in Berlin, Rudolf Zielenziger Collection, Leo Baeck Institute, New York.

ers Chorus that celebrated Palestinian and Jewish music from Brandmann, Rothmüller, Chajes, Engel, Schoenberg, and Gladstein, that I commissioned three works with music for the theatre by living Jewish musicians, that there were performances of the complete incidental music for *Midsummer Night's Dream,* and the most important symphonies and overtures by Mendelssohn, that the *Verklärte Nacht* [Transfigured Night] by Arnold Schoenberg was performed, and that finally each year witnesses performances of one or two biblical oratorios from Handel.[52]

This classification was not unusual in works by Jewish musicians in the early twentieth century,[53] and even outside the League, there were Jewish scholars who treated his music as such in the 1930s. In a letter dated March 10, 1937, Max Ettinger, discussing the repertoire of the new World Center of Jewish Music in Palestine wrote: 'Strictly speaking, music by Jews can be valuable and significant without necessarily being Jewish. Accordingly, Handel is the most obvious example of a non-Jew whose compositions contain a great deal of Jewish material.'[54] This treatment of Handel's music, especially his oratorios, as Jewish may also have been influenced by Handel's recognized connection to the synagogue at the time.

Martin O. Stern, in fact, remembers Handel's music being employed in the synagogue during the Third Reich:

> When I was about ten, one of our maids, with Mother's permission, took me with her to Sunday services in a Lutheran church near our house. After a few minutes, my mind wandered agreeably once again, until suddenly I was brought up short—indeed, startled—by the choir and organ intoning a hymn that I had first heard in Temple: the words were different, but the tune was exactly the same. How could they use a Jewish melody? Surely this indicated that these two religions, and perhaps others, had much in common, and that too much emphasis was placed on their differences. The melody was Händel's 'Hail! The conquering hero comes' from his opera [oratorio] *Judas Maccabeus.* It seems that at that time Judaism was, in my mind, more identified with certain music than with particular rituals or teachings.[55]

As late as 1961, a number of European congregations intoned portions of the Hallel prayer to the strains of 'See, the conqu'ring hero comes' on Passover, a fitting gesture given the chorus

---

52 Quoted in Philip Bohlman, *The World Centre for Jewish Music in Palestine 1936–1940: Jewish: Musical Life on the Eve of WWII* (Oxford: Clarendon Press, 1992), 167–68.

53 See ibid., 208.

54 Quoted in ibid., 208–09.

55 Martin O. Stern, 'How do you like America?', Leo Baeck Institute, New York, 69. Stern grew up in Essen during the Nazi period.

and the holiday's analogous celebration of freedom.[56] Even today, the melody of Handel's popular chorus serves as the basis of a Hannukah song, according to an article entitled 'Getting a Handel on Hanukkah.'[57] Some scholars during the Third Reich also maintained that Handel's music had a 'strong influence' on synagogue song in general. [58] Certainly this association with the synagogue and appropriation of Handel's oratorios as Jewish music increased Handel's popularity in the League. It also defied the government's own attempts to restore the composer to his rightful place in the German pantheon of musical masters. For our purposes, however, it represents yet another paradox in the search for Jewish music in Nazi Germany: League leaders contributed to a Jewish repertoire, that some did not even believe could exist outside Palestine, with the music of a perceived Aryan composer. Meanwhile, thanks again to the flexibility of music in reception, they generally viewed the music of Mendelssohn, which the Nazi regime censored as Jewish, as German or General Literature.

Contradictions, such as these, more than anything else, characterized Jewish music in practice during the Third Reich. In this way, the League's musical activity flies in the face of fixed two-dimensional definitions of Jewish music from the past and underscores the need for scholars to allow for the ironies and paradoxes of Jewish music in various contexts. This approach is important, not only because fixed ideas of Jewish music are fundamentally flawed, but also because they are dangerous. During the Third Reich, such musical categories, though seemingly innocuous, helped reinforce the idea that Jews were a separate people. This mindset helped pave the way for Nazi genocide by helping to mentally prepare Germans for the removal and eventual extermination of this perceived alien racial group.

For a time, the League offered some protection from this end. But on 11 September, 1941, the League was dissolved. As reason for the liquidation of the League, the secret police cited Paragraph 1 of the Reich president's order of 28 February 1933—for the 'protection of people and state.'[59] Many League members had already emigrated. Some former members credit the League with giving them the material and emotional support they needed to face leaving their homes. Alice Levie, the wife of the general secretary and later leader of the League, Werner Levie, explains that 'as long as one was employed, one could prepare for his emigration.'[60]

---

56   Alexander L. Ringer, 'Handel and the Jews', *Music and Letters*, 42 (1961), 29.

57   'Getting a Handel on Hanukkah', http://www.ehsmusic.org (accessed 25 January, 2011).

58   Antoine Lilienfeld-Lewenz, 'Judas Makkabäus, Samson, Belsazar: Die biblischen Texte in Händels Oratorien', *Der Schild*, 8 February 1935, Fritz-Wisten-Archiv, Akademie der Künste, Berlin.

59   The secret police declared, 'Auf Grund des [paragraph] 1 der Verordnung des Reichspräsidenten zum Schutze von Volk und Staat vom 28. 2. 33 löse ich mit dem heutigen Tage den Jüdischen Kulturbund in Deutschland e.V., Berlin, auf.' Letter from secret police, 11 September 1941, Vereinsregister Berlin, Leo Baeck Institute, New York.

60   'solange man beschäftigt war, konnte man sich auf seine Auswanderung vorbereiten,' Alice Levie, in

But the League has also been viewed in a more negative light. To exist, League leaders had to collaborate with the enemy and even lend legitimacy to the regime's plans as a means of propaganda. Not only that, certain scholars and surviving members wonder if more Jews might have left Germany in time if the League had not numbed them to reality—making them feel as if their situation were better than it really was. The historian Alan Steinweis, for one, wrote, 'By providing Jewish artists and audiences with an outlet for creative expression, the *Kulturbund* rendered Jewish existence in National Socialist Germany somewhat less desperate than it otherwise might have been, thereby lulling German Jews into a tragically false sense of security about the future.'[61] It is this idea that has recently inspired some of the worst criticism of the League: Martin Goldsmith, for example, has posed the question as to whether there might have been fewer Jewish deaths had the Jewish Kulturbund not existed.[62] My work on the issue of Jewish music in Nazi Germany has taught me to approach such questions with caution. The League served too many different functions for too many different people, to be seen now, with the luxury of hindsight, as wholly positive or negative. To understand the history of events as well as ideas, such as Jewish music, we must not demand resolution but rather allow for this tension and the resulting contradictions.

Henryk M. Broder and Eike Geisel, *Premiere und Pogrom: der Jüdische Kulturbund 1933–1941* (Berlin: Wolf Jobst Siedler Verlag GmbH, 1992), 158.

61   Alan E. Steinweis, 'Hans Hinkel and German Jewry, 1933–1941', in *Theatrical Performance during the Holocaust: Texts, Documents, Memoirs*, ed. Rebecca Rovit and Alvin Goldfarb (Baltimore: Johns Hopkins University Press, 1999), 23.

62   Goldsmith, 298.

Joshua S. Walden

'Olden Melodies Return'

Memory in Joseph Achron's *Hebrew Melody*[1]

The title of *Hebrew Melody*, a composition for accompanied violin written in 1911 by the Russian-Jewish composer Joseph Achron, can be interpreted to have both particular and universal levels of reference. On a small scale, this title indicates that the piece represents the tune of an individual traditional song or dance; the word 'Hebrew' might denote its derivation from Jewish culture, or that it has a text in Hebrew. Because this tune is not identified as belonging to a specific prayer, lullaby, or other traditional genre, however, the title also can be understood as generic, that is, as suggesting that the piece is a representation of the general category of 'Hebrew' melodies, and thus that it depicts elements that might be considered to be essential components of European Jewish culture. In fact, *Hebrew Melody*, Achron's opus 33, was the first of a number of pieces the composer wrote for violin based on Ashkenazi traditional music during the early twentieth century. His later works in the genre also had titles referring to Jewish culture, for example *Hebrew Dance* and *Hebrew Lullaby* (opus 35, nos. 1 and 2), *Sher* (opus 42), and *Märchen* (opus 46). *Hebrew Melody* would become the most popular of these pieces, and was republished in several editions and performed widely.

With a title that does not refer to details of the source music's original text or its sociological or ritual function, but simply to the Hebrew language or 'Hebrew,' i.e., Jewish, people, and to 'melody,' a quality shared by almost all traditional music, *Hebrew Melody* was considered by many listeners and musicians to evoke Ashkenazi Jewish culture. The work was recorded by numerous prominent violinists, used in film, adapted as a popular song and a concert aria, and reconceived for an electronic instrument. As such, it was reinterpreted over time: in the early years of its performance, it appealed to audiences who were familiar with a still vibrant Eastern European Jewish culture; in its later guises, it took on a retrospective, even memorializing character. As populations of Eastern European Jewish communities diminished through emigration, exile, and genocide, the work was reinterpreted by some as a

---

[1]   Some of this material has appeared in an alternate form in Joshua Walden, 'Music of the "*folksneshome*": "Hebrew Melody" and Changing Musical Representations of Jewish Culture in the Early Twentieth Century Ashkenazi Diaspora', *Journal of Modern Jewish Studies*, 8.2 (July 2009), 151–71.

musical memory of rapidly disappearing ways of life, and by others as a symbol of the promise of Palestine as a new 'homeland.'

Achron, a violinist who studied with Leopold Auer at the St. Petersburg Conservatory,
wrote *Hebrew Melody* shortly after he became a member of the Society for Jewish Folk Music.[2] The Society had been founded in 1908 as a consortium of ethnographers and composers
who aimed to renew Jewish culture by promoting the collection and transcription of Eastern
European Jewish traditional music and the development of a Jewish national style of art
music composition. Inspired by these forward-looking aims of study and artistic creation,
Achron built his first composition for the Society on a traditional melody he initially notated
in the manner of an ethnographic transcription, but rather than being based on the recent
work of ethnographers, *Hebrew Melody* was founded mainly on Achron's personal memory.
He dedicated the composition 'To the memory of my father,' and the inspiration for the
work harkens back to Achron's youth. Achron described visiting a Warsaw synagogue during
his childhood and hearing a prayer melody during the service, and reported that his recollection of this tune, as filtered through the intervening years, became the source for *Hebrew
Melody*.[3] Thus, *Hebrew Melody* was from the start presented as a product of memory. During
the history of the reception and performance of *Hebrew Melody* from the decade of its creation to the period after the Second World War, however, musicians and listeners frequently
reinterpreted the tone of the work's depiction of memory, as well as the sources of its musical recollection, as the conditions and locations of Diaspora life changed in Europe and the
United States.

ACHRON'S SOURCE MELODY AND COMPOSITION

In the first printed score of *Hebrew Melody*, Achron and his publishers incorporated a transcription of the work's source melody, the tune apparently sung in his childhood synagogue, notated
as a solo line without accompaniment above the composition, in the style of ethnographic transcriptions such as those created and compiled by Joel Engel, Susman Kiselgof, and the other
ethnographers involved in the Society for Jewish Folk Music.[4] *Hebrew Melody* was re-edited

---

2   For a detailed discussions of the Society for Jewish Folk Music and Achron's relationship with the
    organization, see Jascha Nemtsov, *Die Neue Jüdische Schule in der Musik* (Wiesbaden: Harrassowitz
    Verlag, 2004); Beate Schröder-Nauenburg, *Der Eintritt des Jüdischen in die Welt der Kunstmusik: Die
    Anfänge der Neuen Jüdischen Schule: werkanalytischen Studien* (Wiesbaden: Harrassowitz Verlag, 2007);
    and Walden, 151–71.

3   Philip Moddel, *Joseph Achron* (Tel Aviv: Israeli Music Publication Limited, 1966), 15.

4   Engel and Kiselgof were instrumental in the founding of the Society for Jewish Folk Music, and

and published at least three times after its first edition, and in each of these versions the source melody transcription continues to appear in small print at the top of the first page.[5] Although the language and precise wording of the expressive markings and performance instructions throughout the score varied in each of its editions, the short musical passage was always introduced with a caption identifying it as a traditional melodic theme on which the larger piece was based, transcribed in musical notation from the oral tradition by Achron. In the 1921 edition created by Leopold Auer, for example, the caption reads: 'Original version of the melody in this transcription as recorded by the author.' The publication of a transcription in the score of a composition based on traditional music was a common feature of Achron's works: the printed versions of *Sher* and *Hebrew Lullaby* open with melodic transcriptions attributed to the fieldwork collections of Kiselgof, and *Hebrew Dance* also incorporates a small-print transcription, credited to Hirsch Kopït, another folk music collector and member of the Society.

Achron offers no prescriptive performance instructions over his 'original version,' simply a descriptive tempo marking and the 'ideal' pitches and durations. He depicts the melody in a generic form, as a transcription of a melodic type derived from listening to a particular performance. Since the publication of folk-song collections such as the 1818 *Deutsche Lieder für Jung und Alt*, one of the earliest books of German language folk-song texts with melodic transcriptions, anthologies of traditional music commonly presented their artefacts in just such a quasi-objective manner.[6] Jewish folk-song collectors of the early twentieth century produced transcriptions in a similar style in compendia including Y.L. Cahan's *Yidishe Folklider mit melodies* (1912) and Fritz Mordechai Kaufmann's *Die schönsten Lieder der Ostjuden* (1920).[7]

---

conducted extensive fieldwork to collect Hasidic folk music from Russian Jewish communities. See Lyudmilla Sholokhova, 'Jewish Musical Ethnography in the Russian Empire: Ideology and Chronology', in *Jüdische Kunstmusik im 20. Jahrhundert: Quellenlage, Entstehungsgeschichte, Stilanalysen*, ed. Jascha Nemtsov (Wiesbaden: Harrassowitz Verlag, 2006); Lyudmila Sholokhova, 'Zinoviy Kiselhof as a Founder of Jewish Musical Folklore Studies in the Russian Empire at the Beginning of the 20th Century', in *Klesmer, Klassik, jiddisches Lied: Jüdische Musikkultur in Osteuropa*, ed. Karl E. Grözinger (Wiesbaden: Harrassowitz Verlag, 2004); and Walden.

5   The first published version of *Hebrew Melody* was released in 1914 by the publishing division of the St. Petersburg Society for Jewish Folk Music. The second edition was printed by G. Schirmer in 1918, and annotated with bowings, fingerings, and other instructions by Efrem Zimbalist, Achron's classmate in Leopold Auer's violin studio at the St. Petersburg Conservatory. The third, published by Carl Fischer in 1921, was edited by Auer; and the fourth, published again by Carl Fischer in 1933, was edited by another Auer student and friend of Achron, Jascha Heifetz.

6   Republished in *Deutsche Lieder für Jung und Alt*, ed. Lisa Feurzig (Middleton, Wisconson: A-R Editions, Inc., 2002).

7   Y.L. Cahan, *Yidishe folkslider mit melodyes*, ed. Max Weinreich (New York: YIVO Institute for Jewish Research, 1957); and Fritz Mordechai Kaufmann, *Die schönsten Lieder der Ostjuden: Siebenundvierzig ausgewählte Volklieder*, ed. Achim Freudenstein and Karsten Troyke (Frankfurt am Main: Edermünde, 2001).

Despite including the melodic transcription as evidence of the basis of *Hebrew Melody* in the memory of a religious song, Achron does not limit himself in his composition to following narrowly the formal structure of the transcription, but develops it, creating an expansive work that employs formal and melodic repetition and variation and a wild, virtuosic cadenza. The transcription of the original melody, in the key of A minor, is in binary form: a (bars 1–16) – b (17–32) (Example 1; in this discussion, lowercase letters describe the form of the transcription, and uppercase letters designate sections of Achron's composition). The a section is in two parts, consisting of a phrase ending on an E, the fifth scale degree (bar 8), answered by an ornamented repetition of the same material, ending on the tonic pitch A (bar 16). The b section is also a melody repeated in two parts, again ending on E in the first half (bar 24) and finally on A (bar 32). The concluding three bars of each phrase in the b section (bars 22–24 and 30–32) echo the final three bars of each phrase in the a section (bars 6–8 and 14–16), except for one difference: in the b section, the fourth scale degree D is raised to D#. This produces an augmented second between the third and fourth scale degrees in A minor. This scale, which Mark Slobin calls the 'raised fourth scale,' is also known as the *Mi sheberakh* synagogue scale.[8]

Example 1: Joseph Achron, *Hebrew Melody*, opening transcription.

---

8   Mark Slobin, 'The Evolution of a Musical Symbol in Jewish Culture', in *Studies in Jewish Folklore: Proceedings of a Regional Conference of the Association for Jewish Studies Held at the Spertus College of Judaica, Chicago, May 1–3, 1977*, ed. Frank Talmage (Cambridge, MA: Association for Jewish Studies, 1980), 314. See also *Jewish Instrumental Folk Music: The Collections and Writings of Moshe Beregovski*, ed. and trans. Mark Slobin, Robert A Rothstein and Michael Alpert (Syracuse: Syracuse University Press, 2001), 15.

Achron's composition, by contrast, is structured in a basic three-part form, A – B – A; more closely, the form breaks down as A (bars 1–23) – A' (24–40) – B (41–57) – B' (58–73) – Cadenza (74) – A (75–87) – Coda (88–108). The work, in A minor like the transcription on which it is based, modulates to C minor in the B' section, after which follows the cadenza, beginning on a diminished 7th chord on the new leading tone B natural and ending on a G major chord. In a short transitional passage (bars 75–79), the harmony returns to A minor for the final A section and coda. Each larger section of Achron's work incorporates the equivalent half of the transcription. Thus, after a six-bar introduction in which the piano plays a chant-like melody in octaves in a low tessitura, section A represents the sixteen bars of the corresponding section a of the transcription, followed by a repetition an octave higher in A'. The melody here closely imitates its source, though the final pitch A in each statement is held for an additional bar, extending the phrases to seventeen bars and counteracting the listener's expectations of the hypermeter.

Sections B and B' are based on the sixteen-bar section b of the transcription. Section B comprises a close imitation of the corresponding passage, but again with a lengthening of the final pitch that brings the hypermeter off-kilter by creating a seventeen-bar phrase. In section B', Achron maintains the basic melodic and rhythmic contours of the second half of his transcription, but alters the pitches and increases the sense of rhythmic motion, with strings of nervous, energetic triplet semiquavers and demisemiquavers marked in Heifetz's edition, 'In slightly accelerated and restless tempo.' As this seventeen-bar passage progresses, the original melody gradually becomes obscured and the swirling patterns speed to sextuplet demisemiquavers and trilled crotchets (example 2).

Example 2: Joseph Achron, *Hebrew Melody*, violin part, bars 58–73.

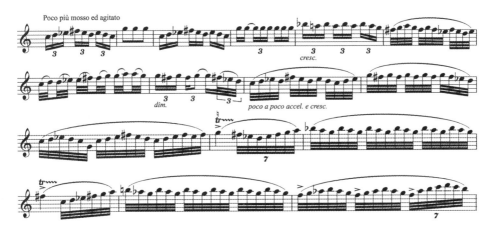

The cadenza is unaccompanied, and marked with dotted bar lines in the violin part, to assist the performer in counting beats, but at the same to indicate that the cadenza should be considered free and unbarred, in the style of a free fantasia (example 3).

Example 3: Joseph Achron, *Hebrew Melody*, Cadenza.

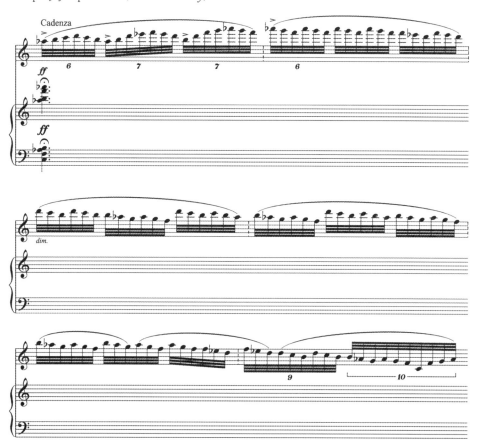

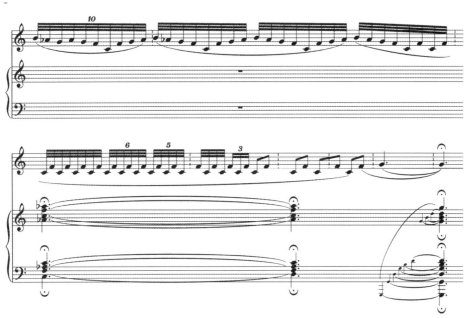

Demisemiquaver notes in groups of six, seven, eight, and nine swirl rapidly at a *fortissimo* dynamic between the second A flat high on the E-string and the low C on the G-string. After the bravura fireworks begin to die down over a decrescendo to *mezzoforte*, the piano enters on a sustained chord, as the violin plays alternating Cs and Fs in gradually slower rhythmic groupings of eight demisemiquavers, then six, then four, followed by semiquavers, quavers, and finally a sustained G, stopped an octave up the G-string, at the dynamic level *piano*. The piano concludes the cadenza with a rolled G-major chord spanning five octaves, played as an unbarred arpeggio. The cadenza thus begins in a passionate, fiery manner, as though the violinist has become possessed by the chant, and then slowly decreases in pitch, dynamic, and tempo to a quiet, sustained chord evocative of exhaustion at the conclusion of a trance. The final A section of *Hebrew Melody* does not repeat the entire a section of the transcription again, but instead, after a five-bar transitional phrase, reiterates the first eight bars of the melody in a high tessitura on the E-string and then elides into an extended coda of dream-like trills and turns that rise upward in pitch and become increasingly quiet. The work ends on the G-string, with an unaccompanied restatement of the melody's closing bars. In the final bar, the piano plays a pianissimo chord as the violin fades out under a fermata.

If the small-print source music in the sheet music of *Hebrew Melody* depicts a folkloric artefact in its ideal form, the score that follows is notated prescriptively with ornaments and performance instructions, and constitutes a highly varied and elaborated setting of similar musical materials. Whereas the original melody is printed without any performance indications other than a tempo marking, the composition was published with many performance instructions. The opening phrase of the violin part in Heifetz's edition (bars 7–23, which follow the six-bar introductory solo for the piano), for example, is copiously annotated with dynamic marks, hairpin crescendos and decrescendos, and detailed instructions for the violinist's left hand, including fingerings, slides, and the suggestion to play in a high position on the G-string. Heifetz also incorporates expressive directions such as 'with full lamenting tone' (bar 7) and 'with expression' (bar 15), as well as indications for the violinist's right hand, including tenuto and accent markings and slurred bowings.

    In a surprising deviation between the scores, the tempo indication in the opening transcription differs from that in the music of *Hebrew Melody*. Although the melodic artefact is labelled 'Moderate,' with an indication that the quaver equals 92 beats per minute on the metronome, the duet is marked 'Tranquil and mournfully,' the quaver equalling 72–80 in Heifetz's version. In editions by Zimbalist and Auer, the tempo of the duet is even slower, at quaver equalling 60–63. Achron's *Hebrew Melody* seems, then, to be an expressive reflection on a recollection from his past, the melody he offers in the opening a transcription. Although his transcription is depicted as an 'ideal' and descriptive version of the melody, it can be presumed that when it was performed, its singers might at times have adopted slower tempos, and even tranquil and mournful tones; the tempo indication that Achron chooses to ascribe to his ethnographic transcription serves less as a reliable indication of ritual tradition than as a scientific control, contrasting to the melancholy tempo indication that opens the setting of this melody as a chamber work. Indeed, the melodic transcription functions as a foil to the duet *Hebrew Melody*. Unadorned and moderate in small typeface, its seeming generic quality stands in stark contrast to the work that follows it, which is embellished and lamenting and even provokes the passionate outburst of the cadenza. The supposedly objective representation of the transcription thus enhances the expressive nature of Achron's treatment in the composition of his memory of a musical experience from his youth.

THE EARLY RECORDING HISTORY OF HEBREW MELODY

In the early years after its composition, *Hebrew Melody* was frequently performed during lecture recitals arranged by the Society for Jewish Folk Music and its offshoots. In a 1922 concert, for example, the Moscow Society for Jewish Music presented a lecture on Jewish music-making by Engel, and featured performances of *Hebrew Melody* and art songs and chamber works based on Jewish traditional themes by Engel, Alexander Krein, Moshe Milner, and Mikhail Gnesin.[9]

---

9   See the reproduction of this concert announcement in Nemtsov, 91.

In other performances beginning in the 1920s, *Hebrew Melody* often came to be incorporated by professional violinists such as Jascha Heifetz and Mischa Elman into more traditional recital formats; these performers brought the work to international audiences in concerts that featured canonic Classical and Baroque works, as well as other pieces based on folk music and contemporary compositions.

Although *Hebrew Melody* has received only intermittent attention from violinists since the mid-1950s, the work was a common feature in the performing and recording repertoire of a number of internationally recognized violinists during the first half of the twentieth century.[10] *Hebrew Melody* was most frequently performed by violinists who had trained in Auer's studio; indeed, Auer considered *Hebrew Melody* to be an important contribution to violin performance pedagogy.[11] His pupil Zimbalist produced one of the editions of the work, and his other students Mischa Elman, Toscha Seidel, and Jascha Heifetz recorded the work and performed it with orchestral and piano accompaniment all around the world.

Elman made three discs of *Hebrew Melody*: the first was a Victor recording from 1944 with the pianist Louis Mittman, the second was made by Decca in 1957 with the pianist Joseph Seiger, and the third was made by Vanguard, again with Seiger, probably in the early 1960s.[12] Another available recording captures Elman's live performance of *Hebrew Melody* in Los Angeles in 1945. Toscha Seidel recorded the piece at least once, in 1929; on this disc, whose B-side features Schubert's *Ave Maria*, Seidel is probably accompanied by the pianist Philip Goodman.[13] Jascha Heifetz's recordings of the work span three decades: in his earliest, made in 1917, he was accompanied by an orchestra conducted by Josef Pasternak; the next Heifetz made in 1926 in duet with the pianist Isidor Achron, the brother of the composer, who frequently travelled and performed with Heifetz; and the final recording was completed in 1946 in Hollywood, with the pianist Emanuel Bay.[14] Heifetz additionally recorded *Hebrew*

---

10   I am indebted to the British Library Sound Archive for providing me with the Edison Fellowship, and to Jonathan Summers, Classical Music Curator at the Sound Archive, for his advice as I conducted research into these and other recordings.

11   Leopold Auer, *Violin Master Works and Their Interpretation* (New York: Carl Fischer, Inc., 1925), 180.

12   The following are the cataloguing numbers for the recordings: Victor 11-9111, Matrix D4RC 533; US London LL 1467, Matrix ARL 3081; Vanguard VRS 1099, CSD 2137, Vanguard Classics OVC 8030.

13   Columbia 9761, Matrix 98615. The *Columbia Master Book Discography* also lists an earlier recording by Seidel, made with accompanist Francisco Longo in 1923, and identified as Matrix 98061, release number 9027-M. Tim Brooks and Brian A.L. Rust, *Columbia Master Book Discography* (Westport, CT and London: Greenwood Press, 1999).

14   The cataloguing numbers of these recordings are listed chronologically as follows: Matrix C-21268-3; Matrix CVE-27034-3; and Matrix D6-RC-5637-2A. For comparative analyses of these recordings, see Joshua S. Walden, 'Performing the Rural: Sonic Signifiers in Early-Twentieth-Century Recordings of Folk Music Arrangements for Violin', in *Before and After Music: Proceedings from the 10th International*

Lullaby in 1922, and *Hebrew Dance* in 1924.[15] *Hebrew Melody* also appeared on disks by two of the prominent pupils of the Romanian violinist Carl Flesch: in 1940 it became one of the few recordings made by the young violinist Joseph Hassid before his untimely death (Hassid was accompanied by Gerald Moore); and in 1942, Decca produced a performance of the work by Ida Haendel, accompanied by her sister Alice Haendel, with Henryk Wieniawski's *Scherzo and Tarantella* on the B-side.[16]

These violinists produced interpretations of *Hebrew Melody* that vary in conspicuous ways. They adopt sometimes significantly different tempos, for example: when the speed is determined at the entrance of the violin in bar 7, the approximate tempos range between as fast as 72 to the quaver, as in the recordings of Heifetz in 1917 and Hassid in 1940, and as slow as 50 to the quaver in Elman's recording of 1956, with the other recordings around the mid-point of these extremes, generally at slightly above or below 60 to the quaver. Almost all of these violinists play at fluctuating tempos, as they invariably interpret the work in a dramatic rubato style. Many of these recordings exhibit fluidity not only of tempo but also of rhythmic interpretation, as, for example, Seidel and Elman in each of his recordings play freely the pattern of oscillating semiquavers that first appears in bar 11 and recurs frequently (for example in bars 19, 28, and 36, though Seidel cuts bars 24–48), so that the rhythms written as duple semiquavers sound almost like unpredictable and syncopated patterns of triplet demisemiquavers.

The cadenza is a site of notable variation between performances; some of these violinists play it rapidly and steadily as a set of virtuosic runs, while others play more quixotically, as a free fantasy. Hassid, Haendel, and Heifetz adopt the former technique, performing the cadenza at a generally unfaltering breakneck speed. Elman and Seidel, on the other hand, do not play the demisemiquavers of the cadenza at equal lengths, but hold particular pitches slightly longer than they are notated, making the passage rhythmically and metrically unpredictable. In his 1956 recording, for instance, Elman suddenly holds back between the sixth and seventh pitches of the nonuplet in the middle of the cadenza, sliding from B to D and holding the D longer than is prescribed in the score. On the rising and falling pattern that follows, Elman lengthens the highest and lowest pitches, B and C, thus emphasizing the oscillating pattern in an impulsive, jaunty manner. He omits the second group of octuplets in this pattern, and then, at the start of the trill-like alternating pattern of fourths between C and F, he perches on the first note, marking the final gesture of the cadenza.

Congress of the International Project on Musical Signification, Vilnius, 21–25 October, 2008, ed. Lina Navickaitė-Martinelli (Vilnius/Helsinki: Lithuanian Academy of Music and Theatre, Unweb, International Semiotics Institute).

15   Heifetz recorded *Hebrew Lullaby* with pianist Samuel Chotzinoff, Matrix B-27034-1; and *Hebrew Dance* with Isidor Achron, Matrix C-30931-2.

16   Joseph Hassid: HMV C321, Matrix 2EA 9051. Ida Haendel: Decca K 1047, Matrix AR 7145.

Despite the differences between these performances of the cadenza, the recordings all exhibit a shared point of interpretation at the end of this passage. Achron notates the gradual loss of tempo here by slowing the frequency of the alternating pattern of C-F, as described above, from demisemiquavers beamed in decreasing numbers, to semiquavers beamed in one set of three and then one set of two, and finally to three pairs of quavers. None of the violinists take this rhythmic patterning literally; instead they all play the alternating notes as a rapid trill of some length, undetermined by the score, that gradually slows down in speed, until the final note, a held G. Rather than playing these rhythms with pedantic accuracy, these violinists interpret the passage as a decrescendo on a shimmering trill that heralds the end of the passionate dream-like cadenza.

In the principal recordings of *Hebrew Melody* from this era, the violinists also share a propensity to play slides frequently between neighbouring notes. While the locations of these slides vary between individual performances, all the recordings exhibit slides at a few specific points, including up to the D at the start of bar 12, and to the E at the start of bar 17. Slides are a typical expressive gesture that can be heard commonly in recordings of violin playing from the first half of the twentieth century; they often project a Romantic aesthetic mode by recalling the sounds of the human voice sighing or singing. Daniel Leech-Wilkinson writes that slides are also a common feature in performances of lullabies during this period. With reference to developmental psychology, he explains that the technique elicits in listeners an intuitive association with 'motherese,' a term that describes the way mothers (and other adults) typically speak with babies and young children.[17] The slides in these recordings may evoke the work's basis in a childhood memory, and in this way suggest the nostalgic effects of remembering a youth brought up among Eastern European Jewish traditions.

LATER VERSIONS OF HEBREW MELODY

Hebrew Melody achieved widespread popularity during the 1920s and 1930s, in part as a result of its virtuosity and the fact that its title, with its lack of specificity and resulting broad field of reference, resulted in its common interpretation as a general representation of Diaspora Jewish culture. The seeming universality of the work's subject also opened it to a range of perceived meanings, and later artists appropriated the piece for a variety of aims, recontextualizing the melody and thus reinterpreting its source. In one example, it was employed to convey a Zionist message as the soundtrack to the short film *Hebrew Melody*, created in 1935 by a

---

17   Daniel Leech-Wilkinson, 'Portamento and Musical Meaning', *Journal of Musicological Research* (December 2006), 233–61.

Berlin-based production company. *Hebrew Melody* was filmed in Jerusalem's Old Town and the surrounding hillside, and in the film, the subject of the composition no longer appears to be the traditional music of Eastern European religious Jewry, but the political cause of the creation of a Jewish homeland in Palestine, and the sentimentality Jerusalem's landscape inspires in the visitor. In the film, the Hebrew melody of Achron's title is conceived to be an anthem of Palestine itself, reverberating across the Biblical landscape. The director of *Hebrew Melody*, Helmar Lersky, and the cinematographer, Walter Kristeller, were both German Zionists who had settled in Palestine around 1933.[18] The film features the Jewish violinist Andreas Weißgerber, a former child prodigy born in 1900 in a small Jewish town near Chernowitz, Ukraine. The filmmakers worked under the auspices of the Jüdischer Kulturbund, which had been initiated in 1933 by the recently elected National Socialist party, as an institution under which Jews could form a ghettoized cultural life, with orchestras, publishing presses, theatres, and other social venues employing Jews and aimed at Jewish audiences.[19]

Hebrew Melody combines the techniques of documentary filmmaking with musical nationalism in its illustration of Palestine as the Jewish homeland. In the spirit of travel documentary and ethnography, the producers filmed *Hebrew Melody* with the aim of bringing images of distant Palestine home to curious viewers in Germany. At the start of the film, Weißgerber explores the urban Jerusalem market place and then travels by car to the countryside. There the sight of the craggy terrain, the rural farmhands, and the view of Jerusalem on the horizon, inspire him to take up his violin in an impromptu rendition of *Hebrew Melody*. In this way, Achron's elegiac rendering of a traditional religious melody he had learned in Warsaw becomes anchored to scenes of the legendary Jewish Holy Land, as though it emanates from the landscape. Weißgerber's performance appears to be a spontaneous act of spiritual inspiration. He plays at an extremely slow tempo, accompanied by an invisible orchestra. He opens with a dramatic rubato, slowing down and speeding up expressively at will, and finally settling on an unstable, slowly lilting tempo. When he reaches the cadenza, the screen turns black, and a shot fades in showing his fingers on the neck of the violin, as if to indicate that in the heat of his passionate playing, Weißgerber has lost conscious control; his fingers flail wildly on the violin, seemingly expressing his emotional response to his visit to Jerusalem. The producers of *Hebrew Melody* thus employ Achron's composition as a medium for conveying a propagandist message advertising Palestine as an idyllic location that will in-

---

18   Horst J.P. Bergmeier, Ejal Jakob Eisler, and Rainer E. Lotz, *Vorbei – Beyond Recall: Dokumentation jüdischen Musiklebens* (Hambergen: Bear Family Records, 2001), 389.

19   Philip V. Bohlman, 'Music, Modernity, and the Foreign in New Germany', *Modernism/Modernity* 1.1 (1994), 128. See also Philip V. Bohlman, 'Musik als Widerstand: jüdische Musik in Deutschland 1933–1940', *Jahrbuch für Volksliedforschung* 40 (1995), 49–74.

spire Jewish visitors and potential immigrants; the piece is conjured not as the memory of the Eastern European Jewish 'homeland,' but as a remnant of the origins of the Jewish ur-culture of a far more distant, biblical past, in a desert landscape.

Achron's *Hebrew Melody* was transformed in similar ways by composers and performers in another location with a growing population of members of the Jewish Diaspora, America, where it was twice arranged into songs with lyrics that referred not to the melody's Eastern European origins, but again to the biblical Jewish homeland in the Middle East. One version, an aria with a text written by Achron's wife Marie Rap-hoph for the Russian singer Nina Koshetz, was published in 1929 in a sheet music edition released by Carl Fischer, with lyrics published in English, Yiddish, Russian, and German. Achron's music is transposed in this new version to G minor, to accommodate the vocal range identified in the sheet music as 'High Voice,' but the form of the work remains generally the same. The first four verses, sung to the A and A' sections of the melody, repeat the lines 'Olden melodies return,/ Floating softly over hearts that burn.' In sentimental and nostalgic language, Rap-hoph's lyrics express that in these 'olden melodies' can be heard the 'wails of the lowly,/ sayings most holy'; 'Israel's pain' as it echoes over the earth; and the Jews' 'glory denied/ and a folk's long-buried pride.' The two remaining verses, in the B section, further emphasize the Zionist message, which becomes personal as the text turns to a first person plaint: 'The nobility in every soul/ And the love for Zion's sacred goal/ Within me rise/ Till the tears come blinding to my eyes./ And the flooding tears, the ancient groan,/ Welling upward reach to Heaven's throne,/ Where the Lord of earth and sky/ Harks to that exceeding bitter cry.'

In the B' section, in the place of Achron's increasingly wild violin part, Rap-hoph instructs the singer to perform the melody on extended melismatic vocalizations of the syllable 'Ah,' as the piano accompanies with undulating triplet semiquavers. The violin cadenza is condensed into a single bar of decreasing volume and speed, as the melody, at a rhythm of one beat of triplet semiquavers followed by two beats of demisemiquavers, descends almost two octaves and past two augmented second intervals. The voice settles on a two-bar F, while the accompaniment plays a slowly rolled chord, as it does in Achron's original version. The cadenza here becomes a realization of the 'exceeding bitter cry' that evokes the singer's yearning for 'Zion's sacred goal,' as according to the lyrics, she weeps and calls out toward God. The cadenza is followed by the repetition of the first two verses, followed by a wordless coda, vocalized at increasingly quiet dynamics. In the final six bars, Rap-hoph gives the singer, now unaccompanied on the final iteration of the opening theme, the instruction to hum the melody an octave lower, interpreted *ad libitum*. This arrangement thus maintains the sense of the cadenza as an evocation of overwhelming spiritual feelings, as the vocalization represents the expression of emotions so powerful that they cannot be put into words.

Another popular song written to the tune of *Hebrew Melody*, adapted for the Jewish singer Seymour Rechtzeit, offers a similar Diaspora anthem about a distant melody that resonates from afar and expresses the longings of a Jew living in exile for the Holy Land in Palestine. Rechtzeit recorded the song with Abraham Ellstein's orchestra, on a 78-rpm disc (the B-side featured a song written to the melody of Pablo Sarasate's work inspired by Romany tradition-al music, *Zigeunerweisen*). The recording was produced by Banner Records (catalogue number B-519); the precise date is unknown, but it appears to be from the 1940s, the decade in which Rechtzeit co-founded Banner Records with Victor Selzman.

This arrangement features melodramatic lyrics expressing a call to return to the Israel he has lost:

> 'Sounds are heard,/ From far-off East, there,/ Sounds enveloped in yearning/ With love from a heart that yearns./ An echo is heard,/ Come back from that time,/ When the an-cestors from once-upon-a-time/ Gave us their treasures./ [...] Parting from you/ was very difficult,/ being with you/ was my goal, my desire./ [...] I won't leave you,/ Lovely bride of Israel.'[20]

The Hebrew melody of the title is a sound that emanates from this distant space, and embod-ies the artistic theme of Jewish yearning for the biblical homeland; it reminds the singer of Israel, referred to as the bride that he was forced, with great difficulty, to leave behind as he moved away in exile, and now has as his goal and desire to recover.

While the lyrics of Rechtzeit's version of *Hebrew Melody* convey the fictional idealization of Palestine through the metaphor of a lost bride, however, the song's orchestral accompaniment features an ensemble of piano and multiple string and wind instruments, performing in a style resembling both the idioms of European Romantic Lieder and American Tin Pan Alley. A muted trumpet can be heard over the orchestra, before the entry of a solo violin, playing a sentimental version of the original violin part. The violin plays high-pitched trills as Rechtzeit sings the closing line about his 'bride.' Rechtzeit's *Hebrew Melody* thus represents both the yearning for a Jewish nation tied to a specific, ancient land, and the effects of cultural assimi-lation and appropriation caused by emigration to the New World. Although this version of the work dispenses with the purportedly religious origins of the melody Achron transcribed, it capitalizes on the nostalgic affect, and the generic breadth of the representation as indicated by the title. Like the 'olden melodies' in Rap-hoph's aria, the melody in Rechtzeit's song be-

---

20   'Klangen, es heren zikh/ fun vayten mizrekh dort/ Klangen ayngehilt in a benkshaft/ Mit libe fun a harts vos benkt./ Hert zikh a vider kol,/ Kum tsurik tsu yene mol/ Vi di uves fun amol./ Zeyer oysres hoben uns geshenkt/ [...] Sheyden fun dir/ iz geven zeyr shver,/ mit dir tsu zayn/ iz geven mayn tsiel, mayn beger/ [...] Lozen vel ikh dikh nit,/ Sheyne kale fun Yisroel.' I am grateful to Dr. Judith Schelly for her help with this transcription from the original recording.

comes an echo from the East. At the same time, this melody becomes 'assimilated' to its new musical context, attuned to the jazz rhythms of the New World. Rechtzeit's song is an emblem of the idealized Jewish homeland, but also, by incorporating American jazz techniques in the band arrangement, embodies the change and assimilation undergone by Jews and their artistic creations during their emigration and resettlement in the Diaspora during this period.

Three decades after World War II, *Hebrew Melody* appeared in a new context in which its quality as a memory of a melody from a distant time and place became even further emphasized. The work was performed as part of the concert and recording repertoire of the virtuoso theremin player Clara Rockmore, who as a child had been a violinist in Auer's studio. Since its invention by Leon Theremin, the instrument was commonly associated with ethereal voices, ghosts, and the subconscious, due to its wailing, eerie timbres and the technique by which one performs the instrument, requiring the musician to stand still and unmoving, and subtly shift hands and fingers in the air above the machine in a manner that resembles the conducting of a séance. It is of course for this reason that the theremin is most frequently heard in scores of science fiction and horror films, such as Miklós Rózsa's score to Alfred Hitchcock's movie *Spellbound*. Rockmore recorded *Hebrew Melody* in 1977 on an album created by the electronic instrument inventor Robert Moog. In Rockmore's hands, the piece is transformed into a distant, ethereal voice. A surviving video recording of her performance of the work shows Rockmore standing as though in a trance, as she conjures the wailing melody from the theremin. In the context of well-known associations between the theremin and the ethereal, and its use in film to signify ghosts and the subconscious, her performance evokes a sound emanating from a mystical, distant time and place, a conjured memory, like Rap-hoph's 'olden melodies' and Rechtzeit's echo 'come back from that time' of his ancestors.

The expression of memory played a salient role in the history of *Hebrew Melody* from its conception through the 1970s, impacting its composition and performance, as well as its arrangement in song, incorporation into film, and integration into the theremin repertoire. What changed dramatically, however, was the way in which the act of memory was represented, as well as the purported source of the memory depicted by the composition. Whereas Achron reportedly recalled a childhood visit to a Warsaw synagogue in creating his composition, later reinterpretations of the work depicted responses to memories of the landscape and people of the biblical 'homeland' in Palestine, and the Jewish victims of exile and World War II. This history reveals some of the ways in which musicians' and audiences' perceptions of works of music based on Ashkenazi Jewish traditional themes varied in response to the changing circumstances of the Eastern European Jewish populations and the gradual resettlement throughout the Diaspora during the first half of the twentieth century.

Ben Winters

Swearing an Oath

Korngold, Film, and the Sound of Resistance?

Recalling a series of photographs taken of his Austrian-Jewish parents and their friends in Bolivian exile in the 1940s—dressed in traditional costume and surrounded by overt symbols of Austrian nationality—Leo Spitzer noted that:

> Taken not very long after the conclusion of the war—after Auschwitz, the death camps, and confirmation of extensive Austrian involvement and collaboration in the Final So-lution—their depictions of enthusiastic celebrations of Austrian nationality strike me as disturbing and distressing examples of denial, if not amnesia.[1]

Given Austria's comparative unwillingness to face its fascist past until relatively recently, one can understand Spitzer's unease. For what image of Austria and Austrians does this present? A reluctance, perhaps, even among those forced to leave, to acknowledge the influence of such expressions of nationalism on the country's own fascist leanings; a nostalgia or *Heimweh* (homesickness) that is capable of selectively forgetting the pre-war years of political turmoil and replacing them with an idealized image of a peaceful nation subjected to Nazi invasion? Such a negative attitude towards nostalgia might remind us of the kind of critiques offered by Christopher Lasch, for whom nostalgia was, in its almost paradoxical belief in progress, 'the abdication of memory.'[2] Svetlana Boym, too, has written of her long prejudice against the phenomenon; that 'unreflected nostalgia breeds monsters.'[3] Yet, Spitzer goes on to mention that

1   Leo Spitzer, 'Persistent Memory: Central European Refugees in an Andean Land', 373–396 *in Exile and Creativity: Signposts, Travelers, Outsiders, Backward Glances,* ed. Susan Rubin Suleiman (Durham: Duke University Press, 1998), 374.
2   Christopher Lasch, *The True and Only Heaven: Progress and its Critics* (New York: Norton & Co, 1991), 82–117.
3   Svetlana Boym, *The Future of Nostalgia* (New York: Basic Books, 2001), xvi.

For the refugees within them to proclaim 'Austrianness'—to reclaim an identification with an Austrian republic after the Anschluss, Nazi rule, and the defeat of the German Reich— was also to reassert rightful belonging within a body politic and cultural tradition from which the Nazis had attempted to sever them.[4]

Spitzer thus presents us with two extreme interpretations of the kind of nostalgia practiced by Jewish Austrian exiles: one of which suggests a simplified, almost deluded, view of the past; while the other implies a positive act of resistance to the forces of European fascism, if at a necessary distance.

The activities of the Austrian composer Erich Wolfgang Korngold might be usefully ex- plored in similar terms. As a Jewish émigré, forced from European concert and operatic life by the Nazis, and eventually driven from his home in Vienna by the *Anschluß*, his was a career that was channelled into the emerging genre of the Hollywood film score. Living in Califor- nian exile from 1938 until his death in 1957, Korngold's only real artistic output between 1938 and 1946 was via the medium of film. It is hardly surprising, then, that his film scores reveal similar expressions of 'Austrianness' to those recognised by Spitzer in the photographs of his parents and their friends at their Austrian Club in La Paz. Furthermore, that same question- ing of this nostalgic tendency can be levelled at Korngold. Is the score to *The Adventures of Robin Hood* (William Keighley/Michael Curtiz, 1938)—a film often interpreted specifically as anti-fascist—an act of resistance; a show of defiance that allows the composer to declare his loyalty to a country struggling under the yoke of an oppressor? Or might it encourage a deeply flawed view of Korngold's homeland to take root, one that is at odds with the realities of Austrofascism, and one that is shaped by, and helps to determine in turn, the fantastical and simplified narratives of Hollywood?

In this chapter, I explore Korngold's evocation of Austria in his film scores as an expression of his nostalgia and *Heimweh*, question the pressure exerted by Hollywood's idea of Europe on its filmmakers, and consider to what extent Korngold's nostalgia was a general feature of his compositional style rather than a specific response to exile. In so doing, I suggest that the ostensible act of resistance represented by the score to *The Adventures of Robin Hood* is, in fact, capable of colluding with fascist appropriations of conservative Austrian culture; that it might be said to represent Korngold's rose-tinted construction of a mythic and timeless Austria with which he could more easily identify; and that, in tying contemporary Austria to the narrative conventions of Hollywood, it helped blind Korngold's contemporaries to Austria's complicity in its slide towards Nazism.

---

4   Spitzer, 374.

NOSTALGIA AND HOLLYWOOD

Nostalgia is a surprisingly recent word. Coined in a 1688 Swiss medical thesis by Johannes Hofer, it was a Greek translation of the German term *Heimweh* that combined *nostos* (return home) and *algos* (pain). It was an attempt to turn a well-observed phenomenon in displaced soldiers and exiles into a medical condition that could be treated and cured—generally by a return home. By the nineteenth century, however, it denoted loss in a far less specific way, a condition of the mind that was no longer tied to a definite place, and therefore could no longer be cured: in short, it became a chronic condition of Romanticism, and was explored by numerous writers and composers, often manifested as an inconsolable yearning (*Sehnsucht*) for childhood (as in Schumann's *Kinderszenen*, for example). The modern usage of the term nostalgia was certainly set by the 1920s, when it was addressed in a major study of 'collective memory' by the French sociologist Maurice Halbwachs. Halbwachs argued that memory was a social construct, and that nostalgia was 'a retrospective mirage, a reconstruction of the past based on the point of view of the present and constituted within the elements of the present.'[5] Most importantly, though, nostalgia represented an escape from the constraints of time, an exercise of individual freedom that allowed the subject to selectively remember positive experiences and make life bearable. As Suzanne Vromen notes, however, there was also a further side to Halbwach's notion of nostalgia, one that returns perhaps to the word's original meaning: 'Here nostalgia is interpreted not in terms of a desire to return to a previous stage of life but as regret for a loss of place, for a sense of belonging and for permanence.'[6] For many Austrian exiles in the 1930s, and for Korngold too, this nostalgia for a loss of place was particularly potent.

In her biography of her husband, Luzi Korngold writes of the couple's initial sense of homesickness on their first trip to Hollywood in 1934. Having arrived in New York, they set out on the cross-country train journey to California, during which Luzi comforted herself with the thought that:

> it is only for a short time, and then we'll go back to Europe, to our Austria with its meadows, forests and brooks; no doubt, a quiet homesickness had gripped us already on the journey to California.[7]

---

5   Suzanne Vromen, 'Maurice Halbwachs and the Concept of Nostalgia', *Knowledge and Society: Studies in the Sociology of Culture Past and Present* Vol. 6 (1986): 55–66, 61.

6   Vromen, 64.

7   Luzi Korngold, *Erich Wolfgang Korngold: Ein Lebensbild* (Vienna: Lafite, 1967), 65. My translation.

Similarly, of their first visit to the Warner Bros. back lot, she writes of suddenly finding herself in a Viennese suburban alleyway. So deceptive was the imitation that her heart began to beat faster; but upon entering a confectionary 'shop', she and Erich soon realised that the street scene was nothing more than a sentimental façade.[8] Luzi acknowledged that since California became their permanent home in February 1938, many of her initial reactions had changed, and that the couple had 'learnt to establish a homeland within our four walls and to feel at home,'[9] yet unsurprisingly they seem to have socialised primarily with other Austrian and German exiles, such as Max Reinhardt and Helen Thimig, William Dieterle, Salka Viertel, and even someone of such different aesthetic outlook as Arnold Schoenberg.

With Korngold's musical career tied exclusively to his work for Hollywood (his vow not to write 'his' music again until the war's end suggests a lost, nostalgic state), it is perhaps unsurprising that his scores should betray evidence of a deep attachment to his homeland—a vision of *Alt Wien*, as Leon Botstein might term it,[10] that he would later reincorporate into his concert works. Cinema, as Elisabeth Bronfen has argued, is evidently a potent cultural space in which concepts like 'home' can be explored. As she points out:

> We feel ourselves at home in the world of cinema because it represents such an unequivocally illusionary world, defamiliarizing our everyday reality by using the image repertoire of familiar fairy-tale and adventure stories. In so doing, this illusory world offers us precisely the sense of belonging that we seek to negotiate through notions like home.[11]

While Korngold's musical language was steeped in the Viennese traditions handed down by his teacher Zemlinsky, and shaped by his father's love of Mahler and Johann Strauss, many of his scores for Warner Bros. offered the opportunity to make more specific allusions, and thus partake of the potency of cinema to create a sense of home. Some of these films featured Austrian characters or settings,[12] offering a ready-made excuse for evoking a nostalgic Viennese sound: *Kings Row* (Sam Wood, 1942), for instance, is based on Henry Bellamann's novel about small-town American life, but it offered Korngold an opportunity to allude to Johann

---

8   Luzi Korngold, 66.

9   Luzi Korngold, 65.

10   Leon Botstein, 'Gustav Mahler's Vienna', in *The Mahler Companion,* ed. Donald Mitchell and Andrew Nicholson (Oxford: Oxford University Press, 1999), 6–38.

11   Elisabeth Brofen, *Home in Hollywood: The Imaginary Geography of Cinema* (New York: Columbia University Press, 2004), 76.

12   Korngold also made use of Strauss waltzes in the party scenes of *The Constant Nymph (Künstlerleben,* Op. 316) and *Devotion* (though the use of *Accelerationen* Op. 234 is anachronistic, since it dates from 1860, while the film is set in the 1840s).

Strauss II's waltz, *Wiener Blut* when Parris Mitchell leaves his home to study psychoanalysis in turn-of-the-century Vienna.

The film also featured a Viennese girl—who turns Parris's head with a lilting musical turn of phrase—and her benevolent, *gemütlich* father (who looks so like Julius Korngold that it is difficult not to see in him an idealised version of the irascible critic). Indeed, *Kings Row* might be considered typical of Hollywood's attitude to Europe. As Thomas Elsaesser has demonstrated in his examination of the mobility of artists between Europe and Hollywood, movie moguls had fixed ideas about how Americans viewed the old world. Émigrés like Ernst Lubitsch 'found Hollywood hungering for images of a Europe fashioned out of nostalgia, class difference, and romantic fantasy […]. In this context, Vienna became an important reference point, the master sign and key signifier of 'Europe' to America.'[13] Korngold's popularity with Hal Wallis, the executive in charge of production at Warner Bros., might be traced as much to his ability to conjure up this evocative world of old Vienna as to the other qualities inherent in his music.

Particularly curious in this regard is *Juarez* (William Dieterle, 1939), a film that in dealing with the struggle for Mexico's freedom from the French imperialist influence of Louis Napoleon might well have been calculated by Warners as a deliberate appeal to Mexico and Latin America to help see off the Nazi threat.[14] The Hapsburg Archduke Maximillian of Austria, though a foreign interloper duped by a rigged plebiscite into believing he is wanted by the Mexican people as Emperor, is certainly painted sympathetically in contrast with the honest, but ultimately ruthless Benito Juarez. And it is in no small measure due to Korngold's music that this is the case. While Juarez has little music to call his own, and in some places he and his followers are associated with thematic material that can be linked closely with the evil ruler in Korngold's 1928 opera *Das Wunder der Heliane*,[15] Maximillian is by contrast bathed in some of Korngold's richest melodies. The love theme composed for Maximillian and Carlotta, which eventually entered the concert hall as the second subject of the Violin Concerto's first movement, helps to skew our sympathies in favour of this rather over-privileged and naïve Emperor, whose bungling attempts to quash the revolutionary fervour of his new subjects result in more bloodshed—violence that is scored as 'action' by Korngold rather than with any sense of tragedy or pathos. While the film may be titled *Juarez*, with Paul Muni in the title role receiving top billing, it is clear that Korngold's sympathies lie with Brian Aherne's portrayal of his countryman.

---

13 Thomas Elsaesser, 'Ethnicity, Authenticity, and Exile: A Counterfeit Trade?', in *Home, Exile, Homeland: Film, Media, and the Politics of Place*, ed. Hamid Naficy (New York: Routledge, 1999), 111.

14 See Michael E. Birdwell, *Celluloid Soldiers: The Warner Bros. Campaign against Nazism* (New York: New York University Press, 1999), 66.

15 The scene where Juarez confronts Uradi appears to use material from the crowd scene at the beginning of Act III of *Heliane*.

Perhaps even more revealing, though, are those films without Viennese connections that, nevertheless, seem to be 'Austrified' by Korngold's music. The 1937 film *The Prince and the Pauper*, for example, based on the Mark Twain novel and set in an idealised Tudor England, seems an early attempt at the creation of a musical *Alt Wien* even before Korngold's physical links with Vienna were severed. There is an allusion to Johann Strauss II's *Kaiser-Walzer*,[16] and the forest scene following the climactic duel includes a virtual quotation of the opening of the fourth movement of Mahler's Seventh Symphony, a work whose Viennese premiere in 1909 the young Korngold could conceivably have attended with his father.

Similarly, *The Sea Hawk* (Michael Curtiz, 1940), seems to align Errol Flynn's Captain Thorpe with the Rosenkavalier of Strauss's opera, or at least the fanfare that announces his arrival in Act II for the presentation of the rose; while *The Private Lives of Elizabeth and Essex* (Michael Curtiz, 1939), in quoting from a piece Korngold wrote in 1916 for the Austrian Empress, appears to interpret Elizabethan royalty in openly twentieth-century terms.[17]

THE ADVENTURES OF ROBIN HOOD

The most obvious 'Austrification' process, however, in a film with ostensibly no links to Austria occurs in the first score Korngold wrote in official exile, *The Adventures of Robin Hood*. The remarkable circumstances surrounding Korngold's involvement with the film and its role in saving the lives of the composer and his family are relatively well known and need not be revisited here.[18] Suffice it to say that the fate of Austria was constantly on Korngold's mind throughout the period of the score's composition (from February through to mid-April 1938), and the film's themes of racial oppression, injustice, and resistance to an outside aggressor may have seemed peculiarly relevant. Indeed, it has long been considered appropriate to read the film through the lens of contemporary events: Robin's band of men swears an oath to 'fight to the death against our Norman oppressors,' and the film has often been labelled antifascist as a result. Michael Birdwell, for example, places the film firmly within the context of Harry Warner's personal crusade against National Socialism, which prompted him to pull Warner Bros. out of Germany as early as 1934, long before the other studios followed suit, and

---

16   An allusion to bars. 9-11 (Walzer I) can be heard when Tom talks to Father Andrew, although just before this moment there is an equally strong allusion to the love scene in Berlioz's *Romeo et Juliet* (see bars. 277–79 in the Berlioz).

17   *Kaiserin Zita-Hymne*. Having said that, Korngold also attempts a kind of pseudo-historical pastiche, with nods to English national colour, in both *The Sea Hawk* and *Elizabeth and Essex*.

18   See my *Erich Wolfgang Korngold's The Adventures of Robin Hood: A Film Score Guide* (Lanham, MD.: Scarecrow Press, 2007), 75–79.

to make covert antifascist and interventionist films in defiance of Hollywood censorship bodies and the US State Department—films such as *The Life of Emile Zola* and *Sergeant York*.[19] Released in May 1938 by Warner Bros., *The Adventures of Robin Hood* seems to anticipate the resistance movements of Nazi-occupied countries. Robin and his men fight a guerrilla campaign to rid England of the danger represented by Prince John and seek to restore King Richard to the throne, a character who, in being held prisoner, prompts the opening line of dialogue 'News has come from Vienna'—an almost unbelievably apt beginning to the film given contemporary events in Austria.

Yet, for all the parallels and symbolism in dialogue and plot, it is the score that provides some of the clearest indicators for seeing a contemporary Austria encoded in the film, something not lost on members of the Warner Bros. orchestra, who dubbed it 'Robin Hood in the Vienna Woods.' Korngold's contemporary comments, however, reveal a curiously defensive attitude towards such questions, and imply a conscious break with the past. In an interview with *The New York Times* shortly after the film's release, the composer denied rumours that the score used music from his then unproduced opera *Die Kathrin*. As Thornton Delehanty reported,

> Professor Korngold shivered the timbers on the Warners lot with a mixture of rage and mirth [...] [he] railed at the idiocy which would entertain [such a thought]. But more than that, his personal feelings [were] very badly damaged. 'Could anyone think I would use something I had already written?' he asked, with an appalled expression. 'Even if such a thing were possible, it would be cheating.'[20]

Perhaps this is an example of the composer's legendary wit, because the *Robin Hood* score did, in fact, quote extensively from music he had already written (more so than any other of his film scores)—and, furthermore, also alluded strongly to *Die Kathrin*. Moreover, the material re-used in *Robin Hood* evokes a specifically Viennese milieu. Themes from the concert overture *Sursum Corda*, for instance, were used for Robin and for the love between Robin and Maid Marian, while extended sections were adapted to accompany the fight sequences.[21] Although *Sursum Corda*, which was dedicated to Richard Strauss, was the young composer's first real failure when premiered in 1919, it nevertheless dates from the height of Korngold's fame: quoting it must have been a reminder of happier times. The *Robin Hood* score also alludes to some of the composer's earliest musical experiences in Vienna, notably to Mahler's *Des Knaben Wunderhorn* and the 7th Symphony (the opening of King Richard's theme refer-

---

19 See Birdwell, *Celluloid Soldiers*.
20 Thornton Delehanty, 'A Score for Robin Hood', *New York Times* May 22 1938.
21 See Winters, 97–102.

ences the song 'Das himmlische Leben', while the 7ᵗʰ Symphony's final brass statement can be clearly heard in the love theme. Likewise the score also alludes to Viennese music of the present; the first act of *Die Kathrin*, whose Viennese premiere was ultimately delayed until 1950, is referenced in many of the score's fanfares.

By far the most compelling evidence, though, for *Robin Hood*'s musical evocation of a mythic Vienna, is Korngold's use of a waltz tune called 'Miß Austria' (a curious Anglo-Germanic title). This had been composed for Korngold's completion of the unfinished Leo Fall operetta, *Rosen aus Florida*, in 1928 as part of a 'beauty contest of nations' in which 'Miß Austria' appeared on stage preceded by a violinist in traditional Viennese costume. Korngold used this tune in *Robin Hood* as the basis for a condensed waltz sequence in the style of Johann Strauss II, written to accompany the banqueting scenes in Sherwood Forest. Furthermore, when turned into a march associated with the merry men, this theme also opened and closed the film. In scenes evoking the typically Viennese love of nature and good food, the use of a melody associated specifically with an operetta evocation of *Alt Wien* was surely not accidental. Korngold worked on the score during the period around the *Anschluß* in March, and while it remains a possibility that the decision to use this melody was made before the period of Austria's final days, none of the extant undated sketches for the score held at the Library of Congress feature this melody. In any case, a homesick Korngold, worried for his family's safety, could hardly have failed to see its significance when heard in its new context.

AUSTROFASCISM

Yet what the score for *The Adventures of Robin Hood* reveals most clearly is the exiled Korngold's sentimental attachment to an idea that never really existed,[22] a Vienna created by the world of Strauss waltzes and operetta that masked a more unsavoury world of nascent fascist organisations and anti-Semitism. The nostalgic *Alt Wien* suggested by Strauss's melancholy, dreamy waltzes, after all, was a late-nineteenth-century construction created in response to the demographic and physical changes the city underwent in the 1850s and 60s.[23] Looking back to a pre-industrial society free of the economic burdens suffered after the financial crisis of 1873, it also implicitly evoked a Vienna free of much of its Jewish population. This became even more marked after the First World War when, to quote Botstein:

---

22   Indeed, Svetlana Boym suggests that nostalgia 'is a longing for a home that no longer exists or has never existed.' *The Future of Nostalgia*, xiii.
23   See Botstein, 6–38.

An imagined bygone Vienna came into being that mirrored a vanished Italianate grace, the civility of a romanticized eighteenth century, a colourful but extinct aristocracy, a baroque love of ornament, a pre-modern sense of wit, and a construct of classicism powerful enough to debunk the claims of an ascetic modern functional or rational aesthetic.[24]

Running alongside this invented nostalgia, not coincidentally perhaps, we can also trace the beginnings of Austrofascism in general and the Austrian Nazi party in particular, origins that stretch back to the activities of Georg von Schönerer in the 1880s. Indeed, just a few years after Korngold's birth in 1897—a year in which Franz Joseph finally ratified the election of the anti-Semitic Mayor of Vienna, Karl Lueger—a nationalist German Workers' Party sprang into existence with claims to racial and cultural superiority over Czechs and Jews, eventually adopting the name *Deutsche Nationalsozialistische Arbeiterpartei* a few months before the founding of the Germans' own Nazi party in January 1919. Although Austrian Nazism was mired in destructive in-fighting, hampered by weak leaders, and achieved only modest electoral gains prior to its temporary seizing of power for all of 6 hours before Germany marched in on 12 March 1938, it was not the only Austrian political party with a fascist ideology. The *Heimwehr*, for instance, though only mildly anti-Semitic (with the exception of the radical Styrian branch), were the Nazi's chief fascist opposition, both in terms of electoral victories and paramilitary activities. Yet, far more insidious because of their outward respectability, were the *Heimwehr*'s erstwhile allies, the ruling Christian Socialist regimes of Dollfuss and Schuschnigg. Following the social unrest of 1933 and 1934, the Christian Socialists abandoned parliamentary democracy and created a *Ständestaat*, a name redolent of pre-industrial society, complete with an umbrella Fatherland Front organisation, membership of which was required to gain employment.[25] Though officially it rejected exaggerated racism, the Fatherland Front made no attempt to staunch the kind of cultural anti-Semitism advocated by Karl Lueger, and embraced many of the outward features of Nazism: Instead of a *Hakenkreuz*, for instance, it had a similar *Krückenkreuz* symbol; its paramilitary organisations were in many ways indistinguishable from the SS; and it had its own Youth movement. By 1933 the Nazis had been outlawed in Austria, and, following a failed putsch that killed Dollfuss in July 1934,

---

24   Leon Botstein, 'Strauss and the Viennese Critics (1896–1924): Reviews by Gustav Schoenaich, Robert Hirschfeld, Guido Adler, Max Kalbeck, Julius Korngold, and Karl Klaus', in *Richard Strauss and his World,* ed. Bryan Gilliam (Princeton: Princeton University Press, 1992), 311–71.

25   According to Jill Lewis, this move towards fascism was motivated by Dollfuss's attempts to defeat the Socialists and undermine the strength of the working class, rather than a desperate attempt by conservatives to appease the Heimwehr or defeat the Nazi party, as is often assumed. See 'Austria: "Heimwehr", "NSDAP" and the "Christian Social" State', in *The Fascism Reader,* ed. Aristotle A Kallis (London: Routledge, 2003), 212–22.

were in disarray, yet the period still remains one in which fascist ideology was omnipresent in Austrian life, where the majority of Austrians favoured an economically-motivated *Anschluß* with Germany, and where anti-Semitism was tolerated if not actively encouraged. Nazism, therefore, did not suddenly arrive in 1938 on the back of a German invasion; indeed, Alfred Persche (a prominent Austrian Nazi) claimed after the war that as many as 80% of the population were sympathisers.[26]

The enlightened England of Richard the Lionheart that Robin Hood and his followers seek to restore in the film thus had little in common with the everyday reality of independent Austria's political and social unrest, or its economic misery of the previous 20 years. Ironically, when considered with Korngold's score, the England of good King Richard seems to resonate more with the view of a mythical pre-industrial Austria as the centre of Germanic culture that the Nazis and other pan-German groups were interested in promoting. We can even read *The Adventures of Robin Hood* and its score as complicit in an idealised fascist view of Austrian society. Although, as Pamela Potter has suggested in her revisionist account of National Socialist music aesthetics, there was no unified Hitler-driven conception of what constituted Nazi music.[27] Camille Crittenden notes that the Nazis certainly utilised the music of Johann Strauss to help smooth the transition from Österreich to *Ostmark*: the Reich Theatre Festival Weeks of 1938 and 1939, for instance, included performances of *Der Zigenuerbaron* and *Eine Nacht in Venedig*.[28] Though Strauss was also a symbol of Viennese rivalry with Berlin, the Nazis evidently felt the image of the composer to be ideologically appropriate for the task;[29] indeed, Strauss's own relationship with Judaism was, to say the least, complicated.[30]

26   Bruce F Pauley, *Hitler and the Forgotten Nazis; A History of Austrian National Socialism* (Chapel Hill: University of North Carolina Press, 1981), xiv.

27   As she notes, modernism was not rejected per se as has been assumed, and the government also retreated from its anti-jazz measures. See Pamela Potter, 'What is 'Nazi Music'?', *The Musical Quarterly* Vol. 88 No. 3 (Fall 2005), 428–455.

28   See Camille Crittenden, *Johann Strauss and Vienna: Operetta and the Politics of Popular Culture* (Cambridge: Cambridge University Press, 2000), 106.

29   Even Korngold, as an assimilated Jew, never lost his faith in the music of *Alt Wien,* remarking in 1933 that 'The *Fledermaus* score is equal to the most inspired *Lustspiel* music of any nation, [...] indeed it need not shy away from the greatest comparison with Mozart. [...]That Vienna could still give the world Johann Strauss and his *Fledermaus* after Haydn, Mozart, Beethoven, and Schubert, should fill us all with hope for an easier, happier future even in these dark times.' Quoted in Crittenden, 168.

30   Crittenden points out that Johann Strauss was often compared with Karl Lueger as rulers of the masses (though she points out that the comparison is an unlikely one); however, Strauss was known to have sketched a satiric waltz song with an anti-Semitic text (102), and created Jewish parody figures in *Die Fledermaus* (143) and *Der Zigenuerbaron,* though in the latter case Crittenden notes that the anti-Semitic caricature of Zsupán may be as much to do with the singer, Girardi (185–6). Strauss was, however, one-eighth Jewish, a fact that forced Goebbels to authorize the falsification of his birth records (104).

Korngold's use of an overtly Viennese musical vocabulary that carries strong links to the operetta and dance idiom of Strauss and his later Viennese successors thus threatens to ally the score for *Robin Hood* with those constructions of Austrian culture appropriated by the Nazis—though Korngold's Jewishness would have precluded Nazi critics from accepting such a view. Robin and his men, the outlawed representatives of the natural world, in fighting to protect an idyllic and diatonically-characterised countryside from the modernising chromaticised world of the economically-inept Normans, could be just as easily interpreted as outlawed Austrian Nazis, who in their period of civil unrest had suddenly developed an interest in democracy and were often described as 'freedom fighters' in the Nazi press. The film ends, after all, not with the establishment of a democratic nation, but with a restoration of an old order, like the Austrian *Ständestaat*, with Robin as a Nazi *Gauleiter* awarded lands and rule.

Given the difficulties in identifying a unified aesthetic fascist ideology with regards to music, this radical interpretation of *Robin Hood* should perhaps not be taken too far; in any case, the composer certainly cannot be blamed for sharing, in part, the musical tastes of those Nazis with musical influence in Austria—though Korngold's music had also been oddly allied with the anti-Krenek position of Nazi activists back in 1927.[31] Nor does Korngold's romantic musical language necessarily preclude it acting as a force for resistance, no matter how persuasive Adorno's counterclaims for modernism may be. Where Korngold's scores might be regarded as slightly disingenuous in their impact on the contemporary movie-going public, though, is in allying these mythical Hollywood worlds—where happy endings are obligatory and where wrong-doers are brought to justice—with a musical view of old Austria. If, as might conceivably have been Korngold's intention, the *Robin Hood* score drew attention to the situation in present day Austria, it also gave the impression of the country's status, long before it was officially proclaimed as such by the Allies, as the Nazis' first victim.

The Moscow Declaration of 30 October 1943 named Austria as 'the first free country to fall victim to Hitlerite aggression' and thanks to Cold War pressures,[32] this pronouncement was enshrined in the State Treaty of 1955, when, as Hella Pick notes, 'without any concern for historical truth, the four powers [USA, Britain, Soviet Union, France] [...] conspired with Austria's leaders to endow this relaunch of the Second Austrian Republic with a clean bill of health.'[33] As Margarete Lamb-Faffelberger notes, this victim status infiltrated all areas of Austrian society, including even those ex-Nazis threatened by Allied demands for strict dena-

---

31 Julius Korngold's ferocious attack on Krenek's *Jonny spielt auf,* which was matched by propaganda in the Nazi press, famously prompted the Austrian Tobacco Company to produce two rival cigarettes named 'Jonny' and 'Heliane.' See Brendan Carroll, *The Last Prodigy: A Biography of Erich Wolfgang Korngold* (Portland, Ore.: Amadeus Press, 1997), 199.

32 See Günther Bischof, *Austria in the First Cold War 1945–55* (London: Macmillan, 1999).

33 Hella Pick, *Guilty Victim: Austria from the Holocaust to Haider* (London: I B Tauris, 2000), 31.

zification (which was ultimately never as comprehensive as it had been in Germany). Thus, government and academic elites were largely preserved: Egon Schwarz, for example, notes that in the fields of German, Theatre Studies and Folklore, 22 out of a total of 24 post-war professors had been members of the NSDAP and SS.[34] Moreover, legitimate Austrian victims were treated shamefully by the state: In 1953 Chancellor Julius Raab rejected demands by Jews for reparations and resettlement, since the Austrian state was deemed to have suffered under the aggressive acts of its Nazi occupiers.[35] Austria's complicity in its descent into Nazism only began to be questioned in the 1980s with the appearance of studies such as Bruce F. Pauley's *Hitler and the Forgotten Nazis: A History of Austrian National Socialism* (1981), which opened with the provocative statement that 'outrages committed against Austrian Jews by Austrian Nazis during and after 1938 were on the whole worse than those perpetrated by German Nazis against the Jews of Germany.'[36] Five years later the 'big lie'[37] of Austria's status as first victim started to be acknowledged openly during Kurt Waldheim's 1986 election campaign, in which the President's questionable war record was examined.

Korngold's film scores, by allying a musical vision of Austria to the anti-fascist products produced by Warner Bros., perhaps also ran the danger of whitewashing Austrofascism as a German import that, once eradicated, would allow the restoration of a chivalrous, rural, *Alt Wien*—a world akin to the mythical reign of *Robin Hood*'s Richard the Lionheart. Korngold's political views are generally assumed to be all but non-existent[38] and the composer was hardly alone in choosing to place his faith in music rather than politics, yet there is a degree to which his music is arguably complicit in the idealized images of Austria (implied or actual) presented in the cinema. This view of the composer may be supported or ameliorated, depending on one's perspective, by placing these exile years in the wider context of Korngold's

---

34   Egon Schwarz, 'Austria: Quite a Normal Nation', *New German Critique* No. 93 (Autumn 2004), 184. Post-war Austrian musicology also faced similar problems. During the Nazi period, Mozart scholar Erich Schenk, while head of the musicology department at the University of Vienna, became involved in Hitler's and Alfred Rosenberg's plans for an elite university, the *Hohe Schule der Partei,* and provided Herbert Gerigk with racial details of Jews who had received their doctorates in Vienna. After the war, he remained director of the musicology institute until 1971, and in the late 1950s he even became rector at the University. See Pamela Potter, 'Musicology Under Hitler: New Sources in Context,' *Journal of the American Musicological Society* Vol. 40 No. 1 (Spring 1996), 70–113.

35   Margarete Lamb-Faffelberger, 'Beyond *The Sound of Music:* The Quest for Cultural Identity in Modern Austria', *The German Quarterly* Vol. 76 No. 3 (Summer 2003), 289–99.

36   Pauley, xiii.

37   Lamb-Faffelberger, 290.

38   When continually asked of his opinion of Hitler upon arriving in America to work on arranging Mendelssohn's *Midsummer Night's Dream* music for Max Reinhardt's film in 1934, he finally remarked simply that he thought Mendelssohn would outlive him. See Luzi Korngold, 64.

compositional output, which I offer by way of conclusion. Korngold's music, after all, did not appear to change fundamentally in response to his exile; rather, exile seems to have made more apparent the inherently nostalgic aspects of the composer's style evident throughout his career. While this might imply that his nostalgia should not be considered a deluded act of amnesia towards the recent past (as Spitzer worried about with the photos of his parents), it might also suggest that, in being a more general feature of the composer's musical proclivities, the negative associations of 'nostalgia' threaten more than just the film scores.

KORNGOLD'S PRE-WAR NOSTALGIA

Korngold's nostalgic love for his native Vienna, and its musical traditions, is displayed in his works long before the political situation in Austria drove him from the country. His greatest success, *Die tote Stadt*, which was composed in his late teens and early twenties, takes the notion of an idealised past as its central tenet. The opera is not only deeply nostalgic in tone, but also uses the story of a man obsessed with his dead wife to invoke stylised musical snapshots of the past;[39] indeed, in its portrayal of the romantic Paul, with his 'temple of memories' and attachments to sentimental old love songs, it is easy to lose sight of the fact that by the time of its double premiere in Hamburg and Cologne in 1920 the opera's composer was still only a young man in his early 20s, whose music had been previously perceived by some as constituting a dangerous strain of Viennese modernism.[40] For all its atmospheric passages built on quartal harmony—the critic Josef Reitler (a friend of Korngold's father) praised its progressive harmonic vocabulary[41]—*Die tote Stadt* arguably remains dominated by two nostalgic phenomenal songs, Marietta's Lute Song 'Glück, das mir verblieb' and Pierrot's Tanzlied 'Mein Sehnen, mein Wähnen', sung by the character Fritz. Fritz's Pierrot song, though supposedly about the Rhine, is essentially a languorous Viennese waltz, whose text speaks of yearning

---

39 Benjamin Goose argues that Marietta's lute song, 'Glück, das mir verblieb', was interpreted by contemporary critics as 'folksong.' See 'Opera for Sale: Folksong, Sentimentality and the Market', *Journal of the Royal Musical Association* Vol. 133 No. 2 (2008), 189–219.

40 A *New York Times* review of the Sinfonietta referred to the new-found euphony that replaced the 'cacophony and incoherence of what has come to be called [...] "the music of the future" heard in his *Schauspiel* Overture' ('Philharmonic Concert. Korngold's Sinfonietta and Wagner Compositions Performed', 11 December 1914), though *Current Opinion* indicated that other reviews of the Sinfonietta assailed it as a monstrosity of ultra-modernism. See 'Arresting Career of the Youngest Creative Musical Genius', Vol. LXI No. 5 (November 1916).

41 See Andreas Giger, 'Tradition in Post World-War-I Vienna: The Role of the Vienna State Opera from 1919–1924', *International Review of the Aesthetics and Sociology of Music*, Vol. 28 No. 2 (December 1997), 197.

and dreaming to return to the past. Upon hearing it at the first Viennese performance, Luzi Korngold noted how Richard Mayr's singing, and the acclamation that greeted it, triggered a memory of her Grandfather's 50th jubilee at the Burgtheater (something she witnessed as a four year old),[42] a testament to the nostalgic power of this moment. Similarly, like Pierrot's lied, 'Glück, das mir verblieb' is a song that reminds Paul of happier times, so much so that he joins in its singing in order to wallow in remembered bliss, and to further cement in the figure of Marietta the image of his dead wife, Marie. Although one could argue that the opera is *about* nostalgia rather than inherently nostalgic,[43] it is tempting indeed to see both these standout numbers of the opera not merely as the reflection of Paul's dreamy and love-sick state, or Fritz's efforts to win the favour of Marietta, but as an expression of Korngold's own attachment to an idealized past—something he undoubtedly shared with his Viennese audience. Indeed, the opera's enormous success surely owed a great deal to its apparent nostalgia for the passing of an old world, offering a fragmented and war-weary European society an illusory wholeness.

In the early 1920s, Korngold was also part of a group of composers that felt the need to make a statement against the dodecaphony of the Second Viennese School, and to assert their status as the true inheritors of Vienna's musical past: along with Joseph Marx, for example, he became artistic director of an addendum to the 1923 Salzburg Festival devoted to Austrian music, which included works by Hans Gál, Alexander Zemlinsky, and Julius Bittner (among others).[44] Similarly, although Korngold turned emphatically to the world of Viennese operetta in the late 1920s partly for reasons of financial and artistic security,[45] it cannot be denied that in adapting works by Strauss and Leo Fall he discovered an instant affinity for the genre's musical language.[46] Indeed, Luzi relates how Korngold had restored a duet in *Eine Nacht in Venedig* because it was his favourite number in the operetta, only to discover from Frau Adele Strauss that it had also been her husband's.[47] When the call from Hollywood came in 1934, this most traditional of Viennese institutions dominated Korngold's artistic life, influencing even the concert works from this period (See the waltz finale to the 2nd String Quartet

---

42   Luzi Korngold, 33.

43   See Ben Winters, 'Strangling Blondes: Nineteenth-Century Femininity and Korngold's *Die tote Stadt*', *Cambridge Opera Journal* Vol. 23 No. 1-2 (March-July 2011): 51-82.

44   Carroll, 157–58.

45   This was in response to the lukewarm reception of his 1927 opera, *Das Wunder der Heliane*. See Andreas Giger, 'A Matter of Principle: The Consequences for Korngold's Career,' *The Journal of Musicology*, Vol. 16 No. 4 (Autumn 1998), 545–64.

46   Julius Korngold even credits his son with initiating a Strauss renaissance. See Julius Korngold, *Die Korngolds in Wien* (Zürich: M & T Verlag, 1991), 287–88.

47   Luzi Korngold, 37.

of 1934). Likewise, *Die Kathrin*—Korngold's fifth and, ultimately, last opera—seems to approach the easy melodiousness of operetta. Subtitled 'a folk opera', its musical language is far more diatonic, in the first act at least, than the intense chromaticism of *Heliane*, and moves towards the musical language that Korngold employed in several of the film scores, notably *Robin Hood*.

The composer's relationship with his native Vienna, however, undoubtedly altered as a result of his years in exile, although his affection for the city remained undimmed (as his *Sonnett für Wien*, Op. 41 reveals). Though he attempted a return after the war, bringing with him works retaining their Viennese origins yet covered with a coat of Hollywood gloss,[48] he was left disappointed by the response he received. In many cases it was far from hostile,[49] but it certainly did not approach the success of the early 1920s, and Korngold noted in a somewhat bitter letter to Joseph Marx in 1952 the wave of hostility and spitefulness from the art-snobs encountered on his last visit there.[50] Korngold, after all, was a romantic with no desire to show the grim actualities of everyday life in his music, a position he articulated in 1953:

> I, myself, do not believe in the mistaken thesis that art should mirror its time […] No, I am much more inclined to believe the opposite: the genuine artist creates at a distance from his own time, even for a time beyond. The true creative artist does not wish to recreate for his fellow man the headlines screaming of atom bombs, murder, and sensationalism found in the daily paper. Rather, for his fellow man, he will know how to take and uplift him into the purer realm of phantasy.[51]

And so the composer returned to Los Angeles, where the dream world of Hollywood undoubtedly had offered a far more palatable vision of his homeland than the reality of a semi-fascist state, unification with the Third Reich, and finally ten years of allied occupation. Exiled from an Austria to which he would never return on a permanent basis, he could perhaps take comfort in the world his film music helped create, and the sentimental wisdom its characters espoused. Thus in the Korngold-scored film, *Juarez*, Dr. Basch, talking of the Austrian vines growing in Mexico, offered the exiled composer an image with which he could conceivably identify, a panacea for the homesick Austrian: 'wine is a living thing […] and no matter

---

48 Nearly all the post-war works feature material used in the film scores. See Winters, *Erich Wolfgang Korngold's The Adventures of Robin Hood*, 48–49. The passage featuring the Strauss allusion in *The Prince and the Pauper* was re-used in Korngold's *Passover Psalm Op. 30* (1941).

49 The premieres of the Symphonic Serenade (under Furtwängler) and the Symphony attracted a number of positive reactions in the Viennese press.

50 833/32– 5 in the Austrian National Library's collection of Musical Letters.

51 From the introduction to Ulric Devaré's book *Faith in Music*. Quoted in Carroll, 358–59.

how far a plant is carried, something of its homeland—its sun, its soil, its seasons—will remain in the vine, and the wine from the vine, forever.' The language used here is ironic indeed given the criticisms of the Nazis, who accused Korngold and his fellow so-called 'degenerate' Jewish composers of a cultural 'rootlessness'—of merely imitating Austro-Germanic culture, rather than being rooted in its soil—but it neatly encapsulates the composer's relationship with Viennese culture.[52]

Korngold's nostalgia (either as an expression of *Heimweh* for Austria or as a more generalized romantic notion, typical of the generation born around 1900) was certainly an essential part of his musical persona.[53] While its presence in the film scores as part of Warner Bros.' anti-fascist narratives may be variously interpreted as an act of resistance on the one hand, or a misleading simplification of Austrofascism on the other, it cannot be denied that Korngold was anything other than true to his own vision of what art should seek to accomplish. Our view of him, therefore, may ultimately depend on which of Spitzer's responses chimes more with our critical sympathies.

---

52   A criticism that, as Bryan Gilliam has recognised, bears a striking resemblance to the left-wing Frankfurt School thinking of Adorno, who attacked film music as debasing authentic musical gestures. See Bryan Gilliam, 'A Viennese Opera Composer in Hollywood: Korngold's Double Exile in America', 223–42 in *Driven into Paradise: The Musical Migration from Nazi Germany to the United States,* ed. Reinhold Brinkmann and Christoph Wolff (Berkeley: University of California Press, 1999), 229.
53   See Lasch, 107.

Magnar Breivik

From Surabaya to Ellis Island

On two versions of Kurt Weill's 'Surabaya-Johnny'

Kurt Weill (1900–1950) was among the large number of European musicians who emigrated to the USA during the 1930s. The circumstances of his departure from Germany are well known. His musical play *Der Silbersee, Ein Wintermärchen* (Georg Kaiser) was premiered in Leipzig, Erfurt, and Magdeburg concurrently on 18 February 1933, just over two weeks after Hitler's attainment of power and only nine days before the arson attack on the Reichstag. Weill had already been mercilessly attacked in the Nazi press for his Jewish origins, his left-wing political sympathies and as a modernist dallying with jazz. So it is hardly surprising that due to Nazi protests, *Der Silbersee* was withdrawn from all three theatres at the beginning of March. On 21 March, Weill fled to France, leaving most of his former life and belongings behind. After a transitional stay in Paris and a few months in London, Weill arrived in America on 10 September 1935, together with his wife Lotte Lenya.

Were it not for these disastrous political events, Weill would probably never have left his native country. Like so many members of Jewish families that had lived on German soil for centuries, Weill had definitely regarded himself as a German. From the *Dreigroschenoper* (*Threepenny Opera*) of 1928, and even before that, the notion of artistic success had become strongly attached to his name. Yet there are reasons to believe that Weill did not regard his forced move as just a temporary getaway to a safe haven in times of harassment and persecution. Probably he also saw it as a step towards what might turn into a permanent and promising new life. The reasons for such expectations were certainly complex, but no doubt the European *Amerikanismus* of the 1920s—according to which America was seen as epitomizing the modern life style *per se* in a free country with open-minded people and ample opportunities for everyone had intrigued Kurt Weill for quite some time.[1] Together with Bertolt Brecht, he had launched no less than four music-theatre pieces that provided an ironic commentary on American society: *Mahagonny Songspiel* (1927), *Happy End* (1929), *Aufstieg und Fall der Stadt Mahagonny* (1930), and *Die sieben Todsünden* (1933). There are also reasons to believe

---

1   A theme that is famously celebrated at the close of Krenek's *Jonny spielt auf,* arguably the most popular opera in the latter part of the Weimar Republic.

that Weill saw greater potential in appealing to a supposedly more uninhibited musical public across the Atlantic than had ever seemed the case in Europe. Moreover, his writings expose optimism concerning the American stage as a prolific arena for the development of inventive musical-theatre projects furthering the artistic experiences he had pursued with Brecht and others back in Berlin. In the notes for the original cast recording of his 'American opera' *Street Scene* (Elmer Rice/Langston Hughes) 1947, Weill writes:

> [...] My first Broadway show, *Johnny Johnson* [1936], was still a continuation of the for-mula which I had tried out in Europe. But through this show I learned a great deal about Broadway and its audience. I discovered that a vast, unexploited field lay between grand opera and musical comedy, although the ground was already well prepared. I discovered that there was a highly receptive audience with a great sensitivity for music and a great capacity for emotions. I discovered also that there was a rich collection of young singers with great acting talent, full of ambition and eager to work, but frustrated by the lack of outlets for their talents. The more I studied this situation the more I became convinced of the possibility to develop out of this material a musical theatre which could eventually grow into something like an American opera [...][2]

Weill's words in a letter to the editor of *Life Magazine,* which in February 1947 had published a feature story on *Street Scene* and its allegedly 'German composer,' are typical for his affirma-tive attitude towards his new existence, both as an artist and as a human being:

> Although I was born in Germany, I do not consider myself a 'German composer.' The Na-zis obviously did not consider me as such either, and I left their country (an arrangement which suited both me and my rulers admirably) in 1933. I am an American citizen, and during my dozen years in this country I have composed exclusively for the American stage [...]. I would appreciate your straightening out your readers on this matter.[3]

This quotation also makes clear his conviction that the Nazis had stolen his national identity and that he did not wish Germany to take any credit for his fame as a prolific composer in the New World. The words 'I am an American' are often attributed to Kurt Weill, being seen as another token of his readiness to acquire a new nationality. However, the connection between Weill and this declaration is probably more due to the fact that he, like so many other famous

---

2   Kurt Weill, 'Two Dreams Come True', in *Street Scene: A Sourcebook,* ed. Joanna Lee, Edward Harsh, and Kim Kowalke (New York: Kurt Weill Foundation for Music, 1996), 26.

3   Facsimile in *Street Scene: A Sourcebook*, 25.

people who had successfully obtained American citizenship, participated in a series called 'I am an American' on NBC, in 1941.[4]

Weill's early tonal language may be described as expressionist, as for instance in his First Symphony (1921), soon developing into the kind of expanded tonality that is heard in his transparent Concerto for Violin and Wind Orchestra of 1924. This type of extended tonality that unfolds within a clear-cut and concentrated formal design was typical for the *Neue Sachlichkeit* at the time, and is consequently also found in composers such as Hindemith and Stravinsky. A distinctive trait in this kind of musical procedure is that the intervals of fourths and fifths tend to dominate the score at the expense of thirds and sixths, a tendency that helps to blur the feeling of a traditional major-minor tonality. It may be useful to have this observation in mind whenever Kurt Weill's further stylistic development is concerned. Just to mention one of Weill's later trademarks, his favoured use of triads with added sixths (for instance in the form of c-g-a-e) that may point towards major and minor at one and the same time, must be seen as a procedure actually rooted in his earlier superimpositions of fourths and fifths, not merely as some trivial, popular-music colouring.

One of the most well-known examples of Weill's added-sixth formations is heard already in the first three notes of the 'The Ballad of Mack the Knife' (C-major: e-g-a). This song, originally 'Die Moritat von Mackie Messer,' comes right after the overture of *Die Dreigroschenoper*, Weill's second collaboration with Brecht. This piece, one of the greatest sensations in musical-theatre history, became a turning point in the composer's career, as one of the earliest of his compositions that was heavily influenced by popular-music idioms. Hence, *Die Dreigroschenoper* stands out as an elucidating example of Weill's aim to face the challenge of making a fruitful amalgamation between so-called serious, contemporary, modernist music and popular music, including dance music and the exciting new idioms of jazz. One of the important driving forces seems to have been that he saw a strong potential for reaching out to a new musical-theatre public through such a stylistic fusion, at a time when the art of opera needed a thorough renewal and the notorious rift between contemporary art and so-called ordinary people seemed to be expanding to a threatening degree. According to the ideals of *Gebrauchsmusik*, Weill's consideration for the consumer became one of the important guiding stars for each new piece. Yet at the same time, his adaptation of popular-music idioms in the 1920s also created another kind of distance, since this stylistic mixture, which included so many 'wrong notes in the right place', became one of the most prominent musical *Verfremdung* (alienation/estrangement) devices in his and Brecht's collaborations. Hence, a gap was still maintained, but now particularly between his own musical-theatre songs and the mass-

---

4   See *Kurt Weill. Musik und musikalisches Theater: Gesammelte Schriften,* ed. Stephen Hinton and Jürgen Schebera (Mainz: Schott Musik International, 2000), 491–97.

produced *Schlagermusik* for the vastly expanding gramophone industry of the time. Generally, Weill made a point of describing the kind of *Gebrauchsmusik* he wished to promote not
as 'superficially seductive like the gramophone hit.' Due to its ethical and social content, this
music should rather be 'bitter, accusing, in its mildest form ironic.'[5]

In 1929, the year after their huge *Dreigroschen* success, Weill and Brecht started working
on the songs for a new project, undoubtedly with the same broad and enthusiastic public
in mind. Entitled *Happy End,* it was based on an American short story by Elisabeth Hauptmann.[6] Hauptmann had allegedly encountered the story in *The J. & L. Weekly* of Saint Louis,
and now had re-worked it under the pseudonym of Dorothy Lane.[7] Despite the fact that
this work included musical numbers that would later be regarded as amongst the most un-
forgettable songs composed by Brecht and Weill, the piece was a flop. It was criticised on two
counts. First, the play was deemed to be inadequate—a suspiciously thin story about some
Chicago gangsters and the Salvation Army leading to a quite trivial happy ending of reconciliation.[8] Second, the piece also included some agitprop numbers that did not go down well
with Berlin audiences at the time. After three performances *Happy End* disappeared from the
stage, and Weill's score was not revived until 1958.[9] Nevertheless, despite its initial failure, the
work contains a number of very important numbers, not least the soon-to-be famous song
'Surabaya-Johnny' alongside the 'Bilbao-Song' and 'Matrosen-Tango.'

Brecht had already written the text to 'Surabaya-Johnny' in 1926, for the piece *Kalkutta,
4. Mai,* which was a revision of Lion Feuchtwanger's drama *Warren Hastings, Governour von
Indien* (1915). According to Brecht scholar Albrecht Dümling, in *Kalkutta, 4. Mai,* the 'Song
von Surabaya-Johnny' is performed by an adventurous Lady Marjorie Hike in the palace of the
British governor to the accompaniment of a banjo. She 'sings and tap-dances' this sentimental
folk-song, according to the scene instructions, with the objective of preventing an assault upon

---

5   See Kurt Weill, 'Die Oper—wohin? Gebrauchsmusik und ihre Grenzen', *Musik und musikalisches
     Theater: Gesammelte Schriften,* 92–96.

6   The author Elisabeth Hauptmann (1897–1973) began collaborating with Brecht in 1924, and in additi-
     on to *Happy End*, she is purported to have contributed substantially to both the *Mahagonny Songspiel*
     and *Die Dreigroschenoper.*

7   According to Forster Hirsh, *Kurt Weill on Stage: From Berlin to Broadway* (New York: Limelight Edi-
     tions, 2003), 57, many years later Hauptmann admitted that she had made up both the magazine and
     the author: 'There is no "Dorothy Lane"; there was no magazine story,' she said.

8   As Hirsh also points out 'Characters and milieu bear a striking resemblance to *Guys and Dolls,* the
     1950 musical by Frank Loesser, Abe Burrows, and Jo Swerling based on a story by Damon Runyon,
     'The Idyll of Miss Sarah Brown,' which was not published until 1932 […]', 57.

9   See Mario R. Mercado, *Kurt Weill: A Guide To His Works* (New York: Kurt Weill Foundation for Mu-
     sic, Inc., 1994), 76.

the ruthless governor.[10] Dümling points out that Brecht's text is based on a ballad by Rudyard Kipling, 'Mary, Pity Women', of which Elisabeth Hauptmann had already made a 'rough translation' that Brecht re-worked into 'Maria, Fürsprecherin der Frauen' ('Maria, advocate of women').[11] Kipling mentioned the story of an elderly bar lady in a London pub as the source for his ballad. Dümling highlights several striking similarities between the verbal expressions in Kipling's and Brecht's texts. However, in the Kipling ballad, the man is anonymous, whereas in Brecht's song, his name is Surabaya-Johnny.[12]

In *Happy End* 'Das Lied vom Surabaya-Johnny', now with music by Kurt Weill, assumed a function similar to its purpose in *Kalkutta, 4. Mai:* One of the protagonists, Halleluja-Lillian of the Salvation Army, prevents gangster boss Bill Cracker from committing a break-in through her singing.[13] Together with songs like 'Jenny, die Seeräuberbraut' (*Die Dreigroschenoper*), 'J'attends un navire' (*Marie Galante*, 1934), 'Aggie's Song' (*Johnny Johnson*) 'My Ship' (*One Touch of Venus*, 1943), and 'Somehow I Never Could Believe' (*Street Scene*), 'Surabaya-Johnny' is one of Kurt Weill's many songs depicting an unhappy, lonely, and longing woman. In the colonial *Kalkutta,* Brecht's initial surroundings for the ruthless bloke called Johnny, Surabaya, Burma, and Punjab are not situated that far away. However, in the context of the 'American' *Happy End,* the person with the nickname 'Surabaya-Johnny' gives the impression of belonging to any sort of undependable vagrant who may come from any mysterious, unknown territory far away—why not from a place with the exotic and intriguingly melodious name of Surabaya?

In the song each of the three stanzas is divided into three sections as a two-section verse followed by a recurring refrain. The three sections may be regarded as displaying three stages of womanly love: The *first section* (a) deals with the woman's sweet memories of once upon a time having fallen in love, the *second section* (b) with the exasperated accusations against her lover who turned out to be hugely deceptive and notoriously unfaithful, and then follows the recurring *third section* (c) describing her unhappy, yet deep and self-sacrificing love that seems to last after all. 'Ich liebe dich' is repeated seven times throughout the text. Undoubtedly the highly emotional and all-too-human text may account for the fact that there are so many recordings and exceedingly individual interpretations of this song:

---

10 See Albrecht Dümling, 'Surabaya-Johnny', in *Brecht Handbuch, Band 2, Gedichte,* ed. Jan Knopf (Stuttgart/Weimar: Verlag J.B. Metzler, 2001), 136.

11 At one stage, the song was considered for inclusion in *Die Dreigroschenoper,* but this idea was subsequently abandoned.

12 Dümling, 136–37.

13 Dümling, 137.

I

a) *Ich war jung, Gott, erst sechzehn Jahre.*
Du kamest von Burma herauf.
Du sagtest, ich solle mit dir gehen,
Du kamest für alles auf.
Ich fragte nach deiner Stellung.
Du sagtest, so wahr ich hier steh',
Du hättest zu tun mit der Eisenbahn
Und nicht zu tun mit der See.

b) *Du sagtest viel Johnny,*
Kein Wort war wahr, Johnny.
Du hast mich betrogen, Johnny, zur ersten Stund.
Ich hasse dich so, Johnny,
Wie du da stehst und grinst, Johnny.
Nimm doch die Pfeife aus dem Maul, du Hund!

c) *Surabaya-Johnny, warum bist du so roh?*
Surabaya-Johnny, mein Gott und ich liebe dich so.
Surabaya-Johnny, warum bin ich nicht froh?
Du hast kein Herz, Johnny, und ich liebe dich so!

II

a) *Zuerst war es immer Sonntag.*
Das war, bis ich mitging mit dir.
Aber dann, schon nach zwei Wochen,
War dir nichts mehr recht an mir.
Hinauf und hinab durch den Pandschab,
Den Fluss entlang bis zur See:
Ich sehe schon aus im Spiegel
Wie eine Vierzigjährige.

b) *Du wolltest nicht Liebe, Johnny,*
Du wolltest Geld, Johnny.
Ich aber sah, Johnny, nur auf deinen Mund.
Du verlangtest alles, Johnny.

Ich gab dir mehr, Johnny.
Nimm doch die Pfeife aus dem Maul, du Hund!

c) *Surabaya-Johnny, Warum bist du so roh?*
Surabaya-Johnny, mein Gott und ich liebe dich so.
Surabaya-Johnny, warum bin ich nicht froh?
Du hast kein Herz, Johnny, und ich liebe dich so!

III
a) *Ich habe es nicht beachtet,*
Warum du den Namen hast.
Doch an der ganzen langen Küste
Warst du ein bekannter Gast.
Eines Morgens, in einem Six-Pence-Bett,
Werd' ich donnern hören die See;
Und du gehst, ohne etwas zu sagen,
Und ein Schiff liegt unten am Kai.

b) *Du hast kein Herz, Johnny,*
Du bist ein Schuft, Johnny.
Du gehst jetzt weg, Johnny, sag mir den Grund!
Ich liebe dich doch, Johnny,
Wie am ersten Tag, Johnny.
Nimm doch die Pfeife aus dem Maul, du Hund!

c) *Surabaya-Johnny, Warum bist du so roh?*
Surabaya-Johnny, mein Gott und ich liebe dich so.
Surabaya-Johnny, warum bin ich nicht froh?
Du hast kein Herz, Johnny, und ich liebe dich so![14]

The accompaniment of the first section is very typical of Kurt Weill during the late 1920s and early 1930s. The opening consists of a repeated ostinato pattern including the use of organ points, harmonically comprising a dominant-chord formation:

---

14 © With kind permission by Universal Edition A.G., Wien.

Example 1: Kurt Weill, 'Surabaya-Johnny,' opening bars, manuscript 1929© With kind permission from Universal Edition A.G., Wien.

The opening chord, divided between the right hand and the left hand of the piano-version manuscript, may be seen both as a dominant chord based on F sharp and a C-sharp minor chord with a seventh on the top of a dissonant organ point of F sharp, or as an E-major chord on the top of an F-sharp organ point. The inclusion of C sharp in the voice, typical of Weill's aforementioned predilection for added sixths, highlights the ambiguity between C-sharp minor and E major as far as the melody is concerned. Nevertheless, from a theoretical point of view, the composer obviously regarded E major as the basic key, since one can see 'nach Es-Dur transponieren' ('to be transposed into E flat-major') written on the top right of his manuscript, as is demonstrated by the full-score version of the opening of Surabaya-Johnny:

Example 2: Kurt Weill, 'Surabaya-Johnny', *Happy End. Komödie mit Music,* opening bars, full score. © With kind permission from Universal Edition A.G., Wien.

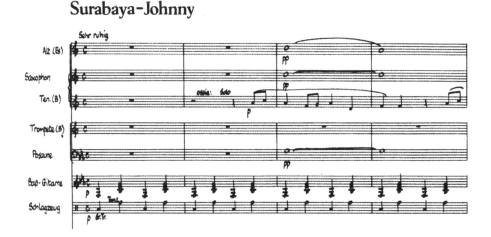

Both versions share a basic trait that from the start there is a dominant-sounding chord that does not function as a dominant according to traditional harmony. It rather acts as an unresolved chord, which may be interpreted as depicting the unfulfilled emotions and discontented situation of the poetical I: At the present point in her life sombre dissonances are shadowing her early memories of an innocent love that later would prove sadly unfortunate. This kind of a semi-dissonant, harmonically unresolved ostinato pattern is often found in Weill's songs at the time, especially when unsettled emotions, bitterness, but also impatience and restlessness, are involved.[15]

The next section (b) of the song reveals the other side of the coin—the unfaithful scoundrel that Surabaya-Johnny soon turned out to be. The poetical I is confronting him with his deceptive character through furious accusations. Now she is fully determined—no harmonic ambiguity here—every bar includes a strong statement and a pointed musical cadence. In the two first stanzas all this is combined with extra intensification by means of a change from quadruple to triple meter:

Example 3: Kurt Weill, 'Surabaya-Johnny', bars 19–20, song-piano manuscript, 1929. © With kind permission from Universal Edition A.G., Wien.

---

15 'Jenny, die Seeräuberbraut' and the first part of the 'Alabama Song' (*Aufstieg und Fall der Stadt Mahagonny*) may serve as two well-known examples.

Through the change of meter from 4/4 to 3/4, the accusations follow each other becoming more plaintively sad, but also more densely breathless and hence more uncontrolled: 'Du sagtest viel, Johnny. Kein Wort war wahr, Johnny[…]' ('You said a lot, Johnny, not a word was true, Johnny') In the third and last stanza, however, Weill keeps the quadruple meter by adding rests in a way that makes the text of these bars more decided and irrefutable: 'Du hast kein Herz, Johnny. Du bist ein Schuft, Johnny[…]' ('You have no heart, Johnny, you're a scoundrel, Johnny […]'

In the last section (c), the recurring refrain of 'Surabaya-Johnny, Warum bist du so roh? Surabaya-Johnny, mein Gott und ich liebe dich so!' ('Surabaya-Johnny, why are you so callous? Surabaya-Johnny, my God and I love you so!'), the resigned yet longing love on the part of the unhappy woman is described through the opening notes in major tonality immediately twisted into minor, another trait typical of Kurt Weill, both at the time and in the years to come. The three opening notes are identical with the added-sixth formation introducing 'Mackie Messer,' one more trait characteristic of the composer. Descending chromatics in the accompaniment, all fading out in E-major tonality with an open, added sixth in the melody: 'Du hast kein Herz, Johnny, und ich liebe dich so.' ('You've got no heart, Johnny, and I love you so much.')

When Weill arrived in the USA in 1935, the gradual development towards a more accessible musical language had been taking place for some years. As has already been suggested, to a considerable degree this process was inspired by his views on the social functions of up-to-date musical theatre. When Weill suddenly found himself on the Broadway-theatre scene, he met a public used to American musical-theatre traditions based on the American language and founded on American popular songs, not a Berlin public rooted in opera, operetta, and cabaret. This meant new and quite significant challenges, not only determined by the American vernacular of popular music but also by the commercial system upon which the theatrical productions on Broadway were based. Consequently, through the last part of Weill's life, his style developed towards a musical language that was supposed to be more readily accessible to the American public. Yet it is important to keep in mind that Weill never abandoned what he saw as his life-long position as an innovator of the musical theatre. This meant that through most of his pieces he tried to challenge the traditional limits even of Broadway musical theatre, both as far as music and the conception of genre were concerned. His aforementioned notes for the recording of his opera for Broadway, *Street Scene*, written only a couple of years before his untimely death, are typical of his attitude:

> Ever since I made up my mind at the age of 19, that my special field of activity would be the theatre, I have tried continuously to solve, in my own way, the form-problems of the musical theatre, and through the years I have approached these problems from all different angles.[16]

---

16   Kurt Weill, 'Two Dreams Come True', *Street Scene: A Sourcebook*, 26.

A second piano-song version of 'Surabaya-Johnny', probably written in the early 1940s, provides an interesting glimpse into the process of change in Weill's musical style during the final part of his life in the USA. This 'American' arrangement of the song, possibly for Lotte Lenya, was not published. The new version may have served as the material for a recording of *Six Songs by Kurt Weill,* made by Bost Records in 1942/43,[17] but the certainty of purpose for this particular arrangement is still questioned. The recording consisted of two songs each from Weill's periods in America, France, and Germany respectively: 'Lost in the Stars,' 'Lover Man', 'J'attends un navire,' 'Complainte de la Seine,' 'Soerabaja Johnny'[18], and 'Wie man sich bettet.' The songs are interpreted by Lotte Lenya, and the director of Bost Records, Herbert Borchardt,[19] claims that Kurt Weill is sitting at the piano.[20]

Weill always hesitated to write a melody for some upcoming song before he had in his hands what he saw as a text with a potential for musical interpretation. A composer's capacity for mastering a text by remoulding it due to his or her artistic visions was perhaps the most powerful driving force behind the development of his remarkable talent as a musical-theatre composer. In connection with his last Brecht-collaboration, the 'ballet chantée' *Die sieben Todsünden* (1933), Weill wrote that 'every text I've set looks entirely different once it has been swept through my music.'[21] These words give emphasis to his view that a composer really has the power to change a text in a fundamental way through the music. Furthermore, Weill's statement must also imply that if a composer makes a new version of his own music to a text, then he or she will also inevitably be presenting a new version of that particular text. Hence, one interesting question pertaining to 'Surabaya-Johnny' is whether the two musical versions made in Germany and USA respectively also present different interpretations of Brecht's words.

In the 1940s version in Example 4, the former tempo designation 'Sehr ruhig (blues)'[22] (see Ex. 1) has been changed into the more neutral *Andante cantabile.* The '2 verses' written above the tempo marking may of course refer to a foreshortening due to the limited space of a recording, but there may also be other reasons for keeping just two verses of a rather comprehensive song in a foreign language.[23] The most obvious difference in this version of

---

17   The recording may be heard on *Kurt Weill: from Berlin to Broadway* on Pearl (GEMM CDS 9189).
18   Soerabaja was the former name of Surabaya.
19   Herbert Borchardt (1906–2000) was a friend of Weill's and a fellow refugee
20   See 'Recording Kurt Weill: […] Herbert Borchardt remembers'(interview conducted by David Farneth and Kim Kowalke), *Kurt Weill Newsletter, Volume 23, Number 1,* Spring 2005, New York, 8–12.
21   Kurt Weill in an unpublished letter to Erika Neher, made available in Johanna Lee and Kim Kowalke (eds.) *Die 7 Todsünden/The 7 Deadly Sins: A Sourcebook* (New York: The Kurt Weill Foundation for Music, 1997), 5.
22   The 'blues' qualification of the tempo was omitted in the full-score version.
23   In the recording Lenya sings the first and third stanza, and the tonality is D-flat major.

'Surabaya-Johnny' compared to the initial one, however, is plainly seen and heard already from the start. The dissonant organ point is now gone: an unmistakable E-flat major, albeit still with an added sixth, tones down any possible harmonic ambiguity. In this harmonic context, the added sixth gives more the impression of reflecting a popular-music convention rather than as being part of a more complex harmonic structure. Yet one should bear in mind that this added sixth is actually rooted in a harmonically more complex style typical for Weill's development during the 1920s. Accordingly, with the composer's compositional development in mind, the added sixth even here may be regarded as more structural than ornamental. In this version, we are in an undisputable major mode, and the slow and march-like ostinato accompaniment of the 1929-version is now made lighter, more flowing, and more flexible, almost as if it is imitating a piano *berceuse*. The right-hand doubling of the melody one octave above the singing voice, which is harmonized by fifths, fourths, and thirds, adds to the impression of increased transparency and lightness.

Example 4: Kurt Weill, 'Surabaya-Johnny', opening bars, song-piano manuscript, early 1940s. © With kind permission from Universal Edition A.G., Wien.

In the second section, contrary to the 1929-version, Weill sticks to the quadruple meter all the way through, which means that there is no change of meter at all in this new arrangement:

Example 5: Kurt Weill, 'Surabaya-Johnny', bars 18–21, song-piano manuscript, early 1940s. © With kind permission from Universal Edition A.G., Wien.

The lack of the initial changing meter from 4/4 to 3/4 fits in well with the smoothness of this arrangement as a whole, and the rest on the third beat cools down both the breathless misery and the accusing intensity that had been so characteristic in two first stanzas of the 1929 version.[24] It even looks as if Weill wants to prevent any restless interpretation by adding *Tranquillo*. In other words, he quite deliberately seems to prefer a rather different mode of expression than before.

The haunting refrain, with the allegedly hopeless situation of being trapped in the love for a rascal, now sounds less discouraging, not least due to Weill's continuous use of an accompaniment loosening up the former tendency towards rhythmical monotony. He applies a slightly syncopated rhythmical pattern reminiscent of a slow-paced Latin-American dance:

Example 6: Kurt Weill, 'Surabaya-Johnny', bars 31–34, song-piano manuscript, early 1940s. © With kind permission by Universal Edition A.G., Wien.

24 In the recording, where the quadruple meter also is kept throughout the song, Lenya seems to have a wish to counteract the evenness by bridging the gaping rests through a compensating tempo increase justified by an impatient *parlando* interpretation.

A comparison between the two versions of 'Surabaya-Johnny', the first one written in Germany and the other in the USA, thus shows a change in Weill's musical style within one and the same song. In the second version, the harmonic structure is less dissonant and more conventional then in the first one. The irregularity of a change of meter in the first version has been abandoned, and the greyish monotony of the accompaniment has been replaced by a greater degree of lightness and flexibility. The music has beyond doubt become less 'bitter and accusing.'[25] This change inevitably also affects Brecht's text: the unhappy woman who has fallen in love with the crook Surabaya-Johnny now appears less bitter and accusing as well. The character of the song as a whole has rather changed in the direction of displaying nostalgic memories and vain complaints concluded by a cheerless affirmation of eternal love.

As already suggested, the development of Kurt Weill's musical style towards greater accessibility cannot be explained only through his situation as a refugee or his being a person in exile. Developments and changes took place throughout Weill's entire compositional career, and the alterations are probably more due to his position as a dedicated musical-theatre composer rather than as a 20th-century modernist composer in the traditional European sense. Within the confinements of his basic views and his musical capacity, he would therefore meet what he saw as the actual challenges of a new theatre piece, be it in Berlin, Paris or New York. Nevertheless, half of Kurt Weill's career as a mature composer took place during his exile in USA, so the artistic conditions of the continent to which he had been expatriated inevitably had a most substantial impact upon his musical production and consequently on his musical style. 'Surabaya-Johnny,' emigrating from fictive America in *Happy End* to real America via Ellis Island, thus also becomes a tiny but telling case study of the influence of artistic exile on a composer's musical style.

Weill's stylistic changes did not imply that he renounced on his search for verbal depths and genuinely human drama. This is more than just obvious in what he regarded to represent the very zenith of his achievements as a composer, the aforementioned Broadway opera *Street Scene*. In pieces such as *Die Dreigroschenoper, Happy End,* and *Aufstieg und Fall der Stadt Mahagonny* back in Berlin, he had endeavoured to include the characteristics of popular music in his current language of serious music. In *Street Scene* he goes the other way round, as he imposes the operatic traditions of his native Europe upon the musical-theatre conventions of his new adopted homeland. Perhaps this piece, more than any of his other works, displays the mixed artistic identity caused by his European background and his American destination. No wonder that it was in connection with precisely this work that he had to correct *Life Magazine*, as mentioned above—the journal which had been careless enough to present him as a 'German composer.'

---

25   Cf. note 4.

James Parsons

Hanns Eisler's *Hollywooder Liederbuch* and 'the new stuff of life'

One would have little difficulty making the case that history has treated Hanns Eisler's *Hollywooder Liederbuch* cavalierly. Not only is the work's densely-dialectical method off-putting, but the malleability with which the composer engages with history is as bracing as it is demanding. Indeed, the Songbook's most conspicuous feature is the way it confronts—but just as often confounds—the conventions of German song, a trait Eisler signals at the outset with the work's name.[1] While on first inspection the word *Liederbuch* is innocuous, the reference to the California *Traumstadt* prompts apprehensions, especially when one recalls the Lied's place at the crossroads of German Romanticism, according to Thomas Mann, 'a nationally unique and incomparable product'.[2] How is one to square (or should one try) 'the miracle of the German Lied,' as Mann goes on to typify this body of music, with the crass commercialism widely thought to emanate from Hollywood's chief commodity, a subject that clearly absorbed Eisler's friend, sometime collaborator, and fellow California exile Theodor W. Adorno?[3] Small wonder many have viewed Eisler's title, and the entire collection, as improb-

A richly rewarding National Endowment for the Humanities seminar directed by Russell Berman at Stanford University during the summer of 2007 provided the congenial opportunity to develop many of the insights I gather here. I include the three music examples below through the kind offices of Deutscher Verlag für Musik, Leipzig, copyright holder. Reprinted with the permission of the publisher. I derive the examples from Hanns Eisler, *Lieder für eine Singstimme und Klavier*, series 1, vol. 16 of *Hanns Eisler Gesammelte Werke*, ed. Stephanie Eisler and Manfred Grabs (Leipzig: VEB Deutscher Verlag für Musik, 1988).

1 On the *Partitur-Entwurf* of the first song Eisler composed, 'Der Sohn I,' dated '30 May 1942 Hollywood' (Hanns-Eisler-Archiv, 337, Archiv der Akademie der Künste, Berlin), he originally calls the collection a 'Liederbüchlein Hollywood,' that is Little Hollywood Songbook. During three Berlin visits the Eisler Archiv staff has made working there a rare pleasure.

2 Thomas Mann, 'Germany and the Germans', in *Death in Venice, Tonio Kröger, and Other Writings*, ed. Frederick A. Lubich (New York: Continuum, 1999), 314. Mann delivered the address on 29 May 1945 at the Library of Congress.

3 In his *Dialectic of Enlightenment: Philosophical Fragments* (1944), ed. Gunzelin Schmid Noerr, trans. Edmund Jephcott (Stanford: Stanford University Press 2002), written with Max Horkheimer, Adorno and Horkheimer begin the frequently-quoted chapter 'The Culture Industry: Enlightenment as Mass Deception', with the observation (94–95) that 'culture today is infecting everything with sameness.'

able. Questions proliferate. Is the Hollywood Songbook a *Liederkreis*, a collection, a succession of songs about which musical or narrative coherence is relevant, or a tuneful omnibus dating (save for Nos. 46 and 47) from Eisler's first fifteen months in California? Is it accurate to speak of a larger whole? To rephrase Gertrude Stein, is there any there, there?

The number of songs and poets comprising the collection (see Table 1 for a summary of the Songbook's contents) ostensibly yield a hodgepodge, a supposition I believe is erroneous.[4] I argue that the plethora of poems and diverse musical styles *is* the point—one that invites Eisler to create a hybrid song cycle-collection while critically assessing what a *Liederzyklus* is. In contrast to most cycles—or at least the most celebrated yet atypical example, Beethoven's *An die ferne Geliebte* (1816)—Eisler eschews closure.[5] After the forty-seventh song, he affixes two more plus a succession of unpublished fragments, a nebulous alliance the composer designates with the word 'Anhang' (appendix). Eisler amplifies his Lieder by other means, setting not a single poet but nine (Robert Schumann's 1840 *Myrthen*, Op. 25, includes seven). Bertolt Brecht, Eisler's long-time friend, leads with twenty-eight texts, followed by Blaise Pascal with two. Single contributions come from Johann Wolfgang Goethe, Joseph Eichendorff, Ar-

---

Two paragraphs later: 'Automobiles, bombs, and films hold the totality together until their leveling element demonstrates its power against the very system of injustice it served. For the present the technology of the culture industry confines itself to standardization and mass production and sacrifices what once distinguished the logic of the work from that of society.' Yet to read such a pronouncement as nothing more than a withering indictment, in much the same way one might assume that Eisler in his *Hollywooder Liederbuch* would pander to nascent opportunism, is to underestimate each man's dedication to dialectical thought. David Jenemann, *Adorno in America* (Minneapolis and London: University of Minnesota Press, 2007), offers a richly-argued corrective to what has tended to be a one-dimensional take on Adorno. As it happens, Eisler (by way of Brecht) was not immune to the realities of the Hollywood 'dream factory.' The concluding couplet of Brecht's *Fünf Elegien*, set by Eisler as No. 25, compares the California riches of gold and oil. Far greater is the fortune that comes from 'dreams of happiness that one inscribes here on celluloid.'

4   Thus I gladly discard the question of whether or not the Songbook is a cycle or collection, agreeing with Ruth Bingham, *The Song Cycle in German-Speaking Countries 1790–1840: Approaches to a Changing Genre* (PhD diss., Cornell University Press, 1993) when she questions the premise that there is any worthwhile distinction between a cycle and a collection. With greater knowledge of the nineteenth-century song cycle, Bingham posits (22, 26–28), 'the 'cycle-versus-collection' question may ultimately prove to be irrelevant, its main function to reveal how ambiguous the boundaries between the two are.'

5   As Barbara Turchin, 'The Nineteenth-Century *Wanderlieder* Cycle', *The Journal of Musicology* 5 (1987), 498–525, and a number of scholars recently have shown, most twentieth-century musicologists viewed Beethoven's *An die ferne Geliebte* as paradigmatic. Fuelling this venerable misunderstanding was an incomplete awareness of a much larger repertory and the fact the cycle's recapitulatory-like ending turns out to be rare among contemporaneous song cycles. See Turchin, especially 513–14, and Bingham, *The Song Cycle in German-Speaking Countries*.

thur Rimbaud, Berthold Viertel, Eisler himself, the Bible, and Eisler helps himself to Eduard Mörike (German translations of five Anacreon fragments) and six by Friedrich Hölderlin. Along with Brecht's *Five Elegies*, the Mörike and Hölderlin groupings, discretely delineated as they are, engender sub-cycles within the larger whole. Four songs are in English, another in French. Outwardly incompatible, the non-German texts are a moving reminder of the refugee's plight. There are further purposes. Adorno, with whom Eisler would write the book *Composing for the Films* (1947), points the way toward one of these in his *Minima Moralia* when he juxtaposes two aphorisms. 'Anti-Semitism is the rumour about the Jews' and 'Foreign words [*Fremdwörter*] are the Jews of language.'[6] Implicit in both is an indictment of the idea then pervading Nazi Germany that Jews are at once transient corrupters (both Adorno's and Eisler's fathers were Jewish) and defilers of the German language.[7]

How the listener responds to Eisler's Songbook depends to a considerable degree on one's experience with and understanding of the conventions of German song, above all those relating to the nineteenth century, the genre's heyday. Whereas the early Romantics approached the cycle with malleability, twentieth-century critics have favoured procrustean principles that, ironically enough, have impeded understanding not only of the nineteenth-century *Liederkreis* but those from the following century, erroneously insisting that a cycle exhibit narrative coherence, fixed order, and other hallmarks of organic unity.[8] Just as Adorno turns to non-German expressions 'to release their explosive force: not to deny what is foreign in them' in his essay 'On the Use of Foreign Words' (early 1930s), Eisler exploits an analogous volatility in his French and English songs.[9] What he achieves matches the dialectic potential of Brecht's *Verfremdungseffekt*, one the poet-playwright summarizes in 1949 as 'designed to free socially-conditioned phenomena from the stamp of familiarity which protects them against our grasp today' and thereby 'per-

---

6   Theodor Adorno, *Minima Moralia: Reflexionen aus dem beschädigten Leben* (Berlin: Suhrkamp, 1951), 200. Adorno began the work in 1944 when he and Eisler were concluding their film music study. For the English translation, which I have amended, see Adorno, *Minima Moralia: Reflections on a Damaged Life*, trans. E. F. N. Jephcott (London and New York: Verso, 2005), 110.

7   For a more thorough account of the supercilious attempt to maintain the 'purity' of the German language, see, C. J. Wells, *German: A Linguistic History* (Oxford: Oxford University Press, 1986), 395–396, and *Handbook of Language and Ethnic Identity*, ed. Joshua A. Fishman (Oxford: Oxford University Press, 1999) 287–294.

8   In addition to Turchin's path-breaking work, the most impressive work has been by Bingham, *The Song Cycle in German-Speaking Countries*. David Ferris, *Schumann's Eichendorff Liederkreis and the Genre of the Romantic Cycle* (Oxford: Oxford University Press, 2000), makes a striking contribution while at the same time continuing Bingham's work of debunking such organicist notions as predetermined order as well as the expectation of narrative and musical unity.

9   Adorno, 'On the Use of Foreign Words', in *Notes on Literature*, ed. Rolf Tiedemann, trans. Shierry Weber Nicholsen, 2 vols. (New York: Columbia University Press, 1991–1992), 2:286.

mits us to recognize its subject, but at the same time makes it seem unfamiliar.'[10] The effect also 'allows the theatre to make use in its representations of the new social scientific method known as dialectical materialism. In order to unearth society's laws of motion this method treats social situations as processes, and traces out all their inconsistencies.' The statement mirrors Eisler's strategy. 'It regards nothing as existing,' Brecht continues, 'except in so far as it changes, in other words is in disharmony with itself.'[11] Eisler's endorsement of this position comes from an essay published in 1962, the year of his death. 'If I identify myself completely with the text, empathize with it, hover behind it, well, that's dreadful,' he writes. 'A composer has to view the text in a way full of contradictions. The tragic element is interpreted by me cheerfully. . . . If ever I am praised for anything, it will be for resisting the text.'[12]

Eisler uncovers constructive defiance in a variety of ways. Plotting the unpredictable potential of the non-German songs, it is necessary to locate their position and take into account their interaction with the lone French and four English ones. Before doing so, it is worth stressing that the sequence of songs presented in the table may reflect nothing more than order of composition. The work's open-endedness, together with the possibility that the 'cycle-versus-collection question' is superfluous, suggests that order, too, is beside the point. One purpose of juxtaposing these languages is to set them in relief, thereby making the familiar unfamiliar and the unfamiliar familiar. Less clear is the range of languages themselves, that is, German, French, and English. The forced migration that is exile affords the most compelling explanation, both the composer's own and his knowledge of the experiences of others during his travels to New York City and Los Angeles, not to mention Denmark, France, London, Prague, Spain, and Mexico City. Obviously, the small number of individuals lucky enough to have relocated to California did not find their lives magically transformed. As Lion Feuchtwanger, another California émigré, remarked in 1943, 'The sufferings of banishment have only rare heroic moments.'[13] The linguistic commingling of No. 27, 'L'automne californien,' by Austrian writer and director Berthold Viertel,[14] featuring a French title and

---

10 Bertolt Brecht, 'A Short Organum for the Theatre', *Brecht on Theatre: The Development of an Aesthetic*, trans. and ed. John Willett (London: Methuen, 1964), 192.

11 'Short Organum', *Brecht on Theatre*, 193.

12 Quoted from Hanns-Werner Heister, 'Hollywood and Home: Hanns Eisler's "Hölderlin-Fragmente" for Voice and Piano', in *Hanns Eisler: A Miscellany*, compiled and ed. David Blake (Australia [New York, N.Y.]: Harwood, 1995), 210.

13 Lion Feuchtwanger, 'The Working Problems of the Writer in Exile', a speech at the Writer's Congress, UCLA, in October 1943; quoted from *Altogether Elsewhere: Writers on Exile,* ed. Marc Robinson (San Diego: Harvest Books, 1994), 257.

14 For a brief biography of Viertel, see Werner Röder and Herbert Strauss, *Biographisches Handbuch der deutschsprachigen Emigration nach 1933* (Munich and New York: K. G. Saur, 1980–1983), 2, pt. 2, 1191–92.

German text, succinctly brings the refugee's most pressing concern into view: the challenge of communication. To the extent that most Americans pondered such issues in 1942, they might have drawn on a telling vignette from a film released that year, *Casablanca*. Mr. and Mrs. Leuchtag have gathered at Rick's Café Américain to celebrate their departure to the United States. As the characters reveal, it is their agreement to speak only English, 'so we should feel at home ven ve get to America.' They then share a charmingly mangled exchange about the time: 'Liebchen, uh, sweetness heart, what watch?' Mrs. Leuchtag's response: 'Ten watch.' His reply: 'Such much?'[15] Viertel's poem and Eisler's music pursue a different path. On one level the title, joined as it is with German poetry, anticipates the French of 'Rimbaud Gedicht' (No. 44). More pertinently, at least for Viertel, like many who fled Hitler's Germany (he had returned to Berlin from California only to leave again in 1933), he arrived in America by way of France. The Los Angeles setting and French title (bearing also the parenthetical 'Kalifornischer Herbst') pithily articulate the linguistic and geographic disconnect. While the text specifies only a ladder propped up against a fig tree in the California autumn and the anticipation of returning to the colder climate of the liberated homeland ('in kältere Breiten heimgegangen'), the two venues could not be further apart.

Eisler ably captures Viertel's spatial disjunction (see Ex. 1). Reminiscent of the lone exile, the unaccompanied voice begins the song moving largely by chromatic descent while in the next bar the piano's left hand counters with an ascending arpeggio.[16] Vivid text-painting is one by-product of the voice and piano's initial interplay; it also delineates the dual directions one can climb on a ladder and the distance between California and the longed-for *Heimat*. Eisler bolsters the second goal by placing Viertel's three-line, four-strophe poem within an elastic musical form. Throughout Eisler adroitly toys with the listeners' expectations. In twice repeating the music of the first and second strophes and the piano interlude, with its precipitous rise in register, modified strophic emerges—at least as this point—as a viable option. Only when one is ready to render a verdict on form does the composer shift gears. Beginning with the same note in the voice as did the two A sections, instead of descending it ascends, thereby launching a ten-bar B unit. The return of A (in fact A", bar 39) signals the likelihood of AABA form, one Eisler again thwarts with a truncated reprise of B (bar 47); thus the form is AA'BA"B'. It is easy enough to explain the cat and mouse game. Form is one way Eisler

---

15   Directed by Michael Curtiz; see http://www.godamongdirectors.com/scripts/casablanca.pdf.

16   One could argue that loneliness in the twentieth-century is most intense when it takes place among others. Isaiah Berlin conflates exile and loneliness in his *Crooked Timber of Humanity: Chapters in the History of Ideas*, ed. Henry Hardy (London: John Murray, 1990), 38–9. 'To be lonely is to be among men who do not know what you mean. Exile, solitude, is to find yourself among people whose words, gestures, handwriting are alien to your own, whose behaviour, reactions, feelings, instinctive responses, and thoughts and pleasures and pains, are too remote from yours.'

has of obliging the listener to experience the limbo German exiles in American then were feeling. Not knowing the war's outcome when composing the song in January 1943, Eisler transfers that uncertainty to the work's formal design, one that enables him to highlight by musical means some intriguing textual parallelisms. For example, the composer employs the same musical material to describe the fig tree after its leaves turn yellow (bars 5-8) and the peace that all hope will come. Yellow of course symbolizes cowardice, an implication one only gains reading the text retrospectively in light of Eisler's music. Equally germane, yellow leaves soon fall, the very wish that Eisler and Viertel held most dear for the forces then controlling Germany. Combining in the music for the poem's last strophe, the A and B sections, like interlocking rungs on a ladder, Eisler links California and the snow-covered country to which he longs to return. The one may be temporary and the other only an imaginative possibility, yet *both* are home.

Hindsight plays a substantial role in the Hollywood songs; in the event, the composer's mode of resisting the text most clearly comes into view in hindsight. Similarly, the Songbook's *raison d'être* emerges gradually, or to make an analogy that ironically resonates in the third song, 'An den kleinen Radioapparat,' like a hard-to-tune-in radio station. As the text of the third song implies and the titles and subjects of the seventh and ninth confirm, a journey is underway. Yet in contrast to most *Wanderlieder*, Eisler obscures the excursion's starting point. In No. 1 the setting is night, a lack of clarity Brecht stresses by suppressing further identification of son and mother. As a great deal of German literature confirms, night is when the individual embarks on the journey of self discovery: 'Holy, inexpressible, mysterious night,' Novalis affirms in his 1798 *Hymnen an die Nacht*.[17] Although few have accused Brecht, the poet of Eisler's first song, of being a Romantic, there is little doubt he is troping a favourite Romantic theme, for both strophes brood over night's restorative yet mysterious realm. The last line is all-important: 'Er wär noch auf der See'—he was still at sea. Lacking fixed location, the poem casts all adrift (see Ex. 2).[18]

---

17 Novalis, *Schriften*, 4 vols. (Stuttgart: W. Kohlhammer, 1960–75), 1:130.
18 The text transmitted in Ex. 2 is in part in error. It reads 'Er sei auf der See.' Eisler's wording is as given above. The text is corrected in the 2008 edition of the *Hollywooder Liederbuch*; see further below, fn. 36.

Example 1. Eisler: 'L'automne californien (Kalifornische Herbst) © by kind permission from Deutscher Verlag für Musik, Leipzig

L'automne californien ⟨Kalifornischer Herbst⟩
(Berthold Viertel)

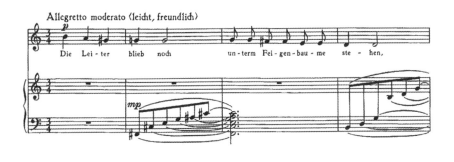

Example 2. Eisler: 'Der Sohn' © by kind permission from Deutscher Verlag für Musik, Leipzig

Der Sohn
〈Bertolt Brecht〉

Example 3. Eisler: 'Epitaph auf einen in der Flandernschlacht Gefallenen' © by kind permission from Deutscher Verlag für Musik, Leipzig.

Epitaph auf einen in der Flandernschlacht Gefallenen
⟨Bertolt Brecht⟩

The first explicit date, 1942 (i.e. included in the title of a poem), occurs in No. 6 and the first to a specific location (Lapland) in No. 9, at which point one learns how far the journey has progressed. (The tacitly understood point of origin is Germany.) Annulling time and place, the first seventeen poems (all by Brecht) treat the immediate concerns of daily life. Only in Nos. 10 and 11 does one learn the meaning of these conflicting revelations: *all* can feel the misery of one, an association Eisler highlights by musical means. No. 10 is a stylized *Kampflied*, or fighting song, a type of music Eisler describes in his 1932 'On Revolutionary Music.' Such a song, Eisler remarks, is 'easily understood, vigorous, and accurate in attitude.'[19] Ease of comprehension derives from driving rhythms, slowly-changing repetitive harmonies, and minor-key modally inflected melodies. The very characteristics typify the Songbook's tenth song, although paradoxically for the soldiers no longer are alive to fight. In No. 11 (see Ex. 3) Eisler creates a depiction of isolation worthy of 'Der Leiermann,' the final Lied from Schubert's *Winterreise*. Schubert's song provides Eisler with a probable model. Like Schubert's, with its famous drone fifths symbolizing the hurdy-gurdy named in the song's title, Eisler's similarly features drone fifths. Whereas Schubert retains the same fifths throughout, Eisler moves to other notes. In a gambit unique to this song, Eisler begins and ends with the same sonority (D-flat-A-flat in the left hand, C-F, with the C descending to B-natural on the next beat in the right) and the same combination of pitches return halfway through. In an eight-bar Lied Eisler sounds his drone during almost a third. Harmonic closure is not the aim but rather the illusion of death in sound. Beginning and ending on the same open fifth, the song goes nowhere: it expires beneath its own lack of momentum.

Throughout the Songbook the journey's meaning accrues by musical means. In the first song (see again, Ex. 2), 'Der Sohn,' Eisler quickly traverses the twelve notes of the chromatic scale, a gambit suggesting the compositional method of his erstwhile teacher Schoenberg, with whom he broke in 1926. In much the same way that Eisler advocates montage in *Composing for the Films*,[20] what he achieves in this song is equally multilayered, starting with the inventive way he places himself within the larger narrative of the *Hollywooder Liederbuch* as the son named in the song's title. At the conclusion, when Brecht's poem returns to the word 'son' for the third and last time, Eisler employs a collection of eight pitches: A, D, E-flat, C, B, B-flat, E-natural, and G, letters which, in the German system for naming pitches spell out the name Arnold Schönberg. Comparing this citation with one from the year before, the composer's *Vierzehn Arten den Regen zu beschreiben*, Op. 70, there is little doubt Eisler means

---

19 Hanns Eisler, 'On Revolutionary Music', trans. in *Hanns Eisler: A Rebel in Music. Selected Writings*, ed. Manfred Grabs, trans. Marjorie Meyer (London Kahn & Averill, 1978), 60.

20 [Theodor W. Adorno and] Hanns Eisler, *Composing for the Films* (New York: Oxford University Press, 1947), 71–79.

the Songbook allusion privately. In the earlier work, there is the unequivocal twelve-tone construction, the dedication to Schoenberg on his seventieth birthday, plus the same instrumental ensemble Schoenberg uses in his *Pierrot Lunaire*. Most significantly, Eisler calls the first number 'Anagramm' and, throughout the movement the musical letters of Schoenberg's name are proclaimed in half and whole notes. Whereas the earlier citation is conspicuous, the one from the Songbook is not. In avoiding in this song and elsewhere strict adherence to the twelve-tone method, Eisler asserts his own identity while implicating the listener, forcing one to reflect on the trajectory of the ever-accumulating array of songs. In short, Eisler expects us to engage with texts and music and, in the process, to be changed.

No narrator clarifies the superfluity of personalities or locales. Time also is elastic and seldom linear. The past shapes the present as much as the future. In a newspaper article written with Ernst Bloch in 1938, 'Die Kunst zu erben,' Eisler insists the artist must engage 'in the selection and preparation' of 'material suited […] to a fight.' Such a struggle is not the result of uncritical acceptance; rather it 'commits one to a thorough critical processing of our historical heritage.' And in this, 'the living relation to the past of the progressive person of today plays an absolutely decisive part.'[21] Just as the Songbook is open-ended, demanding the involvement of those who hear it, the meaning one extracts likewise is dynamic. Is it coincidence that when Eisler was at work on the *Liederbuch,* the Germany he previously had known was daily disappearing? All that one can answer is that the day he began the work, the British Royal Air Force launched its first 1,000-bomber raid over Cologne.[22] In a certain sense, one may think of the range of texts and the multiplicity of musical styles informing the Songbook as building blocks salvaged from Eisler's own past, artfully reassembled to construct something new. How one responds is up to each listener. The sole requirement, as Eisler discloses in the text of his own invention (No. 46), is of 'considering the question from every angle.' One way to attain that goal is by advancing the story line on different planes, not always in sync, the one textual the other musical. The first two Hollywood songs involve human relationships, the first the aforementioned mother and son, the second a father and son. Following the third song, which concerns a screech-owl living in the willows, only in the fourth does he summon elegiac effulgence. So self-effacing is the keyboard that, were it not for its harmonic vocabulary, one might think it from the eighteenth century. In one deft move, Eisler summons the musical past, not as an agent of nostalgia but as a means to elucidate the present. The piano's constant Ds add

---

21 In Hanns Eisler, *Musik und Politik: Schriften 1924–1948,* ed. Günter Mayer, Hanns Eisler *Gesammelte Werke,* ser. III vol. 1 (Leipzig: VEB Deutscher Verlag für Musik, 1973), 407. Originally published in *Die neue Weltbühne,* 6 January 1938.

22 See further, Martin Gilbert, *The Second World War: A Complete History* (New York: Henry Holt, 2004), 328–29.

meaning to an otherwise tranquil song. First, they remind that the song's warmth is not in the service of one of the Lied's familiar topics—twilight's glow, the clasp of a lover's hand—but a modern contrivance. Even so, the radio provides the only connection to other humans. Revealingly, the climax occurs in the one bar where the piano's Ds go mute, a harbinger of the character's fear that the radio again will fall silent.

Throughout his Hollywood songs, Eisler calls on the past, sometimes artfully, other times in a more straightforward manner. In No. 8, 'Über den Selbstmord,' at the line 'Und die ganze Winterzeit dazu, das ist gefährlich' (and the whole of wintertime, that, too, is dangerous), he quotes the opening song of *Winterreise*. Eisler intends more than the shared imagery of winter. Since Schubert's Lied is strophic and the phrase begins the first and second phrases, one hears it six times. The quotation's purpose is not the denial of fixed meaning, but rather music as a kind of first person—a means to engage with memory. Complex and multi-layered as memory is, so too is Eisler's Schubert paraphrase. In making it, he cites not only Schubert but also the wellspring of German song (Schubert the acknowledged 'Prince of Song'), the array of poetical references populating Wilhelm Müller's text, and the past more generally. In so doing Eisler succeeds in writing himself into his ongoing song drama—he is after all the final creative authority here. Moreover, as Richard Terdiman argues, memory always involves a 'then' and 'now,' a reality particularly acute when Eisler was composing his Lieder. Terdiman insists: 'the recession of that past, the disappearance of [a] felt or securely remembered connection with it' oftentimes leaves individuals in the present with 'a kind of depthless enigma.'[23] However fragmentary and fleeting the outcome, there is little doubt that Eisler metaphorically collapses time in his *Hollywooder Liederbuch*, distilling the then of 1942-43 with past and future. But more is at stake here than Eisler writing himself into the Songbook. Grappling with a world gone mad, he struggles to reconstruct the unity of not only his own self but the selves of others too. In such a way he implicates all who would listen to his songs, a course of action not without precedence. As Marcel Proust maintains in his *Remembrance of Things Past*, 'every reader is, while he is reading, the reader of his own self.'[24]

Crowding meaning into a solitary bar of a single song, as he does in No. 8, Eisler distils a larger concern. In the last sentence of his 1947 *Doctor Faustus*, Thomas Mann reflects: 'May God have mercy on your poor soul, my friend, my fatherland.'[25] The musical citations in Eisler's *Liederbuch*, unlike the texts themselves, are exclusively to German music, a tactic en-

23   Richard Terdiman, *Present Past: Modernity and the Memory Crisis* (Ithaca: Cornell University Press, 1993), 299.

24   Marcel Proust, *Remembrance of Things Past*, trans. C. K. Scott-Moncrieff and Terrence Kilmartin, 3 vols. (New York: Random House, c1981.), 3:949.

25   Thomas Mann, *Doctor Faustus: The Life of the German Composer Adrian Leverkühn As Told by a Friend*, trans. John E. Woods (New York: Vintage International, 1999), 534.

suring music's association with a specifically-constructed past and the loss of that past. Eisler poignantly expresses this in No. 33, 'Erinnerung an Eichendorff und Schumann,' a setting of the opening quatrain of an Eichendorff poem famous from Schumann's Op. 39 *Liederkreis* ('In der Fremde,' No. 1). The four lines tell of a 'homeland beyond those streaks of red,' connoting on the one hand a country awash in blood and, in the single word 'beyond,' the hope of moving past so disquieting a reality. The final line, with its insistence that 'nobody knows me here,' speaks to the exile's isolation. In the best Hegelian tradition—and Eisler venerates Hegel above all philosophers—the song defines itself in terms of what it is not, or, more specifically, by what it does not contain, reverberating with absence given that not so much as a motif from Schumann's song intrudes on Eisler's. Too, Eisler does not set Eichendorff's poem in full, only half of it. Eisler's ending heightens the abrupt conclusion. Unlike many of the songs' attention-grabbing endings this one halts *in medias res*, allowing the past to encroach as fragment and phantom. This is anything but a non-Freudian slip, to coin a phrase. Having mentioned Freud, he proves useful given that what Eisler achieves is an arresting example of Freud's *unheimlich*, a word suggesting a special form of fright. *Der Heim* is 'the home'; *heimlich* is 'home-like' or 'familiar'; something *unheimlich* literally is 'unhomely,' a concept that loses some of its richness in the usual English translation uncanny.[26] Discomfort and fright ensue because the thing denoted simultaneously is and is not familiar. A ready example is Heine and Schubert's 'Doppelgänger,' a song where poet and composer define a realm by what is lacking rather than what is present—namely, the stranger standing before a house where his beloved once lived yet no longer does. In his 'Recollection of Eichendorff and Schumann,' Eisler augments the uncanny. Having throughout the *Liederbuch* accustomed one to expect a reference to Germany's musical past, the absence of such here is even more disturbing because the musing on Schumann and Eichendorff is at a double disconnect from afar and in exile.

Eisler at last declares his cycle's objective: how one is to be at home with one's self when one's former home no longer is at hand. How should one remember a *Heimat* transformed by war, 'beyond those streaks of red'? Eisler could not have answered this question during the years 1942 to 1943 and so his trek is uncanny. There is more. Homeward journeys of the self have enjoyed a venerable history in German letters. In that they have, Eisler again draws on the past. And an imposing past it is, with examples of the *Bildungsroman* by Wieland and Goethe on down to Thomas Mann. Although too late to pursue this matter in detail, Eisler's musical *Bildungsroman* avails itself of many of the characteristics employed by these writers.[27]

---

26   For Freud's essay in English translation see *Romantic Writings*, ed. Stephen Bygrave, (London and New York: Routledge, 1996), 318–25.

27   Although there are many studies devoted to the *Bildungsroman*, here I recommend just one, that by

These include a dual emphasis on inwardness and outwardness, the main character's ultimate integration with the world at large, the *Bildungsroman* as a specifically German genre, the manner in which a single life symbolizes all others, and the way the 'harmonic development' of one can inspire the spiritual and intellectual completion of all. This last point was of considerable importance during the period before German national unification (in 1871), especially the belief that a shared literature, and music— namely the Lied—could inspire national unity.[28] In his *Hollywooder Liederbuch*, Eisler repeatedly finds either a poetical or a musical way to mirror these and other *Bildungsroman* conventions. Yet the journey of self-cultivation mandates both teleological advancement and ultimate homecoming. Has Eisler embarked on a voyage for which no ending is possible?

As has been noted, Eisler is an admirer of the philosher Hegel. It is not surprising, then, that Eisler writes Hegel into his Songbook, in No. 46, when he sings of 'considering the question from every angle,' and thus sums up the Hegelian dialectic in a mere six words. As a philosophical method, one objective of the dialectic is to show the necessity of development from one stage of consciousness or history to a higher state. Hegel helps to explain the interior cycles Eisler includes within his larger one. According to Hegel, 'philosophy is a [...] circle rounded and complete in itself. [...] The single circle, because of its real totality, burst through the limits imposed by its special medium, and gives rise to a wider medium. The whole of philosophy in this way resembles a circle of circles.'[29] Elsewhere, advancement plays a part, just as does the idea of 'considering the question from every angle.' The array of musical styles reflects this last point, just as does the passing back and forth between past and present, the universalizing of individual identity, and the mutability of Eisler's first-person musical narrator. Even in 'resisting the text,' the composer finds an additional way to 'consider the question from every angle' and thus satisfy Hegel. The Songbook's open-endedness mirrors the potential for future development—in this case the return home on which the journey of self-development rests. Like Hegel's circles, bursting through constraints to become something else, Eisler's nonending permits him to use the song cycle to shatter the traditional limits imposed by closure. As Barbara Herrnstein Smith observes, an 'open-ended conclusion will [...] affirm its own irresolution and compel the reader to participate in it.' Such works ask, 'What do we know?

M. H. Abrams, 'The Circuitous Journey: Through Alienation to Reintegration', *Natural Supernaturalism: Tradition and Revolution in Romantic Literature* (New York: W. W. Norton, 1971), 197–255.

28   I explore a few of the ways in which the Lied contributed to German-nation building in the introduction to *The Cambridge Companion to the Lied*, ed. James Parsons (Cambridge: Cambridge University Press, 2004), 10–11.

29   *The Logic of Hegel*, 2nd ed. trans. by William Wallace (Oxford: Clarendon Press, 1892), quoted from sect. 15, introduction,. 24. *The Logic* is part one of *Encyklopädie der philosophischen Wissenschaften im Grundrisse* (3rd. ed., 1830).

How can we be sure we know it?' They question the validity and even the possibility of unas-
sailable verities [...] of final words.'[30] In this way, Eisler's lack of closure asserts that while the
journey is not over, one cannot positively say it one day may not be.

For Adorno, exile is a dire condition. 'Every intellectual in emigration,' he writes, 'is, without exception, mutilated.'[31] (I would be the first to admit that reading such a statement literally denies its dialectical power and therefore is not what Adorno intends.) What emerges
from the Hollywood Songbook suggests a more nuanced response. While the Songbook's
organization suggests something continually cut short, my own view is that Eisler uses song
to combat Nazism and that he does so in a way where the many disruptions effect not mu-
tilation but its opposite. Song had long provided Eisler with the means to engage in social
criticism. As he insists in a 1930 song for Brecht's *Die Massnahme*, 'Change the world, it needs
it!'[32] Ernst Bloch sheds penetrating light on Eisler's method in an English-language article
published some four years before the Songbook.

> The German refugee writer brings his roots with him: a mature language, an old culture.
> And he remains faithful to them not by making museum-pieces out of them, but by test-
> ing and quickening his powers of expression on the new stuff of life. [...] It will remain,
> insofar as it succeeds, a deeply original creation, fostered by double but not divided loyal-
> ties—by memory and a vigorous faith in the future. [...] We are creating on the frontier
> of two epochs. We, German writers in America, are frontier-men in a doubly legitimate
> sense—both temporally and spatially and we are working at the one necessary task: the
> realization of the rights of man.[33]

In his *Hollywooder Liederbuch*, far from suffering injury, Eisler continually toils for 'the rights
of man,' not by making a fetish of the past, but 'by testing and quickening his powers of expression on the new stuff of life.' His loyalties are 'double' and 'not divided,' stimulated 'by
memory,' yet also 'a vigorous faith in the future.' This is not to suggest that exile did not leave
its mark. Past studies of the songs Eisler composed during his time in California have tended
to focus on the various subunits.[34] Although I have had to be selective in what I consider, I

30 Barbara Herrnstein Smith, *Poetic Closure: A Study of How Poems End* (Chicago: University of Chicago
    Press, 1968), 233.
31 *Minima Moralia*, trans. Jephcott, 33.
32 This is the English translation of Eisler's song 'Ändere die Welt, sie braucht es,' composed for Brecht's
    play.
33 Ernst Bloch, 'Disrupted Language, Disputed Culture', *Direction* 2/8 (December 1939), 36; the essay
    appears on pages 16–17 and 36.
34 Although too late in this study to mount a full rehearsal of the secondary literature devoted to the

nevertheless hope that a few of the work's larger concerns have emerged with greater clarity. Edward Said's well-known and eloquent reflection on Adorno's response to exile is equally germane to Eisler and his *Hollywooder Liederbuch*. 'To follow Adorno,' Said writes, 'is to stand away from "home" in order to look at it with the exile's detachment.' Through a variety of techniques, but above all his penchant for juxtaposing arresting extremes, Eisler, to use his own words, seeks a similar 'resistance.' As Said continues, the exile knows that 'homes are always provisional. Borders and barriers, which enclose us within the safety of familiar territory, can also become prisons […] Exiles cross borders, break barriers of thought and experience.'[35] Like Adorno, Eisler refuses the confinement of the familiar.

Table 1: Hanns Eisler's *Hollywooder Liederbuch*

	Title	Date	Poet
1.	Der Sohn I	May 1942	Bertolt Brecht
2.	Der Sohn II	May 1942	Brecht
3.	In den Weiden	May 1942	Brecht
4.	An den kleinen Radioapparat	May 1942	Brecht
5.	Frühling	11 Jun3 1942	Brecht
6.	Speisekammer 1942	June (?) 1942	Brecht
7.	Auf der Flucht	June-July 1942	Brecht
8.	Über den Selbstmord	July 1942	Brecht
9.	Die Flucht	7 July 1942	Brecht
10.	Gedenktafel für 4000 Soldaten	July 1942	Brecht
11.	Epitaph auf einen in der Flandernschlacht Gefallen	July 1942	Brecht
12.	Spruch	July 1942	Brecht
13.	Panzerschlacht	summer 1942	Brecht
14.	Ostersonntag	23 July 1942	Brecht
15.	Der Kirschdieb	26 July 1942	Brecht
16.	Hotelzimmer 1942	3 August 1942	Brecht
17.	Die Maske des Bösen	September 1942	Brecht

Zwei Lieder nach Worten von Pascal [*Pensées*, Nos. 169 and 171, trans. W. F. Trotter]

	Title	Date	Poet
18.	Despite these miseries[i]	12 September 1942	Blaise Pascal
19.	The only thing which consoles us[i]	14 September 1942	Pascal

Hollywooder Liederbuch, a refreshing exception to the statement above is that by Markus Roth, *Der Gesang als Asyl: Analytische Studien zu Hanns Eislers Hollywood-Liederbuch*, Sinefonia vol. 7, ed. Claus-Steffen Mahnkopf and Johannes Menke (Hofheim: Wolke Verlag, 2007).

35   Edward W. Said, 'Reflections on Exile', in *Reflections on Exile and Other Essays* (Cambridge, MA: Harvard University Press, 2000), 184–85.

Fünf Elegien

21.	Unter den grünen Pfefferbäumen	September 1942	Brecht
22.	Die Stadt ist nach den Engeln genannt	20 September 1942	Brecht
23.	Jeden Morgen, mein Brot zu verdienen	25 September 1942	Brecht
24.	Diese Stadt hat mich belehrt	September-October 1942	Brecht
25.	In den Hügeln wird Gold gefunden	September-October 1942	Brecht
26.	Die letzte Elegie	Begun 15 September 1942	Brecht

27.	L'automne californien (sung in German)	January 1943	Berthold Viertel

Anakreontische-Fragmente by Eduard Mörike, ed. Eisler

28.	Geselligkeit betreffend	March-April 1943	Mörike/Eisler
29.	Dir auch wurde Sehnsucht nach der Heimat tödlich	March-April 1943	Mörike/Eisler
30.	Die Unwürde des Alterns	March-April 1943	Mörike/Eisler
31.	Später Triumph	March-April 1943	Mörike/Eisler
32.	In der Frühe	18 April 1943	Mörike/Eisler

33.	Erinnerung an Eichendorff und Schumann	19 April 1943	Joseph Eichendorff

Hölderlin-Fragmente (Friedrich Hölderlin), ed. Eisler

34.	An die Hoffnung[iii]	20 April 1943	Hölderlin/Eisler
35.	Andenken	3 June 1943	Hölderlin/Eisler
36.	Elegie 1943	10 June 1943	Hölderlin/Eisler
37.	Die Heimat	21 June 1943	Hölderlin/Eisler
38.	An einen Stadt	22 June 1943	Hölderlin/Eisler
39.	Erinnerung	2 August 1943	Hölderlin/Eisler

40.	Der Mensch, vom Weibe geboren	mid 1943	Bible (Martin Luther trans.),textual montage from Job 14.1, Exodus 12.7 & 23

41.	Vom Sprengen des Gartens	August 1943	Brecht
42.	Die Heimkehr	August 1943	Brecht
43.	Die Landschaft des Exils	2 September 1943	Brecht
44.	Rimbaud Gedicht[ii]	28 December 1943	Arthur Rimbaud
45.	Der Schatzgräber	1944	Johann Wolfgang Goethe
46.	Nightmare[i]	1947	Eisler
47.	Hollywood-Elegie Nr. 7[i]	1947	Brecht

Anhang

	Sprüche [fragment; together with contrapuntal fragments]	1943	
	In Sturmesnacht	4 June 1943	Brecht
	Deutsches Miserere[iv]	June 1943	Brecht

---

[i]   Sung in English
[ii] Sung in French
[iii] Eisler transforms this song with minimal alteration to the vocal line as No. 4 of his 1961-62 *Ernste Gesänge*, a song cycle of seven Lieder for baritone and string orchestra
[iv] Included by Eisler in music for Brecht's play *Schweyk im zweiten Weltkrieg* (1943–59; Warsaw, 1957), No. 19

Consecutive shaded Lieder indicate obvious and possible interior subgroupings.[36]

---

36   The table is a distillation of research I have carried out at the Hanns-Eisler Archiv, Archiv der Akademie der Künste, Berlin, as well as information culled from the "Notes" section of Hanns Eisler, *Hollywooder Liederbuch*, corrected reprint of the first ed. with annotation by Oliver Dahin and Peter Deeg (Leipzig: Deutscher Verlag für Musik, 2008), 97-100.

Juliane Brand

Karl Weigl's Final Years, 1938–1949

A Story of Perseverance

In 1938 the Viennese composer Karl Weigl was made an exile. Expelled from the geographic, cultural, and spiritual homeland that had until then defined him, his life thereafter followed the template charted by all exile survivors from Nazi Europe. In both its singularities and its commonalities with others, his story illustrates a period in human history when individuals were at once powerless to change their circumstances and yet faced with boundless choices on how to live within those circumstances.

An account of his story could open on the bright Sunday in March 1938 when German troops marched into Vienna to unprogrammed demonstrations of enthusiasm. The account could just as reasonably have opened five years earlier, in January 1933, with Hitler's *Machtergreifung* in neighbouring Germany—or even in 1918, on the day a young woman named Vally Pick appeared at Weigl's door to begin private composition studies. Without doubt, Karl Weigl may never have escaped Nazi Austria had it not been for the energy and determination of the woman who became his second wife.

Wherever the retelling of an exile story is begun, it will be fragmentary and discontinuous. Much documentary evidence is lost, and of what is extant much was selectively preserved by those wishing to pre-empt posthumous interpretation. Narrators may try to resist the temptation to smooth over gaps and ignore discordances, but any retracing of someone else's story is only one of several that could be constructed. Just as any retelling of a story is shaped by the nature and provenance of information at hand, it is as inevitably shaped by the personality, sensibilities, and choices of the narrator. My wish is that the retelling here may add the nuance and poignancy of one more lived experience to the exile story template.

What follows is a retelling of the final eleven years in the life of one exiled Viennese musician. Karl Weigl was a bred-in-the-bone Austrian, a man born and raised in Vienna of Hungarian-born parents, which on paper made him for the first twenty-two years of his life a citizen of Hungary and then, for the next fifteen, a citizen of Austria—until in 1938 he was stripped of all nationality. He was a man whose religion was on paper for the first forty-five years of his life *israelitisch* (though he never went to synagogue), and then for the next dozen years (still on paper, for he never went to church), a Swedenborgian Protestant—until in 1938 he was assigned to a Judaism to which he felt less connection than to the Quaker community that would help him escape Austria. Perhaps most important, he was a man who had grown up in Central European traditions and spoke mellow, Austrian-inflected German—until in 1938 he was forced to learn, understand, and speak the languages of an entirely new culture.

Weigl had learned his compositional craft at the Conservatorium der Gesellschaft der Musikfreunde (later the k.k. Akademie für Musik und darstellende Kunst) with Robert Fuchs and Hermann Grädener, and he earned his PhD in musicology under Guido Adler at the University of Vienna in May 1903 for his dissertation on the life and work of Emanuel Aloys Förster (1748–1823).[1] For a brief time after that Weigl was part of the ferment of new music in Vienna. He worked as a repetiteur under Mahler at the Vienna Opera 1904–1906, and during that time he joined Schoenberg and Zemlinsky in the short-lived Verein schaffender Tonkünstler. Occasionally some of his songs and chamber music were performed in small Viennese venues. But he was just a young local talent until his Symphony No. 1 was premiered at the 1910 ADMV Tonkünstlerfest in Zurich to enthusiastic critical response.[2]

On the strength merely of that scheduled performance in an important international forum, Universal Edition (UE) offered Weigl a standard 10-year contract, which was signed on 11 February 1910 and entitled UE to *Prioritätsrecht* (first right of refusal) to all of Weigl's non-dramatic works. Soon his works began to be performed throughout central Europe. At the peak of his career, major string quartet groups of the day (among them the Rosé, Kolbe, Gottesmann, and Busch Quartets) included his chamber works in their repertoire, Ignaz Friedman played his Piano Concerto, and Hanna Schwarz and Elisabeth Schumann programmed his

---

1   Weigl's graduation certificate from the Conservatorium, dated 15 July 1902, gives him the highest passing grade (*vorzüglich*, or excellent) and notes his receiving that year's silver medal for composition. Two years after completing his PhD, Weigl was asked to contribute an article on his thesis topic. See Karl Weigl, 'Emanuel Aloys Förster', *Sammelbände der Internationalen Musikgesellschaft* 6, no. 2 (January –March 1905), 274–314. For more background information on Weigl, visit www.karlweigl.org.

2   Weigl's Symphony No. 1, completed in 1908, was performed by the Zurich Tonhalle Orchestra, conducted by Volkmar Andreae, on 28 May 1910, as part of that year's ADMV Tonkünstlerfest. See reviews by, among others, H.W. Draber in *Die Germania* (Berlin, 1 June 1910), *Heidelberger Tagblatt* (1 June 1910), and *Grazer Tagespost* (2 June 1910); also see *Signale für die Musikalische Welt* (1910), 876; Alexander Weißmann in *Württemberger Zeitung* (30 May 1910); Paul Bekker, 'Das 46. Tonkünstler-Fest des Allgemeinen Deutschen Musikvereins in Zürich (27.–31. Mai 1910)', *Die Musik*, 10 (1910), 372–77; E. von Binzer, 'Musikbriefe: Zürich, 46. Tonkünstler-Versammlung des Allgemeinen Deutschen Musikvereins 27.–31. Mai 1910', *Neue Zeitschrift für Musik* (1910), 123–25; Oswald Kühn, 'Vom Tonkünstlerfest in Zürich', *Neue Musik-Zeitung* 18, no. 31 (1910), 379–381; Leopold Schmidt, 'Vom Zürcher Tonkünstlerfest', *Berliner Zeitung* (27 May 1910); and Walter Paetow, 'Das Deutsch-Schweizerische Tonkünstlerfest', *Tägliche Rundschau,* Berlin 128 (4 June 1910), 511.

lieder. In 1928 he received the honorary title of Professor. In his musical language Weigl maintained a traditional Austro-German approach to syntax and tonality, and he worked in large,
expansive Brucknerian forms. Not surprisingly, by the mid–1920s he came to be seen as a
conservative composer. Until 1933, however, he was able to live comfortably from performance
royalties and private teaching. Then his career, like those of many who depended on performances and income in Germany, began to flag. Increasingly he relied on private teaching. His
last work to be published in Europe, the String Quartet No. 5 in G Major op. 31, dedicated to
the Busch Quartet and premiered by them in Vienna on 23 November 1934, appeared in 1936.

In a diary he kept from 1 January 1934 until ten days before going into exile in September
1938, Weigl laconically charted the slow decline in his career. The diary gives a good overview
of daily activities and concerns. Though the jottings are telegraphic, Weigl rarely missed a day
(or if he did, he filled in the skipped days afterwards, as changes in ink tint or thickness occasionally indicate). Almost all but Sunday entries—that day is usually devoted to hikes and
outings—begin with a reference to Arbeit, or work. As Weigl used the word, Arbeit invariably refers to musical work—sketching, composing, orchestrating, or copying out scores and
parts. Often Weigl notched off the day's allotment of work merely with the abbreviation Arb
or by carrying the reference over from a line above with a crow's-feet symbol; he seems usually to have worked on only one composition at a time, and he generally named the work in
progress only upon first beginning and then again after completing it.[3]

In addition to tracking his compositional work, Weigl used the diary to record meetings
with friends and colleagues, weekend outings and hikes, and evening activities—occasionally
a concert but more often gatherings with friends at their home or *bei uns* (at our place). Only
occasionally does he note facts of daily life such as the weather, a tiff with his wife *(Krach m[it]
V[ally]),* or the state of his mood. Almost never does he refer to conditions in the larger world,
much less to political events. There are, however, several significant exceptions. Early in 1937,
in taking stock of the year just past, he wrote:

[A]m not proud of the past year; as to work, only the last movements of the 4th Symphony; long hiatus for months now; many sketches. External conditions bleaker than ever;
threat of a new European war immediate (from Spain). Serious increase of anti-Semitism;
no chance of a [...] performance any time soon.[4]

---

3   The notebook in which Weigl documented his daily activities, approximately 7.5 inches high by 12
    inches wide, bears a small label with the dates: 1934—1935—1936—1937—1938. MSS 73, The Papers of
    Karl Weigl in the Irving S. Gilmore Music Library of Yale University, Series VIII, Box 29, Folder 926
    (in future Karl Weigl Papers, YU); to access the finding aid for the Weigl Papers, see http://hdl.handle.
    net/10079/fa/music.mss.0073.
4   '[M]it dem abgelaufenen Jahr [...] wenig zufrieden; von Arbeiten nur die letzten Sätze der IV. Sym-

He mentions having been in despair in September, and though he refers to growing public recognition, he ends the year's summary with the words: Zukunftdunkel (Future dark). A year later, summarizing the year 1937, he again notes 'bleak external conditions (war in Spain) [...], Nazis in Germany, Anti-Semitism in Austria.'[5]

Even during the unsettling first two months of 1938, as Austrian autonomy eroded, Weigl, if we are to believe the diary, held fast to his customary schedule and habits. However much he may have been affected, as he writes to his friend Ernst Bacon, by the 'äußeren Verhältnisse, die allerdings tief in das Privatleben eingreifen' (external events that are admittedly reaching deep into one's private life),[6] in the diary he notes that he played some of his music for Egon Petri (2 March), met with Willem Mengelberg (4 March), and attended two Petri concerts (7 and 8 March) as well as a rehearsal (7 March) for a performance of the orchestrated version of his *Bilder und Geschichten,* scheduled for performance on 10 March in the Großer Ehrbarsaal with the Wiener Konzertorchester under Rudolf Fellner. Then on Wednesday 9 March, starkly interrupting this private record, comes the word 'Abstimmung!' (plebiscite!), a reference to Chancellor Kurt von Schuschnigg's announcement of a national vote with which he hoped to resist Germany's pressure for unification.[7]

Two days later, on 11 March, the day the Viennese came to call Black Friday, the Austrian government fell. Countless memoirs describe the effect of Schuschnigg's voice interrupting RAVAG radio broadcasting, at ten minutes before 8 p.m., to announce his resignation and the name of his successor, the Austrian Nazi Arthur Seyß-Inquart. In the hours that followed, people milled in the streets, waiting to hear whether the Austrian president, Wilhelm Miklas, would stand firm. Just short of midnight he too resigned, and with that the Austrian National-Socialist Party—that is to say, Germany—controlled the government. Weigl's diary indicates that he tried to start that day, too, as usual, with Arbeit.[8] But it must have been im-

---

phonie; seit Monaten große Pause; viele Skizzen. Äußere Verhältnisse trüber denn je; Gefahr eines neuen europäischen Krieges unmittelbar drohend (aus Spanien). Starkes Anwachsen des Antisemitismus; dzt. keine Möglichkeit einer [illegible word] Aufführung.' Entry dated 3 January 1937.

5   'Trostlose äußere Verhältnisse (Krieg in Spanien [...], Nazi in Deutschland, Antisemitismus in Oesterr[eich].' Entry dated 31 December 1937.

6   Letter dated 13 January 1938, Ernst Bacon Papers, Special Collections M0906, Stanford University. Ernst Bacon (1898–1990) studied with Weigl in the 1920s and became a good friend. After the 1938 Anschluss he was one of Weigl's most committed supporters.

7   For two detailed accounts of the Austrian experience in March 1938, see *1938—Anatomie eines Jahres,* ed. Thomas Chorherr (Vienna: Verlag Carl Ueberreuter, 1987), and *Dokumentationsarchiv des österreichischen Widerstandes, "Anschluss" 1938: Eine Dokumentation,* ed. Heinz Arnberger, Winfried R. Garscha, et al. (Vienna: Österreichischer Bundesverlag, 1988).

8   A crows'-foot carry-over of *Arb* is followed by an exclamation point and a faintly scrawled and heavily abbreviated phrase that might be *Erinnyentanz,* the piano piece he had been working on as of January of that year.

possible. The entry turns to the events of the day, which he seems to have jotted down as they occurred: first 'Abstimmung' (another parliamentary vote)—that was early in the day. Then 'Abdankung!' (abdication!)—the exclamation point after the word is splay-nibbed with agitation. And, finally, 'Musterprüfung der NSDAP' (draft call for National-Socialist troops)—he would not have known about that till the early hours. It seems probable that the Weigls, like so many Austrians, never went to bed that night.

Scrawled untidily amidst these political references are names of friends to whom Weigl wrote immediately after these cataclysmic events.[9] Amongst these was Toni Stolper, who together with her husband, Gustav Stolper, had emigrated to New York in 1933. There she founded the Selfhelp for German Refugees, as well as working with the refugee organization American Council for Émigrés from the Professions. Writing to Stolper, Weigl explained, 'By the time you receive this letter you will long since know that Hitler has vanquished Austria. [...] [M]uch as it pains us, we will need to familiarize ourselves with the thought of emigration. And as I believe that, were the worst to happen, the U.S. offers the only possible solution, I turn to you for advice on how to go about this.'[10] Over the next few months, the Weigls sent sheaves of letters to an ever-widening circle of friends and friends of friends, asking about job prospects in England and the United States and begging for advice. In turn,

---

9   Weigl used his customary abbreviation for letter, *Bf* (for *Brief*); the names entered, some underlined, include those of his childhood friend Kate Kempner, who had emigrated to the United States several years earlier; the harpsichordist Alice Ehlers, who had left Vienna for the United States in 1936; someone named Sternheim; and the economist Antonie (Toni) Stolper. Two other names remain to be deciphered.

10   'Wenn Sie dieser Brief erreicht, wissen Sie schon längst von Hitlers Sieg über Österreich! [...] Aber trotzdem müssen wir—wie sehr es uns schmerzt—uns mit dem Gedanken der Auswanderung vertraut machen. Da ich glaube, dass im Ernstfall nur U.S.A. in Betracht kommt, bitte ich zunächst um Ihren Rat, wie das anzupacken wäre.' This letter and others from Weigl, as well as some carbon copies of Stolper's letters to him, are preserved in the Toni and Gustav Stolper Collection AR 7212 F AR 7212, Leo Baeck Institute, New York (in future Stolper Collection, LBI). Four letters from Stolper to Weigl are available in the Karl Weigl Papers, YU; two others from this time are in the Karl Weigl Foundation archives, San Rafael, California (in future KWF). Stolper's first response to Weigl, dated 4 April 1938, is reproduced (on the basis of a copy in the Stolper Collection, LBI, the original apparently lost) in *Sources Relating to the History of Emigre Musicians 1933–1950*, vol. 2, New York, ed. Horst Weber and Stefan Dreese (Munich: Saur Verlag, 2005), 377–79. Her efforts to help the Weigls are also substantiated in her correspondence with her brother, Karl Kassowitz, a former student of both Alban Berg and Weigl, and her close friend Lilly Toch; see Ernst Toch Archive, 1, Performing Arts Special Collections, University of California, Los Angeles; finding aid at http://content.cdlib.org/view?docId=ft0z09n428&chunk.id=c02-1.2.9.2.8&query=toni%20stolper&brand=oac. For her reminiscences from this time, see Toni Stolper, *Ein Leben in Brennpunkten unserer Zeit, Wien, Berlin, New York: Gustav Stolper 1888–1947* (Tübingen: Rainer Wunderlich Verlag, 1960).

such good friends as Arnold Schoenberg, Artur Bodanzky, Ernst Toch, and above all Ernst Bacon, made enquiries on their behalf.

While the Weigls waited for responses—letters between Europe and the United States at that time required between ten and fourteen days to arrive to their destination—Nazi hysteria in Vienna steadily increased. Less than two months after Schuschnigg had declared that 'an abyss separates Austria from National Socialism', Austria was Nazi.[11] All the laws Hitler's government had incrementally put in place in Germany over the previous five years had become, virtually overnight, Austrian law. The Weigls were spared being picked up in a neighbourhood sweep—it probably helped that they lived in the central first district, though their home on Rudolfsplatz was just across the river from the second, the 'Jewish' district—but they had their share of pounding fists on the door and abusive behaviour on the streets. Moreover, within two weeks of the *Anschluß*, both Weigls had lost most of their students. As Weigl told Tess Simpson, the secretary and de facto head of the Society for the Protection of Science and Learning, the British relief agency set up in 1933 to assist prominent German scholars, artists, and intellectuals:

For the same reason we both (my wife and I) lost almost all our pupils within 2 weeks, the foreigners leaving Vienna, the others having no money left for music-theory or piano-studies. So we have to look out for being able to live and work otherwise [sic]. As I have different former pupils in England and in the U.S.A., and working-permits f[or] i[nstance] in Holland or Switzerland are still more hopeless to be obtained, I think that only these first two countries come in consideration. May I therefore give you some names of best-known musicians who would be able to warrant for my musical qualification as composer and teacher as f[or] i[nstance]: Adolf Busch, Artur Schnabel, Rudi Serkin, Georg Széll, Bruno Walter, Emmy Heim, Lady Susi Jeans, etc.—or some of my former pupils: (Englishers or well-known as artists) Dr. W.K. Stanton (dir[ector] of the music department of the Radio Birmingham); Dr. J.H. Alden (organist at St. Martins in the Fields); Mrs. Al[ice] Ehlers (the cembalist [...]); Dr. Mosco Carner [...] music-critic; Mr. F. Waldman (conductor and piano-accompanist of the Joos-Ballet [...]), etc.[12]

---

11   J.L. Garvin, 'The Austrian Drama: a mighty event not war but warning Herr Hitler and Dr. Schuschnigg the inner history of the crisis', *The Observer*, 13 March 1938, 16.

12   Letter dated 26 March 1938 (photocopy of carbon copy, KWF), one of the first letters Weigl penned in English. It is reproduced here almost in its entirety because it is representative of many similar letters Weigl sent out. For more information about the Society for the Protection of Science and Learning, see Esther Simpson, *Refugee Scholars: Conversations with Tess Simpson* (London: Moorland Publishing, 1992).

Given his economic situation, Weigl saw no alternative but to emigrate. The thought that it might be fatal to remain in Austria was at that time still inconceivable to almost everyone. The worst that Weigl feared is probably summed up in the letter he wrote to his Dutz-friend Schoenberg: 'You know how it is here, that my remaining here would mean not only isolation but also the impossibility of making a living. So, away!'[13] And yet the information he began receiving in answer to his letters was at first uniformly discouraging. Tess Simpson's response, which reached the Weigls on 4 April, apparently stated—so Vally wrote to a friend the next day—that the chances of getting a work permit in England were 'as good as impossible'.[14] A similar reaction came from the composer Frederick Jacobi, with whom Weigl had been in contact since the early 1930s and who in 1936 had succeeded Rubin Goldmark as professor of composition at the Juilliard School of Music. Responding to a letter from Weigl dated 9 April that referred to the restrictive immigration policies in England, Jacobi declared the circumstances in his country to be no better:

> I can well understand your desire to come to America now. Under the circumstances it is perhaps the wisest thing to do. But the situation here is really very, very difficult. We have many of our own excellent musicians unable to find employment and economic conditions here at this moment are not at all favorable. [...] If you should decide to come to America you must be prepared for considerable difficulty and for a wait of perhaps a considerable lapse of time before you find anything.[15]

Jacobi concluded his letter wishing that 'I did not have to write you so pessimistically, for we all understand the situation perfectly.'[16] But that was the problem: No one outside Austria understood even remotely how dangerous it was for his or her Austrian friends to remain in a Nazi-controlled country. Even Toni Stolper, a native of Vienna, was unable to correctly gauge the changes the city had undergone since the *Anschluß*. In a letter of 24 June 1938 she

---

13   'Du weißt, wie es hier steht, daß Hierbleiben für mich nicht nur Vereinsamung bedeutet sondern auch die Unmöglichkeit eines weiteren Erwerbes. Also weg!' Letter of 31 March 1938, Arnold Schoenberg Collection, Library of Congress.

14   Vally Weigl's letter, dated 5 April 1938, is addressed to 'Mimi' (photocopy of carbon copy, KWF).

15   Letter dated 21 April 1938 (Karl Weigl Papers, YU). It is quite likely that Weigl would have known that Jacobi had helped the Viennese composer Paul Pisk (1893-1990) to emigrate to the United States in 1936; see Elliott Antokoletz, 'A Survivor of the Vienna Schoenberg Circle: An Interview with Paul A. Pisk', *Tempo* 154 (September 1985), 20–21. For a survey of Jacobi's life and career, see Anton Wagner, 'Frederick Jacobi and Herman Voaden: The Prodigal Son', www.lib.unb.ca/Texts/Theatre/voaden/the-prodigalson_article.htm; accessed 4 April 2009.

16   Letter to Jacobi, 21 April 1938.

recommended the option—suggested by Leonard Pick, a distant relative of Vally Weigl, who lived in the United States—that for the time being Weigl leave Vally and their son, Wolfi, in Vienna and emigrate alone:

> This has much to recommend it. Alone you will be much more unencumbered, can travel if necessary, and only you will need to incur the high expenses of life in America. [...] I can imagine that separating would not be an easy decision for the three of you, but many other immigrants have chosen this path to great advantage.[17]

LOGISTICS OF EMIGRATION

Fleeing with false papers was one option for leaving Austria. Otto Leichter, an important figure in the Austrian Socialist Workers Party and the husband of Vally's sister, Käthe Pick Leichter, did so three days after the *Anschluß*.[18] Some other good friends of the Weigls fled a few weeks after the *Anschluß* for Sweden, later informing the Weigls that:

> Mitzi and I, by our precipitate decision (to which, however, we had no choice, given the warnings of informed persons), were certainly spared the terrors and indignities to which others were subjected—indeed, the decision saved my life, for at the very hour of arriving [in Sweden …] our apartment, like our beloved Kahlenbergerdorf, was taken over.[19]

---

17 'Diese Anschauung hat praktisch zweifellos viel fuer sich. Sie sind hier beweglicher, wenn Sie allein sind, koennen reisen, wenn es noetig ist, und der teure amerikanische Boden wird zunaechst nur fuer Sie in Anspruch genommen. […] Ich kann mir denken, dass eine Trennung fuer alle drei kein leichter Entschluss ist, aber viele der Einwanderer haben denselben Vorgang mit Nutzen gewaehlt.' (Stolper Collection, LBI) Stolper cites the example of Fritz Stiedry, whose wife held off coming to New York until he was offered the position of conductor for the just founded New Friends of Music. Amongst the European community, Stiedry's luck in being offered this position within four weeks of arriving in New York became the legendary exception to the rule of the exile experience; in an earlier letter to Weigl, Toni Stolper referred to Stiedry as a *Glückspilz*, a lucky chap.

18 Otto Leichter's first attempt to leave Vienna on 14 March 1938 with a newly acquired false passport was thwarted when he was turned back at the Austrian border with Yugoslavia; on the following day he tried again and this time made it over the border to Czechoslovakia, and from there by stages to temporary safety in Paris.

19 'Mitzi und ich, wir haben sicher durch unseren raschen Entschluss, zu dem wir allerdings durch Warnungen Bestinformierter geradezu gezwungen wurden, nicht nur aller Schauer und Entwürdigungen erspart, denen die Zurückgebliebenen aller Schattierung ausgesetzt waren, mehr noch, der Entschluss hat mein Leben gerettet, denn zur Stunde unserer Ankunft [...] wurde ich schon gesucht, war das liebe Kahlenbergerdorf schon ebenso beschlagnahmt wie unsere Wohnung.' Letter dated 25

The Weigls chose legal emigration. But if anything was needed to add urgency to their preparations, it was the arrest, on 30 May, of Vally's sister, Käthe Leichter, who had decided not to accompany her husband and hoped to achieve legal Ausreise for herself and the two sons, Otto and Franz. As one of the first European women to earn a PhD in law, Käthe Leichter had made a name for herself writing on the subject of women's work, and she had been appointed head of the women's division of the Vienna Arbeiterkammer, a governmental agency for labour and social affairs. Realizing the impossibility of legal emigration, she had decided to leave to Vienna illegally but was picked up by the Gestapo on the very day, almost certainly because she was betrayed by a family acquaintance. Initially held in a succession of Viennese prisons, she was subsequently held for more than two years in the concentration camp Ravensbrück; in early 1942 she was transferred to a so-called psychiatric institution, Bernburg an der Saale, where she was murdered in March of that year.[20]

Those who tried to leave Austria legally faced many hurdles and, especially in the beginning, enormous confusion. The various agencies previously responsible for *Ausreise* were now charged with establishing new requirements and adding extra powers to existing ones, but bureaucrats were unsure about the new laws and incapable of dealing with the surge of applicants. Undoubtedly many of the new procedures were devised, at quite junior bureaucratic levels, as means of harassment. But at the policy level of administration it seems clear that the new National-Socialist government was impersonally motivated above all to rid the country of Jews and strip them of financial assets. In late August 1938, when it became clear that chaotic conditions were hindering both goals, Adolf Eichmann was put in charge of a new Zentralstelle für jüdische Auswanderung, a central office for Jewish emigration, which consolidated agencies and streamlined the exit process.

Those in the first wave of applicants, however, had to find their way through the bureaucratic thicket by means of painful, time-consuming trial and error. At the time the Weigls be-

---

February 1940 from friends named Mitzi and Otto (no surname available), who found refuge in Stockholm (Karl Weigl Papers, YU).

20 Fur further details on Käthe Leichter, see Herbert Steiner, *Käthe Leichter: Leben und Werke* (Vienna: Europa Verlag, 1973); Rochelle G. Saidel, *The Jewish Women of Ravensbrück Concentration Camp* (Madison: University of Wisconsin Press, 2004); and the heart-wrenching collection of letters written to her from Paris by her husband, Otto Leichter, *Briefe ohne Antwort: Aufzeichnungen aus dem Pariser Exil für Käthe Leichter 1938–1939* (Vienna: Böhlau Verlag, 2003). See also Otto Leichter, *Zwischen zwei Diktaturen: Österreichs Revolutionäre Sozialisten 1934–1938* (Vienna: Europa Verlag, 1968); and the memoir of one of the Leichter sons, Henry O. Leichter, *Eine Kindheit: Wien—Zürich—Paris—USA* (Vienna: Böhlau Verlag, 1995). For a discussion of the relationship between Käthe Leichter and her sister, see Margit Wolfsberger, 'Käthe Leichter und Vally Weigl: Zwei Schwestern, zwei Autobiographien, eine schwierige Beziehung', in *Give Them Music: Musiktherapie im Exil am Beispiel von Vally Weigl*, ed. Elena Fitzthum and Primavera Gruber (Vienna: Edition Praesens, 1993), 70–81.

gan the process, shortly after the *Anschluß*, they would have had to sort through much contra-dictory information. Every required document necessitated going to a different office several times, first to procure a form, then to hand it in. Every application required stamps, costing anywhere between eighty groschen and three schillings; many applications called for copies of other documents; and face-to-face meetings with officials were also sometimes mandatory. The offices involved in the process were scattered all over the central districts of Vienna, and most had restricted hours. Prospective emigrants faced long waits everywhere, as seen in photographs that show people queuing outside offices all night.[21] With the successful acquisition of each new piece of paper or stamp of approval, applicants had to make a designated number of copies, affix new stamps to each copy, and get all the copies notarized. Then the process started over for the next document. In letters to friends and in the diary, Weigl's handwriting, not good at the best of times, was often downright illegible during this period. Occasionally he apologizes, as in a letter to Toni Stolper: 'Please excuse the poor handwriting; my nerves are a bit ragged at the moment!'[22]

The two most important documents needed to leave Austria were the so-called *Steuerliche Unbedenklichkeitsbescheinigung*—the fiscal, or tax, clearance certificate—and the official exit permit. Both involved a great many intermediary documents, including many for which Jews had to reapply even if those they already possessed had not expired. Weigl's previous *Heimatschein*, or certificate of domicile, which attested his right of legal residence in Vienna, had been issued in 1913 and had no expiration date, but he had to apply for a new one.[23] It was also necessary to certify having paid all local, district, municipal, and national taxes. On 17 June 1938 Weigl received a statement from the tax office of the first Vienna district, where he lived, indicating that he had a credit of 40.86 Reichsmark.[24]

Another important intermediary step involved the *Reichsfluchtsteuer* (usually translated as the Flight Tax), which was based on a December 1931 emergency decree that had gone into effect in Germany during the Weimar period to counter the threat of currency loss during

---

21   See, for example, the photograph reproduced in 'Central Office for Jewish Emigration in Vienna: Wilhelm Hoettl, Testimony Given for the Trial of Adolf Eichmann', www.holocaustresearchproject. org/nazioccupation/hoetll.html; accessed 30 May 2009.

22   'Entschuldigen Sie die schlechte Schrift; die Nerven sind derzeit etwas in Unordnung!' Letter dated the Saturday before Easter, Ostersamstag 1938 [16 April 1938] (Stolper Collection, LBI).

23   Copies of Weigl's post-Anschluß Heimatschein, dated 30 May 1938, as well as the other documents described below, are located in KWF.

24   According to this document he had paid 81.44 Reichsmark to cover taxes of 27.06 Reichsmark on his 1937 salary of 2,000 schillings, and an additional 13.52 for the first two quarters of 1938. A subsequent *Empfangschein* (confirmation receipt) dated 29 July 1938 indicates that he paid an additional 40.40 Reichsmark to the same office for taxes owed in June 1938.

those catastrophic economic times; when the National Socialists took power they reoriented the law towards Jews trying to emigrate. An incomplete collection of bank statements and other documents among the extant Weigl family papers indicates that, like many exiles and despite stringent attempts to prevent out-of-country transfers, the Weigls were able to spirit some funds out of Austria prior to leaving. On 28 March they sent the bulk of the funds at their disposal—from two Vienna bank accounts and German rail and British war bonds—to their friend Primus Bon in Switzerland. By the time they stopped off in Basel on their passage into exile, Bon had arranged for the Bank für Anlagewerte in Zurich to cut one cheque for $1,799.78 (this was sent to the New York address of Dr. Wilhelm Eitner, a Viennese friend of the Weigls who had emigrated to the United States in the 1920s) and another cheque for $1,000 to cover immediate expenses (this, in addition to ten pounds in English currency, was remitted to them in Basel by messenger). With these funds the Weigls were able to make the journey and survive in New York during the initial year of exile. In later years Vally Weigl wrote that her savings from working in Amsterdam in 1921 had provided the 'emergency backlog' to 'start life anew' in exile: 'The night after the *Anschluss* I transferred it to the father of one of our students in Switzerland [Primus Bon] who later could send it to us in New York, so we had then not only the 10 Marks we could take along in leaving Vienna and felt not quite as lost and insecure.'[25]

On 8 July 1938 Weigl acquired the fiscal clearance certificate. The document, illegibly signed by an otherwise nameless bureaucrat, has an oddly personal cast, reading, in part: 'I have no objections against the exit of Professor Dr. Karl Weigl [...] and his wife Valerie, née Pick [...] and his children [sic] Wolfgang Johannes.'[26] This document was valid for one month. In mid-April Weigl had thought that they could survive in Vienna for perhaps two to three months. Instead, it had taken three months just to achieve financial clearance.

The second and final major hurdle for leaving Austria, the actual exit permit, for which the *Steuerliche Unbedenklichkeitsbescheinigung* was both prerequisite and companion piece, required Weigl's taking his passport to the Wanderungsamt, the office for emigration. There he got a stamp confirming that on 14 July he had been 'seen at the Wanderungsamt'. With

---

25　Vally Weigl, undated typewritten manuscript titled 'Early Childhood Recollections' (KWF). Vally Weigl may have been referring to the 934 Swiss francs (a bit more than 200 contemporary U.S. dollars) that she deposited in her name to the Swiss Kreditanstalt in Zurich on 16 December 1937 and 17 March 1938.

26　'Gegen die Ausreise des Prof. Dr. Karl Weigl, Wien, I. Rudolfspl[atz] 1, geboren am 6. II. 1881 in Wien, und seiner Ehefrau Valerie geborene Pick, geboren am 11. IX. 1894 in Wien, und seiner Kinder [sic] Wolfgang Johannes, geboren am 1. VIII. 1926, habe ich keine Bedenken.' According to the notary who authorized the carbon copy that Weigl retained in his possession, the signature of the official who granted the exit permission was 'unleserlich' (illegible) on the original document.

that stamp in place he was allowed to apply for passport renewal—required even though his passport should not have expired until 1940. The renewal stamped into the Weigl family's passports four days later, on 18 July, gave permission to the passport holders to travel to 'all countries on earth'. On that same day, on the facing page of the passport—but from a different office—they got the stamp giving permission for einnmalige Ausreise (one-time exit) to 'all of Europe, North and South America, and Australia'.

U.S. IMMIGRATION REQUIREMENTS

It is by now well documented that the U.S. State Department required its consulates to keep immigration below the existing quotas; these quotas, which had been in place since 1924, remained in effect for the duration of the European refugee crisis. In 1917 the U.S. Congress had passed a bill 'Regulating Immigration of Aliens to, and Residence of Aliens in, the United States', in which for the first time the country's open-door policy was overturned in favour of quotas based on recent immigration numbers; the 1917 quota figures were revised in 1920 and again in 1924, but there they stayed, even after the international conference of thirty-two countries in Evian, France, in July 1938, which had been called by President Roosevelt. Although by late 1938 applications for U.S. visas from Central Europe (mostly Jews in Germany and Austria) numbered 125,000, the maximum number of immigrants from those two countries remained at 27,370 per year, the combined Austrian (1,413) and German (25,957) quotas.[27]

---

27   This figure is given in various sources, including President Herbert Hoover's Proclamation 1872 of 22 March 1929, 'On the National Original Immigration Quotas', reproduced in Michael C. LeMay and Elliot Robert Barkan, *U.S. Immigration and Naturalization Laws and Issues* (Westport, CT: Greenwood Press, 1999), 163–64; for an online source see also Laura M. Miller, 'Proclamation on Immigration Quotas (28 April 1938)', *Dictionary of American History* (The Gale Group Inc., 2003, www.encyclopedia.com/doc/1G2-3401804817.html; accessed 29 July 2009); and Suzanne Stone, 'Refugee Crisis of 1938' (http://history.sandiego.edu/gen/st/~stone/Refugee.html; accessed 4 November 2008). The extensive body of literature dealing with US policy towards Jewish refugees includes Henry Feingold, *The Politics of Rescue: The Roosevelt Administration and the Holocaust, 1938–1945* (New Brunswick, NJ: Rutgers University Press, 1970); Saul S. Friedman, *No Haven for the Oppressed: United States Policy toward Jewish Refugees, 1938–1945* (Detroit, MI: Wayne State University Press, 1973); Michael C. LeMay, ed., *The Gatekeepers: Comparative Immigration Policy* (New York: Praeger, 1989); David S. Wyman, *Paper Walls: America and the Refugee Crisis, 1938–1941* (New York: Panthean Books, 1985); and Bat-Ami Zucker, *In Search of Refuge: Jews and U.S. Consuls in Nazi Germany, 1933–1941* (London: Vallentine Mitchell, 2001). See also Melissa Jane Taylor, 'Bureaucratic Response to Human Tragedy: American Consuls and the Jewish Plight in Vienna, 1938–1941', *Holocaust and Genocide Studies* 21, no. 2 (2007), 243–67.

The Weigls were fortunate that John C. Wiley, U.S. consul general in Vienna from December 1937 until 18 July 1938, was more sensitive to the humanitarian aspect of the refugee crisis than many of his colleagues; he seems, in fact, to have walked a fine line, keeping to just within State Department guidelines but stretching as many points as he could.[28] No less important was the support of his wife, the sculptor Irena Wiley, who in her memoirs recounts that her husband ordered twenty-four assorted telephone directories from New York and Chicago to help would-be U.S. immigrants locate relatives who might be willing to sponsor their application. Given the impossibility of helping everyone, Irena Wiley concentrated her efforts on artists. A number of exiles, including, perhaps most prominently, Sigmund Freud, owed their escape from Vienna to her. Karl Weigl met several times with 'Mrs. Wiley'—the first occasion noted in the diary was on 25 April—and took her advice that he write to musicians with positions at U.S. academic institutions. She seems also to have initiated the Weigls' contact with the Vienna Quaker Center, which made herculean efforts to help endangered Austrians. Emma Cadbury, the American head of the Vienna Quaker Center, not only helped the Weigls with their immigration applications but later also provided introductions to Quakers in the New York area.[29]

The crucial requirement for a U.S. visa was an affidavit of support from a legal U.S. citizen or resident who vouched for the émigré and declared 'that I am willing and able to receive, maintain, support, and be responsible for the aliens mentioned above while they remain in the United States, and hereby assume such obligations, guaranteeing that none of them will at any time become a burden on the United States or any State, County, City, Village or Municipality of the United States.' Above all it was the public charge clause—one of the oldest and still debated components of U.S. immigration policy—that most often served to justify the rejection of applications for asylum.[30] All through April, May, and June Weigl trawled for affidavits. Several acquaintances that declared themselves prepared to sign affidavits for the family did not meet immigration service standards.[31] Others to whom they applied refused

---

28   The Papers of John Cooper Wiley, including diplomatic files, general correspondence, personal documents, and writings, are available at the Franklin D. Roosevelt Presidential Library and Museum.

29   For more on Irena [Baruch] Wiley, see her memoir, *Around the Globe in Twenty Years: An Artist at Large in the Diplomatic World* (New York: David McKay, 1962), 78. For a general overview of Quaker contributions to the Jewish refugee effort, see Hans A. Schmitt, *Quakers and Nazis: Inner Light in Outer Darkness* (Columbia: University of Missouri Press, 1997). Emma Cadbury enclosed cards of introduction in a letter dated 26 September 1938 (KWF), which she sent Karl and Vally Weigl after they had left Vienna and were making their way to England.

30   See, for example, James R. Edwards Jr., 'Public Charge Doctrine: A Fundamental Principle of American Immigration Policy', *Center for Immigration Studies* (May 2001), http://www.cis.org/articles/2001/back701.html; accessed 8 March 2008.

31   One of the Weigls' acquaintances in New York, Albert Tanzer, owner of the export firm Pan-America

outright, as in this response from a Mrs. Ina Younkers, with whom the Weigls had spent time in Vienna the previous year:

> I regret to say it is impossible for me to sign an affidavit for you. I am afraid your information is not correct if you have been told that this is merely a formality. Our government is very precise and exacting now about affidavits due to the large increase in immigration, and it expects the signers to be financially responsible 'for any persons entering the country on such affidavits.' Also I am sorry to say I do not think it would be at all easy for you to find a suitable position here unless you were directly recommended to one by your friends or pupils. We are in the midst of a serious business depression in the United States and all artists face a very severe struggle for existence.[32]

In the end it was a total stranger who in July came through with affidavits for the Weigl family: the New York businessman Ira Hirschmann, a vice president of Bloomingdale's and founder in 1936 of a successful non-profit organization, New Friends of Music, that sponsored performances of chamber music.[33]

In one more Kafkaesque turn in the path to exile, Weigl was required to obtain formal certification from the Israelitische Kultusgemeinde (IKG), first established in 1852 by decree of Emperor Franz Josef I as the main spiritual, cultural, and educational centre for

---

Fur Corporation, was willing to sign an affidavit for Karl Weigl's mother but failed, as he tells them in a letter of 29 August 1938 (KWF), *'weil ich nicht die erforderlichen Qualifikationen besitze'* (because I do not possess the required qualifications).

32 Typed letter without envelope, dated 20 May 1938 (KWF).

33 Later, Hirschmann was a prominent member of the War Refugee Board and helped to rescue Jewish refugees while serving as President Roosevelt's special envoy to Turkey in 1944. See the Ira Hirschmann Papers, 1934–1969, New York Public Library, Music Division (www.nypl.org/research/manuscripts/music/mushirschmann.xml). Also see various books by Ira Hirschmann, including his posthumously published *Obligato: Untold Tales from a Life with Music* (New York: Fromm International, 1994) and his *Life Line to a Promised Land* (New York: Vanguard Press, 1946), which he dedicated 'To the survivors of Hitler's hate, who will most deeply love, and live for, freedom.' Several items of correspondence (Karl Weigl Papers, YU, and KWF) attest to a loosely maintained connection between Hirschmann and the Weigls after their arrival in New York. According to Kurt Adler (1905–1988), the conductor and long-time director of the San Francisco Opera, it was Irena Wiley who persuaded Ira Hirschmann to issue the affidavits for the Weigl family; see Adler, 'Dear M & A (a letter from Kurt Adler, Conductor and Chorusmaster of the Metropolitan Opera; Advisory Board Karl Weigl Memorial Fund)', *Music & Artists* 1, no. 4 (1968): 26–27, and the four-page typescript draft for this article, with handwritten additions (KWF). Adler, who had studied with Weigl in the 1920s, went into American exile on the same boat, the SS Statendam, that took the Weigls from Southampton to New York in October 1938. He remained a strong supporter of Weigl for the rest of his life.

Vienna's Jewish community, that he was a Jew. This document was apparently required by a Viennese Militärbehörde (military agency). The simple half sheet of paper carrying the certification was issued to Weigl upon submission of unspecified documents (presumably including his birth certificate), notarized by the IKG on 29 August 1938, and approved one day later with a stamp from the Wehrbezirks-Kommando (defence commando) of Vienna.[34]

In the midst of the multiple document chases and worries of that summer came a new difficulty: Vally fell ill. For a few weeks after she was diagnosed with pleurisy on 2 July, Weigl's diary contains almost daily references to her steadily worsening condition. On 1 August he was finally able to note that she was better, and three weeks later, on 23 August, she travelled by train to Semmering, a mountain town, about one hundred kilometres south of Vienna, that was a popular spot for recuperating lung patients. While away, Vally Weigl sent copious advice and directives on what was to be packed, what sold, and what given away. All these letters to her husband are in English, as the Weigls assiduously practiced what they hoped would become their new *Umgangssprache;* one of Vally's first letters closes with the words 'For today kindest regards and write every day about everything, will you? Your English was very good, only you still mix up then and than. Ever yours, Vally.'[35]

One week after her return, on 7 September, the Weigls finally received, stamped into their passports, the three precious U.S. immigration visas and three corresponding immigrant identification card numbers. On 5 September the central tax office had extended for one more month Weigl's *Steuerliche Unbedenklichkeitsbescheinigung.* And ship passage from England to New York was secured and paid for, as Weigl noted in the diary on 10 August. Now it remained only to make the rounds of the consulates to obtain transit papers for Switzerland, France, and England. On 9 September the transit visa for England came through—'Good for single journey only'; three days later the passports were stamped by the French consul in Vienna for transit *sans arrêt;* and one day after that, on 13 September, the family received their transit visa for Switzerland, for '*einmalige Reise durch die Schweiz ohne Aufenthalt*'.

Even today, to anyone deciphering passages in Weigl's diary, the anxiety emanating from the telegraphic entries is palpable. Yet there are no complaints to be found, and hardly any indications of his feelings. On 20 June 1938, for example, the day his daughter married Gerhart Piers in Switzerland—the couple had left Vienna on 29 March, taking Karl Weigl's com-

---

34   After the Anschluß the IKG was co-opted by the National-Socialist government to collaborate in the forced expulsion and deportation of Jews. For more information on the IKG, see Felicitas Heimann-Jelinek, Lothar Hölbling, and Ingo Zechner, *Ordnung muss sein: Das Archiv der Israelitischen Kultusgemeinde Wien* (Vienna: Jüdisches Museum Wien, 2007).

35   Letter from Vally Weigl to Karl Weigl, dated 25 August 1938 (KWF).

positional autographs with them for safekeeping—he comments only by underlining a few words: '*Marias Hochzeit ohne mein Dasein*' (Maria's wedding without my presence).

In August the diary begins to include farewells to close friends; on 29 August Weigl took what may well have been the last hike in his beloved Wienerwald; the outing was marked by a thunderstorm. (One can only speculate as to whether this sent his spirits soaring or might rather have symbolized the terrors of departure.) The words '*z[um] letztenmal*' (for the last time) and '*z[um] Abschied*' (for good-bye) appear often during the remaining diary entries, which end on 5 September. And then, ten days later, on an unremarkable Thursday morning, 15 September 1938, the Weigl family boarded a train to Switzerland.

SUCCESSFUL EXILE?

The Weigls could consider themselves lucky to be among those who had been allowed to immigrate legally into the United States.[36] They had had a great deal of help from others, but they needed to draw on all their reserves of resourcefulness and perseverance. While preparing feverishly for emigration, they had surely also to battle grief and anger. They might have been forgiven for thinking that existential worries would ease once they reached safety. But though he soon knew the extent of the dangers that had been eluded, Weigl would never again, in the years that remained, feel economic security.

Weigl was almost fifty-eight when he left Vienna. He arrived in New York virtually incognito, and he was granted only eleven years to try to re-establish himself. Age at time of arrival and subsequent life span were undoubtedly important factors for all exiles (see table 1 for a partial comparative list of exiles from Weigl's circle). But apart from these two factors—and luck—the chances for a successful new life seem above all to have depended on the personality of the exile himself. Karl and Vally Weigl responded to the *Anschluß* with pragmatism and energy. They consulted with family and friends on emigration, pro and con—the diary once mentions 'plan postponed'—but within days of the German invasion on 12 March they had arranged for English tutoring and begun daily piano practice; Weigl occasionally made a note of this, as on 28 March: '*Immer Englisch u. Klavier*' (Always English and piano). Toni Stolper repeatedly urged them to practice their English: 'For the time being I can only keep repeating

---

36 The actual number of immigrants varies with the source consulted. According to Peter Eppell, *Österreicher im Exil, USA 1938–1945: Eine Dokumentation,* vol. 1 (Vienna: Dokumentationsarchiv des österreichischen Widerstandes, 1995), 28, possibly circa 30,000 Austrians entered the United States between March 1938 and December 1941, when the United States declared war on Germany; that same source cites the number given by the Israelitische Kultusgemeinde in Vienna for the period between 13 March and mid-November 1941 as 28,615.

my most important piece of advice: that learning English remains your top priority. Nothing you do or don't do in the meantime is nearly as important.'[37]

From the diary and other sources, it is clear that Weigl understood that he would have to begin anew. Moreover, he understood that if anything were to see him through, it would be not his composer's contributions but his musical expertise and abilities as a performer and teacher. What he called his *Arbeitsfeld,* his sphere of activity, would never again be the same. Writing to Jacobi, he listed the different kinds of jobs for which—'according to my abilities', as he modestly qualified—he might be considered: '[A]s lecturer or music teacher (theory, composition, history, conductor's preparation, etc.) at some university or college; as piano accompanist, or examiner, referent [sic] at some music publishers, whatever.'[38]

A number of letters Weigl addressed to 'Dear Sir', or *'Sehr geehrter Herr Professor'* include suggestions of this sort. In most of these letters Weigl also described Vally Weigl's qualifications as pianist and teacher, usually in terms similar to those he used in his first letter to Tess Simpson: 'As to my wife, Valerie Weigl, she has not only her States-examination for piano and music-theory and was assistant teacher of the famous Prof. Robert in Vienna; but she also worked as translator for English, German, French (a little Italian and Dutch) in Amsterdam and would consent to take what job ever as teacher for piano or harmony, as translater [sic] or secretary, as lady-companion or travelling-companion, whatever obtainable.'[39] Weigl never referred to his wife's credentials as a composer (she had studied composition with him), but then she did not begin composing seriously until she was in the United States.[40]

Even while still in Vienna Weigl started preparing for the new kind of audience he anticipated that he might encounter. In drafts for music appreciation lectures, he summarized Austro-German music history, describing what it would take for the United States to build 'a nationwide audience of listeners who will know how to listen to music.'[41] Here he revealed a

---

37   'Einstweilen kann ich nur immer und immer wieder meine wichtigsten Rat wiederholen: alle Kraefte eingesetzt fuer das Studium des Englischen. Nichts, was Sie in der Zwischenzeit tun oder nicht tun, ist annaehernd so wichtig.' Letter dated 24 June 1938 (Karl Weigl Papers, YU).

38   Letter to Frederick Jacobi of 9 April 1938 (carbon copy, Karl Weigl Papers, YU).

39   Letter dated 26 March 1938 (carbon copy, Karl Weigl Papers, YU).

40   By the end of her life she had completed a large corpus of works, many of which have been performed and recorded. For more information on Vally Weigl, see www.karlweigl.org. Also see Sophie Fetthauer, 'Vally Weigl', *Lexikon verfolgter Musiker und Musikerinnen der NS-Zeit,* http://cmslib.rrz. uni- hamburg.de:6292/receive/lexm_lexmperson_00001012;jsessionid=r2u665b89y7s?wcmsID=0003, a still on-going project of the Musikwissenschaftliches Institut, University of Hamburg; and *Give Them Music: Musiktherapie im Exil—Am Beispiel von Vally Weigl,* Wiener Beiträge zur Musiktherapie 6, ed. Elena Fitzhum and Primavera Gruber (Vienna: Praesens, 2003).

41   Typescript titled 'Appreciation of Music,' in notebook of undated writings (Karl Weigl Papers, YU, box 25, folder 817).

widely held preconception that the land offering sanctuary was culturally backward; émigrés to England shared the same feelings as well. Beyond preconceptions, however, these drafts also highlight Weigl's determination to try to make a musical difference—if not through his own works, then through teaching.

THE REALITY OF EXILE

Ernst Krenek once said that the most painful part of exile was 'echolessness'—the lack of resonance for one's own sensibilities and traditions.[42] For Weigl, too, this was a major component of exile. In the beginning, however, the Weigls, like most exiles, were mostly preoccupied with the need to make a living. America's charitable response to refugees was beginning to fray by the end of 1938, but many aid organizations and individuals reached out to help them. '[I]n fact,' Vally wrote to her son, Wolfi, less than two weeks after the family arrived in New York, 'almost everyone here has welcomed us most kindly. How immensely good that feels, after the inhumane, demeaning treatment under the Nazis, eh? — You feel it too, right? — All three of us must be sure never to forget that about this country and its people!'[43] Vally needed to communicate with her son in writing because, just five days after the family disembarked in New York, he had been sent to board with a Quaker family in Connecticut, where he started school.[44] Toni Stolper had turned to the Quaker community for help in making these arrangements for the Weigls' son.[45] Apart from a few holidays, the boy never again made his home with his parents.

---

42 Ernst Krenek, 'America's Influence on Its Composer', *Perspectives of New Music* 8, no. 2 (Spring–Summer 1970), 112–17, translated by Don Harran, from Krenek, 'Amerika's Einfluss auf eingewanderte Komponisten', *Musica* 12 (1959), 757–61.

43 '[Ü]berhaupt fast alle Leute hier kommen uns ungemein lieb entgegen. Wie wohltuend ist das nach der menschenunwürdigen Behandlung unter den Nazis, gelt!? — Du spürst's ja auch, nicht wahr? — Und das wollen wir dem Land und seinen Bewohnern alle drei nie vergessen!' From Vally's letter to John Weigl, dated 20 October 1938 (KWF).

44 In New York the Weigls became members of the Wider Quaker Fellowship. Vally Weigl maintained strong connections to the Quaker community for the rest of her life.

45 On 16 September 1938 Toni Stolper had written to the Weigls' Vienna address, also sending a copy of the letter to the SS Statendam: 'I hope that before you leave you and your wife will receive the good news I was just told by your friend Mrs. La Farge. She suggests that your son be placed for a few months at an apparently excellent private school, Glenacres School in Roxbury, Connecticut. Her husband taught at this school and is a friend of the director, Mr. Martin, who lived in Germany for six years and is happy to accept a well-recommended immigrant child. It appears that Mr. Martin will pay your son's tuition costs and Mrs. La Farge his living expenses.' (Ich moechte gern, dass Sie und Ihre Frau vor der Abreise die erfreuliche Nachricht erhalten, die mir eben Ihre Freundin, Mrs. La Farge, gibt. Sie schlaegt vor, dass Ihr Sohn fuer einige Monate auf ihre Kosten in einer anscheinen aus-

Karl and Vally Weigl came to the United States with somewhere in the region of $2,800. They hoped that this sum, which seems to have been the extent of their savings, would see them through the first fourteen or fifteen months. For the entire first year of exile their address was 'care of' a Mrs. Oschlag; they were not able to move into an apartment of their own until September 1939. For almost the first two years the only work either of them could find was part-time private teaching.[46] Weigl did not get a steady job until fall 1940, when he was appointed to a position at the Julius Hartt School of Music in Hartford, Connecticut. Between 16 September 1940 and 14 June 1941 he taught ten to eleven hours a week there for a total salary of $1,800, paid in ten monthly instalments. The position was secured for him by the Emergency Committee in Aid of Displaced Foreign Scholars an organization formed in New York in May 1933 by American academicians wishing to help relocate exiled European scholars, and partially underwritten by the Oberlaender Trust.[47] After this job ended in June 1941, Weigl again experienced a hiatus of almost nine months before a new temporary and part-time position was cobbled together for him at the New York Public Library. This position, again partially funded by the Oberlaender Trust, as well as by the National Committee for Refugee Musicians, was actively promoted by Carleton Sprague Smith (1905–1994), chief of the music division of the New York Public Library 1931–1959; Sprague Smith had studied with Weigl in Vienna 1928–1930 while completing his musicology dissertation at the University of Vienna, and he thought highly of his former teacher.[48] The end of Weigl's New York Public

---

gezeichneten Privatschule, Glenacres School in Roxbury, Connecticut, untergebracht wird. Ihr Mann hat an dieser Schule selbst unterrichtet und ist mit dem Leiter, Mr. Martin, befreundet. Dieser hat sechs Jahre in Deutschland gelebt und ist mit Freuden bereit, ein gut empfohlenes Emigrantenkind aufzunehmen. Er scheint, dass Mr. Martin die Kosten fuer den Lehrfreiplatz und Mrs. La Farge die fuer den Unterhalt Ihres Sohnes tragen wollen.) (Karl Weigl Papers, YU).

46   Among Weigl's first students in New York was the internationally renowned violinist Roman Totenberg, who had relocated to New York from Paris a short time earlier and wished to deepen his understanding of harmony and counterpoint (private interview, 12 June 2003).

47   Upon its dissolution in 1946 the Emergency Committee donated the voluminous papers documenting its activities to the New York Public Library; see www.nypl.org/research/chss/spe/rbk/faids/ Emergency/index.html. For more details about the Oberlaender Trust, which belonged to the National Carl Schurz Association, another organization actively involved in aiding refugees in the later 1930s and 1940s, see the collection of materials housed at the Balch Institute for Ethnic Studies of the Historical Society of Pennsylvania, www.balchinstitute.org/manuscript_guide/html/german.html; see also Hanns Gramm, *The Oberlaender Trust, 1931–1953* (Philadelphia: The Carl Schurz Memorial Foundation, 1956).

48   For more information on Sprague Smith, see, among other sources, John Shepard, 'The Legacy of Carleton Sprague Smith: Pan-American Holdings in the Music Division of the New York Public Library for the Performing Arts', www.britannica.com/bps/additionalcontent/18/20478413/the-legacy-of-carleton-sprague-smith-panamerican-holdings-in-the-music-division-of-the-new-york-public-

Library job in February 1943 overlapped with his beginning a three-month stint of teaching for $100 a month at the Settlement Music School in Philadelphia, whose director, the Dutch-born violinist Johann Grolle, was a pioneer of arts education in the United States. When that position ended in June there was another spell of uncertainty before Brooklyn College hired Weigl in September of that year as a part-time 'lecturer and coach in a course on special music problems' for a remuneration of $40 a month; the Oberlaender Trust again helped to defray the cost of the salary. Vally Weigl during these years also held a number of part-time teaching jobs, including at the American Theatre Wing and Birch Wathen School in New York. In September 1942 she began teaching piano two days a week at Westtown School in Pennsylvania, where her contract renewal soon seems to have become routine. Several years after Weigl's death she would retrain as a music therapist, earn an MA in 1953 from the Teacher's College, Columbia University, and become a pioneer in the field.

Weigl had no choice but to spend most of his eleven years of exile teaching, or looking for teaching work. He also had no choice but to be more active as a performer than he had been in Vienna, and he and Vally often appeared together in four-hand piano performances at musicales in private homes and educational institutions. Yet from the start of the American years, Weigl carved out time to compose. His compositional output in Europe had slowed noticeably in the years immediately preceding emigration, probably reflecting discouragement. Once emigration was unavoidable, however, he not only applied himself energetically to the tasks of transition but also regained energy for composing.

It would seem that, at least initially, he approached composing in exile as pragmatically as he had approached establishing himself as a composer when he was a young man. During that period his first works had been single songs (as opposed to the song sets and cycles and, above all, large orchestral works that he composed in his mature European period). Now, in exile, his first works were again single songs. One of these—possibly his first on an English text—is the setting of a boisterous text by Charlotte Storm titled 'The Glorious Vagabond'. Similarly defiant in tone is the early 1939 song 'The Refugee' which he dedicated to the Friends Service Committee; the poem ends with the words 'I am outcast, a refugee, and Christ is born a Jew!' His first larger work in exile was the energetic Piano Trio, dedicated to Ira Hirschmann, followed by the String Quartet No. 6. For the first two years, he thus limited himself almost entirely to short works for modest performance forces.[49] This practical approach paid off: a number of his smaller works, both new and old, were performed fairly regularly during his

---

library-for-the-performing-arts, accessed 5 March 2008; and Israel J. Katz, Richard J. Wolfe, and Male-na Kuss, eds. *Libraries, History, Diplomacy, and the Performing Arts: Essays in Honor of Carleton Sprague Smith*, ed. Israel J. Katz, Richard J. Wolfe and Malena Kuss (New York: Pendragon Press, 1991).

49   For more information on individual Weigl works, see www.karlweigl.org.

American years in small public venues, private homes, and occasionally on the radio. (See table 2 for a list of performances and performance venues from one representative year, 1941.)

Yet Weigl regarded himself above all as a symphonic composer. And we see that already in the spring of 1939 he began writing again for orchestra. Initially even these works—the twenty-minute orchestral work *Old Vienna* (originally titled *Dances from Vienna*); a seven-minute overture for small orchestra *Music for the Young* (originally titled *Boy Scouts Overture*); and, in the following year, a short *Summer Evening Music* for string orchestra—show that he kept practical considerations of length and substance in mind. Not until 1940 did he tackle a more substantial work, the Rhapsody for piano and large orchestra. And then, for three years starting in 1942, he worked on the fifty-minute Symphony No. 5, which he titled Apocalyptic Symphony. He dedicated this work, completed just before VE-Day, 'to the Peoples of the United Nations'.[50]

Ironically, completing this symphony coincided with learning that his position at the Brooklyn Academy would end that spring. Maurice Lieberman, chair of the Department of Music, was, as he explained in a letter of 11 June 1945, unable to renew Weigl's contract because one of the school's permanent staff members had now returned from the armed forces. Although by no means an uncommon experience amongst exiles in the immediate post-war period, this news may well have contributed to Weigl's serious illness that spring, from which he recovered only to succumb to a severe depression. He had reason to despair, finding himself, at the age of sixty-four, yet again without a means of earning his livelihood, and again with no expectation of hearing his latest new work performed. That fall, however, Weigl was offered a position at the Boston Conservatory of Music, and in the three years remaining to him, despite long days of teaching and a tiring weekly commute, he managed to complete another handful of significant works.

Among the few choices open to Weigl in his last years was whether or not to remain in the United States after the defeat of Nazism. Austria, unlike Germany, was remiss in encouraging its émigrés to return after 1945, but many nevertheless did so, or tried to. The Weigls never considered returning to Europe. They had applied for U.S. citizenship shortly after arriving, and both became citizens in January 1944. Both of Weigl's children had settled in the new country, and there were two grandchildren before Karl Weigl died in 1949. Equally important, he had learned to love the natural beauties of the United States. Living less than one short New York city block from Central Park had done much to mitigate the loss of his

---

50   On a copyist's copy of the full score Weigl originally wrote: 'Dedicated to the People of the United States, In Memory of Franklin Delano Roosevelt'. Some time after, he covered the Roosevelt reference with a strip of paper and changed the first part of the original dedication to read: 'Dedicated to the Peoples of the United Nations'. (KWF)

beloved Wienerwald, and frequent outings to the Adirondacks and a trip to the mountains of the West cemented his connection to the new homeland.

*

Presumably most composers write with the hope for applause and recognition, but even more important for many may be the very act of composing. Like all exile survivors, Weigl recognized how profoundly his life had been redirected by external circumstances. His several serious depressions attest that he was occasionally paralyzed by the conviction that his life was one of strangled potential. Though during his last eleven years he was never free from economic worry, and labouring harder than he ever had before, his corpus of completed works testifies to his having refused to allow the echolessness of exile or the near-extinction of his name to interfere with the pursuit of his chosen craft.

Weigl's last works—particularly the last big orchestral work, Symphony No. 6, and the String Quartet No. 8, which he finished just three months before his death—reflect the consistently meticulously crafted and personal musical language that he had made his own. Increasingly after reaching maturity as a composer in the 1920s, and even while losing his foundational cultural support, first at home and then in exile, he had become less interested in works written by contemporaries. Indeed, he can be said to have become impervious to new directions and technical means once he had discovered the interrelationship between technique and emotional content that made music 'work' for him. The traditional, organic, and masterful architectural structures that Weigl developed in his mature compositions reflect his belief, as he once wrote in a draft for a talk on music appreciation, that the soul of music 'is immortal and undergoes different reincarnations.'[51] It could be argued that in continuing to compose works for large orchestra that he knew had but slim chances of being performed, to say nothing of continuing to compose in an 'unfashionable' style, Weigl chose to run counter to what common sense would have dictated. But undoubtedly he had chosen to follow his inner compass.

How the composer himself may have regarded the matter can perhaps be conjectured from a 1945 letter to Vally, in which he took stock:

> I know that in addition to all the other difficulties I also have to compete with the younger generation. Nevertheless I believe that, at least potentially, I was their equal, or would have been, if not for—etc.

---

51 Typescript titled 'On the Teaching of Music Appreciation', n.d. (Karl Weigl Papers, YU, box 25, folder 818). Weigl was, as many of his students have documented, a dedicated teacher. The extant drafts for lectures to lay audiences also show him to have been dedicated to helping untrained listeners to, as he puts it in this lecture, 'find a suitable path into the beautiful wilderness of music.' Surely joining this goal would also have been that of nurturing listeners who would, by understanding music like his, be able to resonate to with it.

It is the situation, scarcely to be envied, of Baumeister Solness, thwarted in his development but yet able to earn the laurel wreath [*Kranz*]—as recently demonstrated.[52]

In comparing himself to Ibsen's Baumeister Solness, the Master Builder—who achieved his early ambitions by surpassing his elders but then himself begins to be surpassed by, and eventually falls victim to, the younger generation—Weigl seems to indicate that he knew he was no longer a player in the competitive arena. At the moment of this writing, with Symphony No. 5 just completed, he may even have thought that he had reached his creative end; after all, Solness falls to his death in trying to place a *Kranz,* or laurel wreath, on his last building. Nevertheless, Weigl expressed confidence that he has once again earned a master's laurels. Surely in striving, as he did with each new work, for another reincarnation of music's immutable essence—for the unattainable perfection of a master builder—he lived a life not just of perseverance but also of choice.

TABLE 1:

	came to U.S.	at age
Karl Weigl (1881–1949)	1938	57
FRIENDS AND MUSICIANS FROM HIS GENERATION OR EARLIER		
Alexander Zemlinsky (1871–1942)	1938	67
Arnold Schoenberg (1874–1951)	1934	60
Alfred Einstein (1880-1952)	1938	58
Béla Bartók (1881-1945)	1940	59
Igor Stravinsky (1882–1971)	1939	57
Fritz Stiedry (1883–1978)	1937	54
Bruno Eisner (1884-1978)	1936	52
YOUNGER FRIENDS AND *STUDENTS		
Karl Kassowitz (1886-1978—1968?)	1934	48
Alice Ehlers (1887-1981)	1936	49
Ernst Toch (1887–1974)	1934	47
Antonie (Toni) Stolper (1890-1988)	1933	43
Karol Rathaus (1895–1954)	1938	43
*Erich Wolfgang Korngold (1897–1957)	1934/1938	37/39

---

52 'Ich weiß, dass ich zu allen anderen Schwierigkeiten auch noch den Kampf gegen eine jüngere Generation zu bestehen habe. Trotz allem glaube ich, dass ich potentiell mindestens eben so viel gewesen bin oder geworden wäre, wenn nicht'—etc. Es ist die wenig beneidenswerte Lage eines in der Entwicklung gehemmten Baumeister Solness, der aber immerhin noch imstande ist, den Kranz auf seiner höchsten Person zu tragen—wie sich vor kurzem gezeigt hat.' Letter to Vally Weigl, dated 5 July 1945 (KWF).

Otto Leichter (1897–1973)	1940	43
*Hanns Eisler (1898–1962)	1938	40
Ernst Krenek (1900-1991)	1938	38
Hans T. David (1902-1967)	1938	36
*Kurt Adler (1905–1988)	1938	33
*Peter Paul Fuchs (1907–2007)	1938	31
*Roman Totenberg (1911–2012)	1937	26
*Alfred Mann (1917–2006)	1938	16
Paul Doktor (1919–1989)	1947	28
*Lukas Foss (1922–2009)	1937	15

MUSICIAN FRIENDS FROM WEIGL'S GENERATION	CAME TO ENGLAND	AT AGE
Hans Gál (1890–1987)	1938	48
Karl Rankl (1898–1968)	1939	41
*Ernst Gombrich (1900–2001)	1936	36
*Frederic Waldman (1902-1995)	1935	33

TABLE 2: Performances of music by Weigl 1941

3 Jan 1941   Sonata for viola and piano
Hartford, Connecticut, Julius Hartt Musical School of Music
Alfred Kohn, viola; Karl Weigl and Irene Kahn, piano

2 Feb 1941   Two Songs from Phantasus
Chicago, Sherwood Symphony Orchestra, cond. P. Marinus Paulsen
Maria Hussa, soprano; Beverly Watts, piano

21 Feb 1941   Two Night Phantasies; Sonata for viola
New Jersey, WHOM radio broadcast
William Schoen, viola; Harriet Serr and Karl Weigl, piano

23 Feb [1941]   Notturno for violin and piano; Norwegian Dance for piano duet; Two Pieces
for cello and piano
New Jersey, WHOM radio broadcast
Hebert Sorkin, violin; George Finckel, cello; Karl Weigl and Vally Weigl, piano

6 Apr 1941   Demonstration of Music by Karl Weigl
New York, Musicale at the home of Mr. and Mrs. Maurice Heaton
Karl Weigl, piano

8 Apr 1941   Sonata No. 2 for violin and piano; 4 songs for contralto and piano; Five Songs
for soprano and string quartet
New York, Musicale at the home of Mrs. H. A. Guinzburg
Alice Howland, Ruth Kisch-Arndt, Roman Totenberg, Elsie Stein String Quartet, and Karl
Weigl, piano

8 May 1941   Pictures and Tales; Adagio from Sonata No. 1 for violin and piano; 4 songs for
contralto and piano; String Quartet No. 5 in G Major
New York, Musicale at the home of Mrs. Emil Goldmark
Karl and Vally Weigl, piano; Elsie Stein, violin; Ruth Kisch-Arndt, contralto; Elsie Stein String
Quartet

17 May 1941   Panel Discussion: The Europe We Left; Tea
New York, Picnic Supper & Musical program by the Cooperative Art Work Shop
Karl and Vally Weigl, piano; Alice Gerstl-Duschak and Dr. Gottfried Duschak, singers

4 Jun 1941   5 Songs for soprano and string quartet
New York, YMCA, New Collegium Musicum
Alice Howland, soprano; Irene Jacobi, piano; Elsie Stein String Quartet; Josef Wagner, piano;
Erich Simon, clarinet; Fritz Jahoda, piano; Anthony Scott, bass

17 Jun 1941   Pictures and Tales
New York, Dinner meeting for the American Committee for Christian Refugees, Inc.
Karl and Vally Weigl, piano

7 Nov 1941   Pictures and Tales
Westtown, Pennsylvania, Westtown School
Karl and Vally Weigl, piano

26 Nov 1941   Variations on an Eight-Measure Theme
New York, YMCA, New Collegium Musicum
Charles Rosen, piano

29 Nov 1941   Pictures and Tales
Englewood, New Jersey, Dwight School: Piano Duet Recital by Dr. & Mrs. Karl Weigl
Karl and Vally Weigl, piano

Kristof Boucquet

The Transformation of Viktor Ullmann's Compositional Language

In April 1929, at the Music Festival of the International Society for Contemporary Music in Geneva, the Austrian-born Jewish composer Viktor Ullmann gained international acclaim for his *Schönberg-Variationen für Klavier*. Almost fifteen years later, in the autumn of 1943, Ullmann's sixth piano sonata was performed in quite different circumstances, as part of one of the events of the *Freizeitgestaltung* or leisure organization for the internees of the Theresienstadt concentration camp. In August 1944 Ullmann finished a seventh and last piano sonata, only a few weeks before he was deported to Auschwitz, where he was killed in the gas chambers on 18 October 1944. From the beginning of international recognition in 1929 until the violent suppression of his work by the Nazis, Ullmann's constantly changing life circumstances faithfully reflected the turbulent political and cultural climate of his times. The title of one of his journals, *Der fremde Passagier* (the strange passenger), reveals Ullmann's feeling of being a traveller on a never-ending journey. The evolution of his compositional language was also subjected to a succession of transformations, from an essentially adaptive stage during which Ullmann closely followed the example of his teachers, to the foundation of a personal mode of expression. Since the rediscovery of Ullmann as a composer with the Amsterdam première of *Der Kaiser von Atlantis* in 1975, authors such as Ingo Schultz and Verena Naegele have attempted to reconstruct Ullmann's biography on the basis of the few surviving documents.[1] Very little has been written about Ullmann's compositional language, with the exception of *Der Kaiser von Atlantis*, without doubt the most impressive work from Ullmann's Theresienstadt period.[2] Here too, the loss of many early compositions is the main reason for the difficulties in retracing Ullmann's compositional evolution. His piano compositions offer the most promising perspective for an investigation of this evolution since, apart from the *Schönberg-Variations*, Ullmann's seven piano sonatas have been preserved in their

---

1   Ingo Schultz, *Viktor Ullmann—Leben und Werk* (Stuttgart: J. B. Metzler Verlag, 2008); Verena Naegele, *Viktor Ullmann—Komponieren in verlorener Zeit* (Cologne: Dittrich Verlag, 2002).

2   Only Ingo Schultz, in his recently published monograph *Viktor Ullmann—Leben und Werk*, offers a balanced view of Ullmann's compositional evolution as a whole, with sufficient attention being paid to all of the surviving major compositions.

entirety. Between the earliest surviving version of the *Schönberg-Variations* from the Geneva Festival and the first piano sonata from 1936, there is nevertheless a gap of seven years in which Ullmann's compositional aesthetics underwent a radical transformation. Little is known about the different stages of this transformation, for most of his compositions from this period are lost. Some insights may nevertheless be gained from his letters and from the articles written by Ullmann during these years for journals such as *Anbruch* and *Der Auftakt*.[3] As a preliminary to a thorough investigation of the metamorphosis in Ullmann's compositional outlook, this essay attempts to offer a general description of the essential characteristics of this transformation, choosing Ullmann's piano compositions and published articles as a point of departure.

When in 1909, as an eleven-year-old boy, Ullmann moved from his birthplace Teschen to Vienna, he quickly became absorbed in the many cultural and artistic movements of Vienna's pre-war period. With his fellow students Josef Travníček and Hanns Eisler at the Rasumovsky Gymnasium in Vienna's Kundmanngasse, young Ullmann shared a keen interest in the music of Gustav Mahler and the writings of Karl Kraus. From 1914 onwards, he received lessons in composition from Josef Polnauer, a former student of Arnold Schoenberg. Through his teacher Ullmann became acquainted with Schoenberg's recent works. Early evidence of this is offered by Ullmann's own attempt at composing a *Kammersymphonie* for seventeen instruments, of which only a few bars have been preserved in his correspondence with Anny Wottitz.[4] Following his military service at the Italian front during the last years of World War I, Ullmann returned to Vienna and registered for Schoenberg's seminar for composition in October 1918. Until May 1919, he was given lessons in counterpoint, harmony, form, instrumentation and analysis. Ullmann also actively participated in Schoenberg's *Verein für musikalische Privataufführungen* (Society for Private Musical Performances). Even after his departure for Prague in May 1919, Ullmann remained part of the Schoenberg circle. Heinrich Jalowetz, another of Schoenberg's early students, became Ullmann's new composition teacher in Prague. In 1920 Ullmann succeeded Anton Webern as a choir director at the Neues Deutsches Theater under the supervision of Alexander Zemlinsky, where he assisted with the preparations for a Prague performance of Schoenberg's *Gurrelieder* in 1921.

Given these close associations with Schoenberg and his pupils, it is not surprising to find that Ullmann's own compositions from this period respond in many ways to Schoenberg's compositional innovations. This is best illustrated by Ullmann's *Schönberg-Variations*, dedi-

---

3   His most important articles from this period include 'Zur Frage der modernen Vokalmusik' (*Der Auftakt* 9, 1929), 'Alban Berg' (*Anbruch* 12, 1930), 'Arnold Schönberg. Zum 50. [60.] Geburtstag' (*Bohemia*, 13 September 1934), 'Zur Charakteristik der Tonarten' (*Anbruch* 9, 1935) and 'Gustav Mahler' (*Tempo* 15, 1935).

4   Ingo Schultz, 'Viktor Ullmann und Arnold Schönberg: Dokumente aus den Jahren 1917–1919', *Journal of the Arnold Schönberg Center*, Vol. 2 (2000), 169–70.

cated to his first teacher Josef Polnauer. A first version of this work originated in 1926 and consisted of twenty-one variations and a concluding double fugue. In its second version, the work was reduced to five variations and a double fugue. Ullmann's radical reduction of the number of variations was most likely prompted by the negative reviews on the occasion of its first performance in 1926. These negative comments had mainly to do with the extravagant length of the work. In the journal *Bohemia*, one of the critics wrote: 'Ullmann varies a theme by Schönberg as long as there is manuscript paper available; he even has reserves for a monumental double fugue.'[5] The second, reduced version was presented at the Geneva Festival on 6 April 1929 by the pianist Franz Langer. In 1933–34 Ullmann wrote a third version of this work, now consisting of nine variations and fugue. In this form it was published in 1939 as *Variationen und Doppelfuge über ein Thema von Arnold Schönberg für Klavier op. 3a*. Opus number 3b was reserved for the arrangement for orchestra, completed in the same period as the third piano version. With this orchestral arrangement, Ullmann won the Emil Hertzka-award in 1934. A second arrangement of the *Schönberg-Variations*, this time for string quartet, was discovered in 1998 in the Houghton Library of Harvard University. With this string quartet version, dated 'Prague, 9 April 1939' and dedicated to the Kolisch Quartet, Ullmann probably hoped to raise interest in his work in the United States.[6] Ullmann's continued preoccupation with his *Schönberg-Variations* may have been motivated by the very positive reception of its second version by the international press during the Geneva Festival in 1929. In his report of this Festival for *The Musical Times*, Edwin Evans wrote:

> Viktor Ullmann gave us Five Variations and Double Fugue on a small pianoforte piece by Schönberg, which Prof. Franz Langer interpreted with so much spirit that even those who confessed that Schönberg was a sealed book to them were impressed. Both the piece which served as theme and the Variations reared upon it are ejaculatory, semi-pugnacious music, and it was exhilarating to see the pianist, pausing on a note of exclamation, gaze at the pianoforte as if expecting it to retort with something equally pungent. But joking apart, there was something compelling about it, and many made a note to take an early opportunity to study the work.[7]

---

5 'Ullmann variiert ein Thema von Schönberg, solange Notenpapier vorhanden ist, und er hat noch Vorrat für eine weitausholende Doppelfuge', F. Adler, *Bohemia*, 18 May 1926, quoted in Christian Hoesch, 'Preface' to the edition of Ullmann's *Variationen und Doppelfuge op. 3a über ein Thema von Arnold Schönberg (op. 19/4)* (Mainz: Schott ED 8433, 2004), 4.
6 Hoesch, 'Preface', 6–7.
7 Edwin Evans, 'Geneva Festival', *Musical Times* (May 1929), 440.

When the work was repeated in a broadcast recital in Frankfurt am Main, Theodor W. Adorno was more critical of Ullmann's work, describing the variations as 'not as good as their reputation would have it; more adaptations of their theme with constantly changing character, rather than penetrating into the real compositional substance.' He nevertheless praised the work as being attractively composed and imaginative.[8]

The theme of Ullmann's *Variations* is the fourth of Schoenberg's *Sechs Klavierstücke* op. 19 from 1911.[9] These aphoristic pieces were written by Schoenberg during his period of free atonality, whereas in 1926, the year of the first version of Ullmann's *Variations*, Schoenberg himself had already developed his twelve-tone method. Following the nature of the theme, Ullmann's variation cycle is atonal. It is not a twelve-tone composition, although the work manifests many similarities to Schoenberg's newly discovered technique. These similarities can be explained by the observation that both Schoenberg's twelve-tone method and Ullmann's *Variations* were intended to revive pre-classical and polyphonic compositional techniques. The fifth of Ullmann's *Variations* is a canon in three voices, of which the theme is derived from the inverted retrograde of the second phrase of Schoenberg's piece. The seventh variation is a passacaglia based on a recurring bass pattern. This descending chromatic bass pattern in the low register of the piano immediately evokes the dark, ominous atmosphere from the eighth melodrama 'Nacht' from *Pierrot Lunaire*, a piece which in its strict voice-leading pattern is often considered as a forerunner of Schoenberg's twelve-tone composition.[10] Apart from these voice-leading techniques, which reflect Ullmann's reception of the polyphonic tradition through the example of Schoenberg, the formal designation of a number of Ullmann's variations also refers to the period of Bach: the fourth variation is called 'quasi Gavotte' and the eight variation is in the 'Tempo di Menuetto', two musical dance forms that also appear in Schoenberg's Suite for piano op. 25, his first full-fledged twelve-tone composition.

If we consider the compositional technique of Ullmann's first variation in greater detail, the similarity with Schoenberg's contemporaneous compositions is even more striking (see music examples 1.1 and 1.2). The right hand melody of the first variation is an exact inversion of the original theme, starting from the identical opening tone F. At the same time, this inversion is combined with the retrograde of the original melody: the left hand of the first

8   Theodor W. Adorno, 'Frankfurter Opern- und Konzertkritiken—April 1930', *Gesammelte Schriften Band 19: Musikalische Schriften VI*, ed. Rolf Tiedemann (Frankfurt: Suhrkamp, 1984), 175: 'Danach die Klaviervariationen von Viktor Ullmann über das vierte Klavierstück aus Schönbergs opus 19; nicht so gut wie ihr Ruf; ihr Thema mehr in wechselnden Charakteren umschreibend als in kompositorischem Angriff eindringend; [...] allerdings hübsch gesetzt und einfallsreich.'

9   In my discussion of this work, I will refer to the third and final version for piano, published in 1939.

10   Bryan R. Simms, *The Atonal Music of Arnold Schoenberg 1908–1923* (Oxford: Oxford University Press, 2000), 135–39.

variation opens with A-sharp from bar 4 of the original theme and continues with the tones preceding this A-sharp in the original theme. A modified version of this retrograde theme will later serve as the second theme of the concluding double fugue. The harmonic material of the theme is varied through transposition: the left hand figure of bar 4 of the theme is transposed up a major second in bar 17 of the first variation, whereas the chordal material of the left hand of bar 6 is transposed down a major second in bar 19. The techniques of inversion, retrograde and transposition are usually associated with Schoenberg's treatment of the series in twelve-tone composition. Ullmann's point of departure is not a twelve-tone series, but an existing theme, that is nevertheless subjected to the same compositional principles. Ullmann's full awareness of Schoenberg's newly discovered techniques is evident from the fact that in bar 20, the third possibility (besides inversion and retrograde) of the treatment of the series in twelve-tone music is introduced: the theme starting in the left hand in bar 20 is the inverted retrograde (in transposition) of the thematic segment in bars 3–4 of the original theme.

Example 1.1: Schönberg-Variations, bars 1–9 © With kind permission from Schott Verlag, Mainz.

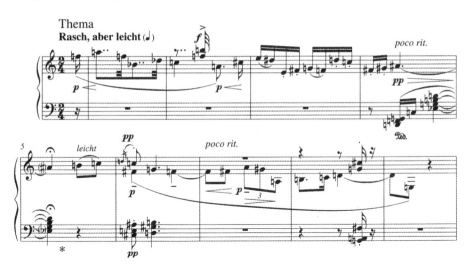

Example 1.2: Schönberg-Variations, bars 14–22 © With kind permission from Schott Verlag, Mainz.

Ullmann's *Variations* clearly demonstrate the influence of Schoenberg and his pupils on his early compositional career, an influence Ullmann himself described in a letter to Karl Reiner from 25 August 1938: 'To the Schönberg school, I owe strict, i.e. logical architecture and the penchant for adventures in the world of sound.'[11] While this kind of compositional logic remained characteristic of Ullmann's later compositions, soon after the *Schönberg-Variations* Ullmann developed a more personal sound or harmonic idiom. He described the purpose of this compositional transformation in the same letter to Karl Reiner: 'It is my intention to explore the unexhausted possibilities of tonal, functional harmony, or to fill the gap between the romantic and 'atonal' harmony.'[12]

Ullmann's renouncement of a strictly atonal language and his development of a specific kind of functional tonality can be explained in several ways. Firstly, his interest in Schoenberg gradually narrowed to the early, tonal works of this composer, still written in the romantic tradition. Symptomatic in this respect is his homage to Schoenberg published in *Bohemia* on the occasion of the composer's sixtieth birthday in 1934, in which he writes far more favour-

---

11 'Der Schönbergschule verdanke ich strenge—will sagen logische Architektonik und Liebe zu den Abenteuern der Klangwelt', quoted in Konrad Richter, 'Einführung in die Kompositionsprinzipien der Klaviersonaten Viktor Ullmanns', *"Lebe im Augenblick, lebe in der Ewigkeit" —Die Referate des Symposions aus Anlaß des 100. Geburtstags von Viktor Ullmann in Berlin am 31. Oktober/1. November 1998,* ed. Hans-Günter Klein (Saarbrücken: Pfau Verlag, 2000), 103.

12 'Es mag darum gehen, die unerschöpften Bereiche der tonal funktionellen Harmonik zu ergründen oder die Kluft zwischen der romantischen und der "atonalen" Harmonik auszufüllen', quoted in Richter, 106.

ably on Schoenberg's early period and on his qualities as a teacher and spiritual leader than on the works of his later atonal and twelve-tone periods.[13] Ullmann may have realized that the language of Schoenberg's early works still provided several unexploited possibilities within tonality. In fact, Schoenberg himself would occasionally return to this form of extended tonality in his American years, for instance in his *Variations on a Recitative for Organ* op. 40 from 1941, in which he systematically investigated the properties of the fourth chords of his first *Kammersymphonie* op. 9 from 1906.[14]

Secondly, Ullmann's close contact with Alexander Zemlinsky in Prague during the 1920s, his longstanding admiration for Mahler and his growing appreciation of the music of Alban Berg all may have contributed to his development of a personal tonal language. His article on Alban Berg, published in *Anbruch* in 1930, is a clear testimony of the changes in his musical allegiance: in this text, Ullmann expresses doubts whether Schoenberg's strict twelve-tone method (designated as 'the great taboo') will ever form the basis of a future common musical language. Alban Berg, on the other hand, is praised as the founder of a true synthesis: 'Under his hands, the material is no longer subject to discussion and we forget the distinction between tonality, atonality or twelve-tone method. Schönberg has once compared tonality with water, atonality with wine. Berg performs the miracle of transformation: both elements become similar, they permeate each other.'[15] Through this synthesis, Berg's music also restored the relationship with the public.

A third reason for Ullmann's elaboration of a characteristic tonal system may relate to his strong interest in anthroposophy. Between 1931 and 1933, Ullmann renounced all musical activity in order to keep a small anthroposophical bookshop in Stuttgart. Many authors have already pointed to the impact of specific anthroposophical ideas on several of Ullmann's writings and opera libretti, and on his general philosophy of life.[16] The role of the anthroposophical philosophy and of the influence of his friend and anthroposophist Alois Hába on the development of Ullmann's compositional language is however a subject that still needs closer investigation.[17]

---

13   Viktor Ullmann, 'Arnold Schönberg—Zum 50. [60.] Geburtstag', *Bohemia*, 13 September 1934, 5.

14   See in this respect Gerhard Luchterhandt, *'Viele ungenutzte Möglichkeiten'—Die Ambivalenz der Tonalität in Werk und Lehre Arnold Schönbergs* (Mainz: Schott, 2008), 261–301.

15   Viktor Ullmann, 'Alban Berg', *Anbruch*, 12 (1930) No. 2, 50: 'Unter dieser Hand wird das Material der Diskussion entrückt und wir vergessen, daß es hier "Tonalität", dort "Atonalität" oder Zwölftonsystem heißt. Schönberg hat einmal Tonalität mit Wasser, Atonalität mit Wein verglichen. Berg tut das Wunder der Verwandlung: Die beiden Elemente werden einander ähnlich, sie durchdringen einander.'

16   Jan Dostal, 'Ullmann als Anthroposoph', *Viktor Ullmann Materialien*, ed. Hans-Günter Klein (Hamburg: Von Bockel Verlag, 1995), 126–29; Robert Kolben, 'Viktor Ullmann und die Anthroposophie', *Viktor Ullmann—Die Referate des Symposions anlässlich des 50. Todestags 14–16. Oktober 1994 in Dornach und ergänzende Studien*, ed. Hans-Günter Klein (Hamburg: Von Bockel Verlag, 1996), 39–54.

17   One article in Czech explores the relationship between the two composers. See Vlasta Reittererová, 'Alois Hába a Viktor Ullmann - doteky života a díla,' *Hudební věda*, 1994, (vol. 31, no. 1), 3–24.

Example 2: Piano Sonata No. 1, first movement, bars 1–17 ©With kind permission from Schott Verlag, Mainz.

The first results of Ullmann's new harmonic orientation are manifested in his first piano sonata, finished in Prague on 8 April 1936. This work is dedicated to Franz Langer, the interpreter of the *Schönberg-Variations* at the Geneva Festival. The sonata was played at the Festival of the International Society for Contemporary Music in New York in 1941, only a year before Ullmann was deported to Theresienstadt. A change in its harmonic vocabulary is immediately apparent in the opening passage with the striking presentation of the chords of G-flat major and C major in bars 2 and 5 respectively (music example 2).

These chords are tritone related, a relationship that is also expressed melodically in the upper voice of bars 5 and 6. Within a tonal context, these chords could represent the Neapolitan and the dominant of F-major or f-minor. This interpretation is supported by the appearance of the f-minor chord in bar 9 and by the final cadence of this movement in F major. Within the context of the first bars, however, these chords hardly function as Neapolitan and dominant harmonies. The movement opens with a French sixth type of chord, which through its specific position underlines the two tritone intervals.[18] The whole-tone content of this chord is complemented by the alternative whole-tone dialogue between right and left hand in the passage in bars 7–8. In general, the whole-tone scale features prominently in Ullmann's new harmonic language. Even more important is the presence of chords constructed of fourths, perfect fourths as well as diminished and augmented fourths. A chord of this type appears in the first half of bar 14. Depending on whether the tone A-sharp or B is interpreted as a harmonic tone, this chord can be read as a fourth combination of F – A-sharp – E-flat – A – D or as a combination of F – B – E-flat – A – D.

In a perceptive article about the compositional techniques in Ullmann's piano sonatas, the editor of these works Konrad Richter has observed that the frequent use of these fourth chords results from Ullmann's selection of a specific group of overtones (overtones 8–14), not unlike Scriabin's 'mystic chord'.[19] Richter has pointed to the almost identical structure of the mystic chord at the opening of Scriabin's seventh piano sonata with the chord in the opening bars of the second movement of Ullmann's first piano sonata. This second movement, dedicated to Gustav Mahler in commemoration of the twenty-fifth anniversary of his death, is also remarkable for its use of a specific palindromic contrapuntal technique (music examples 3.1 and 3.2). The movement consists of an ABA'-form in which the second A-part is not a repetition, but an almost exact retrograde of the first A-part. As a result, this movement ends with the same notes with which it began, although the contrasting middle part does not

---

18   In his analysis of Ullmann's first piano sonata, Ingo Schultz discovers in the pitch content of the chords of bar 1 a tribute to Alban Berg and Gustav Mahler, by reinterpreting the German tone names as letters from these composers' names; see Schultz, 162–63.

19   Richter, 103–20.

participate in this palindromic structure. The tradition of this technique reaches back to the early contrapuntal masters and was revived by Schoenberg in pieces like 'Der Mondfleck' from *Pierrot Lunaire* and by Alban Berg in almost all of his major compositions.[20]

Example 3.1: Piano Sonata No. 1, second movement, bars 1–5 © With kind permission from Schott Verlag, Mainz.

Example 3.2: Piano Sonata No. 1, second movement, bars 64–68 © With kind permission from Schott Verlag, Mainz.

The presence of this palindromic structure in Ullmann's first piano sonata demonstrates that, in spite of the new harmonic context, Ullmann did not abandon his penchant for contrapuntal forms. Other elements in Ullmann's piano sonatas also suggest a continuation of the compositional techniques of his earlier *Schönberg-Variations*. Several movements unfold as a series of variations on a theme, for instance the second movement of the second piano sonata, based on a Moravian folk song recorded by Leós Janáček, or the third movement of the third piano sonata, based on an early piano piece by Mozart (K3). These Mozart variations are followed by a fugue, another formal element that connects them with the earlier *Schönberg-Variations*. The finale of the fourth piano sonata is even constructed as a triple fugue, a clear testimony to Ullmann's undiminished interest in intricate contrapuntal forms.

---

20   See for instance the discussion of retrograde motion in Berg's *Wozzeck* in Douglas Jarman, *Alban Berg: Wozzeck* (Cambridge: Cambridge University Press, 1989), 62–4.

Of Ullmann's seven piano sonatas, the last three were written during his Theresienstadt period. Ullmann arrived in Theresienstadt on 8 September 1942 and soon became involved in the *Freizeitgestaltung* as a composer, musical director, pianist and critic. As has already been remarked by several scholars, there is no notable change in Ullmann's Theresienstadt compositions; they follow the path set out in the compositions of the preceding Prague period. In an often-quoted passage from his essay *Goethe und Ghetto*, Ullmann himself has pointed to the positive influence of Theresienstadt on his musical productivity: 'All that I would stress is that Theresienstadt has helped, not hindered, me in my musical work, that we certainly did not sit down by the waters of Babylon and weep, and that our desire for culture was commensurate with our desire for life.'[21] This 'desire for life' is noticeable in the opening movement of the fifth sonata, a work finished in Theresienstadt on 27 June 1943 and dedicated to Ullmann's wife, Elisabeth. The opening movement carries the subtitle '*Von meiner Jugend*' and sounds remarkably joyful in its first C-major theme (music example 4.1). In an earlier article 'Zur Charakteristik der Tonarten', Ullmann had identified the key of C-major with the origin of light and with victory, in imitation of Goethe's theory on the psychology of colours. This theory, in which each colour had its own emotional or spiritual quality, was later adapted to 'tone colours' by theorists such as Josef Matthias Hauer and Hermann Beckh. Ullmann accepted these associations of tonal keys with spiritual moods as a universal law and found its corroboration in many examples from music literature. In 'Zur Charakteristik der Tonarten', the 'light' and 'victory' connotations of C-major are illustrated by the passage 'Es werde Licht' in Haydn's *Schöpfung* and by Wagner's *Meistersinger*.[22] In the opening bars of his fifth piano sonata, this key is coloured by the appearance of F-sharp and B-flat. According to Richter, these pitches, constituting the eleventh and fourteenth overtones of C, are the hallmark of Ullmann's tonal language.[23] Other characteristics of this language also reappear, as for instance the minor triad with added major seventh on the strong beats of bar 29 and the succession of perfect and augmented fourths in the arpeggio-figure of the first half of bar 29 (music example 4.2). In bar 31, the second theme is introduced in the region of e-minor. This melancholic waltz-theme sounds as a nostalgic reminiscence of a bygone era.

21 'Zu betonen ist nur, daß ich in meiner musikalischen Arbeit durch Theresienstadt gefördert und nicht etwa gehemmt worden bin, daß wir keineswegs nur klagend an Babylons Flüssen saßen und daß unser Kulturwille unserem Lebenswille adäquat war', quoted in Viktor Ullmann, *26 Kritiken über musikalische Veranstaltungen in Theresienstadt*, ed. Ingo Schultz (Hamburg: Von Bockel Verlag, 1993), 93.
22 Viktor Ullmann, 'Zur Charakteristik der Tonarten', *Anbruch*, 1935, No. 9, 244–46.
23 Richter, 112.

Example 4.1: Piano Sonata No. 5, first movement, bars 1–7 © With kind permission from Schott Verlag, Mainz.

Example 4.2: Piano Sonata No. 5, first movement, bars 28–31 © With kind permission from Schott Verlag, Mainz.

In his Theresienstadt compositions, Ullmann continued to use complex contrapuntal forms. A particularly famous example is the concluding fugue of his seventh and last piano sonata, in which Ullmann combines the theme of the Hebrew song 'Rachel' by Yehuda Sharret with three other musical references, the Hussite Song 'You who are God's warriors', the chorale melody 'Nun danket alle Gott' and the B-A-C-H motive. Another telling example in this respect is the third movement of this seventh piano sonata (music example 5). As in the slow movement of the first sonata, the main theme of this movement has a palindromic structure: starting in bar 9, the music goes backwards until bar 16, where the opening notes of the melody are reached. In the subsequent section from bar 17 onwards, the same melody serves as the bass pattern, on which a new melody is constructed with material from the first section.

Example 5: Piano Sonata No. 7, third movement, bars 1–21 © With kind permission from Schott Verlag, Mainz.

When we consider, by way of conclusion, the evolution of Ullmann's compositional language from the early *Schönberg-Variations* to the seventh piano sonata, we encounter important elements of change as well as of continuity. The harmonic dimension presents the most radical change, from the early adaptation of Schoenberg's atonal language to the foundation of an individual tonal system. Two unifying factors throughout this development are the techniques of 'polyphony' and 'variation', by which Ullmann proved himself an admirer of German tradition from Bach to Mahler, Schoenberg and Berg. Especially the variation form continued to preoccupy Ullmann's compositional thinking. On a personal level, this form reflects the way Ullmann interpreted his own development as an artist and a human being. Of the now lost second string quartet written in 1935, the first movement in variation form was called *selbstportrait* (self portrait). On a more metaphysical level, this technique can be interpreted as a musical expression of Ullmann's belief in the interrelationship and transformation of all human life. This idea finds its expression in one of the aphorisms from Ullmann's journal *Der fremde Passagier*: 'Theme with variations—the metamorphoses of individuality through several earthly existences.'[24] This succession of metamorphoses had to result in a victory of form or spirit over the burdens of matter. Ullmann expressed this vision most clearly in his essay *Goethe und Ghetto*, in which he writes:

> For me Theresienstadt has been, and remains, an education in form. Previously, when one did not feel the weight and pressure of material life, because modern conveniences—those wonders of civilization—had dispelled them, it was easy to create beautiful forms. Here, where matter has to be overcome through form even in daily life, where everything of an artistic nature is the very antithesis of one's environment—here, true mastery lies in seeing, with Schiller, that the secret of the art-work lies in the eradication of matter through form: which is presumably, indeed, the mission of man altogether, not only of aesthetic man but also of ethical man.[25]

In this way, the evolution of Ullmann's compositional language testifies to his enduring faith in the cultural transformation and elevation of the human spirit, even under circumstances in which physical and spiritual life was constantly under threat.

---

24 'Thema mit Variationen—die Metamorphosen der Individualität in verschiedenen Erdenleben', in
    Viktor Ullmann Materialien, 123.
25 'Theresienstadt war und ist für mich Schule der Form. Früher, wo man Wucht und Last des stofflichen
    Lebens nicht fühlte, weil der Komfort, diese Magie der Zivilisation, sie verdrängte, war es leicht,
    die schöne Form zu schaffen. Hier, wo man auch in täglichen Leben den Stoff durch die Form zu
    überwinden hat, wo alles Musische im vollen Gegensatz zur Umwelt steht: Hier ist die wahre Meister-
    schaft, wenn man mit Schiller das Geheimnis des Kunstwerks darin sieht: den Stoff durch die Form
    zu vertilgen—was ja vermutlich die Mission des Menschen überhaupt ist, nicht nur des ästhetischen,
    sondern auch des ethischen Menschen', quoted in Ullmann, *26 Kritiken*, 92–3.

Katarzyna Naliwajek-Mazurek

Nazi Censorship in Music, Warsaw 1941

Since the end of World War II, problems connected with Nazi music policy have been subjected to considerable analysis. Yet in recent decades, a much more nuanced view of this multifaceted issue has emerged. In 1995, for example, Leon Botstein commented upon the 'paradoxes and ironies' surrounding the appropriation of Beethoven's music during the war by the Nazis in public propaganda events and—on the other hand—by the Allied anti-Nazi propaganda. At the same time, he noted that not only was this music often performed by the Jüdischer Kulturbund, at least between 1933 and 1936 (as Botstein put it, 'by Jews for Jews'), it was also played in the ghetto in Warsaw 'despite an official ban of the performance by Jews of music by Aryan composers in concerts publicly advertised as featuring only the music of Mendelssohn and Meyerbeer.'[1] Likewise, Erik Levi has highlighted both the discrepancies and the lack of consistency towards music, which were otherwise rather uncharacteristic of Nazi propaganda, and that even at the time of the establishment of the Music Censorship Office (*Reichsmusikprüfstelle*), 'which exercised much tighter control over musical censorship [...], bureaucratic interference did not always prove infallible and there were so many instances when stylistically advanced music somehow managed to slip through the net. Performances of Stravinsky's work in Germany for example, were only officially banned by the regime as late as February 1940.'[2] Pamela M. Potter further questioned the consistency of music censorship in Nazi Germany, referring to a broad array of historical studies, including one by historian Alan Steinweis, who argued that 'music censorship policy in Nazi Germany was amorphous at best, and largely unenforceable given the limited personnel and resources assigned to it. The few government-issued blacklists had a limited distribution and led to no organized measures to ensure that they were honoured.'[3]

---

1   Leon Botstein, 'After Fifty Years: Thoughts on Music and the End of World War II', *Musical Quarterly* (1995), 228. In his article Botstein suggests that Beethoven was performed by the Jüdischer Kulturbund between 1933 and 1941, although the Nazis had in fact placed a ban on them performing his music after 1936. See Lily E. Hirsch's chapter in this book.

2   Erik Levi, 'Atonality, 12-Tone Music and the Third Reich', *Tempo (1991)*, 17. See also Erik. Levi, 'The censorship of Musical Modernism in Germany, 1918–1945', in: *Censorship and Cultural Regulation in the Modern Age*, ed. Beate Müller (Amsterdam: Rodopi 2004), 63–85.

3   Pamela M. Potter, 'What Is "Nazi Music?"', *Musical Quarterly* (2005), 428–55; Alan E. Steinweis, *Art,*

While this lack of consistency explains some of the paradoxes occurring in what was before the war Polish territory, and which was then partly transformed into the General Government (GG) and partly annexed to the Third Reich, the situation there differed substantially from the censorship imposed in the Reich and in other Nazi-occupied countries. Its main categories remained racial and were to a considerable extent determined by the changes to the military context. Yet the ideological borderline was traced not between the modernist, dissonant, atonal and the stylistically acceptable, as was generally the case with regard to the newly construed concept of truly German art, primarily because in the Warsaw or Kraków music milieu, there were practically no composers who could be accused of blatant modernism. Furthermore, Polish culture in general, as the product of Slavic and Jewish *Untermenschen,* was not recognized by the Nazi authorities.[4] This was made evidently clear at a press conference convened on 24 October 1940 when it was stated that:

> Poland is a mass of *Untermenschen.* Poles, Jews, Gypsies should be enumerated in one breath […] A Pole is something impure, something which one should not be concerned with […] All which is good in Poland, has its German roots, as culture […] Reports from the occupied territories should be treated as part of German life and its cultural area.[5]

Many musicians, especially those who were teachers, belonged to the part of Polish society, so-called by the Nazis as the *Führersicht*, that was to be terrorized or liquidated.[6] Yet there

---

Ideology, and Economics in Nazi Germany: The Reich Chambers of Music, Theater, and the Visual Arts (Chapel Hill: University of North Carolina Press, 1993), 138–42.

4   See K. Naliwajek-Mazurek, 'The Racialization and Ghettoization of Music in the General Government', in *Twentieth-Century Music and Politics*, ed. Pauline Fairclough (Farnham: Ashgate, 2013), 191–210.

5   Elke Fröhlich, 'Sytuacja kultury w krajach okupowanych', in *Inter arma non silent Musae. Wojna i kultura 1939–1945*, ed. Czesław Madajczyk (Warsaw: Polski Instytut Wydawniczy, 1982), 213 (English translations of Polish sources are by the author of this chapter).

6   The *Ausserordentliche Befriedungsaktion*, which liquidated the intelligentsia, was introduced in September 1939. In the Nuremberg Tribunal Judgment it was stated that: 'On 30th May, 1940, Frank said at a police conference that he was taking advantage of the offensive in the West which diverted the attention of the world from Poland to liquidate thousands of Poles who would be likely to resist German domination of Poland, including "the leading representatives of the Polish intelligentsia"'. Quoted in *Law Reports of Trials of War Criminals* (London: His Majesty's Stationery Office, 1949), xiv: 34. He stated: 'Der Führer hat mir gesagt. Was wir jetzt an Führerschicht in Polen festgestellt haben, das ist zu liquidieren, was wieder nachwächst, ist von uns sicherzustellen und in einem entsprechenden Zeitraum wieder wegzuschaffen'. ('The Führer told me. What we now stated, as far as the leading class in Poland is concerned, is to ensure that what grows again is liquidated, and it is removed again in an adequate time-span.') C. Madajczyk, *Polityka III Rzeszy w okupowanej Polsce* (Warsaw: Polskie

were others considered useful as orchestral, chamber or band musicians who could be exploited for the Nazi system and play the 'ornamental' role in more and less prominent exhibitions
of the German *Kultur*. The expression 'to slip through the net' referred in this case not only
to the music itself, but primarily to the musicians and their survival. At the same time, the
majority of Polish musicians, persecuted because of their Jewish origin as determined by the
Nuremberg laws, were murdered in Nazi ghettos and camps.[7]

Thus, from the outset, the role of music censorship in the General Government, as far
as former Polish citizens were concerned, was not to ensure that the great German music
cherished by the Nazis would evolve and could be used by Germans for Germans to augment
the glory of the state in the newly occupied territories. Rather it was to secure a suitably low
artistic level of the repertoire played by Poles and for Poles and reinforce its compliance to the
rules of the day divesting music of grand ideas and links to any Polish identity. This censorship was a potent tool of manipulation (which remains the *raison d'être* for censorship in all
eras) and one more refined psychological method of humiliation; it was also made part of
a 'cultural politics', which aimed at proving the traditional superiority of truly German art
and at effecting the extinction of Polish and Polish-Jewish culture.[8] In fact, censorship as an
element of this policy was used to obfuscate essential goals, directed not only against Polish
cultural identity, but towards the extermination of the people.

As early as 16 December 1939, Heinrich Himmler, who spoke of Poles using the expression *Untermenschenvolk des Ostens*, ordered the confiscation of all their musical instruments,
as well as scientific supplies, arms, costumes, coins, stamps and similar collections.[9] Differ-

---

Wydawnictwo Naukowe, 1970), vol. 2, 237. Musicians, as part of the intelligentsia, fell victim to this
extermination policy, for example Marian Burzyński, horn player in the Polish Radio Orchestra, who
was shot in Palmiry near Warsaw in 1939 at the age of 38.

7   See K. Naliwajek-Mazurek, *Chopin inter arma*, Proceedings of Chopin Congress 2010, forthcoming.

8   'In practical terms, Nazi cultural politics in the General Government encompassed various destructive
and plundering actions accompanied by anti-Polish press propaganda and realized from the standpoint of the supposed superiority of German over Polish culture and the supposed dependence of
the latter on the former.' On the other hand, as the Nazis stated, 'all the grassroots penetrating of
Polishness into German [culture] results in the lowering of our level.' Madajczyk, 214. At a conference
with the Directors of the Ministry of Propaganda Departments on 2 November 1939 Goebbels gave
the following directives concerning the occupied Polish territories: 'the goal is to develop the cultural
life of German population and Polish cultural life should not be encouraged in any way' (Deutsches
Zentralarchiv, Reichsministerium für Volksaufklärung und Propaganda, Protokoll der täglichen Kon-
ferenzen des Ministers Dr Goebbels mit den Abteilungsleitern, vol. 1a). Quoted in Madajczyk, 128.

9   Wiesław Głębocki and Karol Mórawski, *Kultura walcząca 1939–1945. Z dziejów kultury polskiej w okresie wojny i okupacji* [*Struggling culture 1939–1945. From the history of Polish Culture during the war and
occupation*] (Warsaw: Wydawnictwo Interpress 1985 (second edition), 301–4. In his *Einige Gedanken
über die Behandlung der Fremdenvölker in Osten* (A Few Thoughts about treating the Foreign Popula-

ent policies were applied in the Reich-incorporated territories (*Eingegliederte Ostgebiete*) and in the General Government. In the NSDAP document *Die Frage der Behandlung der Bevölkerung der ehemaligen polnischen Gebiete nach rassenpolitischen Gesichtspunkten* (*The matter of treating the population of the former Polish territory from the racial-political point of view*) of November 1939, the following instructions were included concerning the population in the *Eingegliederte Ostgebiete*:

> Polish restaurants and cafés – as centres of Polish national life – should be forbidden. Poles are not allowed to frequent German theatres, cabarets and cinema-theatres. Polish theatres, cinema-theatres and other places of cultural entertainment should be closed. There will be no Polish daily newspapers, no Polish books or reviews will be published. For the same reason the Poles are not allowed to own radios and gramophones.[10]

The same document also contains the following order that 'the whole of the Polish intelligentsia [from the Reich-incorporated territories] should be immediately transported to the remaining territory (the notion of Polish intelligentsia encompasses, first of all, Polish priests, teachers [higher schools included], doctors, dentists, veterinarians, officers, higher rank clerks, important merchants and land owners, writers, editors, as well as all persons, that graduated from high schools or universities).' These *Aussiedlungen* and other forms of persecution (often, most effectively, *Vernichtung*) were introduced especially in the Reich-incorporated territories.

In the light of these statements, one might wonder why the Nazis let their more or less Aryan subjects in the General Government entertain themselves in the cafés, whereas the remaining sanctions were applied also there (for example, possession of a radio set was punished by the death penalty in Warsaw)? The answer is contained in the next section of this document, *Treating of Poles and Jews in the remaining [part of] Poland* [i.e. General Government], where the following guidelines are presented:

> Cafés and restaurants, although they had often been the meeting points of nationalistic and intellectual circles in Poland, should not be closed, as the control of them seems to be

---

tion in the East) from 15 May 1940 Himmler added: 'For the non-German population of the East, only four-grade primary schools should exist. The aims of such schools are exclusively: simple counting up to 500 at the highest, writing one's name, and teaching that obedience to Germans, honesty, assiduity and politeness are godly commands. I do not regard reading as necessary' (Głębocki & Mórawski, 302). This policy, albeit slightly modified as far as counting was concerned, was introduced for the non-German inhabitants of the former Polish territories incorporated into the Reich.

10 These guidelines were signed by Erhard Wetzel and Günther Hecht, 25 November 1939. Quoted after Głębocki and Mórawski, 289–94.

easier than over the private gatherings of conspirators, which would necessarily have appeared and in which Polish history so abounds.

It is a pressing necessity to introduce a cultural censorship, taking into account the specific mentality and psyche of the Polish nation from the racial-psychological and political
points of view. Theatres, cinemas and cabarets, because of their great national importance,
should be kept at the lowest level and on a special concession.[11]

In the *Zweijahresbericht des Distriktschefs in Warschau vom 30 IX 1941*, it was stated that: 'Since
no radical solution to the problem of the Polish intelligentsia was achieved, the artistic circles
activity, difficult to police and undoubtedly also political, should be controlled so that it
would allow us a constant monitoring '.[12] On 8 March 1940, General Governor Hans Frank
issued a special decree subjecting all cultural activity in the General Government (GG) to the
control of the Department of Education and Propaganda. Following this, the Department
prepared a circular entitled *Kulturpolitische Richtlinien*, forbidding all cultural activity for Jews
and defining what would be allowed for Poles—'some forms of primitive entertainment'—
whereas 'all concerts, which by the high quality of the programme can bring some artistic
experiences to the public, should be banned. With regard to Polish music, marches, folk and
national songs and all classical music are forbidden. The music programmes in the cafés also
require authorization. Polish artists can play operettas, revues and light comedies for Poles.'[13]
No serious plays or operas were allowed. On the other hand, popular, unsophisticated songs
about love, such as tangos, slow-foxes etc., were allowed to be published in Polish in 1941 in
the so called 'Blue Series' by the Arct Publishing House.

In the autumn of 1940, Frank forbade the publication of books, reviews, calendars and
scores. All associations—scientific, cultural and others were closed, as well as libraries, universities, art schools and secondary schools (except for the schools preparing for certain professions that were deemed useful for the Third Reich, such as *Berufsschulen, Technische Fachschu-
len, Berufspflichtschulen* and *Werkschulen*).[14]

---

11   '[…] hier eine Überwachung leichter erscheint, als in den dann notwendigerweise privaten Zusammen-
     künften von Werschworen, an denen die polnische Geschichte so reich ist.' Głębocki & Mórawski, 116.

12   The German original reads: 'Da keine radikale Lösung des Problems der polnischen Intelligenz durchge-
     führt wurde, musste versucht werden die schwer kontrollierbare und zweifellos auch politische Tätigkeit
     der Künstlerkreise in Bahnen zu lenken die uns eine ständige Überwachung ermöglichen'. Madajczyk, 129.

13   Głębocki and Mórawski, 66–67.

14   Later on, Polish students could study orchestral instruments in the Deutsche Musikschule, a second-
     ary music school opened in the building of Warsaw conservatory, directed by Albert Hösl—composer
     and pedagogue from Munich, though with Polish teaching staff and composer Kazimierz Sikorski as
     its vice-director. Clandestine composition and conducting classes were also given there.

After Polish territory was divided in September 1939 between the Soviet Union and Germany, Warsaw became the most powerful centre of musical activity and resistance. In spite of the terror and different methods of manipulation, the former capital of Poland remained a constant challenge for the German authorities. Yet Nazi censorship, even if considered only with reference to this rebellious city and confined in this chapter to the year 1941, remains a complex issue for two reasons: first because of the constant changes in policy of the Abteilung für Volksaufklärung und Propaganda, and second because the city was divided by the German authorities into three sections, with different laws regulating their existence and differing rights in accessing music.[15] Music censorship, being an integral part of this policy, cannot be discussed separately from this context.

The city was divided by a decree issued by Ludwig Fischer, the Warsaw District Governor, on the 2 October 1940, establishing a ghetto for those that were considered Jewish by the Nazi authorities (already in 1939 numerous inhabitants of the city were forced to leave their houses or flats for the German soldiers and civilians coming from the Reich).[16] Thus from October 1940, three districts: Jewish, German and Polish were to lead a separate existence, whilst the population had to move hastily to other parts of the city. Waldemar Schön, who held the post of Leiter der Abteilung Umsiedlung at the Warsaw District Governor's office and was behind the idea of the ghetto in this city, reported on 20 January 1941:

> It was clear that this project, in the light of specific settlement and extremely complicated conditions of the city of Warsaw, must have seemed at the beginning unrealizable. From many sides protests came, especially from the city board. […] It was alleged that the establishment of the ghetto would result in considerable objections from industry and the economy. […] In the end, however, the transfer of 113,000 Poles and 138,000 Jews was made possible. […] the Jewish quarter is around 403 hectares in size. According to the Jewish Council, which claims to have carried out a census, there are around 410,000 Jews living there, but according to our observations and estimates derived from different quarters, there are in fact between 470,000 and 590,000 Jews.[17]

---

15   K. Naliwajek-Mazurek, 'The Racialization and Ghettoization of Music', 192.

16   See *Eksterminacja Żydów na ziemiach polskich w okresie okupacji hitlerowskiej: zbiór dokumentów*, [Extermination of Jews on Polish territory during Nazi occupation: collection of documents], ed. Tatiana Berenstein, Artur Eisenbach and Adama Rutkowski (Warsaw: Żydowski Instytut Historyczny, 1957), 95–96.

17   The German original reads: 'Es war klar, dass dieser Gedanke bei den besonders gelagerten und äußerst komplizierten Verhältnissen der Stadt Warschau zunächst als undurchführbar anmuten müsste. Einwände wurden von verschiedenen Seiten, insbesondere von der Stadtverwaltung geltend gemacht […]. In ganzen gesehen wurde eine Umgruppierung von 113.000 Polen und 138.000 Juden bewältigt.

A year later, on 10 November 1941, this was followed by the decree of the death penalty for leaving the ghetto without permission (soon extended to those who helped people of Jewish origin).

As in the rest of the GG, shortly after September 1939, any participation in concert and operatic life was prohibited by the Nazi regime to former Polish citizens in Warsaw—a process that was simplified by the fact that the Opera House and Warsaw Philharmonic buildings, together with their instruments and libraries, had been destroyed during September bombardments. Polish cultural institutions (such as the Polish Radio) were dissolved, as well as all orchestras and ensembles. Although Polish musicians attempted to recreate the Philharmonic Orchestra, the idea was turned down by the Nazi authorities. Even the proposal by the temporary Mayor of Warsaw (Kommissaricher Stadtpräsident) Dr. Helmut Otto, to acquire Warsaw Philharmonic musicians for a German orchestra, was rejected.[18] Thus, Polish musicians were denied access to concert halls unless they chose to collaborate and perform for the Nazis in the institutions under their administration, and music by Poles for Poles either took the form of clandestine concerts in private apartments, or was forced to retreat to cafés or churches. Even in the cafés, their choices were strictly controlled; all the programmes organised by cafés, together with the German translation of texts of songs and arias, had to be submitted to the censor.

A concert programme dating from February 1941, with annotations by a Nazi censor from the Abteilung für Volksaufklärung und Propaganda residing with other German authorities in the Brühl Palace,was recently discovered in a private collection and provides evidence which allows us to evaluate what repertoire was banned by the Nazi regime at that time of the war in Warsaw. It belonged to a singer named Zofia Zeyland-Kapuścińska.[19]

On the front page we read: '*Zur Veröffentlichung zugelassen. Auf Grund dieses Programms, ist der Geschäftsunternehmer verpflichtet, eine Benachrichtigung über die Aufführung dieses Programms in seinem Lokal zu übersenden.*'[Accepted for publication. On the basis of this programme, the business entrepreneur is required to send a notification about the performance of this programme to his Café.] Below, this is the following note: '*Es wird darauf hingewiesen,*

[…] Die jüdische Wohnbezirk ist etwa 403 ha gross. Auf diesem Gebiet wohnen nach Angaben des Judenrates, der eine Volkszählung vorgenommen haben will, etwa 410.000 Juden, nach unseren Beobachtungen und Schätzungen, die von verschiedenen Seiten vorgenommen wurden, etwa 470–590.000 Juden.' Berenstein, Eisenbach and Rutkowski, 100–3.

18   K. Naliwajek-Mazurek, 200–1.

19   Biographical details of this singer are currently unavailable. My warmest thanks go to the owners of this document, Bożena and Jacek Wójcik, who inherited it from Jan Michalski (1911–1990) educated as a musician and singer, linked with the Polish Radio before the war who was active in the underground and most probably clandestine musical life.

*das nur in diesem Programm genehmigten Kompositionen zur Aufführung gebracht werden dür-
fen. Jüdische Kompositionen fallen in arischen Unternehmungen grundsätzlich fort.'* [It should
be noted that only compositions approved in this programme can be performed. As a matter
of principle, any Jewish compositions in Aryan enterprises should basically be removed.']
The document with the number 814 placed on the top is dated 8 February 1941 together
with the stamp 'GENEHMIGT [approved]. Der Chef des Distrikts Warschau. Abteilung für
Volksaufklärung und Propaganda, Warschau', with a handwritten date (6/3 41) and an illegible signature or number. This handwritten date and signature signifies that it took almost a
month before the programme was 'corrected' by the censor. The page, covered with numerous
brown-reddish stains, is signed at the bottom by the singer, *'zur Kenntnis genommen'*.

The table of contents is divided into three categories: *Opernarien* (Opera arias)*, Lieder ital-
ienisch gesungen* (Songs performed in Italian) and *Lieder polnisch gesungen* (Songs performed
in Polish). From 12 enumerated operas, all repertoire by Puccini was accepted by the censor,
as well as the arias by Gounod, Mascagni, Strauss and Catalani, whereas both Wagner's arias
(from *Lohengrin* and *Tannhäuser*) were crossed out. Not surprisingly, all seven lighter Italian
songs, such as 'Torna Amore', 'Mal D'Amore' and 'Lolita' by Buzzi-Peccia, 'La Folleta' by
Salvatore Marchesi and 'Stornellatrice' by Respighi, as well as the 'Serenata' by Enrico Toselli
and 'Estrellita' by Manuel Ponce were accepted.

All the songs sung in Polish, with their German translations provided, were analysed in
depth by the censor. Those referring to love were again accepted, whether they were from
German composers, such as 'Still wie die Nacht' ('Cicha jak noc') by Carl Bohm (1844–1920),
or Polish ones, for example 'Cudne oczy' ('Wunderschöne Augen') by Witold Friemann
(1889–1977), 'Serenade' by Jan Gall (1856–1912), 'Mów do mnie jeszcze' ('Sprich noch zu mir'
to words of the famous Polish poet Kazimierz Przerwa-Tetmajer) by Napoleon Rutkowski
(1868–1931), 'Są takie chwile' ('Es gibt Augenblicke') by Aleksander Wielhorski[20], 'Boston' by
Władysław Walentynowicz[21], 'Casanova' and the childish 'Laleczki moje' ('Meine Püppchen')
by Ludomir Różycki (1883–1953), as well as the light-hearted 'Karuzel' ('Das Karussel') by
Stanisław Nawrocki (1894–1950, student of Paderewski)[22], and such popular songs as 'Kochaj

---

20   Born in 1890, this Chopinist and composer was active during the war as pianist in cafés and clandes-
     tine concerts and as pedagogue. He was arrested and although he was among the hostages that were
     to be executed by the Nazis, he survived. He died in 1952. Most of his compositions were burnt in the
     Warsaw Uprising,, see Stanisław Dybowski, *Słownik pianistów polskich*, (Warsaw: Selene, 2003), 727.
21   Born in 1902 in Yaransk, Russia, he died in 1999 in Sopot, Poland, and was a pianist, composer, music
     critic and pedagogue; he played popular music in the cafés during the war (Café Club, Kolorowa,
     Złoty Ul). His pieces for the radio trio comprising Rachoń, Hoherman and Szpilman, and other
     works were lost during the war. Dybowski, 712–14.
22   Nawrocki, who was once called by Paderewski the "Polish Beethoven", participated in the clandestine

a cały świat jest mój' ('Lieb mich und die Welt ist mein') by Ernest R. Ball and 'Wiosna' ('Der Frühling') by Charles Gounod.[23] Both 'Ständchen' by Schubert and 'Traum durch die Dämmerung' by Richard Strauss, referring to corporeal love, were left by the censor, whereas 'Morgen' by the latter was crossed out. This leads one to speculate as to whether the reasons for this are due to the artistic level of this song and its importance for German culture (as Wagner was also not allowed for these *Untermenschen*) or because of its optimistic vision and hope contained in the words 'this earth again breathing with sun'?

Every one of the numerous songs by Grieg ('Łabędź' / 'Ein Schwann', 'Pierwiosnek' / 'Mit einer Primula veris', 'Pierwsze spotkanie' / 'Erstes Begegnen', 'Sen' / 'Ein Traum', 'Na łodzi' / 'Im Kahne', 'Małgorzatk'a / 'Margaretlein', 'Kocham Cię' / 'Ich liebe dich') was accepted by the censor, while the entire Russian repertoire was rejected. In the latter case, one wonders whether the guidelines directed against Russian music were introduced already before the *Unternehmen Barbarossa*. The Nazi attack was originally planned for May 1941, so not surprisingly the Propaganda Office might have found it unpalatable for Russian music to be played during the *Kampf gegen Bolschevismus*. It was probably for this reason that such repertoire was banned, the more so since the texts were the most innocent possible as exemplified in Grechaninov's 'Kołysanka' ('Wiegenlied'), Rachmaninov's 'Bzy' ('Flieder'), Nikolai Tcherepnin's 'Ciebie bym ucałowała' ('Einen Kuss möcht ich dir geben'). At the same time, one could argue that Tchaikovsky's 'Tę kto tęsknotę zna' ('Nur wer die Sehnsucht kennt') and Grechaninov's 'Na pola złote' ('Auf Felder goldig gelb'), evoking longing and suffering, even if again linked to love, could have sounded a little less innocent from the lips of a Polish artist. On the other hand, the same theme of longing and, in that case, typically Polish 'żal' ("das Leid"), although originated by the death of the beloved, constituted perhaps the reason for rejecting Herman Bemberg's 'Indisches Lied'.[24] Or was it rather because the composer was French despite his parents being of German-Argentinean origin?

Of all these interventions from the Nazi censor, one is tragically telling. It concerns a waltz that was extremely popular before and after the war, entitled 'François', composed by Adam

---

concerts and played in the cafés. His pianistic achievements, recorded by the Polish Radio before 1939, were destroyed during Warsaw Uprising. Few of his compositions survived the war; his Symphony in B flat minor, Symphony in F minor, 4 symphonic poems, oratorios, 3 piano concertos, a violin concerto and a cello concerto as well as an opera and several songs and piano pieces were either destroyed during bombardments of Warsaw in 1939 or in the aftermath of Warsaw Uprising. Dybowski, 469–41

23 The titles are quoted here in their Polish and German versions as in the quoted source, irrespective of the actual title.

24 Herman Emanuel Bemberg Ocampo (1859 Buenos Aires–1931 Bern) studied in Paris under Massenet. From his output his songs (Chant Hindou among others) are best known. He is also the author of piano pieces, cantatas and operas

Illustration 1: Front page of the Café Concert Programme with the Nazi censor's annotations.

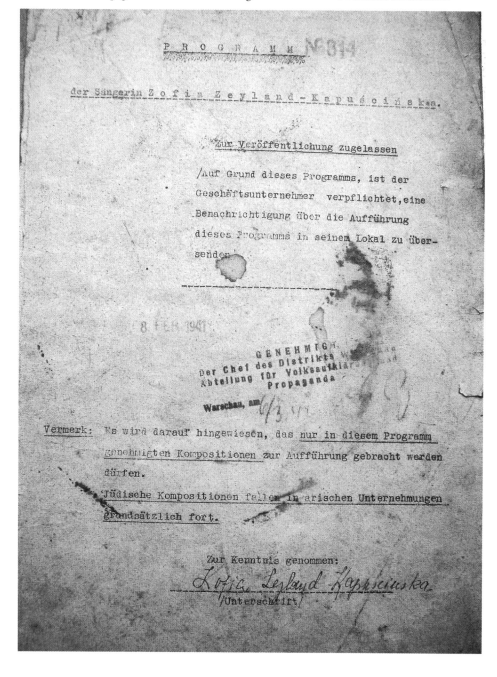

Illustration 2. Inside page of the Café Concert Programme with songs crossed out by the Nazi censor.

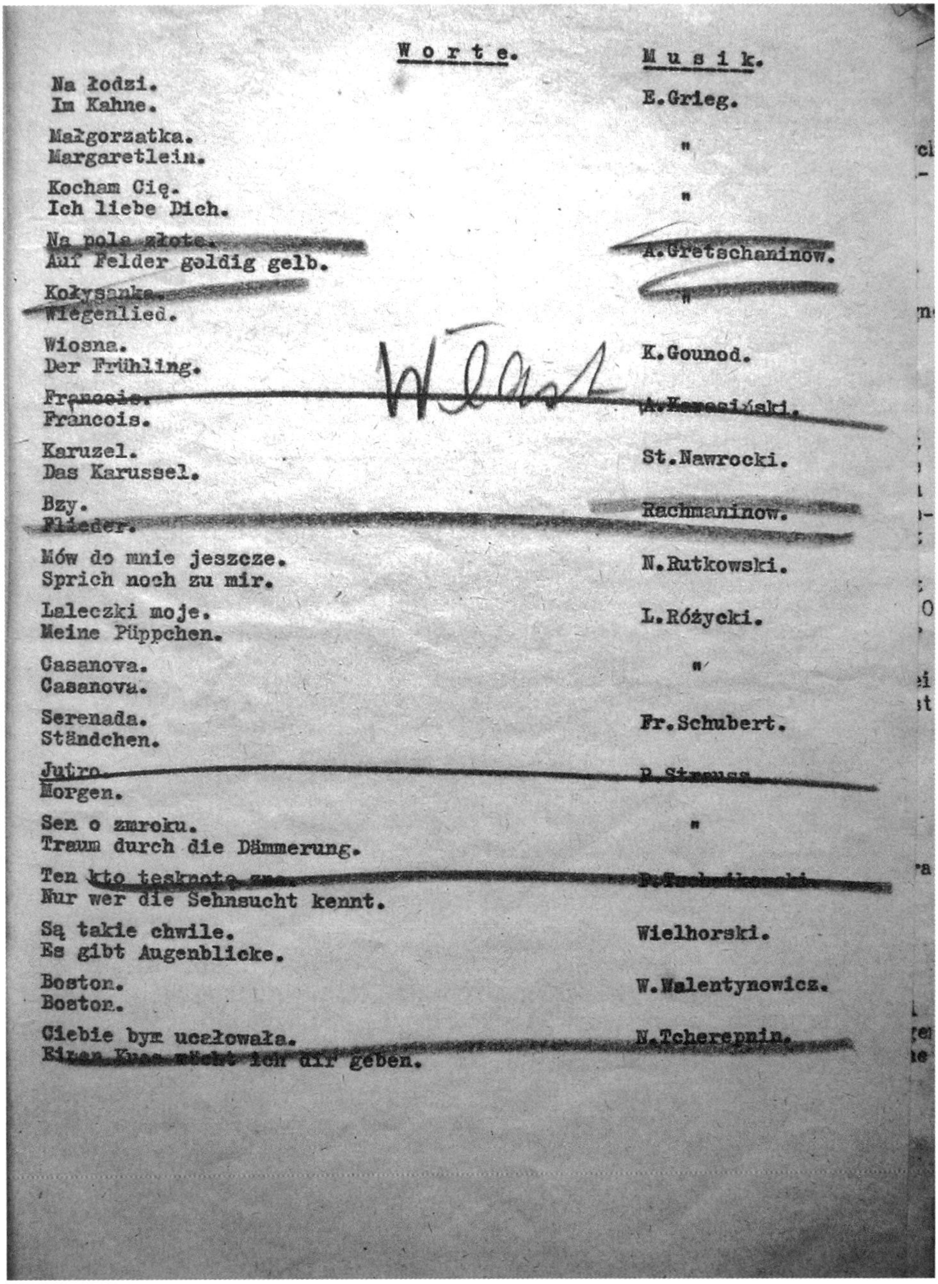

Worte.	Musik.
Na łodzi. Im Kahne.	E.Grieg.
Małgorzatka. Margaretlein.	"
Kocham Cię. Ich liebe Dich.	"
~~Na pola złote.~~ Auf Felder goldig gelb.	~~A.Gretschaninow.~~
~~Kołysanka.~~ ~~Wiegenlied.~~	~~"~~
Wiosna. Der Frühling.	K.Gounod.
~~Fr[illegible]~~ Francois.	~~A.[illegible]ski.~~
Karuzel. Das Karussel.	St.Nawrocki.
Bzy. ~~Flieder.~~	~~Rachmaninow.~~
Mów do mnie jeszcze. Sprich noch zu mir.	N.Rutkowski.
Laleczki moje. Meine Püppchen.	L.Różycki.
Casanova. Casanova.	"
Serenada. Ständchen.	Fr.Schubert.
~~Jutro.~~ Morgen.	~~R.Strauss.~~
Sen o zmroku. Traum durch die Dämmerung.	"
Ten ~~kto tesknote [illegible]~~ Nur wer die Sehnsucht kennt.	~~P.[illegible]~~
Są takie chwile. Es gibt Augenblicke.	Wielhorski.
Boston. Boston.	W.Walentynowicz.
Ciebie bym ucałowała. ~~[illegible]~~ ich dir geben.	~~N.Tcherepnin.~~

Karasiński in 1907, and made famous by Tola Mankiewiczówna and Mieczysław Fogg with the words written in 1934 by Andrzej Włast.[25] And it is precisely the name of this poet, librettist and author of over 2,000 song texts, that prompted the censor to reject the whole song since he was perfectly aware that Włast (originally Gustaw Baumritter, born on 17 March 1895 in Łódź) was of Jewish origin. Neither the waltz 'François' nor its author was able to slip through the net. Around the beginning of 1943, the poet's friends tried to take him out of the Warsaw ghetto, but at the sight of the guards, he panicked, began to run away, and was shot.[26] His text for the song, which was not permitted to be performed in spring 1941 in Warsaw, is an evocation of the charming past. Although it was written before the war, the old waltz could serve in fact as a nostalgic symbol of Polish popular song repertoire history ('Among old scores of grandma / This waltz was preserved / I recollect this soirée at hers / I see it as in my dreams. / Musicians at the piano / Visitors all around and the expression of the poet's wish in its refrain: 'If only once / That time returned / If the hearts of evil men / were aroused by old waltz's 'François' charm').[27]

The censor's choices offer immediate evidence that there was a strict application of several different categories: political (Russian music ostensibly banned, although as we shall see below, this is contradicted by other sources), purely ideological, based on the belief of supremacy of great German art (Wagner not for Poles), and racial (compositions by authors of Jewish origin could not be performed by Poles). Furthermore, any repertory related to nostalgia, grief, past and a bright future was off-limits for the Poles. On the other hand, we can observe how the censor followed the guidelines of a confidential circular sent in 1940 by

---

25   It was the composer's son, Zygmunt Karasiński (born on 2 May 1898 in Warsaw, left Poland in 1968 due to the anti-Semitic campaign of the Communist regime and died on 20 June 1973 in Copenhagen), who arranged this song in this new version and is often quoted as its author. He also created most of the famous Polish songs of the inter-war period with Andrzej Włast's words. Zygmunt Karasiński, violinist, pianist, clarinettist, saxophonist, composer and arranger studied with his father, then violin with Jerzy Jarzębski at the Warsaw conservatory. He accompanied silent films, then played in the first Polish jazz band (with Szymon Kataszek, Jerzy Petersburski, piano, Sam Salwano, percussion). In Warsaw, Karasiński's and Kataszek's Jazz Tango was one of the most popular dance orchestras. In 1941 he founded in Białystok the ensemble Białoruski Jazz (Belorussian Jazz) and played in a revia-jazz group in Lvov. After the war, he worked for the Polish Radio as a composer and arranger.

26   Among his most famous songs are: 'Całuję twoją dłoń, madame' ('I am kissing your hand, Madame'), 'Ja się boję sama spać' ('I fear to sleep alone'), 'Rebeka', 'Tango Milonga', 'Titina, Warszawo ma' ('My Warsaw'), 'Zapomnisz o mnie' ('You will forget me'), 'Już nigdy' ('Never more'), 'Ostatnie tango' ('Last Tango'). See Dariusz Michalski, *Powróćmy jak za dawnych lat... Historia polskiej muzyki rozrywkowej w latach 1900–1939* (Warsaw: Iskry, 2007).

27   'W starych nutach babuni / Walc przechował się ten, / Pomnę wieczorek u niej, Widzę go jak przez sen. Grajek przy fortepianie, Goście snują się w krąg'; 'Gdyby jeszcze raz /Wrócił tamten czas, / Gdyby zbudził serca złych ludzi / Czar modnego walca François.'

the Department of Education and Propaganda of the General Government, which allowed the Poles some forms of primitive entertainment[28] and of the General Governor himself ('as far as Polish artists are concerned, there are no obstacles to lower the level or imbue their programmes with erotic feeling. Nonetheless, all performances representing the life of Polish nation are prohibited').[29]

How could the censor know so well the who-is-who and what was to be banned? It is interesting to note that at least for a certain period, there was no imported German censor in music in Warsaw, as probably such an official was required to understand all the subtleties of Polish cultural life and have a good command of the language. According to the unpublished testimony of singer Janina Godlewska, who was delegated by the Polish charity organization Main Care Council (Rada Główna Opiekuńcza) and by the SiM, "Sztuka i Moda" café ("Art and Fashion", where Panufnik and Lutosławski, among others, performed) to contact the censor:

> This task was given to me, as the censor residing at the Brühl Palace, whose name was Bartz-Borodin, knew me from the time before the war (we performed together at SiM). When the war began, Bartz-Borodin signed the *Volkslist* and became a censor. In our programme propositions we always gave more Polish music than was originally planned. Bartz-Borodin crossed out two-thirds, and the rest was what we needed. Later on, the censor was changed and the post was taken by a German with a Czech name—Janeczek or Janaczek—I also managed to deal with him somehow.[30]

By confronting documents and collating testimonies such as those quoted above with other sources, in particular the propagandistic official press and Polish clandestine publications, one can trace different manifestations and inconsistencies of music censorship policy in Warsaw and its role in the German propaganda. Furthermore, by analysing the content of the propa-

---

28 See Stanisław Lachowicz, *Muzyka w okupowanym Krakowie 1939–1945* [Music in occupied Cracow] (Kraków: Wydawnictwo Literackie, 1988), 12–13.

29 *Okupacja i ruch oporu w Dzienniku Hansa Franka 1939-1945* [Occupation and Resistance in Diary of Hans Frank], vol. I, 1939-1942, ed. Zofia Polubiec; transl. from German by Danuta Dąbrowska and Mieczysław Tomala (Warszawa: Książka i Wiedza, 1970).

30 She was the wife of Andrzej Bogucki who also played at the cafés in Warsaw and created numerous cabaret shows. After her arrival from Lvov to Warsaw in May 1940, she had performed at first with Władysław Szpilman in the Café Dorys up to the moment when he could not no longer leave the ghetto. Later on (February 13th 1943), it was the singer and her husband who helped Szpilman escape from the ghetto (although she does not mention this information in her testimony, we know it thanks to Szpilman himself and the composer Piotr Perkowski, who also helped the pianist).

gandist *Nowy Kurier Warszawski* (*New Warsaw Courier*, *NKW)*, whose target group was the *Polnische Bevölkerung,* it is possible to find out which music was officially sanctioned to be played by Poles for Poles. However, several facts should be taken into account in the interpretation of this source. First of all, the official press, called 'reptile' by the Polish public, was one of most important tools of Nazi propaganda, and the information included there should be read as such. This was already perceptively analysed by the clandestine press. For example, the following statement is made in an editorial on the first page of the most important underground biweekly, *Biuletyn Informacyjny* dated 9 January 1941:

> The name of 'reptile press' is given to newspaper-reptiles, which treacherously inveigle themselves into the skin of the Polish language, to poison with their venomous content the organism of the Polish nation. The language used in these reviews is Polish, but the brain and hand which directs it—German. Its goal is to work in the interests of Germany. The biggest reptile newspaper of the 'Government' is *Nowy Kurier Warszawski* (daily sales of over 150,000 copies, the printing of holiday and Sunday copies—ca. 300,000). Monthly revenue of this daily amounts to over 300,000 zł. [...] All the enumerated reviews are not private property, but are created, directed and financed by special publishing institutions brought into being by the Propaganda Office of the General Government in Cracow. As result, their considerable income goes directly to this German Propaganda Office. Conclusion: who buys reptile newspapers is by the same token financing German propaganda and absorbs a certain dose of propagandistic poison. Yet whether the organism is healthy or the poison small, the systematic application of such a toxic policy always achieves a result. A lack of space does not allow us to present interesting methods of Nazi propaganda, which can make use of a seemingly quite innocent novel, an 'impartially' written article and even a photograph of the Polish army.[31]

As is evident from the quote above, *Biuletyn Informacyjny* brought exact news from the front, informed its readers about the tragedy of the Jewish population, about terror and extermination policies in different places of former Poland, about the losses of Polish science, art etc., of course never mentioned in the propagandistic official press. Inevitably any involvement in such clandestine publications, which were the only source of balanced information, as well as distributing and possessing them, resulted in investigation, tortures, executions or deportations to concentration camps. Nonetheless, *Biuletyn Informacyjny* provides the most detailed information about the extremely varied landscape of cafés where classical music was

---

31   *Biuletyn Informacyjny* [no numbers, nor authors names provided in this clandestine journal] 9 January 1941, The information on the editing had to be limited, for obvious reasons.

performed and illustrates how each one, depending on its particular status, was treated differently by the Nazi authorities.

Several import articles appeared in the *Biuletyn Informacyjn* of 30 January 1941. Under the headline 'Zabawa' (Entertainment), the journal urged Poles not to attend cinemas, the theatre and cabarets since noisy public entertainment was deemed inappropriate, given the tragic conditions of Nazi occupation. An article entitled 'Rok okupacji w Polsce' summarizes a year of occupation in Poland, providing information on closed universities and high schools and the following description of the destruction of Polish culture:

> Instead of the widespread Polish press—we have a German press of low level and the 'reptiles', in place of exquisite dramas and comedies – farces and cabaret, instead of symphonic concerts—orchestras playing in the cafés, which are not allowed to perform Chopin, Paderewski and Moniuszko.[32]

In the article 'Why should we boycott the cinema?', the mechanism of Nazi propaganda and finance is explained:

> After entering Poland, Germans commandeered all the cinema premises, all the films and film cameras. This confiscation has been made for the sake of the German Ministry of Propaganda, which after a while started to screen individual movies. With the purpose of totally surrendering the cinema programmes to the spirit of German propaganda, the appointed directors of cinemas are Germans, Ukrainians and Volksdeutsche. The institution body governing cinemas on behalf of the Ministry of Propaganda is called 'Betriebstelle'. All profits from the theatres are chanelled to this office, and are then transferred to the Ministry of Propaganda in Berlin.[33]

---

32 'A Year of Occupation in Poland', *Biuletyn Informacyjny*, 30 January 1941, 3–4. 'Zamiast szeroko rozpowszechnionej prasy polskiej – mamy na niskim stojącą poziomie prasę niemiecką i 'szmatławce', zamiast wyborowych dramatów i komedyj – farsę i kabaret, zamiast koncertów symfonicznych – orkiestry po kawiarniach, którym nie wolno grać Szopena, Paderewskiego i Moniuszki.'

33 'Dlaczego powinniśmy bojkotować kino?' ('Why should we boycott the cinema?'), *Biuletyn Informacyjny*, 30 January 1941, 14: 'Dlaczego powinniśmy bojkotować kino? Po wkroczeniu do Polski Niemcy zarekwirowali wszystkie lokale kinowe, wszystkie filmy i aparaty filmowe. Konfiskata ta została dokonana na rzecz niemieckiego ministerstwa propagandy, które po pewnym czasie zaczęło uruchamiać poszczególne kina. Celem całkowitego poddania programów kinowych duchowi propagandy niemieckiej wyznacza się na kierowników kin Niemców, Ukraińców lub volksdeutschów. Organem kierującym kinami z ramienia ministerstwa propagandy jest tzw. „Betriebstelle". Do urzędu tego m.in. wpływają wszystkie zyski z kin, które to zyski są z kolei [original ortography: skolei] przekazywane do ministerstwa propagandy w Berlinie.'

When we analyse the programmes of cafés—the only official places where the Polish public could listen to more serious classical music without attending a Nazi-administered institution, the richest programme was performed at the Lardelli Café, where a substantial orchestra of around 60 musicians was conducted by collaborator Adam Dołżycki, and where Germans also used to come. Some of the musicians (among them soloists) probably did not consider it treacherous to perform with him at the beginning, as Dołżycki, of Ukrainian origin, married to a German woman, was a well-known conductor (mainly at the Warsaw Opera house) before the war. His connections with the Nazis became apparent only gradually and particularly after he declared himself as a Ukrainian.[34] Subsequently, clandestine organizations advised soloists not to play there. Exceptions were made for those who were endangered and had no choice, because of their Jewish origin, like the famous singer Ada Sari, or still others because of hiding a Jewish wife, husband or friends who needed this protection for some other reason (the same attitude was adopted in some cases to those who performed in other theatres, especially the most important of them, Theater der Stadt Warschau (Theatre of the City of Warsaw), which will be referred to later in this text). Some testimonies offer evidence that Dołżycki forced musicians to perform for the Germans. Indeed the *Biuletyn Informacyjny* of 30 October 1941 openly urged the Polish public to boycott the concerts there.

For a certain time, there existed another chamber orchestra, albeit one that was of smaller size, created by Zygmunt Latoszewski, which performed at the Café Gastronomia alongside several other ensembles. The *NKW* displayed advertisements and even published reviews of some of these artistic events, interspersed with propaganda. In No. 37, Dołżycki is advertised conducting Scriabin's Symphony No. 2, Schumann, Tchaikovsky, Puccini, Bach, Beethoven, Gluck, Mozart and Paganini. In No. 43, a review of Latoszewski's concert at Gastronomia is placed next to the article entitled 'Do not sell anything to Jews.' The programme included Bach's Toccata and Fugue in d minor orchestrated by Jerzy [sic][35] Padlewski, Grieg's *Holberg Suite*, the Elegy and

---

34   Ukrainians, because of Ukraine being allied to the Nazis, had a special status, and were treated as 'almost Germans' when willing to collaborate.

35   It was in fact Roman, Jerzy's brother, who was the author of the orchestration. Both brothers became victims of the Nazis. Roman Padlewski conductor (7 October 1915 Moscow–16 August 1944 Warsaw), was an eminent composer, violinist, musicologist and music critic and used war pseudonyms R. Kasztan [R. Chestnut], Skorupka [Shell]. One of the most promising of his generation, he was 29 at the moment of his death during the Warsaw Uprising. He was shot on 14 August 1944 in his spine by a German soldier while attempting to disarm the Goliath tracked mine. The tragic fate of the young artist touched also the major part of his musical output. Both orchestral pieces composed during the Nazi occupation (Songs to poems by Jerzy Liebert for soprano and orchestra (1942) and the Violin Concerto (1944), as well as an orchestral setting of Toccata and Fugue D minor and D major by J.S. Bach (1943)) are lost, as well as the incomplete Third String Quartet (1944). These works probably perished in Warsaw when they were burnt by Nazi squads after the Uprising in autumn 1944.

Burlesque from Tchaikovsky's *Serenade* Op. 48, the Waltz from Richard Strauss's *Rosenkavalier* and some unspecified Waltzes by Johann Strauss. Zofia Fedyczkowa performed with the orchestra the 'Hymn to the sun' from *The Golden Cockerel* of Rimsky-Korsakov, an aria from Mozart's *Entführung aus dem Serail*, and 'Waltz Caton' from opera *Casanova* by Ludomir Różycki.

A review of a concert at Lardelli's in No. 49 mentions repertory by Bach, Brahms, Mozart, Gluck, Paganini, Haydn, Mozart, Beethoven, Rimsky-Korsakov's *Scheherazade* and fragments from operas *Rigoletto*, *Ballo in maschera*, *Madama Butterfly*, *Carmen* and Catalani's *La Wally*. Józef Śmidowicz played one of the Brahms Piano Concertos there. The author [A.P.] states that 'It should be recognized that the programmes at Lardelli's are gradually being prepared in a more diligent way, and one should mention that a proper, good programme is difficult to realize nowadays because of the fire, which burnt the Philharmonic and Opera House libraries.' In Nos. 53–58, anti-Semitic propaganda became more intense and aggressive; there are no mentions of performances of serious repertory and for almost two weeks no information about cafés (except for the nightclub Adria which is advertised in No. 63), although German theatres were still open. An explanation for this state of affairs can be found in No. 58, dated 10 March 1941, in an article on the first page entitled 'How did Igo Sym die?' After this actor, a valued Nazi collaborator and Gestapo agent, appointed director of the Theater der Stadt Warschau by the German Propaganda Abteilung, was killed on sentence of an underground court, the cafés were closed for two weeks, around 180 people were arrested, twenty of them were executed, and famous theatre director Leon Schiller and eminent actor Stefan Jaracz were sent to Auschwitz. *Biuletyn Informacyjny* of 13 March notes 'the incommensurability between a killing of an actor, German agent, and the force of repressions' and brings an explanation that the affair served as a pretext to the authorities: 'What is going on there? To answer this question, one should know that at a governors' briefing in the first days of January, Fischer was reprimanded by Frank for the fact that the Warsaw district is the least controlled of all in the General Government. Amongst other matters, Fischer was ordered to liquidate Warsaw's clandestine press within a month, and this is what he strived to achieve during the well-known January arrests.'[36]

NKW's No. 77 of 1 April 1941 brings news of the première of Lehár's operetta *Gipsy Love* at the Theatre of Warsaw City, No. 98 of 27 April 1941 features an article taken from the German press entitled 'Obrazki z Warszawy' (Images from Warsaw, in a series 'What do others write?') in a mocking and threatening tone depicting the 'degenerate' Polish intelligentsia in the cafés.[37] Two days later, a review reflects upon the most appropriate musical genre that should be performed at that time:

---

36 *Biuletyn Informacyjny* 1941, 13 March 1941, 1.
37 'Obrazki z Warszawy', *NKW* 1941, No. 98, 27 April 1941, 2.

Dołżycki plays a lot of suites, that is, a musical form, which is extraordinarily adequate for our times. We have lately heard Grieg's *Peer Gynt*, Spendiarov's *Crimean Sketches*, Bizet's *L'Arlésienne*, *Scènes pittoresques* and *Scènes Napolitaines* of Massenet, then the original suite *Háry Janos* of the talented Hungarian Kodály, full of grotesque thematic and instrumentation ideas […]. Friday's all-Tchaikovsky concert featured the ever fascinating Piano Concerto played by Żurawlew […]. One of the most attractive events of this week was the Tuesday recital of Prof. J. Śmidowicz at the Art House [Dom Sztuki], led by Prof. Woytowicz and promoting in an uncompromising way the chamber music of the purest genre […]. Among other pieces Schumann's *Symphonic Studies* were played.[38]

In No. 104, a concert of Generalgouvernement's Philharmonic Orchestra (in Kraków) is announced on page 3: Dvořák's Cello Concerto (young Józef Mikulski), Overture to Weber's *Oberon*, the *Romantic Suite* by the ardent Nazi Carl Ehrenberg, 'contemporary composer, professor of composition and conducting master class at the Academy of Music in München' and Tchaikovsky's *Capriccio Italien*. On the first anniversary of the General Government's proclamations in autumn 1940, Hans Frank established a symphony orchestra in the opera house at Kraków, as the Philharmonic of the General Government and the Theater der Stadt Warschau (Theatre of the City of Warsaw, in the building of closed Teatr Polski [Polish Theater]). These theatres were originally intended for Germans, but were subsequently partially opened to the Polish public (while, for example, in Lvov after June 1941 concerts that took place in the Opera House were intended for Germans or for Germans and Ukrainians only), mainly with operetta repertoire, and gradually symphonic concerts were introduced.[39]

On 4 May there is a concert of the 'Ukrainian National Choir of the Generalgouvernement' at the Conservatory Hall. Also in May (No. 112, 14 May 1941) in the article 'From

---

38   'Z kawiarnianej estrady' (From the café stage*), NKW No. 100, 29 April 1941, 3.*

39   Hans Frank described his motivations to organize the Philharmonic of the General Government during a meeting of the district and chief officers of the General Government NSDAP held at the Wawel Castle on 18 March 1942: 'We are still cold-bloodedly continuing the fight to attain our goals. Gentlemen, you see how the state organs work; you see that we do not refrain from anything and dozens of people are put up against a wall. It is necessary, just because the healthy mind shows that we cannot spare the blood of foreign nations while the best German blood is sacrificed. […] That is why if any Polish leading forces appear, they should be relentlessly destroyed, and with ruthless energy. This should not be publicized; it should happen tacitly. And if we afford the luxury of allowing the Poles types of philharmonic orchestras, which we present to foreign journalists, it doesn't matter at all. People play music according to our wishes, and when they are no longer useful to us, we shall dissolve the institution.' Frank's remarks, translated from German by the author of this chapter, are similar, though not identical, to the English translation as featured in *Hans Frank's Diary*, ed. Stanisław Piotrowski (Warsaw: Państwowe Wydawnictwo Naukowe, 1961), 255–56.

cafés stage. Concerts', we read about Ada Sari singing Rossini, Bellini, Donizetti, Verdi, Rachmaninov's 'Georgian Song', 'The Rose' and 'The Nightingale' of Rimsky-Korsakov, Reger's 'Lullaby', 'Serenades' by Richard Strauss and Polish composer B. Wallek-Walewski, Johann Strauss's waltzes, arias from operas *Adrianna Lecouvreur*, *Mirella* of Gounod, *Mignon* of Thomas and Donizetti's *Linda*. We can observe that the Russian repertoire crossed out by the censor in the spring of 1941 was still officially reported in the press. At the end of May, a Polish composition (Noskowski's *Step*) appears at Lardelli's next to Smetana's *Vltava* and pieces by Wagner, Schumann, Tchaikovsky, Brahms, Beethoven, Schubert, Schumann, Rachmaninov and Liszt.[40] Also in May, some Polish repertoire was performed at Bolesław Woytowicz's café, amongst other chamber pieces, Szymanowski's String Quartet No. 1 and Jan Ekier's Quartet.[41] Most surprisingly, by the time when Dołżycki was already condemned by the Polish underground as a collaborator, and the *Kampf gegen Bolschevismus* was at stake, a change regarding the ban on Chopin was lifted, at least as far as this café was concerned, where for example on 6 October a piano recital by Józef Śmidowicz featuring works by Beethoven, Chopin, Liszt was held. Furthermore on 20 October, Chopin's F minor Concerto was played by Zbigniew Drzewiecki, and the E minor Concerto was performed by Śmidowicz on 17 November, with Dołżycki conducting in both cases. Surviving publicity posters demonstrate that Concertos by Beethoven and Schumann were also performed at that time.

The situation in the ghetto in 1941 was most succinctly described by Emanuel Ringelblum:

> After the settling of the ghetto, the occupant left the inside cultural activity free. The commissar of the Jewish quarter, advocate Auerswald, did not care much what the Jews are doing in the ghetto; he cared only about one thing: that the Jews must die from hunger.[42] Although the prisoners of the ghetto were not officially allowed to perform non-Jewish music, 'the regulations of the German Propaganda Office, forbidding performance of Aryan composers, are not recognized in the ghetto, 'freedom' is reigning here. They play whatever they like, not paying attention to the censorship allowing only a very restricted number of musical works. Some of the more eminent musicians were hired in schools, where they trained children's vocal ensembles whose performances were very much appreciated by the public.'[43]

---

40 [A.S.] 'Z estrady. Koncerty', *NKW* No. 127, 30 May 1941, 3.

41 *NKW* No. 132, 6 June 1941.

42 Emanuel Ringelblum, *Kronika getta warszawskiego, wrzesień 1939—styczeń 1943*, ed. Artur Eisenbach, translation from Yiddish by Adam Rutkowski (Warsaw: Czytelnik, 1983), 561. Jewish Cultural Organization (IKOR), created by E. Ringelblum, Menachem Linder, Sagan, Sonia Nowogrodzka (eminent pedagogue), Brotsztajn, Mazo, Szyja Rubinowicz, developed cultural activity in the Jewish Social Help organization (ŻSS). See Ringelblum, 560.

43 Ringelblum, 597.

We know very well that this policy was a cruel and perfidious manipulation and that the orchestra, which regardless of basic difficulties, could perform in 1941 under the direction of Marian Neuteich, Szymon Pullman and other eminent musicians, was dissolved by the Nazis at the time that they judged appropriate, on the basis of violation of the previously neglected rule—the noncompliance to the accepted repertoire. This was only a prelude to their extermination. On 16 November 1940, the ghetto was sealed off. Just nine days later, the first concert of the Jewish Symphony Orchestra took place at the Central Judaic Library in Tłomackie Street. On 1 June 1941 the Great Synagogue was reopened there. On 1 October 1941 it was allowed to open elementary schools in the ghetto, while a month later the construction of the extermination camp in Bełżec began, and Fischer's decree on the death penalty for leaving the ghetto without permission followed the opening on 7 December 1941 of the extermination camp in Chełm (Kulmhof) on the Ner river. Earlier though, numerous cafés operated with eminent musicians forced to play there or in the streets; on 2 February the propagandistic *Gazeta Żydowska* brought information that Władysław Szpilman and Artur Gold were to play at the Cafe Nowoczesna (Modern Cafe), No. 51 mentioned that 'the only theatre of the district playing in Polish is open.'[44] In an article entitled *Inter arma musae non silent*, we read the harrowing lines:

> On his 35th birthday Adam Furmański, who was heard in Kiev by Emil Młynarski, and then sponsored by Baron Kronenberg, gave concerts in Warsaw, graduated with distinction from the Conservatory, encouraged by his sponsor to leave to Italy with one condition, to change his religion. Furmański stayed, is accepted at the Warsaw Philharmonic and creates his own orchestra; he is a pioneer and propagator of great art, he is the first to arrive in small towns and cities and is the initiator of children's concerts. Ten years ago, he celebrated his silver jubilee. From many parts of the world, colleagues and students arrived to celebrate their master. Among them Mieczysław Horszowski. [...] Year 1941. Adam Furmański in the Jewish district. [...] and again, as throughout all his life, he puts all his energy, belief and enthusiasm into the new, hard work. With a young musician H. Stromberg, and other musicians, he creates an institution of enormous cultural value—the Jewish Symphonic Orchestra.[45]

There is much more information in *Gazeta Żydowska* concerning different performances, such as in No. 73 an article entitled 'Artistic chronicle: Musical Impressions', where a symphonic concert conducted by Marian Neuteich is described; the review points out the enor-

44   *Gazeta żydowska*, No. 51, 27 June 1941, 3.
45   Ibid.

mous popularity of Tchaikovsky and the 'unfortunately unavoidable' effect due to the use of saxophone instead of horn in the second movement Andante cantabile in his Fifth Symphony. In No. 78, on page 2, more information about missing instruments was included: 'A few instruments (horn, bassoon, oboe) had to be replaced with other instruments. That is why some works were prepared by Pullman for chamber orchestra.' As in other articles, the repertoire is enumerated (Vivaldi, Bach, Haydn, Mozart, Beethoven, Schubert, Tchaikovsky, Brahms, Verdi, Bruckner, Beethoven's *Grosse Fuge*). However, in the light of Emanuel Ringelblum's words, its analysis is not genuinely relevant from the point of view of music censorship—as the real goal behind this 'liberal' smokescreen in the 'liberty' to play (without proper instruments nor scores) was the physical extermination of both musicians and their listeners, and the racial laws in music were used only as pretexts in this criminal plan. A quotation from the memoirs of Stanisław Różycki of 1942 brings an image of the reality in which all intellectual and artistic values were in fact banned for the ghetto population:

> In the cruel fight for a piece of bread, for a few metres of space to live, for maintaining health, forces and life, one cannot devote much energy nor force to spiritual matters. The other things are German restrictions and bans. One cannot publish anything, teach, learn, associate, exchange cultural values. We are cut off from the world: libraries [...], schools, scientific institutions etc. are banned. There are no cinemas, no radio, no contact with the world's culture. Nothing is reaching us, no product of the human soul is reaching us. Not only comestible and industrial merchandise must be smuggled in, but also products of the mind.[46]

German musical activity in 1941 in occupied Poland was thriving, according to Goebbels's guidelines, which stated that Polish cultural life should not be in any way supported, and that the only goal was the development of a programme that was indigenously German.[47] Classical music concerts and opera performances in a music theatre, named Theater der Stadt Warschau were organized first of all by Germans for Germans: soldiers, civilians who worked in numerous offices and their families. German artists coming from the Reich mostly performed there. Probably due to the costs of transportation and the wage demands of German musicians and because they had been in part mobilized, Polish musicians were also gradually asked or, in some cases, forced to play there. Some of the operettas and revues performed by Poles were also available to the Polish public. The work there was considered as collaboration

---

46   Quoted in Berenstein, Eisenbach and Rutkowski, 137.
47   These guidelines were presented at a conference for the Ministry of Propaganda departments' directors on 2 November 1939, see Madajczyk, 128.

and Polish attendance at such events was deemed inappropriate, as in the case of other Nazi-controlled theatres.

Among several newspapers for Germans, the *Warschauer Zeitung* brought information about cultural events *nur für Deutsche* in the GG and other parts of the empire. It is impossible to enumerate here even only those having taken place in Warsaw (by the hour of a concert, we can judge with certainty that it was not intended for Poles, as the curfew for Poles was observed mainly from 8pm; sometimes it was changed even to an earlier hour). November 1941 deserves special attention because of two important festivals—the Deutsche Kulturtage and Mozart-tage. Several operas (for example on 1 November the Staats-Theater des Generalgouvernements featured *Iphigenie in Aulis* of C. W. Gluck, beginning at 19:30, finishing at 22:20)[48], concerts and other events took place and the headline titles of the articles give a good indication of their impact: 'Stark pulsierendes Kulturleben'[49], 'Glanzvoller Anschluss der Kulturtage in Warschau'[50], 'Beethoven-Abend im Theater der SS und Polizei, Elly Ney in Warschau, Klavierabend im Palais Brühl'[51], 'Der Weg der kulturellen Arbeit. Geistige, Bodenständigkeit im GG Hausmusik für Front und Heimat. Ein Aufruf Hermann Abendroths'[52], 'Dank an die volksdeutschen Frauen: Warschaus deutsche Frauen versammelten sich im Theater der Stadt Warschau, um von der Beauftragten der NSDAP für den Fraueneinsatz im Generalgouvernement' and 'Zwei Jahre Warschauer Kulturleben im Zeitungsspiegel', mention of the next performance of *Iphigenie in Aulis*[53], 'Wieder 'Deutsche Kulturtage' in Warschau. Zahlreiche Veranstaltungen vom 26–30. November–Künstler aus dem Reich wirken mit und Deutsches Theater im Ostraum. Mittelalterliche Mysterienspiele in Krakau–Deutsche Ensembles in Warschau–Frontbühnen in Zahlen'[54], 'Elly Ney spielte in Warschau. Beethoven–Mozart–Schubert, Mozarttage des Generalgouvernements vom 8. bis 14. Dezember.'[55] On 22 November, the Stadt Theater performance of *Wiener Blut* Operette is advertised as 'Der Auftrag des deutschen Kulturschaffens im Kriege. Warschaus „Deutsche Kulturtage" feierlich eröffnet —Gouverneur Dr. Fischer gab kulturellen Leistungsbericht, Kulturelle Förderung der Volksdeutschen. Eine Hauptaufgabe der Partei–Distriktsstandorttagung der NSDAP als Abschluss der Warschauer Kulturtage, Ausklang der Mozartwoche. Das „Requiem" als Staatsakt'.[56] The newspaper's 9 December issue features

48   *Warschauer-Zeitung*, 1 November, 1941, 9.
49   *Warschauer-Zeitung*, 3 November 1941, 4.
50   *Warschauer-Zeitung*, 6 November 1941, 5.
51   *Warschauer-Zeitung*, 9 November 1941, 3.
52   *Warschauer-Zeitung*, 12 November 1941 4.
53   *Warschauer-Zeitung*, 6 November 1941, 5–6.
54   *Warschauer-Zeitung*, 13 November 1941, 5.
55   *Warschauer-Zeitung*, 15 November 1941, 4.
56   *Warschauer-Zeitung*, 22 November, 1941, 5

the following articles: 'Stand der Mozartforschung. Kongress der Musikwissenschaftler', programme of Warschauer Mozarttage, advertisement of the festival.[57] Four days later, further Mozart concerts are featured: *Eine kleine Nachtmusik*, *Der Schauspieldirektor*, *Les Petits riens* and the Mozart-Abend at the Staats-Theater des Generalgouvernements and Kammermusik auch in Warschau' (at the Palais Brühl).[58]

This initial attempt at discussing some of the facets of Nazi music censorship in Warsaw in 1941, undertaken in 2008, will be completed by more detailed studies based on documents and press material. The image of music censorship as such, its causes and effects, is closer to reality only when differing rights of access to great art are taken into account. In fact, during more than five years of the most cruel occupation ended by the annihilation of the city by the Nazis, the racially divided musical life in Warsaw was – paradoxically enough – extremely rich and intricate. That is why the examination of bans concerning the repertoire itself is not a sufficient tool for dealing with the facts concerning this tragic chapter in music history. All the evidence cited above suggests that various sources partly contradict and partly reinforce information found elsewhere to form a complex and equivocal image. Such methods may allow for the development of a more nuanced understanding of Nazi music control mechanisms, when applied to other periods of the German occupation of Poland, as the political functions of censorship evolved and were used by the authorities according to their needs to manipulate public opinion at different stages of the war.

One further example from the 'reptile press' serves as a suitable conclusion to this excerpt from a longer story of the censorship of music in Nazi-occupied Warsaw. On the first page of the *NKW* of 27 November 1939 (No. 41) is a report of the visit of the Governor General Hans Frank to Warsaw and the ceremony of the opening of a German school. It quotes Frank's speech: 'Let's get to the realization of historical tasks that await us here, with the invincible eternal German idealism. The school is to become the fortress of Germanism, comparable to a spiritual citadel that is the proud stronghold of Adolf Hitler and his idea.'[59] Below, on the same page, is an article entitled 'Securing of jews' [with lower-case intentionally] property. Jews can possess only one banking account and 2000 złote at most in cash'. On page 2 there is a brief mention of the current activity of Polish artists, entitled 'Ballet and Opera: Sixth Artists' Café'. It describes the opening of a new café in Krucza Street where artists 'will dance whilst others serve the clients'. Next to this, however, is a larger headline entitled 'From hits *[Schlagers]* to shovel *[Od szlagierów do łopaty]'* which presents extremely derogatory remarks about Andrzej Włast:

57 *Warschauer-Zeitung*, 9 December 1941, 4–6.
58 *Warschauer-Zeitung* 13 December 1941, 4.
59 *NKW* No. 41, 27 November 1939, 1.

Once popular in Nalewki circles [name of a street in Warsaw, traditionally inhabited by Jews] the manufacturer of hits *[schlagers]* such as 'O Come my beloved, give me your pale lips', and other rhymes in Częstochowa style [poor poetry], Gustav Baumritter, signing his products under the pseudonym Andrzej Włast, is currently busy in forced labour in Warsaw working with a shovel in his hand. To the former favourite of the 'Shabbes-goyish' public physical work proves good for health and his sense of humour does not leave him, because, as we have heard, he promises his fellow workers that his next hit will be entitled 'And I was like – boom with my shovel.' [in the original this mocking title is rhymed: 'A ja na to – bęc łopatą']60

This example demonstrates perfectly that the analysis of Nazi music censorship policies should be projected against the larger background of the meticulously executed propagandistic action of the German Office of Enlightenment and Propaganda. Not only did it seek to facilitate the racial segregation of the former Second Polish Republic through a virulent anti-Semitic campaign, but it also extolled the cultural superiority of the German nation by denigrating Polish society and demonstrating its inferior aspirations and national character. These propagandistic endeavours went hand in hand with the application of the strategies that enabled these goals to be fulfilled. In this respect, musical censorship was in fact only one of several threads in an intricately contrived propagandistic web which enabled Goebbels and his collaborators to ensnare their more or less willing victims.

---

60   *NKW* No, 41, 27 November 1939, 2.

Erik Levi and Melina Gehring

Paul Hirsch and Alfred Einstein

The trials and tribulations of collaboration in exile

No documentary evidence survives as to exactly when Paul Hirsch (1881–1951) and Alfred Einstein (1880–1952) first became acquainted. The relatively enclosed world of German musicology suggests that they must have known of each other for a number of years even if professional dealings at the outset of their relationship may well have been rather limited. Hirsch was probably the first to have established a national reputation. The son of the Jewish iron founder Ferdinand Hirsch, he grew up in a sufficiently prosperous environment to have been able to indulge in a lifelong passion for collecting rare music and music literature, although he worked professionally as an industrialist. From 1896 onwards, he devoted most of his spare time to assembling a huge library of scores and books, which were housed at his Frankfurt home. During the 1920s, Hirsch nurtured increasingly close links with German musicologists through allowing them direct access to his library and financing the publication of several facsimiles in his collection, which were edited by his professional colleagues.[1] One

---

1   The publications issued under the imprint of the Paul Hirsch Music Library from 1922 to 1930 and published by the Berlin firm of Martin Breslauer were as follows: 1. Francesco Caza, *Tractato vulgare de canto figurato, Mailand 1492*, im Faksimile mit Übersetzung herausgegeben von Johannes Wolf. Mit einem Verzeichnis der nachweisbaren musiktheoretischen Inkunablen (1922); 2. Giovanni Luca Conforti, *Breue et facile maniera d'essercitarsi a far passaggi, Roma 159.3* Im Faksimile mit Übersetzung hrsg. von Johannes Wolf. (1922); 3. *Neujahrsgrüsse empfindsamer Seelen. Eine Sammlung von Liedern mit Melodien und Bilderschmuck aus den Jahren 1770–1800. 75 faksimilierte und mit der Hand kolorierte Blätter.* Herausgegeben von Max Friedlaender (1922); 4. Georg Philipp Telemann, *Drei Dutzend Klavierfantasien.* Herausgegeben von Max Seiffert (1923); 5. Hercole Bottrigari. *Il Desiderio overo de' concerti di varii strumenti musicali. Venetia, 1594.* Mit Einleitung und Anmerkungen herausgegeben von Kathi Meyer (1924); 6. Carl Friedrich Zelter, *15 Lieder* mit einer Einleitung von Moritz Bauer (1924); 7. Giovanni Spataro, *Dilucide et probatissime demonstratione de Maestro Zoanne Spatario musico Bolognese contra certe friuole et uane excusatione da Franchino Gafurio in tuce aducte.*Herausgegeben von Johannes Wolf (1925); 8. Nicolaus Listenius, *Musica Nicolai Listenii: ab authore denuo recognita multisque novis regulis et exemplis adaucta.* Herausgegeben von Georg Schünemann (1927); 9. C.P.E. Bach, *Ein- und dreistimmige kleine Stücke für die Flöte oder Violine und das Klavier [Wq. 82.]* [...] Mit Einführung neu herausgegeben von Richard Hohenemser (1928); 10. Christoph Schultze, *Das bittere Leiden und Sterben unsers Herren und Erlösers Jesu Christi aus dem heiligen Evangelisten Luca: nach den Personen mit 4 Stimmen komponiert.* Herausgegen von Peter Epstein (1930)

indication of the great esteem with which he was held in the musicological world during the 1920s was that a plenary meeting of the directorate of the International Society for Musicology took place at Hirsch's Music Library in Frankfurt on 4 September 1928. As reported in the pages of the journal *Mitteilungen der Internationalen Gesellschaft für Musikwissenschaft*, a host of prominent academics – including Guido Adler, Higinio Anglés, Edward Dent, Rudolf von Ficker, Knud Jeppesen, Wilhelm Merian, Zdeněk Nejedlý, Albert Smijers, Paul Speiser, Peter Wagner and Johannes Wolf – were in attendance at this event.[2]

Alfred Einstein did not enjoy such a privileged background as Hirsch. He was born in Munich and obtained a doctorate in musicology in 1903 at Munich University with a dissertation on German works for the *viola da gamba* from the 16th and 17th centuries.[3] Even though this work was graded *magna cum laude*, his supervisor Adolf Sandberger prevented Einstein from securing his *Habilitation,* the postdoctoral lecture qualification necessary to obtain a chair at a German university. According to Einstein, Sandberger's rejection had largely been prompted by anti-Semitic resentment.[4] Whether or not this was the case, the consequences were significant for Einstein's career since he had to earn his living primarily as a music critic writing for the *Münchner Post* until 1927 and for the *Berliner Tageblatt* from 1927 to 1933. At the same time, Einstein remained a proactive scholar contributing many articles to music journals. Moreover, his appointment as the first editor of the *Zeitschrift für Musikwissenschaft* in 1918, and also his editorship of the *Riemanns Musiklexikon* (9th to 11th editions 1919, 1922 and 1929) gave him a position of considerable influence in the musicological world.

It was a shared devotion for Mozart that brought Hirsch and Einstein closer together. Despite amassing an impressively eclectic amount of material for his library, which encompassed all periods of music from the medieval times to the twentieth century, Hirsch always maintained that the pride and joy of his collection were the early scores and manuscripts by Mozart that he had bought over the years. Indeed as early as 1906, Hirsch had authored a book entitled *Katalog einer Mozart Bibliothek* published in honour of the 150th anniversary of the composer's birth.[5]

---

2   'Bericht über die Sitzung des Direktoriums in Frankfurt a. M. Dienstag, den 4. September 1928 in der Musikbibliothek Paul Hirsch, Neue Mainzerstraße 57', *Mitteilungen der Internationalen Gesellschaft für Musikwissenschaft / Bulletin de la Société internationale de Musicologie*, 1/2 (Jan., 1929), 19–22.

3   Alfred Einstein, *Zur deutschen Literatur für Viola da Gamba im 16. und 17. Jahrhundert* (Leipzig: Breitkopf und Härtel, 1905).

4   Pamela M. Potter, 'From Jewish Exile in Germany to German Scholar in America. Alfred Einstein's Emigration', in *Driven into paradise. The musical migration from Nazi Germany to the United States*, ed. Reinhold Brinkmann and Christoph Wolff (Berkeley: Univ. of California Press, 2001), 302.

5   Paul Hirsch, *Katalog einer Mozart Bibliothek. Zu W. A. Mozarts 150. Geburtstag, 27. Januar 1906* (Frankfurt am Main: 1906).

Einstein's interest in Mozart surfaced somewhat later. The most significant manifestation of his Mozart scholarship during the Weimar Republic was his edition of the score to *Don Giovanni,* published in Leipzig by Ernst Eulenburg in May 1931. This project had actually occupied Einstein since 1923 while he was working as an editor for the Munich-based publishers, Drei Masken Verlag. That it took almost eight years to reach publication can be explained by the fraught economic situation at the time, and by the inaccessibility of the original autograph, which had been deposited at the Paris Conservatoire in 1910.

As he was working on his edition of *Don Giovanni*, Einstein's investment in Mozart scholarship would be intensified through the invitation in 1929 from the publishers Breitkopf and Härtel to prepare a newly revised edition of the Köchel Catalogue of the composer's works. The original commission had gone to the Salzburg-based author and conductor Bernhard Paumgartner, but Paumgartner soon realised that he did not have the time nor the inclination to undertake such a mammoth task. Whether or not it was Paumgartner who suggested Einstein as a suitable replacement, there is no doubt that his colleague relished the challenge not least because so much new information and material about the composer's output had surfaced since the previous edition of the catalogue in 1905 which had offered only slight modifications to Köchel's original work of 1862.

It was fortunate that Einstein was resident in Berlin during the period in which he started work on the Köchel Catalogue, for the German capital housed a substantial proportion of precious manuscripts in the Prussian State Library. In addition, Einstein established close links with the Berlin-based antiquarian dealer Leo Liepmannsohn, who had sold a number of Mozart editions and fragments to libraries and private collectors all over the world. A further advantage for Einstein was that his duties as a music critic necessitated that he travel throughout Germany and Austria on a regular basis reviewing concerts and opera. Such opportunities enabled him to consult many other libraries in both countries which held important Mozart autographs and first editions. It was on one of these occasions that he consulted Paul Hirsch's private library in Frankfurt, making a more extended visit in 1932. These exceptionally cordial meetings between the two men must have acted as a catalyst for an important artistic and professional collaboration that would only come to fruition after both had left Germany as a result of the Nazi take-over.

Einstein in fact spent only six months in Nazi Germany. Soon after Hitler came to power, he was dismissed from his position as a critic at the *Berliner Tageblatt* and was forced to resign his editorship of the *Zeitschrift für Musikwissenschaft*. In July 1933, he left Germany for good, vowing never to return. The traumatic experience he faced during the first months of the Nazi regime inevitably left a residue of bitterness and hostility towards his native country that could never be healed. Yet ironically, exile also proved extraordinarily liberating for his career as an academic.

From the summer of 1933 to 1939, Einstein, together with his family, lived an itinerant existence working primarily in England and Italy before the musicologist finally obtained his first university position in the United States. Yet despite facing an uncertain future after leaving Germany, the mid-1930s proved to be tremendously productive in terms of his written output with the commissioning of several books and numerous articles for various prestigious journals and newspapers. Moreover, departure from Germany in no way disrupted his goal to complete the Köchel Catalogue revisions as quickly and efficiently as possible. Fortunately, despite the fraught political situation, there was much goodwill amongst his international musicologist colleagues who were keen to assist him with his research. Realising that Einstein could never amass the funds necessary for widespread travel, librarians from the United States, Sweden and Russia generously provided him with photocopies of Mozart autographs and scores that he would not have been in a position to see first-hand. Putting to good use his time spent in England, he was able to peruse material both in the British Library and at Cambridge. Furthermore, whilst he was in Italy, Einstein was given access to important Mozart sources in Florence and Bologna. During the winter of 1935/36, he concluded his work on the Köchel Catalogue with an extended stay in Vienna scrutinizing the archives of the Austrian National Library.[6]

Whereas Einstein had already become an exile from Germany in the summer of 1933, Paul Hirsch chose to remain there for at least three years. Doubtless, like many relatively prosperous Jews, initially he may well have regarded Hitler's coming to power as merely reflecting a temporary change in the political climate and thought it would be better to sit it out until a new and different regime took control. Judging by the evidence of the extensive correspondence between Hirsch and Einstein which began in 1934, he continued to be extremely proactive in purchasing more material for his library. Furthermore, he had now established a working relationship with the publishers Bärenreiter who agreed to reprint a number of facsimile editions of his library collection, which had previously been issued by Martin Breslauer in the 1920s.[7] Perhaps reflecting the more nationalistic ideology of the period, it is also worth noting that the only new publication Bärenreiter issued under the imprimatur of the Paul Hirsch Library in 1934 was the *Deutsche Messe* of 1526 by Martin Luther, edited by Hirsch's close colleague Johannes Wolf.[8]

---

6   Alfred Einstein, 'Vorwort zur dritten Auflage', *Chronologisch-Thematisches Verzeichnis Wolfgang Amade Mozarts von Dr Ludwig Ritter von Köchel* (Leipzig: Breitkopf und Härtel, 1937), XXXVIII–XLVII.

7   It is perhaps worth pointing out that the facsimile reprints (C.P.E. Bach, Zelter and Telemann) from the Paul Hirsch Library, now issued by Bärenreiter, were edited by 'Aryan' musicologists whilst those supervised by Jewish scholars never reappeared in the series.

8   M. Luther, *Deutsche Messe. 1526*. Mit einem Geleitwort hrsg. von Johs. Wolf. Veröffentlichungen der Musikbibliothek Paul Hirsch, Frankfurt a. M. vol. II. (Kassel: Bärenreiter, 1934).

Hirsch planned to follow the *Deutsche Messe* with probably his most cherished project—a new edition of Mozart's ten mature quartets, which was to be produced in collaboration with Einstein. The idea may well have been suggested by Einstein as he was working on Mozart sources held at the British Museum. Certainly some of the earliest surviving letters in their correspondence, currently deposited at the British Library, already allude to this possibility. For example, on 24 March 1934, Hirsch sent Einstein a number of photographs of Mozart early editions and sketches which were in his library. Expressing tremendous enthusiasm at the prospect of working together with Einstein on creating a newly corrected edition of the Mozart Quartets, Hirsch confessed that he would not be in a position to issue such a volume under the auspices of his library, but fully intended to discuss the matter with Bärenreiter.[9]

At this stage in their correspondence, Hirsch remained somewhat guarded about the political situation in Germany. This might explain his naïve optimism that he could even persuade Bärenreiter to engage Einstein for such a project, particularly given the virulent anti-Semitic purges that were affecting every aspect of cultural life during that period. Already on 6 April 1934, Hirsch promised Einstein that he hoped to establish a definitive agreement with the publishers for their Mozart project as soon as possible. Presumably Einstein remained more sceptical about the possibility, particularly since he had been prominently targeted in the Nazi press as an enemy of Germany. Nevertheless, Hirsch must have believed that he could overcome such problems since almost a year later on 17 March 1935 he informed Einstein, who was now living in Florence, that he had written to the managing director of Bärenreiter about their edition and suggested that the publishers pay Einstein a fee of between 500 and 1000 marks for his work.[10]

Several letters to Einstein in the following months still allude to the possibility of confirming arrangements for the Mozart edition with Bärenreiter. Yet such a prospect seemed even less likely as time wore on. Whether or not Hirsch realised how implausible it would have been for a German music publisher to risk issuing such an important volume, thanks to the efforts and initiatives of two prominent Jews, is not made explicit in his correspondence with Einstein. But he must have realised by the end of 1935 that there was no future for him in Germany, and that he would have to make plans to leave. Above all, he was increasingly fearful that Nazis might impound his precious library, and all efforts were now directed towards ensuring its survival.

Wisely Hirsch refrained from disclosing any of these thoughts to Einstein, presumably because he now became aware of the possibility that his letters could well have been intercepted by the Gestapo. The plan to leave Germany for Cambridge, England, along with his entire library

---

9   British Library. Hirsch Papers. Correspondence with Alfred Einstein, 24 March 1934.
10 British Library. Hirsch Papers. Correspondence with Alfred Einstein, 17 March 1935.

was therefore hatched in secret over a period of months. With the help of his wife, who carefully wrapped up each item, he managed to take his collection out of the country in several train wagon loads, succeeding at the same time in duping the Nazi authorities as to the enormous value of the collection. Einstein learnt of his colleague's departure to Cambridge in the summer of 1936 and in a letter to Hirsch expressed tremendous joy that he had finally escaped Nazi tyranny:

> [. . .] this is indeed great news, which has triggered delight in everyone of us today! Yet again someone of importance has escaped the lower echelons of society and the country of great perfidy! We cannot wish you any better other than that you, as well as we do, still feel like Germans, yet in a different sense than the Brabants of the Lohengrin from Braunau, and that you are and will stay as happy as we are afar from the Third Reich![11]

Some months later, Hirsch wrote to Einstein on the 13 September 1936 that since the third edition of Köchel Catalogue had not yet been published in Nazi Germany, any bibliographical reference made to material in Hirsch's collection should indicate that his Music Library, formerly in Frankfurt, now resided in Cambridge.[12]

After both men had left their native countries, it was now possible for Einstein and Hirsch to be far more open with each other in their correspondence, particularly with regard to the discussion of the course of events in Nazi Germany. In particular, Einstein did not hold back in venting his fury at what he considered to be the moral cowardice and betrayal of his former musicologist colleagues who had capitulated to the ideology of the Third Reich. Such was the venom and hostility with which he expressed himself regarding the character of certain individuals who subsequently occupied prominent positions in post-war German academic life that after the deposit of the Hirsch correspondence in the British Library in the 1960s, some letters from Einstein to Hirsch, which railed against a number of German musicologists, remained classified for many years.

In comparison to Einstein's rather volatile temperament, Hirsch seems to have acted with greater tact and discretion.[13] No doubt he was anxious not to ruffle too many feathers in his newly adopted country. At the same time, he held firm in his determination to see through several cherished projects, and was keen to lend his support to Einstein in every conceivable way. Of immediate concern was the possibility that Breitkopf and Härtel, fearing repris-

---

11   British Library. Hirsch Papers. Correspondence with Alfred Einstein, 24 June 1936 (all translations provided by the authors).

12   British Library. Hirsch Papers. Correspondence with Alfred Einstein, 13 September 1936.

13   It is worth noting that in a letter to Einstein dated 15 February 1945, Hirsch even contemplated writing a satirical article about Nazi musicologists, but recoiled from the idea, feeling that in the end he did not want to add his own personal venom to the argument.

Illustration 1: advertisement in the British musical press for advance copies of Alfred Einstein's edition of the Mozart Köchel catalogue, 1936

als from the Nazi regime, might after all renege on their agreement to publish Einstein's Köchel catalogue, although the publisher's British agents had already advertised its imminent availability in the summer of 1936 in the *Musical Times* (see illustration 1 below). Certainly the Germans remained extraordinarily tight-lipped about its publication and in the end the Catalogue could only be issued thanks to a special dispensation from the regime.

Once it was published in the summer of 1937, musicologists were expressly forbidden or were too intimidated to review Einstein's work in the German press.[14] Elsewhere, however, the catalogue received widespread coverage and unbounded praise. However, Einstein felt increasingly dissatisfied with his work. Having discovered new material and corrected several mistakes in the published catalogue, by 1939 he had assembled a sufficiently large number of revisions to justify the printing of a fourth edition of the Köchel Catalogue. Yet there was absolutely no question of Breitkopf and Härtel publishing such a volume, given the problems they had already experienced with the project in the mid-1930s. Furthermore, once the war broke out and Einstein had left Europe for good, the prospect of the revisions ever being brought into the public domain seemed even more remote. That they appeared was largely down to a combination of persistence and encouragement from his friend Paul Hirsch, and to the selfless dedication of Geoffrey Sharp, with whom he was on particularly friendly terms, and who was editor of a newly established British journal entitled the *Music Review*.

Sharp's journal, which featured an article by Paul Hirsch on early Mozart editions in its first issue, was an unusual venture and almost unique in British musical journalism at the time for its extensive promotion of articles by exiled musicologists and critics.[15] This reputa-

---

14   For more detailed discussion of the trials and tribulations of issuing Einstein's edition of the Köchel Catalogue in Nazi Germany see Erik Levi, *Mozart and the Nazis* (New Haven & London: Yale University Press, 2010), 121–29.

15   Paul Hirsch, 'Some Early Mozart Editions', *Music Review*, 1(1940), 54–67.

tion, confirmed in an 1942 article in *The Times* which referred to the editor having made his journal 'the home of Continental criticism dispossessed', resulted in Sharp being particularly amenable to Hirsch's suggestion that the *Music Review* might be the ideal forum for the publication of Einstein's revisions.[16] From the surviving correspondence in the Hirsch Papers at the British Library, Einstein readily agreed to the idea:

> It is more than kind of you to say that it would give you pleasure to print my Koechel Supplement in the *Music Review*, the more so as you are ready to meet all my ideas [. . .] and I very much hope that your readiness to let the supplement appear in the language of the main work – a readiness most appreciable in these times – will not cause you any inconvenience. On the other side, I hope that my position against the Third Reich is well enough known, to make sure that such inconvenience should not arise. Still it may be best to keep on the middle line and so to do the right thing. It is no doubt better to bring the many small corrections and additions, in accordance with the main work, in German. The longer notes, which are not many, could be given very well in English.[17]

At the end of his letter, Einstein demonstratively waived aside Sharp's offer of financial recompense for his work with the words 'your offer is one of many kindnesses for which I am indebted to England and English friends. I shall never forget this and shall never be in a position to reciprocate.'[18]

The first instalment of Einstein's revisions was published in the fourth volume of the *Music Review* at the end of 1940 under the title 'Mozartiana und Köcheliana' and ran to 30 pages of closely written typescript. Considering that publication took place at the time when many German refugees had been interned as enemy aliens (a fate incidentally that Hirsch himself was unable to avoid, albeit for a limited amount of time), it is remarkable that Sharp agreed to present Einstein's material in its original language. Highly sensitive to the controversy that might have arisen from this decision, Einstein hoped that readers would not be 'surprised that

---

16 'Musical Reviews: Human Interests', *The Times*, 27 February 1942, 6. See also 'Musical Reviews—Contributors from the Continent', *The Times*, 8 March 1941, 6. In its first five years of existence *The Music Review* published many articles on Mozart by Austro–German refugees. See Paul Hirsch 'Some Early Mozart Editions' (1940), 54–67 and 'More Early Mozart Editions' (1942), 38–45; Hans Redlich 'L'oca del Cairo' (1941), 122–31; Alfred Loewenberg,'Lorenzo da Ponte in London' (1943), 171–89; Egon Wellesz, 'Don Giovanni and the "dramma giacoso"', (1943), 121–26. German-born Alfred Loewenberg, best remembered for his pioneering book *Annals of Opera* (1943), contributed five articles on aspects of Mozart Operas under the title 'Some Stray Notes on Mozart' in *Music & Letters* between 1942 and 1944.
17 British Library. Hirsch Papers. Correspondence S, 16 January 1940.
18 British Library. Hirsch Papers. Correspondence S, 16 January 1940.

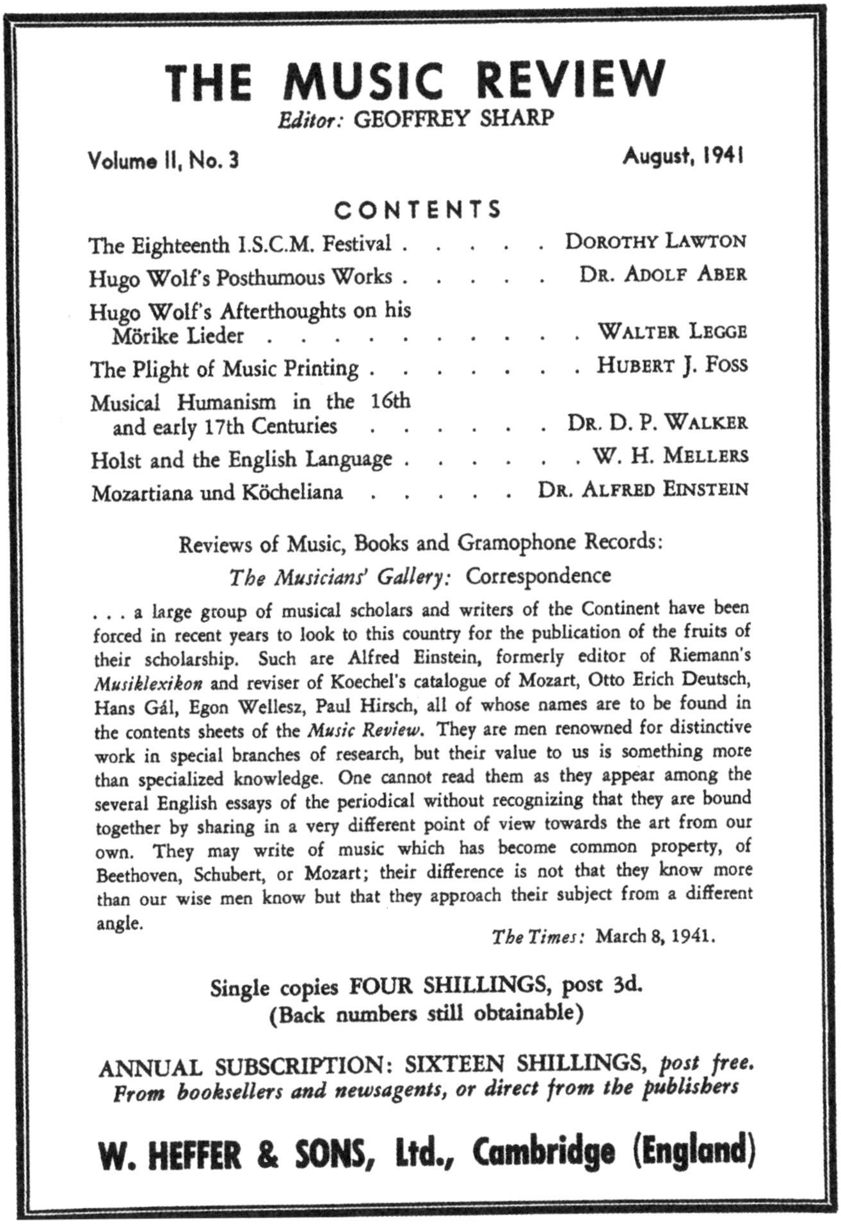
THE MUSIC REVIEW
Editor: GEOFFREY SHARP
Volume II, No. 3
August, 1941
CONTENTS
The Eighteenth I.S.C.M. Festival . . . . . DOROTHY LAWTON
Hugo Wolf's Posthumous Works . . . . . DR. ADOLF ABER
Hugo Wolf's Afterthoughts on his Mörike Lieder . . . . WALTER LEGGE
The Plight of Music Printing . . . . HUBERT J. FOSS
Musical Humanism in the 16th and early 17th Centuries . . . . . . DR. D. P. WALKER
Holst and the English Language . . . . . . W. H. MELLERS
Mozartiana und Köcheliana . . . . . DR. ALFRED EINSTEIN
Reviews of Music, Books and Gramophone Records:
The Musicians' Gallery: Correspondence
. . . a large group of musical scholars and writers of the Continent have been forced in recent years to look to this country for the publication of the fruits of their scholarship. Such are Alfred Einstein, formerly editor of Riemann's *Musiklexikon* and reviser of Koechel's catalogue of Mozart, Otto Erich Deutsch, Hans Gál, Egon Wellesz, Paul Hirsch, all of whose names are to be found in the contents sheets of the *Music Review*. They are men renowned for distinctive work in special branches of research, but their value to us is something more than specialized knowledge. One cannot read them as they appear among the several English essays of the periodical without recognizing that they are bound together by sharing in a very different point of view towards the art from our own. They may write of music which has become common property, of Beethoven, Schubert, or Mozart; their difference is not that they know more than our wise men know but that they approach their subject from a different angle.
The Times: March 8, 1941.
Single copies FOUR SHILLINGS, post 3d.
(Back numbers still obtainable)
ANNUAL SUBSCRIPTION: SIXTEEN SHILLINGS, *post free.*
From booksellers and newsagents, or direct from the publishers
W. HEFFER & SONS, Ltd., Cambridge (England)

Illustration 2: 1941 advertisement for the British journal *Music Review*, featuring articles by émigré musicologists including Alfred Einstein.

the supplement should appear in German in an English periodical, or should not 'take exception to the fact'. He further explained that:

> This course of action has been adopted merely to avoid incongruity between the supplement and the main work, and to permit the retention of the same abbreviations and other bibliographical references. My original intention was to prepare only a few typewritten copies of the supplement and to present them to a few libraries where they would be readily available to students, but when the editor of *The Music Review* kindly offered to place his pages at my disposal, I gratefully welcomed this opportunity of ensuring its wider circulation.[19]

Fortunately for both Einstein and Sharp, there was no obvious backlash against the appearance of the first part of Einstein's supplement in German, an anonymous reviewer in *The Times* merely commenting that 'since Dr Einstein is now debarred from publishing his supplement through the German publishers, Mr Sharp's undertaking must be regarded as an act of disinterested public service.'[20] One year later, the same newspaper was slightly more forthcoming and suggested that in having decided to publish the Einstein supplement, *The Music Review* had salvaged 'a fragment of the shattered European scholarship in music.'[21]

Although the publication of Einstein's Köchel revisions proceeded relatively smoothly, largely thanks to encouragement and support of Paul Hirsch, the project to publish their joint edition of the Mozart Quartets was a much more fraught process. Soon after he arrived in Cambridge, Hirsch began to make contacts with British music publishers, hoping that they would prove more responsive to his proposal than Bärenreiter. Under the circumstances, it seemed perfectly logical to approach in the first instance those Hitler refugees that had already settled in London and were working in music publishing. Initial enquires to Dr Adolf Aber, who had left Germany in 1936 to join Novello, seemed very promising. In fact, on 4 December, Aber wrote to Hirsch in response to his proposal that he 'would be overjoyed' to hire Einstein as the editor of a score of Mozart Quartets.[22] Yet the project dragged on for many years, and the prevarications took their toll on Hirsch's health. Although Einstein had effectively finished the edition by November 1938, no formal agreement between Novello, Hirsch and Einstein was established for the publication until 1943. In the interim period, Hirsch had tried to persuade Max Hinrichsen, another refugee publisher, to take it on. But

19   Alfred Einstein, Preface 'Mozartiana und Köcheliana', *Music Review,* 1 (1940), 314.
20   'The "Music Review"', *The Times,* 12 November 1940, 6.
21   'The "Music Review"—an Optimist's Venture', *The Times,* 14 November 1941, 6.
22   British Library. Hirsch Papers. Correspondence A–E: Adolf Aber, Letter to Paul Hirsch, 4 December 1936.

Hinrichsen proved unreliable, firstly promising to issue the scores and then blaming the paper shortage crisis during the war as an excuse for reneging on his agreement.

Despite all the anxieties caused by all these obstacles, Hirsch was not prepared to relinquish his cherished idea so easily. Determined that their edition should see the light of day, he submitted the text of Einstein's written introduction for publication in the *Music Review* in 1942.[23] Accompanying the article was a footnote from Geoffrey Sharp justifying his decision to print Einstein's article in advance of the scores being published:

> This edition was completed by Dr Einstein some time ago and was to be published as volume XII of the *Publications of the Paul Hirsch Library* at Cambridge. The negatives of the score have been made, but production is at present held up as the necessary quantity of special paper suitable for music-printing is not available. Publication will most probably have to be delayed until after the war; but Dr Einstein's *Preface* contains so many revelations important to the Mozart scholar that its appearance within these covers should serve a useful purpose in itself, besides whetting the appetite for what is to come [...][24]

This strategy seems to have paid off, since it galvanised Novello into securing a definitive agreement with Hirsch, even though, as was already intimated in Sharp's footnote, the eventual publication of the edition had to be postponed until the end of the war.

In a letter to Richard Capell dated 7 January 1939, Hirsch confessed that 'it has for many years been my hope to be able some day to have published these Ten Quartets which I love more than nearly anything else', working in collaboration with a 'first-class authority' such as Einstein.[25] After a period of eleven years and against the background of the defeat of the Nazis, both Hirsch and Einstein could feel an understandable sense of satisfaction that their joint efforts would at last see the light of day.

As victory over the Nazis seemed increasingly likely, especially from 1944 onwards, both Einstein and Hirsch outlined further plans to work together after the end of the war. One proposal was to follow their edition of the Mozart Quartets with a publication devoted to the String Quintets. But despite the fact that relations between the two men remained warm to the end of their lives, neither this nor any other idea for working together really got off the ground. A partial reason for the failure to continue their partnership may well have been down to Einstein's reluctance to resume any form of collaboration with his former German col-

---

23 Alfred Einstein, 'Mozart's Ten Celebrated Quartets: First Authentic Edition: Based on Autographs in the British Museum and on Early Prints', *Music Review*, 3 (1942), 159–69.

24 Einstein, 159.

25 British Library, Hirsch Papers. Correspondence A–E: Letter to Richard Capell, 7 January 1939.

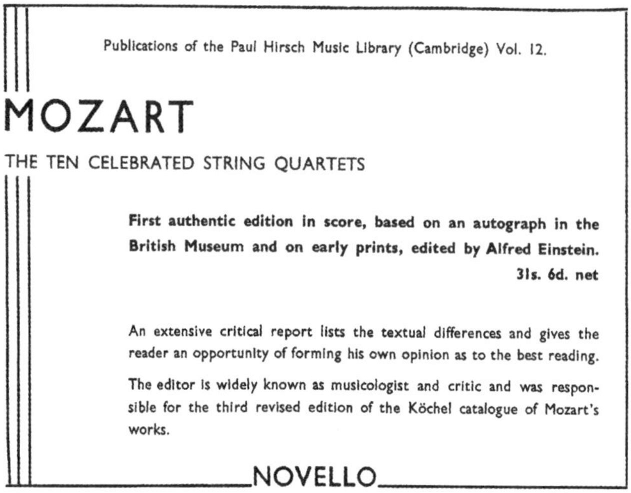

Illustration 3: advertisement for the Hirsch/Einstein edition of the Mozart String Quartets, 1945.

leagues, and his increasing outrage that some British writers on music were given the platform to express views that in his view hardly differed in tone from those postulated by the Nazis.

This latter problem erupted already in 1944. After the first part of Einstein's supplement had appeared in the *Music Review*, a further six instalments were to follow between 1941 and 1945.[26] At the end of the war, Geoffrey Sharp had every intention of bringing together these various sections and offering the supplement in a single publication, once he had received the final section of Einstein's revisions. But Einstein was no longer willing to make further contributions to the *Music Review*, having taken great exception to a passage in an article by Cecil Gray which appeared in the November 1944 issue of the journal. Amidst a flurry of barbs against various modern trends in musical development, Gray had been injudicious enough to have made comments on the current cultural situation in England which included overtly anti-Semitic slurs, in particular the suggestion that an 'enormous influx of Central European refugees, largely of Jewish extraction' had flooded the home market so that it had become 'the happy hunting-ground of a rout of commercial speculators and profiteers.'[27]

The surviving correspondence between Sharp and Einstein reveals the editor's evident discomfort at the nature of Gray's remarks. Yet despite issuing a heartfelt apology that it was never his intention to cause Einstein undue distress, Sharp was nonetheless unprepared to condemn Gray on the basis that writers in his journal were entitled to express their per-

---

26   Alfred Einstein, 'Mozartiana und Köcheliana', *Music Review*, 2 (1941), 68–77, 151–58, 235–42, 324–31; *Music Review*, 4 (1943), 53–61, and *Music Review*, 6 (1945), 238–42.

27   Cecil Gray 'Contingencies', *Music Review*, 5 (1944), 245–46. See also Potter, 311.

sonal opinions. For his part, Einstein denied being personally offended by Gray's remarks, but merely regarded them as a sad indictment of a certain state of mind. He wrote to Sharp on 17 June 1945 that 'Hitlerism in Germany began exactly with remarks like that; and if they are possible in a democratic country even before V-E Day was achieved, the five and more years of 'blood, sweat and tears' have, in my opinion, been wasted.'[28]

Although the *Music Review* published a further article in 1946 by Einstein on the first performance of Mozart's *Entführung* in London, the author was unwilling to change his mind and refused to submit the last instalment of the Köchel supplement to the journal. In the end, the Köchel revisions were incorporated into an entirely new edition of the Mozart thematic catalogue. Yet rather than opting for a British publisher to bring out this volume, Einstein decided that these revisions should be issued together in a new edition that was published in the United States.

Einstein's fears concerning the inherent racism of certain British writers were to be further inflamed by an anonymous article that appeared in the July 1946 edition of the journal *Musical Opinion*. Commenting on the forthcoming music festival of the International Society for Contemporary Music, which was to be held in London, the author was strongly dismissive of the programme and the featured composers. He commented that 'it is a little difficult to know whether some of these gentlemen are representing their country of birth or the USA.' Although apparently relieved that the two composers chosen to represent England at the festival (Elisabeth Lutyens and Alan Rawsthorne) 'at least bear English names', he could not resist adding a xenophobic and anti-Semitic gloss on the whole festival with the remark that 'in these days of the infiltration of "Bergs" and "Steins" into our concert programmes, it would not at all be surprising to find us represented by a Finkelberg from Golders Green (England).'[29]

---

28 Melina Gehring, *Alfred Einstein: Ein Musikwissenschaftler im Exil* (Hamburg: von Bockel, 2007), 136.

29 'Stray Puffs by "Flute"', *Musical Opinion* (July 1946), 295. The same journal had frequently railed against the presence of foreigners in British musical life. For example in February 1946, we find the following remarks: 'But the disquieting fact is that so many refugee guests of this country ignore their hosts […] Your Bulbsteins and Finglegrafs appear here for the first time like a gale, but in reality the net result is as a gentle expulsion of wind from a punctured bicycle tyre.' See 'Commentaries by Mr Urbanus,' *Musical Opinion* (February 1946), 135. In September 1946, the same columnist wrote in somewhat mocking tones: 'So now we are to have British opera at Covent Garden. Our true British blood runs faster at the thought. The musical director, by the way, is Herr Karl Rankl. Following the British tradition the successor to Stanford Robinson as conductor of the BBC Theatre Orchestra is Walter Goehr (our British blood is getting somewhat watery now) who has written or is writing the film music for that very English book Great Expectations. (What you haven't much to cheer about? Did I hear you murmur something about the cuckoo in the nest?)'. See 'Commentaries by Mr Urbanus,' *Musical Opinion* (August 1946), 327.

Equally disconcerting, as far as Einstein was concerned, was a review of Friedrich Blume's book *Wesen und Werden deutscher Musik* which appeared in the July 1947 issue of *Music & Letters*. A particular bone of contention was the reviewer's intimation that Blume had been an active anti-Nazi, a position vigorously challenged by the exiled musicologist.[30]

Yet the final straw came a year later. The problem started with a review of Alfred Einstein's book *Greatness in Music* by Norman Suckling which was published in the *Monthly Musical Record* in 1948.[31] Suckling attacked Einstein for his uncritical approach to great composers such as Beethoven, Brahms and Schubert, suggesting that he had overlooked the fact that they too had occasionally written mediocre music:

> What certainly *is* essential to great music is concentration or condensation [...] Dr. Einstein himself is well aware of this necessity for condensation, and yet displays a typically German inability to discern its absence in his own idols [...][32]

According to Suckling, Einstein had been guilty of a biased approach which by implication undermined the greatness of music originating from other countries. His approach to non-German music was 'almost like that of a doctor studying abnormal psychology' and this had led him 'in a fairly extensive book devoted to musical greatness, to mention Debussy with

---

30 See R.F. review of Blume's *Wesen und Werden deutscher Musik* in *Music & Letters* (July 1947), 279–281. Some excerpts from this review warrant citation here for the staunch way in which the critic defended Blume and the inevitably provocative impact it would have exerted on Einstein: 'The new German Gesellschaft für Musikforschung, at its first conference at Göttingen during April of this year, elected as its President Friedrich Blume, Professor of Musicology at the University of Kiel. I cannot believe that this new organization could have made a better choice, even if nothing else were considered than the fine record of Blume's scientific work under the Nazi dictatorship. Already in 1938 Mr Ernest Newman, in an article on Blume's study *Musik und Rasse*, drew our attention to 'one of the leading living German musical scholars.' He indulges in none of the too customary dithyrambs over Germanic and Nordic music. This noble and daring attempt of Blume's to replace the race nonsense of the Nazis by a sober scientific analysis of the facts was followed by the lecture 'Wesen und Werden deutscher Musik', which he was asked to deliver by order of the higher authorities in 1944 as part of a series of public lectures on 'Die Kunst des Reiches'. Blume, aware both of the support of his anti-Nazi friends and also of possible serious consequences for himself attendant on his adherence to strictly scientific principles, decided to use this opportunity to aim a blow at the official Nazi music propaganda. He could not, of course, in 1944, in a public lecture attended by high Nazi officials, freely say what he really meant. He had to camouflage the true meaning of his words with a certain amount of current phraseology. But anybody who knows a little about Nazi thought on music will very soon grasp his real meaning on reading the pamphlet under review.'
31 See Norman Suckling, 'Musical Greatness', *Monthly Musical Record,* 78 (July/August 1948), 149–53.
32 Suckling, 152.

reluctance, to ignore Fauré altogether, and to include the names of Franck and Borodin only in a list quoted from someone else.'[33] After reading this review, Paul Hirsch wrote a letter of protest to Gerald Abraham, the editor of the *Monthly Musical Record*, expressing strong disapproval of Suckling's article.[34] Four days later, Hirsch sent a copy of this letter to Alfred Einstein with the comment that the 'otherwise sensible Abraham' should not have published such an 'imbecility'. He had already anticipated Abraham's response, which would probably refer to the necessity for an editor to remain as objective as possible, and concluded that while maybe someone else might (publicly) give their opinion on this review, a letter by Hirsch himself would be out of place, as he was still regarded by many as someone from the continent despite the fact that he had been a naturalised Briton for a number of years.[35]

Eight days later, Hirsch sent Einstein another letter, quoting Abraham's response, which claimed to 'sympathise heartily' 'with Hirsch's feelings and suggested that he disagreed almost completely' with Suckling's article. Nevertheless, as had happened some years earlier with Geoffrey Sharp, Abraham defended his right to print the article on the grounds that he felt that the *Monthly Musical Record* 'should publish <u>all</u> musical points of view provided they are intelligent, and I think Suckling's point of view is that of an intelligent—though very eccentric—man, however violently I disagree with it.'[36]

At this juncture, Einstein's reaction to the review remained somewhat neutral, not least because he had not read it. In his letter to Hirsch, he urged his colleague not to respond to Suckling's comments, arguing that the whole issue would soon be forgotten. On the other hand, Einstein expressed both sympathy and solidarity with Hirsch's position, commenting with some irony that 'the neutralized Englishman P. H. should not rise to speak for the hyphenated American A.E.':

It is of no avail, we are 'former Germans' [...] Whoever publishes a book, hereby steps out on the street and has to tolerate the fact that not everyone likes his mug. However, you have to thank Mr. Abraham for his willingness to publish your reply. You might tell him of my standpoint. And tell him that I am 'used to suffering', thanks to my experience with the *Berliner Tageblatt* [...][37]

Einstein's attempt to persuade his colleague not to respond to Suckling's article however backfired. Hirsch's letter of protest to Gerald Abraham had been accepted for publication and

---

33 Suckling, 150 and 153.
34 British Library. Hirsch P. 18, Supplementary Papers, letter to Gerald Abraham sections 4–8, 16 July 1948.
35 British Library. Hirsch Papers. Correspondence with Alfred Einstein, 20 July 1948.
36 British Library. Hirsch P. 18, Supplementary Hirsch Papers, sections 4–8, 28 July 1948.
37 British Library. Hirsch Papers. Correspondence from Einstein to Hirsch, 2 August 1948.

appeared in the September 1948 issue of *Monthly Musical Record*. [38] Not surprisingly, Hirsch staunchly defended Einstein's *Greatness in Music*, and challenged Suckling's evaluations of a number of composers. In addition, he made direct reference to the contentious suggestion regarding Einstein's nationality:

> I do hope that Mr Suckling will not judge my criticism as 'a typically German inability to discern [...]' (I left Germany more than twelve years ago and I feel very much at home in this country by now). [39]

Suckling responded to Hirsch's comments in the October 1948 issue of *Monthly Musical Record*, insisting on his right to discuss works of inferior quality, even if they were penned by composers or poets who are regarded as being sacrosanct. At the same time, he carefully avoided making reference to his insinuations regarding Einstein's 'typically German' qualities. [40]

No further debate ensued with regard to this difference of opinion, but the whole affair had long-lasting consequences for the professional relationship between Hirsch and Einstein. Although both men corresponded avidly with each other to the end of their lives, there was now no possibility whatsoever of them resuming the kind of partnership that had flourished during the 1930s and early 40s. Despite the fact that Hirsch expressed the hope to Einstein that the whole thing would soon blow over and 'that one can [...] go back to normal after what this idiot has said', Einstein remained far more circumspect. [41] Already he had confided to Hirsch in a letter dated 25 August that whilst he was deeply grateful for his support, the publication of Suckling's review had finally convinced him that it was best to sever any further ties with British musicology. [42]

This decision had already been confirmed in a letter dated 25 August 1948 which Einstein drafted to Eric Blom, currently the editor of the forthcoming fifth edition of *Grove's Dictionary of Music and Musicians*. The letter deserves to be quoted in full because it exposes one of the major dilemmas that faced an exiled scholar trying to establish a balanced reputation in a different country:

---

38   British Library. Hirsch Papers. Correspondence with Alfred Einstein, 7 August 1948.
39   Paul Hirsch, 'Correspondence. "Musical Greatness"', *Monthly Musical Record*, 78 (September 1948), 189.
40   N. Suckling, 'Correspondence. "Musical Greatness"', *Monthly Musical Record*, 78 (October 1948), 218.
41   British Library. Hirsch Papers. Correspondence with Alfred Einstein, 16 October 1948.
42   British Library. Hirsch Papers. Letter from Alfred Einstein to Hirsch, 25 August 1948.

My Dear Blom,

I wish I did not have to send you this letter, but it cannot be helped, it has to be written. In the latest issue of "Monthly Musical Record", one Mr Norman Suckling has launched an attack on me, which, I fear, has set an end to my musicological relations with British publishing. I have not read the article but I have been informed that it attacks me, on the grounds of my 'typically German inability to discern'.

Well, I am tired of being blamed for my German extraction. Sometimes, the American press also calls me the 'German scholar', but usually (there are exemptions also here) it does not happen without "*dolus*", because what would become of this country if it only fully accepted the ancestors of those who floated here on the Mayflower.

In England, however, and very particularly in the case of this Suckling, about whom I know nothing apart from that he has written a Fauré biography, the 'German scholar' is meant to be a detraction. I do not want to talk about the ironic fact that around 1933 I was denied my Germanness and at that time was called the Jew Einstein. I also do not mean to say that this detraction is so bad, it just means: non-British. And as a matter of course, Mr Suckling as a Briton has the right to be biased, yet not my humble self. Well, I cannot redress the mistake of not being British.

Mr. Suckling's assault is but the straw that broke the camel's back. I do not take it too seriously. And I do not forget having friends in London and its surrounding areas. But I have become a liability for the musicological public in England. You know that I have not contributed to any British journal for a long time now—the one for Edward Dent in 'The Music Review' was an exemption; I could not deny this request. And you know that my contributing to the 'Grove' is an acknowledgment of my gratitude towards you, I have left no doubt about that from the outset. I have to ask of you—not to retract my hitherto existing contributions, they have been typeset, and I do not want to harm Mac-Millan. But I have to ask you to publish them under a pseudonym; whichever you like, just not mine. I would sneer at myself, were I to, in my typically German inability to discern, appear in an undertaking which can be reckoned a British national enterprise. As always best wishes, your old (German? Jewish? Hyphenated American?) Alfred Einstein[43]

Unfortunately, Blom's response to Einstein's letter has not survived in the Einstein papers at the University of California. Paul Hirsch, however, seems to have been fully aware of Einstein's determination to completely turn his back on British musicology[44], but in a letter dated 13 September 1948 tried in vain to persuade him to change his mind:

---

43   Alfred Einstein Collection I, University of California Berkeley: Einstein to Blom, 25 August 1948.

44   With one exception, Einstein indeed stopped publishing in England. Only his *Schubert: A Musical Portrait* appeared with the Oxford University Press in New York and London in 1951, as well as with Cassell in London in the same year.

I knew you would consent to my (by now published) letter in MMR [*Monthly Musical Record*] [...] But, please do not take it amiss that I say: the consequences you are drawing from Suckling's article are neither legitimate nor logical. This man is not at all a musicologist, but a French lecturer at the University of Newcastle, whom hardly anyone in our 'circle of experts' knows and who has by coincidence written a fanatical book on Fauré. In this country, you can write under your name at anytime, where and how you want to, and your following here is as large as the one in America! Every expert knows and appreciates you, and you may not blame the guild for such a derailment. Gerald Abraham should not have accepted Suckling's article—you have read how he explained himself. That he not only accepted my letter, but expressly asked for it, shows that he realized his mistake.[45]

Hirsch's argument that Norman Suckling was not a musicologist and was hardly known in the relevant circles, and that therefore the British field of musicology should not be held responsible for his particular opinions, seemed persuasive. Yet he signally failed to change Einstein's mind.

Another letter dated 10 October written by Einstein to Eric Blom reaffirmed his determination to maintain his position. Whilst acknowledging that Blom remained well-meaning in his response to the whole episode, Einstein felt that his colleague had not really understood his point of view:

What would you say if in a tolerably esteemed American journal, to which you have contributed yourself, there were published an article which would state among other things: 'Mr Eric Blom, an exponent of the mixture of arrogance and ignorance which is typical of British music writing and criticism?' Now this would be no more true in your case as would be in mine regarding the assertion that I were an exponent of the typically German inability to discern true greatness. I cannot and do not want to defend myself. I have no choice but to withdraw from the English public as much as possible and to restrict my role to being a victim of the enlightened criticism of the United Kingdom, meaning: to be treated as a typical German and an 'exile'.[46]

Einstein broadened his complaint comparing what he perceived to be the different response in Britain accorded to exiles and those that remained in Germany:

---

45   British Library. Hirsch Papers. Correspondence with Alfred Einstein, 13 September 1948.
46   Alfred Einstein Collection I, University of California, Einstein to Blom, 10 October 1948.

Unfortunately it is true that former Nazis in the British public are being treated much better than 'exiles', let's say for example the Privy Councillor and Philharmonic Standarten-führer Furtwängler [Standartenführer being a military rank in both the SA and the SS] or Mr Friedrich Blume who had been understood to have taken on the smell of an heroic adversary of the 'movement' and who had also received rhapsodic plaudits in 'Music and Letters'. (But you will respond that his books or brochures are better than mine after all). I draw the consequences. Indeed it is said that in English fox hunting, the fox is aware of his sportive role, and in this awareness lets the dogs delightfully lacerate him; but at least I am not an English fox. If I am still writing my books in German, this is due to respect for the English language, in which no one of my age learns to be proficient as completely as I would demand from myself.[47] Mr Suckling's attack has not been launched, after all, against my language but against my 'German mentality'. Paul Hirsch's reply took place against my express will. I effectively pointed out to him that it would remain without any impact, as he too is an 'exile', and in three hundred years from now his descendants would not be viewed as pure-blooded, even though they would then be called Hirst or Hughes or Holmes.[48]

Einstein concluded his letter to Blom with a plea that he did not want to be mentioned in the preface to the forthcoming edition of *Grove* and that any of his contributions to the Dictionary should appear anonymously. But when the Dictionary was published after Einstein's death, Blom chose to ignore the first of these requests and made direct reference to his work in the preface:

> The late Dr Alfred Einstein, although he did not wish to be among the contributors, was unfailingly generous in making suggestions regarding his chief special study—the Italian madrigal and its forerunners.[49]

From our vantage point it is difficult to make a balanced judgment of this whole affair. If Einstein's withdrawal from British musicology had been prompted exclusively by the publication of Suckling's article, one might have still wondered—as Paul Hirsch suggests— whether he had not overreacted. Indeed, from the evidence of Einstein's letters to Blom, it is clear that he was far more piqued by Suckling's statement regarding him being 'German' than by

47   While Einstein wrote his books in German, from his *Gluck* (London: J. M. Dent 1936) onwards, all of them were first published in English translations and only later also in the German original.

48   Alfred Einstein Collection I, University of California, Einstein to Blom, 10 October 1948

49   Eric Blom, 'Preface to the Fifth Edition', *Grove's Dictionary of Music and Musicians*, 5th Edition 1954, vol. 1, xiv.

any criticism of his book. At the same time, it is doubtful that this remark alone sparked his outrage. A closer reading of the review reveals that Suckling actually praised Einstein for more thoroughly recognising the achievements of non-German composers than other Germans or Austrians, and even criticizes him for not having pursued such a goal forcefully enough in this particular book. When Suckling accuses the Germans of standing up for their own composers with too much verve and of neglecting, for example, his beloved Fauré, the argument appears to reflect a private matter of taste rather than a politically motivated assault.

For Einstein, however, such distinctions hardly mattered. First of all, he was deeply offended to be regarded—in a British musicological journal—as being 'typically German': This statement directly linked him with former colleagues, with whom he understandably did not want to be associated. Second, and this probably carried even more weight, he felt anger and bitterness towards British musicology for treating people like Friedrich Blume and Wilhelm Furtwängler with sympathy. His position on such matters remained steadfast in that he would simply not countenance any contact with persons or institutions that adopted a lenient attitude towards musicians who remained in Germany from 1933 to 1945, whether they were Nazi party loyalists or merely opportunists. Not even the strong bond of friendship Einstein had developed with Paul Hirsch over the years would persuade him to change his mind. The sustained injustice he had suffered for so long was far too traumatic to allow for a spirit of reconciliation to take the upper hand.

Suzanne Snizek

The Abyss and the Berries

In my sober moments it is clear to me that I am mad. Here I am writing this music, completely superfluous, ridiculous, fantastic music for a flute and two violins, while the world is on the point of coming to an end. Was ever a war more lost than this one now? What shall we do if peace is now concluded? What if none is concluded? Each possibility seems as hopeless as the other […] Yet I hang above the abyss eating berries. How wonderful that there are such berries! Never in my life have I been so grateful for my talent as I am today.[1] (Hans Gál, British internment camp diary entry 12 June, 1940)

HISTORICAL CONTEXT

May 1940 was an extraordinary month in the British national experience. Germany had reached the French shore; the Low Countries (Belgium, Luxembourg, and the Netherlands) had fallen to German occupation. The British, as well as the rest of the world, fully expected their country would soon be invaded, and for the first time since the Napoleonic era, seriously contemplated the possibility of direct attack. Having not experienced an invasion since the year 1066, the British expected armed conflicts to be settled on foreign shores.[2] But in the spring of 1940, German advances on the European mainland shattered this expectation.

When war broke out in September 1939, tribunals were established to evaluate the potential risk of all German and Austrian nationals that were resident in Britain. Of the approximately 73,000 cases heard, only around 569 were deemed 'significant risk' (Category A). Low risk cases were deemed Category B. The vast majority, about 66,000, were classified Category C, or no risk whatsoever. About 55,000 of those assigned to Category C were refugees from Nazi op-

1   Hans Gál, *Musik hinter Stacheldraht,* ed. Eva Fox–Gál and Tony Fox (Bern: Peter Lang), 2003. All excerpts from the Gál diary were translated into English and generously provided by Eva Fox–Gál, and appear by permission. This new English translation is currently awaiting publication.

2   Norman Moss, *Nineteen Weeks* (Boston: Houghton Mifflin, 2003), 188.

pression; of those, about 90 per cent were Jewish refugees.[3] Yet despite these tribunal results, by May 1940 the British government began to intern all male Germans and Austrians between the ages of 16 and 60, including Class C refugees. Ultimately, there were about 25,000 German and Austrian men, and 3,000 women, who would be interned throughout England and the Isle of Man. Additionally, by August 1940, about 4,000 men would be deported to Canada, and 2,000 to Australia.

Most of the British Internment camps were situated near or in the town of Douglas, on the Isle of Man. These included Central Camp (also known as Central Promenade Camp), Metropole, Sefton, Granville, Palace, Onchan, and Hutchinson (which was often considered one of the 'best internment camps,' in terms of conditions).[4] Elsewhere on the island there were Peel at Peveril, Mooragh at Ramsey, and two camps at Rushen.[5]

Composer Hans Gál would be interned first in Huyton Camp, a transit camp near Liverpool, and then in Central Camp which was comprised of 34 extremely overcrowded beachfront houses that held about 2000 internees.[6] Shifting between states of disorganisation, apathy and sheer hostility, the administration did not facilitate concerts here (as did, for example, the administration of Hutchinson Camp), although musical life there turned out to be remarkably active.

Nonetheless, daily life could often be characterised as quite difficult. As relief worker William Ravenscroft Hughes noticed, 'I obtained the impression that Central Promenade is the least well organised and the Commandant and Adjutant strict and unsympathetic.'[7] Even the relatively simple gesture on the part of the administration—allowing the establishment of an internal camp newspaper—was at first refused. As Gál described it, 'from that first day

---

3   At the height of internment (in August 1940), around 14,000 individuals were interned on the Isle of Man. A total of about 25,000 were arrested and interned throughout England and the Isle of Man. Of these, about 4000 were women and children. See Connery Chappell, *Island of Barbed Wire* (London: Robert Hale, 2005), 43. Chappell's figures are based on data from the Manx Museum of the Internment Camps Division of the local government.

4   Hutchinson benefited from both a more sympathetic and accommodating Commandant (Captain H. O Daniel) and a better location. Central, for example, was located directly on the beach front and therefore had very little space for the men to move around. It also lacked adequate larger rooms for communal activities such as classes. Hutchinson not only had more space, but also a built-in quadrangle area in the centre of the camp where concerts and classes could be held. Further, it was kept open longer, and this allowed more time for physical improvements to be made. By the winter of 1940, there was also a large hall, which could be heated and was to be used for various cultural activities, See Ronald Stent, *A BeSpattered Page* (London: Andre Deutsch, 1980) and Chappell, *Island of Barbed Wire* See also visitors reports dating from 1940–41, Friends House Library Archives, London.

5   Chappell, 44.

6   According to visitor Rabbi Schonfeld, about 1700 of these 2000 were Jewish internees. Stent, 183–84.

7   From a report written by Hughes, dated 2 October 1940, Friends House Library Archives.

onwards there have been the same problems as in Huyton; the suspicious reserve towards the enemy aliens that first one has to overcome before one can expect understanding and helpfulness, and the incredible organisational incompetence in the face of the task of looking after two thousand people.'[8]

This chapter examines musical culture that these German and Austrian refugees created while interned. Classical music—especially the German and Viennese masterworks—was often a prominent feature in both the childhood homes and education of these refugees. Daniel Snowman hypothesizes that this prominence partly arises out of a sort of thwarted nationalism: after the humiliating German defeat in the Great War, the German people could still be proud of their internationally renowned musical culture.[9] This culture was, in effect, recreated in the 'empty space' that was British internment—the internees being largely left to their own devices. They therefore quite naturally filled that space with Germanic culture—of which classical music was a central feature.

There were several talented and accomplished émigré composers interned on the Isle of Man during World War II, including Egon Wellesz in Hutchinson Camp, and Franz Reizenstein and Hans Gál in Central Promenade Camp. However, it is in Hans Gál's internment period compositions that one finds a unique portrayal of the collective internment experience as expressed in both his Trio known as the *Huyton Suite* and his Revue entitled *What a Life!*.

HANS GÁL

Hans Gál was born in Brunn am Gebirge, outside Vienna, on 5 August 1890.[10] By the age of nineteen, he had obtained his teaching certificate and was teaching at the New Vienna Conservatory. Gál also studied form and counterpoint with Eusebius Mandyczewski, a close associate of Brahms. Mandyczewski became a close friend and influential musical mentor to him; Gál in fact considered him his 'spiritual father.' By the age of twenty-three, Gál had completed his doctoral dissertation on Beethoven's early period, which was published within Guido Adler's series *Studien zur Musikwissenschaft*.[11] Shortly after, he was awarded the Aus-

---

8   Gál diary, 18 June 1940.

9   Daniel Snowman, *The Hitler Emigrés: The Cultural Impact on Britain of Refugees from Nazism* (London: Chatto & Windus, 2003), 11–13.

10   All biographical details on Gál's life prior to internment are based on http://hansgal.com/ unless otherwise designated. This website is maintained by the Gál family. Last accessed 18 July 2010.

11   Hans Gal, 'Die Stileigentümlichkeiten des jungen Beethoven', *Studien zur Musikwissenchaft* vol.4 (1916), 58–115.

trian State Prize for Composition for his First Symphony in 1915. Despite this recognition, Gál withdrew the work before performance, dismissing it as an 'apprentice work.'

Like many other young men of his generation, Gál's life was interrupted by the Great War and he served in the Austrian army between 21 June 1915 and 30 November 1918. While stationed in Belgrade he wrote *Serbian Dances*, op. 3, a piano duet; he likewise wrote his first opera—*Der Artze der Sobeide*—while in uniform in Italy. This ability to continue to compose—even under unlikely circumstances—would prove highly valuable during a lifetime perforated by political upheaval and personal adversity.

ARTISTIC SUCCESS AND IMPACT OF NAZISM

Gál's early professional ascent could well be described as meteoric. There were twenty-four new performances of ten Gál works in the year 1926 alone—the same year in which Gál received the Art Prize of the City of Vienna. Both his operatic and orchestral works were receiving widespread recognition; the *Overture to a Puppet Play, op. 20*, for example, became an international favourite. The work, as his daughter Eva Fox-Gál notes, 'had over 100 performances in a short time [...] under prominent conductors such as Furtwängler, Keilberth, Szell, Weingartner and Busch.'[12]

By 1930 Gál had been appointed director of the Mainz Conservatory, a prestigious cultural and educational institution in Germany with around one thousand students and a faculty of about seventy. Mainz was apparently not a centre that was strongly supportive of the Nazis, so an SS detachment from Worms reportedly had to be sent to establish control over the city.[13] Nevertheless, by 29 March 1933 Gál—being Jewish—had received his dismissal letter. Additionally, his compositions could no longer be performed or published in Germany. The family left Mainz, first retreating to the greater anonymity of the Black Forest, then returning to Vienna. Throughout this substantial upheaval, Gál continued to compose. However, following the *Anschluß*, the family finally left the Continent, Gál arriving in Britain in March 1938.

Fortunately for Gál, the British musicologist Sir Donald Tovey had been able to arrange a position for the renowned composer: reorganising the Reid Library at the University of

---

12   Anthony Fox and Eva Fox–Gál, http://www.hansgal.com/biography/ll-success.html (last accessed 20 July 2009).

13   Interestingly, the Gál's landlord refused to accept any rent from April to August 1933, 'his own personal protest against the Nazi regime.' Anthony Fox and Eva Fox–Gál, http://www.hansgal.com/biography/15-nazitakeover.html (last accessed 20 July 2009).

Edinburgh. The low-brow nature of the project left Gál unfazed; during this time he also discovered an unpublished Haydn symphony.

In the autumn of 1939, Gál's wife was offered a housekeeping position (which came with accommodation for the entire Gál family) at the cultured home of Sir Herbert Grierson. This allowed Gál to focus on re-establishing himself as a composer. During this productive period he established the Edinburgh Refugee Orchestra, formed a madrigal choir, and befriended other refugee intellectuals, including Max Born (the physicist who would later win the Nobel Prize). He would soon find himself interned with many of his new Edinburgh friends, as well as old friends from the Continent.

BRITISH INTERNMENT

Gál was just beginning to re-establish himself in Britain when he was interned. This situation was tragically mirrored by thousands of Hitler émigrés who were all struggling to rebuild their lives in Britain. The frustration at this point for Gál was considerable. Though the original plan had been to continue on to the United States, the Gáls had voluntarily chosen to stay in Britain. In fact Gál soon came to love his new country, which he dubbed the 'wonderful land that was like a cultivated garden.'[14] Not surprisingly, the experience of internment dealt him a particularly heavy psychological blow, although characteristically he continued to compose whilst being interned.

It is impossible to fully understand the extraordinary nature of these internment musical works without an appreciation of the actual conditions under which they were conceived, written and performed. This is not to imply that their musical merit is of questionable value. Indeed, Gál's internment composition *Huyton Suite*, in this author's estimation, remains under-recognised and deserves much wider attention as a substantial chamber piece of the highest calibre. Likewise, the most 'serious' portions of the camp revue *What a Life!*—specifically, *The Ballade of the German Refugee* and *The Ballade of Poor Jakob*—are significant and valuable works in their own right. In addition, the texts to both of these works are uniquely important, as they were penned by prominent scholars, Otto Erich Deutsch (famed musicologist and creator of the cataloguing system with regard to Schubert's works) and Norbert Elias (internationally renowned sociologist), respectively. The contribution of these two eminent

---

14   From a new English translation (as yet unpublished) of Hans Gál internment diary *Musik hinter Stacheldraht*, edited by Eva Fox-Gál and Richard Dove, 4 May 1940 entry. All Gál diary quotes translated and provided, with permission, by Eva Fox-Gál. Special thanks to Ms. Fox-Gál for her considerable and gracious assistance.

figures requires further explanation. Frequently, the suspension of normal life led internees to undertake projects that lay outside their usual realm of expertise, as there was typically ample time to experiment without the burdens of financial pressure or professional advancement. Thus one finds Elias, the sociologist, writing poetic texts and Gál, the serious composer, writing music for a cabaret; in the same spirit, musician Maryan Ravitz, of the famous popular piano duo Ravitz and Landauer, explored sculpture.[15] One internee later recalled that Ravitz similarly began to experiment musically—'for the first time in his life he learnt to play Bach, which was very interesting because Bach turned out to be played in the rhythms of a Viennese waltz—he couldn't help it.'[16]

IDENTITY OF REFUGEE INTERNEES

Hard data reflecting exactly who the internees were—how many were musicians, professors, and so on—does not exist. Twice a day roll calls often gave inconsistent results; internees often swapped identities when transports were at hand; official records were sloppy, or were lost.[17] Any discussion of collective identity is instead based on a plentiful anecdotal history that offers a consistent, though admittedly unscientific, description and depiction of who the internees were.

It appears that despite great diversity, a disproportionate number of these German and Austrian refugees-turned-internees were established professionals and academics. Such individuals were able to come to Britain in the first place through significant professional or personal connections; they also had the financial means to emigrate. Many of the internees in Central Camp were, as Hans Gál described himself and his circle, 'pampered people.' Most of them were thoroughly assimilated middle-class German and Austrian Jews or—as many described themselves— 'more German than Jewish.'[18] Many German refugees had come of

---

15   Maryan Ravitz (1899–1970) and Walter Landauer (1911–1983) were well known for their piano duo renditions of popular classical melodies. They had settled in Britain in 1935 on the invitation of the Prince of Wales.

16   Klaus E. Hinrichsen interview, Imperial War Museum Sound Records Department, file #0037789/09.

17   In fact, when telegrams arrived at Central Camp they often went unanswered or answered incorrectly because the administration simply had no idea where individuals were. By early July 1940, the internees themselves, desperate for some sense of organization, began to work out a simple but effective index card system—one box listing current internees and their 'house' numbers, while another box detailed release information. According to Gál, 'the authorities are only interested in how many total internees were in the camp and whether the addition or subtraction caused by the most recent arriving or departing transports is correct.' Gál diary, 8 July 1940.

18   Stent, 166. In fact, sixty-eight years later, this phrase was still commonly used by descendants of the internees. Personal phone interviews with the author, between 2007 and 2009.

age either just prior to or during the Weimar Republic (1918–1933). As Peter Gay noted in his classic text *Weimar Culture: The Outsider as Insider*:

> The Weimar Republic, though it gave Jews unprecedented prominence across a wide scope, was not a 'Jewish' republic, as its enemies have so often proclaimed it to be. It would not have been worse if it had been, but Jews taking a significant part in German culture were wholly assimilated. They were Germans. Ernst Cassirer's work on Kant was not a 'Jewish Kant,' Bruno Walter's Beethoven was not a 'Jewish Beethoven.'[19]

At both camps there were other internees—though they are described as a minority—who were not interested in the 'high-brow' camp life, preferring instead to play bridge or listen to popular music. One such popular musical ensemble was Central's Kurt Wolf and his Band, a piano, violin, and accordion trio that played in the camp cafe—for a fee. This fee was a point of philosophical contention for Gál. 'As all work in the camp for the common good done by doctors, chemists, teachers and professors is carried out free of charge, I would find it contrary to professional honour for musicians to put themselves at the level of boot-boys, launderers, sock-darners and hairdressers, who are paid for their services.'[20]

ARRESTS

The arrest process was seemingly arbitrary and notoriously disorganised. Klaus E. Hinrichsen's account of his arrest in Britain illustrates the absurdity and arbitrariness of the process:[21]

> One evening, in the boarding house where I lived, the landlady said, '[...] they are coming for you in the morning.' So I said, 'Why?' She said, 'Well, they came with the name of Walter Bergmann. But they had arrested him already, in the morning. So they said, 'Have you got anybody else?' And she said, 'Yes, I have got Mr. Hinrichsen.'[22]

---

19 Peter Gay, introduction to *Weimar Culture* (London: Penguin, 1968), vii.
20 Gál diary, 27 June 1940.
21 Art historian Klaus E. Hinrichsen left Germany shortly after his arrest by the Gestapo on *Kristallnacht* (9 November 1938); he was released because he was *Mischlinge* (half Jew, half Aryan). He 'found the situation intolerable, the incompatibility of his dual identities being heightened by the threat of his call up to military duty.' In May 1939, he left for a three-month visit to England—ostensibly to visit relatives. He was then interned in late June of 1940. Shulamith Behr and Marian Malet, *Arts in Exile in Britain 1933–45* (Amsterdam: Rodopi, 2005), 31.
22 Klaus E. Hinrichsen interview, Imperial War Museum Sound Records Department, file #0037789/09.

Hans G. Furth was, at that time, a promising young refugee pianist from Vienna.[23] He recalled:

> It wasn't done very decisively. If you got out of your house by 7 o'clock in the morning, you were safe- they would come between 7 and 8 in the morning, you knew this. So my piano teacher said, 'Come to me and have breakfast,' so I left every morning at half past 6 and had breakfast there. I could have avoided it. But after some time, I got tired, and I thought, 'well, why shouldn't they look after me?' [...] And there was one day a note, 'Will you please stay in, so we can get you?' (He laughs) They were polite. So I stayed in, and they got me.[24]

Gál was arrested in Edinburgh by a civilian police officer, and 'given just enough time to pack the necessary things for a few days.'[25] After an uncomfortable yet brief stay at Donaldson Hospital he was sent to Huyton.

HUYTON CAMP

Many of the physical conditions in the so-called 'transit camps,' which included Huyton, were completely inadequate, at best. To understand the conditions, which prevailed in Huy-

---

Walter Bergmann was a continuo player/flautist who would later collaborate on Gál's *Huyton Suite* in Central Camp. He was arrested the morning of 9 July 1940. He was given half an hour to prepare, then he left 'struggling with his heavy case (which presumably included his music, manuscripts and his flute).' Anne Martin, *Musician for a While: A Biography of Walter Bergmann* (Hebden Bridge: Peacock Press, 2002), 43.

23 Furth had converted to Catholicism while a youth in Vienna. While interned, he became acquainted with a group of Carthusian monks. After his release, he studied for seven years to become a Carthusian monk himself, before deciding his fate lay elsewhere. He later worked with Piaget in Geneva, and ultimately became a renowned psychologist and Professor Emeritus at the Catholic University in Washington, DC.

24 Hans Furth, interview by family members, VHS, 31 December 1990. Furth family collection, generously provided by the children of Hans Furth. Special thanks to Peter Furth and David Walker for coordinating this effort and providing the videotape.

25 Internees were typically not aware they would be held indefinitely. A certain 'Dr. M.T.' explained, 'A great trouble was that we had been taken from our homes in such haste and under false pretenses so that we had nothing with us, neither change of clothes nor towels, handkerchiefs, etc. [...] 90 percent of those who were interned together with me still wore the same dress and the same underwear they were in when they were interned.' 7 September 1940 GEC report submitted by Hughes. Unpublished Friends House Library Archives, Box 25.

ton when Gál arrived, one can consider the following description given to Quaker relief worker William Ravenscroft Hughes:

> The arrival at Huyton was without any doubt the most terrible during my whole internment period: You come to a site covered by little houses surrounded by barbed wire in a way that looked not only very ugly, but very formidable too [...]. Then we were directed to our lodgings, small houses, completely empty, neglected and not suitable to be inhabited by human beings'[...]. Then we had to get straw for our palliasses, but as there was not sufficient straw, a great many of us had to sleep on the filthy floor. The whole impression which I got from Huyton when I arrived was most depressing. The internees we met looked not like human beings. They were not shaved, dirty, their suits neglected and filthy. They were pale and thin and had a hopeless look in their eyes.[26]

The 'pale and thin' appearance of these internees is explained by Gál's description of the rations in Huyton. As he said: 'there is nothing to eat. The catering arrangements are in a desperate mess [...] We are constantly being put on half rations [...] there is still no real famine. But there is an atmosphere of hunger revolt in the camp, and the mess hall has acquired the nickname "Starvation Hall".'[27]

The administrative attitude towards the internees is also described by Gál on 26 May 1940:

> Plans are already afoot to establish a camp university. But there is initially opposition from above to everything. It is not allowed for more than ten people to assemble in one room. There are no books, no instruments or apparatus, not even blackboards and chalk. Whatever is suggested to our Captain, the answer is 'impossible.' He finds things difficult enough as it is, and avoids anything that could create complications. But everything that is not foreseen in his 'regulations' creates complications.[28]

Gál also recounted that Huyton's Captain Tanner even 'went around and confiscated musical instruments; he simply snatched the instrument out of the hand of one youth who was sitting on a straw sack playing his clarinet, from another he took a flute and from a third a concertina. Today he took an umbrella from an internee—it was pouring rain at the time—from an

---

26 Statement by 'Dr. M.T.', Unpublished, Friends House Library Archives (GEC report 7 September 1940). Author's note: Internment was intended to exclude the 'invalid and infirm'. However, this was not absolutely followed and sometimes included the infirm (some of whom had recently been released from German concentration camps), the elderly and teens younger than 16.

27 Gál diary, 22 May 1940.

28 Gál diary, 26 May 1940.

internee. It is hard to work out what is in his mind. The most plausible explanation is that he is inebriated.'[29]

HUYTON SUITE

An obvious alternative to scarce sheet music was newly composed music, such as Gál's *Huyton Suite*. Items such as music, books, and instruments were usually confiscated upon internment. Even after restrictions relaxed, paper itself remained scarce. Gál mentions he had enlisted a young person in the camp to draw staff paper for him, later commenting, 'I must be economical with my sketching, as I have only a few pieces of manuscript paper.'[30]

Not surprisingly the *Huyton Suite* contains some moments of deep melancholy. For example, the primary theme of the *Canzonetta* movement, which has a forlorn and haunting quality, is particularly poignant. However, the work as a whole possesses an unshakable optimism, which entirely transcends the dismal place where it was composed. This quality of optimism is a pervasive feature of Gál's personality, and by natural extension, his work. Gál's comments, eight years later, are revealing:

> When I mention the circumstances surrounding any of these compositions, I do it only because they are somewhat picturesque. The title of my trio for flute and two violins is actually 'Huyton Suite.' Huyton is a small village near Liverpool, near the English west coast, where I spent the summer of 1940. This village was then inhabited by thousands of inmates, and there were all kinds of pastimes, but no music, because the instruments were lacking. The only strong musicians with instruments, that I could find, were a flautist and two violinists. It was for them that I wrote this trio, which in a series of performances brought much enjoyment to all the participants. I forgot to mention that the village was surrounded by barbed wire, because its occupants were interned 'enemy aliens.' In itself it was incidentally a mild sort of imprisonment, of which the only harshness was the robbing of one's freedom.[31] *I think I can assure you that the barbed wire, one of the symbols of our*

---

29 Gál diary, 26 May 1940.
30 Gál diary, 4 June 1940.
31 Gál might be tacitly comparing his internment with all the other imprisonments that occurred during the World War II period (especially since this piece was written just three years after the war ended). In this sense such an assessment is, of course, absolutely accurate. However, this should not lead one to assume that the internment was not damaging and profoundly affecting for many internees and their families (as indeed it was for Gál, in fact). As historians David Cesarani and Tony Kushner have pointed out, 'the significance of alien internment in the modern British experience has to be found within its own national context.' See 'Conclusion and Epilogue', in *The Internment of Aliens in Twen-*

modern civilization, has left no noticeable traces in my music; but rather, the beautiful, warm summer days during which it was composed (emphasis mine).[32]

Further, the writing process itself completely captured his imagination. He writes: 'The trio is growing like an asparagus. I have nothing else in my head, I see nothing, hear nothing, do nothing else. My friends laugh that I don't allow myself to be either disturbed or even briefly interrupted even by the loud conversations in the room, by visitors or controversies.'[33]

Despite being consistently and stringently self-critical, Gál was pleased with the finished work, affectionately describing it as 'looking as if it were made of air, light and sunbeams.'[34] *Huyton Suite,* as earlier indicated, was pragmatically scored for two violins and a flute. This instrumentation is unusual since it lacks the low voice that usually serves as a sort of musical anchor. *Huyton Suite* instead has three high voices and a technically challenging, rhythmically entangled texture, which runs the risk of unravelling in performance. Gál was well aware of this risk, but true to his lifelong pragmatic working style, he preferred to write for real world performance opportunities—even if imperfect—rather than imagined ones.

---

tieth Century Britain, ed. David Cesarani and Tony Kushner, (London: Routledge, 1993), 210. Finally, this concert note was clearly not a place where these issues would be examined in any case.

32 Gál, 'Vorliebe für das Trio' (article for a chamber music concert in Wiesbaden), 25 September 1948, Gál family archives. Translated by the author. Many thanks to Eva Fox–Gál and Tony Fox for generously providing this material. This excerpt of the original text is as follows:
'Vorliebe für das Trio, von Hans Gál.
Das erste Kammerkonzert des Städtischen Symphonieorchesters findet am kommenden Dienstag 19.30 Uhr in der Oranien-Aula statt. Auf dem Programm stehen Kompositionen von Hans Gal (Edinburgh), der auch selbst mitwirkt.
Wenn ich die Begleitumstände einer dieser Kompositionen erwähne, so tue ich es bloß, weil sie einigermaßen pittoresker Art sind. Der Titel meines Trios für Flöte und zwei Violinen ist eigentlich „Huyton Suite'. Huyton ist ein Dörfchen in der Nähe von Liverpool, nahe der englischen Westküste, wo ich den Sommer 1940 verbrachte. Dieses Dörfchen war damals von tausenden Insassen bevölkert, und es gab allerhand Kurzweil, aber keine Musik, da es an Instrumenten fehlte. Die einzigen leistungsfähigen Musiker mit Instrumenten, die ich auftreiben konnte, waren ein Flötist und zwei Geiger. Für diese habe ich des Trio geschrieben, das dann in einer Reihe von Aufführungen allen Beteiligten viel Spaß gemacht hat.
Ich habe vergessen zu erwähnen, daß das Dörfchen von Stacheldraht umgeben war, denn seine Insassen waren internierte „feindliche Ausländer". An sich war es übrigens eine milde Art Gefangenschaft, deren einzige Härte die Freiheitsberaubung war. Ich glaube auch versichern zu können, daß der Stacheldraht, eines der Symbole unserer heutigen Zivilisation, keine merklichen Spuren in meiner Musik zurückgelassen hat, sondern eher die schönen, warmen Sommertage, an denen sie erstanden ist.'
33 Gál diary, 7 June 1940.
34 Gál diary, 12 June 1940.

The Huyton Suite ensemble faced many obstacles. First, the original trio was broken up when one violinist was left at Huyton, whilst Gál and the other players were transferred to the Isle of Man. Next, Gál's flautist and one of the violinists were deported to Canada. He then asked an amateur flautist, Dr. Fronzig, to play the part, yet the technical demands proved beyond him, so it was now passed on to Walter Bergmann.[35]

Gál summed up Bergmann, in terms of his flute playing, as a 'good, well trained musician, though without perfect technique.'[36] Ironically, their privately held assessments were basically mutual, with Bergmann describing Gál's piano playing as 'without a great deal of technique but very (musical).'[37] Bergmann and Gál had met in the first days of internment, when they had 'played the Schubert Introduction and Variations on *Trockne Blumen*, op. 160 until they were sick of it because it was the only (flute and piano) music they both knew from memory.'[38]

It appeared that Gál now had his Huyton trio players established: Erich Markowitz (first violin), Hermann Baron (second violin), and Walter Bergmann.[39] However, despite Bergmann's enthusiasm, this personnel arrangement also fell apart. According to Gál, Baron and Bergmann had a major disagreement over tempi and other nuances. Gál tried unsuccessfully to repair the breach, but finally replaced Bergmann with Nicolo Draber.

(Franz) Nicolo Draber (1911–1987) was born in Ostendorf, a German town near Bremen, on 12 April 1911.[40] He was the only son of musicologist and flautist Hermann Wilhelm Draber,

35 Gál diary, 18 July 1940. This, incidentally, was the same Bergmann who was mentioned earlier by Klaus E. Hinrichsen in his account of his arrest. Bergmann (1902–1988) was trained as both a musician and a jurist. Bergmann was imprisoned in Germany by the Nazi authorities. The conditions of this imprisonment were harsh, and included solitary confinement and interrogation. He left Germany on 21 March 1939 and immigrated to Britain with the assistance of British musicologist Edward Dent as well as the Germany Emergency Committee of the Society of Friends. Shortly after arrival, Bergmann was interned and his efforts to build a new life were interrupted. (Erica Bendix, daughter of Walter Bergmann, personal interview by the author conducted at her home, 8 February 2008.) Also see Martin, 23.
36 Gál diary, 18 July 1940.
37 Martin, 43.
38 Ibid.
39 Hermann Baron was a former young violin student of the acclaimed violin teacher, Max Rostal. Baron frequently appeared in chamber music concerts in Central Camp with pianist and composer Franz Reizenstein. After internment, Baron became a well-known UK based music antiquarian. Erich Markowitz, according to Gál, was a mild mannered young violinist. No other details are known of Markowitz at this time.
40 His given name was Franz Nicolo Draber, though he went by 'Nicolo'; later he adopted the British name of Nicolas Frank Debenham. All biographical information for Nicolo Draber is based on the Draber family's unpublished four-page document, unless otherwise noted. Special thanks to the Draber family for allowing me access to this material.

and Gertrud Elizabeth Charlotte Friedburg, who was a 'learned lady of Jewish descent.'[41] After training at the Berlin Musikhochschule, Draber briefly worked as a freelance flautist in Germany. Draber then left Germany in 1933, the year of the Nazi rise to power.[42] Afterwards he worked as a flautist in the Russian cities of Charkov and Kiev from 1933 to October 1937. In 1937 the Soviets decreed that foreigners must leave Russia, so Draber was now forced to leave Russia. However, as his wife and child held Soviet citizenship, they were not permitted to leave with him. After arriving in Britain, Draber was interned.

Draber, at that stage 29 years old, was apparently an extraordinary player. Gál overheard him practising shortly before this point and, excited to hear such fine playing, ran up the stairs to see 'what rare bird had suddenly flown in.' Though Gál was characteristically quite understated, he is effusive in his praise of Draber, routinely referring to him as 'our excellent flautist.'[43]

Gál mentions that rehearsals had to take place exclusively in the evening, as Draber refused to rehearse during office hours on account of a job he held in Camp headquarters. According to Gál, Draber took his work in headquarters 'very seriously,' although exactly what work he was engaged in during his internment remains unclear.[44] However, it is known that Draber later joined the Pioneer Corps of the British army, and eventually did translation work for British intelligence. Given this history, and the fact that he viewed his work in camp headquarters as important enough to limit his musical activity in the camp, it is possible he might have already been quietly doing some sort of translation work that supported the war effort even during his internment period. Despite this limitation on rehearsal scheduling, the premiere performance finally took place at the end of July and was a huge success. Undoubtedly, this success owed much to Draber's considerable talents as a flautist. As Gál wrote of the premiere:

> An experience like this performance is recompense for all kinds of hardship. I can hardly remember any chamber music piece of mine that had such an immediate effect as the *Huyton Suite* did. But then nowhere else can one *find* the audience for whom a piece was so tailor-made and dedicated as this was to my friends and fellow-sufferers. They see themselves in the mirror of this music.[45]

Indeed, there is a musical representation of both a British officer in the camp, and the camp 'roll call,' as played by the flute. Ironically, the premiere performance was interrupted by the *actual* roll call. About this Gál wrote:

41   Draber family archives.
42   Gál diary, 18 July 1940. Gál mentions that Draber 'came from the music college in Berlin.'
43   Gál diary, 18 July 1940.
44   Gál diary, 26 July 1940.
45   Gál diary, 1 August 1940.

We had started a little late, and just as we were in the middle of the finale, at the place that I ascribe (but I told no-one about this) to the whisky-jowled captain, the whistle sounded, summoning us to roll-call. We could easily have played for the few minutes until the end, there wouldn't have been any danger in that, but the audience nevertheless became a little restless, and when a conscientious house occupant, whose duty this is, began to toll a bell wildly on the staircase, that was naturally the end. Everyone scattered in a strange mixture of humour, annoyance and enthusiasm.[46]

This work would ultimately enjoy four extremely successful performances in Central.

At the last performance, a British officer Gál identifies as 'Smith,' was in attendance. Gál noted that Smith was the only English officer at Huyton who was seriously interested in music, and also 'the only one among the officers who associates with us as with equals.'[47] Apparently Smith had earlier heard Gál's song entitled the 'Three Princesses' and had been quite impressed.[48] This officer was probably Lt. Crowle-Smith. Gál's positive impression of Crowle-Smith was later echoed by a relief worker, Wilfred Israel, who noted Crowle-Smith's 'sincerity of conviction and kindness of heart.' Crowle-Smith also remarked to Israel during this visit that 'he had always shown great personal interest in all cases of genuine refugees.'[49]

ART AS ADVANTAGE

Although lack of meaningful occupation was usually the primary psychological challenge for internees, artists in general were able to continue with their work even if under far less than optimal circumstances. In this respect they had a distinct advantage over other internees. In fact, the opportunity to focus on one's art, coupled with the rich intellectual environment, was regarded by some artists, such as young pianist Hans G. Furth, as extremely beneficial.[50]

---

46   Ibid.
47   Gál diary, 13 August 1940.
48   This work is the fourth song from the Five Songs, op. 33. It was performed by the young baritone Hans Karg- Bebenburg and Gál in an earlier camp concert.
49   Wilfred Israel, 'Strictly Confidential Report' dated 31 December 1940, Friends House Library Archives.
50   It should be noted that internment is often viewed in a more benign or even positive light when viewed in hindsight. Contemporaneous accounts are typically more critical. See Walter W. Igersheimer, *Blatant injustice. The story of a Jewish refugee from Nazi Germany imprisoned in Britain and Canada during World War II* (Montreal: McGill–Queen's University Press, 2005) – a book which details the author's considerable ordeal in both British and Canadian internment, as a further case of an account, written immediately after the experience. In Furth's specific case, internment was in Hutchinson, which appears to have been a considerably better overall environment than either Huyton or Central.

This attitude was understandably more prevalent amongst young people who did not yet have careers or financial responsibilities as did the adults.[51] Furthermore, many of these young people had recently arrived in the UK as part of the *Kindertransport*—the camp community thus seemed to become a surrogate family of sorts.

The mentoring young Hans Furth received from the older men, especially Richard Glas, was extremely important to his musical and personal development.[52] Hutchinson Camp appears to have been a more musically and perhaps even emotionally sustaining environment than was his previous life. Furth recalled:

(My internment) was really the highlight of my musical career. I was surrounded by scientists of all kinds, by musicians, by artists. It was the first time I played chamber music [...] We had some violin players and I was very much in demand (as a pianist). And I met a brilliant pianist, Glas, who gave me lessons [...] I really had a great time and had no intention of leaving. Except that eventually people left [...] I was there from May (1940) until March (1941) [...] it was like a University.[53]

Creating music could also be psychologically advantageous under less generous conditions. Gál's later writings on the 'Great Composers'—Mozart, Bach and so on—provide a fascinating window into his own thoughts about the creative process, and illuminate his own personal ability to compose under duress. About these historical figures he wrote, 'Again and again one marvels at the strength of resistance a creative will was able to give to a frail, ailing body, and the meagre encouragement on which such a creative urge could be maintained.' He later continues, 'Creating is the aim and end of the artist's instinct. His struggles and suffering are but passing clouds; the reality is his work [...] the capacity to disregard everything else was a part of their equipment.'[54] This, in fact, was also true of Gál himself.

A connection to music also sustained performers. A cellist, Dr. Fritz Ball, who will be discussed in greater detail later, describes how playing music could be a psychological asset:

---

51 A former Peveril internee recently remarked, 'I was only 21 years of age, eager to make the best of things and probably more adaptable than older men with established professions, jobs, businesses, etc. I then had little patience and sympathy with these people, who I can now see were quite understandably more upset by their predicament than I was.' Fritz Lustig, 'Internment in Peel, July to October 1940,' Manx National Heritage Museum archives.

52 Hinrichsen recalled Glas as 'a very gentle man who was much younger than Ravitz but had quite a following and gave beautiful concerts of early classical music.' Hinrichsen interview, Imperial War Museum Sound Records Department, file #0037789/09.

53 Hans Furth family interview, VHS, 31 December 1990.

54 Hans Gál, *The Musicians World: Great Composers in their Letters* (London: Thames & Hudson, 1965), 448.

In the camp I met a man, with whom I had played chamber music for many years in Berlin. He was, through this internment and other blows of fate, so broken that he had not played a note in years. I asked him if he would play with me but he refused, until the evening of the first concert, when all the inmates were in the theatre and the camp was empty, that he finally gave in to my prodding. And from that day we played together daily, and he was my best accompanist. I could see that the music was freeing him from his depression.[55]

Of course, individual responses to adversity vary. Like Gál, composer and musicologist Egon Wellesz (1885–1974) regarded 1940 as a low point in his life.[56] However, Wellesz (who was interned in Hutchinson) differed from his colleague through the fact that he was silenced, albeit temporarily, by the dislocation and stress of exile and internment. Wellesz, in fact, did not compose anything between 1937 and 1943, but fruitfully shifted his attention from composition to scholarly activity during internment. In this capacity, he fully participated in the cultural life of Hutchinson. According to his friend and fellow internee Dr. Richard Friedenthal:

There were lectures on any possible subject of the world. And since people had nothing to do, they went to any lecture […]. My good friend Egon Wellesz (before internment) did a lecture on Byzantine music and all the times (sic) had perhaps three listeners […]. Now, he had three hundred or five hundred, you know, who eagerly discussed the finer points of Byzantine music.[57]

---

55   The original German text reads as follows: 'Ich traf im Lager einen Herren, mit dem ich früher vor vielen Jahren in Berlin einige male Kammermusik gespielt hatte. Er war damals ein ausgezeichneter Pianist. Aber er war durch seine Internierung und andere Schicksalsschlaege so gebrochen, dass er seit Jahren keine Note mehr angerührt hätte. Ich bat ihm immer wieder mit mir zu spielen, aber er war nicht dazu zu bewegen, bis am Abend des ersten Konzertes, als fast alle Insassen im Theater waren und das Lager fast leer war, er endlich mein Drängen nachgab. Und von da an spielten wir täglich zusammen, und er wurde mein bester Begleiter. Ich konnte sehen, wie die Musik ihn aus seiner Depression befreite.' All Ball memoir excerpts were generously provided by his granddaughter Sandra Ball via e-mail June 2009. These transcriptions are, for the moment, approximate and have been adjusted for syntax and spelling. This unpublished memoir, entitled 'Three Times Interned' (i.e., twice in Germany and once in British internment) was given to Ms. Ball last year, along with the cello that Ball played in Central (Ms. Ball is an amateur cellist herself and today plays on that same cello). After internment Dr. Fritz Ball emigrated to the United States. Special thanks to Ms. Ball for her generous assistance and also to Dr. Alex Fisher (UBC) and Dr. Sonja Boon (Memorial University) for their expertise.
56   Caroline Cepin Benser, *Egon Wellsz: A Biography (1885–1974)* (New York: Peter Lang, 1985), 164–65. Wellesz had been one of Schoenberg's earliest pupils (from 1904–1906) at the University of Vienna. He later created a successful dual career in composing and musicology (specializing in Baroque and Byzantine music) prior to immigrating to Britain.
57   Richard Friedenthal interview, Imperial War Museum Sounds Records Department, file #003963/05.

PHYSICAL CONDITIONS

Despite physical differences between the various internment camps, there were common features. First, there was the obtrusive barbed wire, which sometimes contributed to what was commonly known as 'barbed wire sickness.'[58] As Gál realised, 'how pathologically our perspective has shifted, how terribly inflated this barbed wire has become in our consciousness. Being imprisoned means much more than the loss of physical freedom; it means a clamp around the brain, a pressure that does not leave one, even in one's dreams.'[59]

There were widespread physical deprivations. Access to water for bathing was one such issue.[60] As Gál noted in his diary on 16 May, when he was still at Huyton, 'we have three washrooms with two sinks and one toilet for over a hundred people; that's tight for over a hundred people.' In fact, Gál had his first bath in internment at Central only after three months, when he was given this privilege through the issue of a doctor's note. In Central's first days, as at Huyton, food was limited. Of his first meals in Central, cellist Fritz Ball writes:

> I can hardly follow the gentlemen from Vienna because of their dialect. But their conversation is very interesting. They talk about the Viennese Opera where the conductor worked [...] (and) about Viennese *Konzertleben*. The banker from Berlin knows a lot of people whom I know and he is also interested in Art and Literature, and so we forget in the first few days that we are leaving the table as hungry as when we sat down.[61]

Rampant overcrowding was also a serious issue. A relief worker observed:

> In all the men's camps the prison like precautions are very obtrusive, a high double fence of barbed wire and sentries with fixed bayonets. This method of enclosure is quite inconsistent with the conception of friendly aliens, and has a most depressing effect [...] at Hutchinson, this effect is somewhat mitigated by the fact that there is some room to move about [...] but the five camps along the sea front at Douglas are little better than large cages.[62]

---

58 Panikos Panayi ,'Prisoners of Britain: German Civilian, Military and Naval Internees during the First World War', in '*Totally Un-English?*,' *Britain's Internment of 'Enemy Aliens' in Two World Wars*, ed. Richard Dove (Amsterdam: Rodopi, 2005), 37.

59 Gál diary, 5 July 1940.

60 According to a relief report dated 31 July 1940, 'There are hardly any baths or showers up to now and there is no hot water. Most of the internees have not had a bath for many weeks.' Wilfred Israel, Report, Friends House Library Archives.

61 Fritz Ball Memoir.

62 These 'five camps along the sea front' included Central. 28 October–2 November 1941. Friends visit report, Friends House Library Archives.

Lack of privacy in these camps was absolute. When Gál began to write *Huyton Suite* he observed: 'I have found a patch of shade in the green area on one of the camp sites, where I am reasonably undisturbed; the nearest card-players settled on the grass leaves me a space of perhaps two metres in diameter. For us that is so much that it almost borders on privacy.'[63] Men were typically forced, from lack of space, to even share two to a bed.[64]

PSYCHOLOGICAL CHALLENGES

Most of the internees suffered acutely from the awareness that they were being made helpless at the very time that the need to resist the Nazi regime was most urgent. The irony was that while the refugees were amongst the most unequivocal opponents of Hitler, they were now being looked upon as suspect by the very country that had offered them refuge. Furthermore, they were being made to feel completely useless in internment rather than serving the war effort, which was after all, very much their war.[65]

Incredible though it may seem, Nazis were not separated from refugees in these camps, despite the clear classifications made by the 1939 tribunals. These tribunal evaluations had been completed by the spring of 1940. However, by that point there was widespread anxiety, particularly fanned by the press and some members of Parliament, about the supposed 'fifth column' element within Britain.[66] This fear widely expressed by some newspapers was instru-

---

63 Gál diary, 4 June 1940.

64 Nearly all internment accounts make reference to this. As art historian Klaus E. Hinrichsen later remembered, 'A very unpleasant surprise was that all the rooms had double beds. Now people who had practically never met before […] cannot be asked to share a double bed […] most houses solved the problem by taking off the mattresses […] *(i.e. put them on the floor)*, but then there was very little room to move and you had to climb over people […] ' Hinrichsen Interview, Imperial War Museum Sounds Records Department, file # 0037789/09.

65 Gál comments on this sentiment in his internment diary on 13 May 1940, saying 'Every one of us is worried, with every fibre of our being, about the outcome of this war, which is *our* war, the war against *our* oppressors, against those who have ruined our livelihood, plundered our property and left us unprotected and homeless! And now we are imprisoned because we have been mistaken for the enemy—our enemy!' The fact that approximately one out of every seven German and Austrian refugees would eventually volunteer to fight in the British Pioneer Corps also is evidence of this prevailing sentiment. See National Geographic, 'Churchill's German Army,' http://natgeotv.com/uk/churchills-german-army/about (accessed 13 August 2010). See also Stent, *A BeSpattered Page.*

66 The term 'fifth column' was apparently coined in 1936, during the Spanish civil war. Franco's General Mola boasted of having four columns to attack Madrid (which was being defended by the Republicans) with an additional 'fifth column' which was secretly waiting to join his attack, from within the city. See Angus Calder, *The Myth of the Blitz* (London: Pimlico, 1991), 111.

mental in swaying public opinion towards an acceptance of a mass internment policy. As Gál argues in his diary,

> The war has entered a critical stage, Norway and Holland have fallen, Belgium and France are in the middle of a severe struggle. There has been treason everywhere. In one section of the press there has long been deliberate agitation against the refugees. Are there not other interests and other tendencies behind this measure, which was carried out without any visible preparation and literally overnight, to arrest all 'enemy aliens' in the protected area on Whit Monday? We have enemies in this country, that is beyond doubt. These enemies were Hitler's most loyal friends until the outbreak of war. Are secret forces of this kind now at work, are we, the *apparent* fifth column, ultimately the victims of the *real* one? And what will happen if such forces intervene here in the machinery of state and war?[67]

The *Sunday Dispatch* was almost certainly the hostile 'section of the press' to which Gál referred. This paper was owned by Lord Rothermere, who was an outspoken supporter of Fascism before the war.[68] In 1940 it had led a concerted two-pronged campaign against both resident aliens and Communists, and by mid-April of that year, had featured a provocative article decrying Hitler's 'fifth column in Britain' comprised of 'Fascists, Communists, peace fanatics and alien refugees in league with Berlin and Moscow.'[69]

By spring 1940 there were articles appearing in other newspapers, including the *Daily Telegraph*, largely attributing the swift German success in Norway to a 'Trojan Horse' strategy.[70] Despite this, John Anderson (then Home Secretary) remained determined to avoid mass internment if possible.[71] However, after 9 May the military demanded internment of all male enemy aliens resident within the southeast and east of England (the areas of Britain perceived to be most vulnerable to a German attack). The Cabinet then supported this demand by the military authorities, and on 12 May arrests began.[72]

Sheer disorganization and ineptitude on the part of the British authorities (rather than malice) apparently caused most of the suffering inflicted on the internees. However, this fact does not excuse the very policies that caused the suffering. As Gál observed, 'When it is now explained that it is difficult to separate the wheat from the chaff and for security reasons the

---

67   Gál diary, 13 May 1940.
68   Calder, 111.
69   Ibid.
70   Ibid.
71   Louise London, *Whitehall and the Jews 1933–1948: British Immigration Policy, Jewish Refugees and the Holocaust* (Cambridge: Cambridge University Press, 2000), 170.
72   Ibid.

innocent must suffer along with the guilty, one can only respond that it was after all unnecessary to mix the wheat and chaff together in the first place.'[73] There were estimated to be between 5 and 15 per cent Nazis amongst the Central population. As refugee advocate Dame Margery Corbett Ashby wrote about the problem:

> Rather inadequate division of Nazis and Fascists from Anti-Nazis and Anti- Fascists has been attempted [...] As releases increase the proportion of remaining anti-Nazis to Nazis is reduced. They have again and again been victims of Nazi propaganda, and now, with their own leaders released and with no moral support from their British officers, their situation is increasingly depressing and helpless.[74]

Further, there were reported to be about 150 Nazi concentration camp survivors in Central.[75] Among these was the aforementioned Fritz Ball. According to Gál, Dr. Ball was a 'distinguished law officer and must have been an excellent cellist. His right hand became almost useless in a German concentration camp through frost bite, the fingers are crooked and incapable of gripping anything.'[76] Despite this, Ball relearned how to play his cello after his release from Sachsenhausen, and Gál viewed him as a valued member of Central's chamber music life.
There was a notorious lack of understanding of the Continental political reality by the British administration, from officer down to foot soldier. As Margery Corbett Ashby would lament in 1941, 'almost without exception, the men and women in authority (on the Isle of Man) have, in fact, no knowledge of Continental politics, and the effect of this ignorance and misunderstanding has on the men and women under their charge, who have endured so much and so long for conscience sake, is embittering and deeply depressing.'[77]

HOUSE CONCERTS

An essential aspect of communal *Musikleben* was the 'house concert,' which became a stand-

---

73   Gál diary, 26 May 1940.
74   5 March 1941 report written by M. Corbett Ashby, Friends House Library Archives. Margaret Corbett Ashby was a key figure in progressive political life in Britain for nearly a century. For most of her long life (1882–1981) she was active in defending the civil rights of the oppressed, including immigrants, women, and refugees.
75   Hansard Reports. http://hansard.millbanksystems.com/lords/1940/aug/06/internment-of-aliens (accessed 17 July 2009).
76   Gál continues, 'It is a mystery how he can use the bow, but he manages it, although he is restricted and technical things can easily go wrong.' Gál diary 5 July 1940.
77   5 March 1941 report written by M. Corbett Ashby, Friends House Library Archives.

ard cultural feature of these internment camps. These 'house concerts' were typically free, though tickets were issued to ensure adequate seating. Gál recounted that he and a young talented violinist named Kauffman played their house concert programme four times,

> and we would not lack an audience if we did it twice as often. But the artists would go on strike and I would not make an exception in this case. The people are starved of music. When I play Bach or Beethoven, there is a reverence such as I have rarely experienced in music-making.[78]

The aforementioned cellist Ball also played in house concerts with 'the famous composer' (by which he often referred to Gál in his memoirs—in the following quote he simply refers to him as 'der Komponist'). Ball's memoir reveals both Gál's determination to make music, and the popularity of these house concerts.

> My cello arrived in its case on the 15th of July, but I still had no sheet music. The composer asked me to play with him, and we began to make music together, some pieces from the cello literature and of chamber music, and the next day the Beethoven Sonata and other small pieces, letting me have no rest and announcing an evening concert for us. I asked if I could please have some time to practice, but he waved this off, he thought not, as we did not know how long we would be here together before being transported out (of the camp). So this brings us to our first concert. In the camp we have three Piano sonatas by Beethoven, and two pieces of the *Well Tempered Clavier* by Bach, Beethoven's Sonata in A Major, the *Kol Nidre* by Bruch and two Schubert songs. The room was filled to the last seat. Tickets were made and we had to give the concert three times. On the last night, the room was so full that it was difficult to move my bow.[79]

---

78   Gál diary, 27 June 1940.
79   Ball memoir. The original text is as follows: 'Am 15. Juli erhalte ich mein Cello im Kasten zugesandt, aber ich habe noch keine Noten. Sofort drängt der Komponist mich mit ihm zu spielen, und wir intonieren von begeisterten Zuhörern umgeben, viele Motive aus der Celloliteratur und der Kammermusik, und als ich am nächsten Tage die Beethoven Sonaten und andere Kleinigkeiten erhalte, lässt er mir keine Ruhe und annonciert einen Abend für uns. Ich bitte ihn mir etwas Zeit zu gewähren, dass ich mich erst einspielen kann. Er winkt aber ab, er weiss nicht, wie lange wir hier bleiben, wann man auch uns abtransportieren wird. So bringen wir unser erstes Konzert. Im Lager sind nur drei Klaviersonaten von Beethoven und drei Stuecke aus dem wohltemperierten Klavier von Bach, Beethoven's A-Dur sonate, das Kol Nidrei von Bruch und zwei Schubert Lieder. Der Raum ist bis zum letzten Platz gefüllt. Billets wurden zu den Konzerten ausgegeben, und wir müssen den Abend dreimal wiederholen. Beim letzten Abend ist es so voll in dem Raum, dass ich Muehe habe in den Raum zu gelangen und auszustreichen.' Though Ball does not cite names in his memoirs, it is clear that the 'fa-

RIVALRY AND CONFLICT

Despite internment, competition was still solidly part of the musical process. The substantial stresses of such an experience could also become a fertile breeding ground for interpersonal conflict. Both these aspects were evident on multiple levels and confirmed by several individual accounts, including those of Gál, Bergmann and Ball.

At one point, Central's acting 'music impresario,' Herr Hamburger, asks pianist Alfred Blumen to play at a camp concert.[80] Blumen agrees—but only if the entire concert be given to him. Since Gál was hospitalised by this point, that programming decision was left to 'music committee' member Otto Erich Deutsch.[81] With his ensuing solo debut, Blumen unintentionally stirred up already simmering tensions amongst the interned musicians.

After hearing Blumen, Gál fully acknowledged the man's extraordinary gifts as a pianist. Another internee specifically recalled this concert many years later, saying that Blumen gave his solo concert on a grand piano 'found in the foyers of one of the hotels. There was an audience of hundreds, listening to him playing Schumann, including my father's favourite *Davidsbündlertänze*, and many of the older men were crying uncontrollably.'[82]

Gál also noted that Deutsch was, as a result of this concert, 'the most hated man in the camp—this fine, restrained scholar, who has never made any demands for himself [...] They will never forgive the person who caused Blumen to become the music sensation of the camp.'[83]

Continuo player and flautist Walter Bergmann also wrote of the musical rivalry in the camp. Always a sensitive man, Bergmann noticed a certain amount of what he felt was snobbery from the professional musicians towards him. He felt they initially did not take him seriously, since he had been a lawyer by profession. However, over time Bergmann found his relations with the professional musicians improving as his abilities and training were acknowledged.[84] Ball made the same criticism as Bergmann, saying his concert with Gál on 17 July ended the 'happiest period' of his internment. Ball explains, 'some of the young artists in

---

  mous composer' to whom he refers is indeed Gál, as this same concert is also described in Bergmann's diary. Bergmann writes that he attended a concert on 17 July 1940 played by Dr. Gál and 'a cellist'; the programme included a Bach fugue, a Beethoven Piano Sonata, and some arrangements for cello.

80 Alfred Blumen had enjoyed a high profile solo career before the rise of Nazism. He had been a frequent concerto soloist under the baton of Richard Strauss, including a long tour of South America with the Vienna Philharmonic in 1923. See Alan Sanders, CD liner notes for Testament booklet note, live Richard Strauss concert recording from 1947, SBT21441. CD issued 2008.

81 Gál had been suffering from a serious skin disease which had worsened to the point of requiring hospital care.

82 Michael Kerr, *As Far as I Remember* (Portland: Hart Publishing, 2002), 142.

83 Gál diary, 28 August 1940.

84 Martin, 44.

the camp will not let it rest that the famous composer had performed three evenings in a row with me. Young as they are, they accused me of being a lawyer, that is all, and want to put me in my place by this barrier.'[85]

Ball also expresses some bitterness over the musical committee itself:

A Musical Committee is formed, which no one has chosen, composed, of course, of only Viennese musicians. The committee determines who can take part in the official concerts and who is allowed to use the pianos. I can only use the piano when the rest are taking their walks. The composer, who is also a committee member, becomes ill, unfortunately. That means that the other committee members have all the power.[86]

Ball later says that 'when the ill composer got better, he apologised for the way in which the other members of the music committee had treated me.'

By late August there was deepening conflict between the Music Committee and a number of the musicians. Gál attributes the origins of this 'storm in a teacup' to disgruntled musicians upset with Deutsch's handling of musical affairs while Gál was in hospital.[87] Ball says:

shortly before my release, all musicians in the camp decided to go on strike if the Committee did not step down. An assembly was organized, and they invited me as well. I did go, and listened silently to their discussion. When my opinion was asked, I said only that I had just heard that I was to be released, and I wished to remind the gentlemen that no one came to my aid when I was the first to be forced to retire from so-called public musical life due to the Committee. I still had the satisfaction of being invited to a concert by the same Committee.[88]

---

85   Fritz Ball memoir. The original text is as follows: 'Denn einige junge Kuenstler im Lager lässt es nicht schlafen, dass der berühmte Komponist mit mir drei Abende hinereinander gegeben had. Sie werfen mir, jung wie sie sind, vor, dass ich ein Rechtsanwalt sei, und sie tun alles, um mich an die Wand zu drängen.'

86   Ibid. The original text is as follows: 'Es bildet sich ein Musikkommittee, das niemand gewählt hat, und dieses natürlich nu aus wienern bestehende committee regelt jetzt das öffentliche Musikleben im Lager, indem es vor allen Dingen eigenmächtig entschied, wer an den Öffentlichen Konzerten teil zunehmen habe, und wer an die Berechtigung besitze die Klaviere zu benutzen. Der Komponist, der auch im Committee Mitglied war, erkrankte leider bald. So übten die beiden anderen Mitglieder unbeschrankte Macht aus.'

87   Gál diary, 15 September 1940.

88   Ball memoir. The original text is as follows: 'dass kurz vor meiner Entlassung alle Musiker im Camp erklärten, in Streik zu treten, wenn das Kommitte nicht abtrete. Eine Versammlung wurde veranstaltet, und sie luden auch mich ein. Ich ging auch hin, hoerte stillschweigend zu, um was sie berieten,

WHAT A LIFE!

What a Life!, a bilingual camp revue, took place in September 1940 and enjoyed two highly successful performances. This enterprise completely absorbed Central's artistic community—including Gál, who wrote the music—and ultimately involved many internees as participants.

The multifaceted Dr. Pick doubled as the *opera buffa* singer in this revue as well as serving as a camp cantor—at least until the High Holy days when the two camp 'careers' became unseemly.[89] Another singer in this revue was the aforementioned Hans Karg-Bebenburg.[90] Wolfgang Lesser, then a 17-year-old clarinettist, also performed in *What a Life!*. Lesser had been interned shortly after his arrival in Britain.[91]

Each piece from the revue represents a specific aspect of internment. There is a song to portray the reality of the 'double bed' arrangement, the 'barbed wire,' two songs for housework ('cleaning up' and 'broom song') and so on. Even the noise of musicians practising, which Gál titled the 'Camp Conservatory,' is represented by an amusing mixture of fragments from the classical repertoire. *What a Life!* had serious moments as well, in the 'Ballad for Poor Jakob', and the 'Ballad of the German Refugee'.[92]

Dr. Fritz Ball, who performed in the first show, recalled:

> The revue was excellent. The rehearsals took place in the theatre. All the scenes were played behind barbed wire […] and the whole effect was successful and funny. Our lives in the camp were represented in these scenes, and the concluding scene showed a soldier shouting that we should turn out the light in the room. But it is all dark in the room, except for

---

und als man meine Meinung zu hören wünschte, erklärte ich nur, dass ich gerade gehört habe, dass ich entlassen werden würde und den Herren nur ins Gedächtnis zurückrufen möchte, dass mir keiner zuhilfe gekommen sei, als ich als erster gezwungen war mich wegen des Kommittees vom sogenannten öffentlichen Musikleben zurück zuziehen.'

89 Dr. Pick also led a Buddhist meditation group in Central. Gál diary, 15 September 1940.

90 Gál diary, 26 July 1940. Karg-Bebenburg had been a singer with the State Opera in Linz. Upon release, he worked as a vocal soloist with the 'Entertainment Section of Headquarter Company' within the Pioneer Corps. Fritz Lustig, *Memories of the Pioneer Orchestra* (Imperial War Museum lecture), Manx National Heritage Museum Archives.

91 In 1942 Lesser became a member of the Communist Party of Germany. He then (1943–1947) served in the British Army, followed by formal studies in composition at the East Berlin Hochschule für Musik (1950–1954). In 1971 he became a member of the East German parliament, and later was President of the East German Union of Composers and Musicologists (1985–1989). Gabriele Baumgartner and Dieter Hebig, *Biographisches Handbuch der SBZ/DDR 1945–1990* (Munich: K.G.Saur, 1996/7), 474.

92 These texts were written by Norbert Elias and Otto Erich Deutsch, respectively.

the moon still shining through the window. Finally a sentry 'turns out the moon' [represented on stage by a light that is switched off], while the entire house sings together the refrain of the final song under the little light that can be seen. Naturally there is no lack of pointed jokes against the guards and the officers present laughed heartily.[93]

When Gál was later asked if he, a serious composer, had found it 'somewhat trivial' to write the music for this revue, he said, 'Not at all, because it was such a genuine improvisation, written within days [...] with gifted performers, gifted singers, actors [...] everything there was real, it was a real community.'[94]

On the surface, the revue was intended to be an entertainment. Yet both in process and product, it projected a deeper significance, one that Gál seemed gratified to discover, was apparent to at least some of their audience: 'This morning one (audience member) told me how pricelessly he had enjoyed himself, and how he then cried half the night because it was so dreadful.'[95]

RELEASES

Internees were finally released by virtue of the so-called 'White Papers,' which were issued to facilitate releases. The first was issued in July 1940, the second in late August 1940 and the third issued in late October 1940. By November the government further expanded the release conditions. These White Papers did not address the inherent injustice that was mass internment, and instead focussed on the usefulness of the applicant. As one observer wrote, 'the releases appear to (the internees) to be given or withheld quite arbitrarily, for although loyalty to this country is naturally supposed to be the test for release, it appears that manual usefulness to this country is in practice preferred.'[96]

---

93   Fritz Ball memoir. The original text reads: 'Die Revue war ausgezeichnet. Die Proben fanden im Theater statt. Alle Scenenbilder spielten hinter dem Stacheldraht [...] und das Ganze war sehr gelungen und drollig. Unser Leben im Lager wurde in vielen Bildern dargestellt, und das Schlussbild zeigte wie die Soldaten immer riefen wir sollen das Licht in den Zimmern ausmachen. Es ist aber alles dunkel in den Zimmern und nur der Mond schien von den Fenstern wieder. Schliesslich knipst ein Posten den Mond aus, waehrend das ganze Haus den Refrain des letzten Schlagers, ueber das Bisschen Licht, das man scheinen sieht, mitsingt. Natuerlich fehlte es in der Revue nicht an derben Witzen gegen die Gefangenenwaerter, und die Offiziere, die der Revue beiwohnten lachten kraeftig mit.' Ball would ultimately be released before the second show.
94   Gál interview, Imperial War Museum Sound Records Department, file #004304/04.
95   Gál diary, 3 September 1940.
96   M. Corbett Ashby visitors report dated 5 March 1941. Friends House Library Archives, Box 25.

Many of the musicians were finally released by virtue of the last of the three 'White Papers.'[97] The aforementioned Furth recalled how the release categories became quite elastic:

> The British issued a White Paper, according to various rubrics you could be released. If you were an Anti-Nazi fighter, if you had a job indispensable for the war effort, if you had a family, all sorts of reasons. But I didn't fall under any of them! And I didn't *feel* like going out. I was quite comfortable and looked after. So the Commandant (author's note: Daniel) called me in and said, 'What are you still doing here?'
> 'Well, Sir, I didn't fall under any of the rubric.'
> 'What do you mean; you don't fall under the rubric? You are an excellent pianist!' And so I looked at the rubric: 'World Famous Musicians, Recommended by the Penn Club or the Music Club.'
> So he said, 'Why don't you apply?'
> I said, 'But I am not world famous!'
> He said, 'We-l-l-l…you can say you HOPE to be world famous!'
> So I applied and said, 'Will you release me on the hope of my becoming world famous?'
> And they did (release me), Vaughan Williams was the one who signed it.[98]

By March 1941, many of Hutchinson's musicians and artists had been released. It is revealing that of all the things that could have been requested of the Friends relief effort—clothing, as the camp at Peel requested, agricultural books as Onchan Camp requested—the thing Hutchinson Camp requested was musical instruments, as most of their musicians had by then left, and had taken their instruments with them.[99]

Gál was released early from Central Camp (on 27 September 1940) under a medical hardship category, as he had been suffering from a skin disease. He, in fact, wrote all the music for *What a Life!* directly from his hospital bed.

Gál regarded his internment as unequivocally 'the worst period of his life.'[100] However, he voluntarily stayed a day beyond his official release to give the final performance of *What a Life!*, which reflected through art much of the total experience of this internment—the absurdity, the comradeship, the 'camp conservatory'—and the tragedy of the German refugee.

---

97   Stent, 211.
98   Hans Furth, 31 December 1990, Furth family archives.
99   Friends report 23–30 March 1941, no author, Friends House Library Archives, Box 25.
100 Eva Fox-Gál, personal interview at her home by the author, 10 February 2009.

Malcolm Miller

Music as Memory

Émigré Composers in Britain and their Wartime Experiences

In his book *The Romantic Generation*, Charles Rosen has observed that music's power to evoke memory within its very structure was one of the major innovations of nineteenth-century Romanticism.[1] But this trend intensified during the twentieth and twenty-first centuries. Indeed modernist and post-modernist approaches involving intertextuality and polystylism have led composers to create ever more subtle means of relating music to historical process and historical events. Musical monuments, radical for their time, such as Tippett's *A Child of Our Time* (1938), Benjamin Britten's *War Requiem* (1952), Penderecki's *Threnody to the Victims of Hiroshima* (1960), and John Adams's *On the Transmigration of Souls* (2002), exemplify the interest in the genre of public memorials that tap a collective memory, an interest further reflected by the BBC's relatively recent revival of John Foulds's *World Requiem* (1919–21) composed at the end of the First World War. Allied to such large-scale public works there is a less often discussed, yet no less compelling, repertoire of smaller-scale works that are more personal and autobiographical, and which interweave public and private experience of the trauma of war, specifically World War II and the Holocaust. Such works often offer a deeply reflective approach to the artistic language, which embodies a powerful commentary on history transcending the iconic symbols of public works. One well-known example is Steve Reich's *Different Trains* (1988), for string quartet and electronics, a contrast to the more public and recently premiered commemorative quartet *WTC 9/11*.[2] My chapter focuses on less familiar works by several of the seventy or so refugee composers who came to Britain from Hitler's Europe, works that embody a personal memory of WWII and of the experiences associated with it.

I propose that such works may be divided into three categories: firstly, those composed during the war years, closely connected to events, as expressions of feelings aroused by events,

---

1   See in particular the sections entitled 'Landscape and memory' and 'Music and memory' in Charles Rosen, *The Romantic Generation* (Cambridge, Mass.: Harvard University Press, 1998), 150–74.

2   Reich's *Different Trains*, premiered in 1988, famously interweaves string quartet textures imitating train sounds with electronically recorded extracts from Holocaust survivors' testimonies, with voices of an American Pullman Porter and the composer's governess. *WTC 9/11* (2010) uses similar collage techniques and was premiered in March 2011.

which may also contain extra-music allusions. As examples I shall discuss in detail the *Huyton Suite* Op.92 for two violins and flute, by Hans Gál and works for string quartet by Vilem Tauský, Egon Wellesz, and Berthold Goldschmidt.

The second category concerns works that are composed after the war, at a significant distance from the wartime experience, which are the result of deep reflection on the experiences, and in which musical processes and specific stylistic or thematic allusions locate the narrative and musical drama in the original experiences, refracted through the wide lens of mature personal memory. In this group I include my two main case studies, Berthold Goldschmidt's 3rd String Quartet (1989) and Joseph Horovitz's 5th String Quartet (1966). Finally, there are public musical memorials that extend personal experiences to a collective memorialisation, and are often connected to commemorations.[3]

I intend to look at these three categories in turn, and discuss how far they reflect the three themes of the émigré experience: firstly, the experience of persecution and suffering in Europe; secondly, the migration to a new country with its accompanying feelings of dislocation and loss, strangeness, and struggle; thirdly, the revivifying effect of acculturation, the adaptation to and enrichment of a new culture and society, with its concomitant musical European-British stylistic hybridity, including—in some cases—a heightened awareness of Jewish identity.

Of the wartime works, one of the most interesting is the *Huyton Suite* composed by Hans Gál (1890–1987) during his period of internment at Huyton near Liverpool in June 1940, before being moved to the Isle of Man, where the premiere took place in July of the same year.

Hans Gál's music has enjoyed a worthy revival in the last few years, one that almost matches the resurgence of interest in Berthold Goldschmidt's music from the 1980s. Like Goldschmidt, Gál's career epitomizes that of the émigré generation: in his native Vienna he was one of the most popular opera composers of his day. *Die heilige Ente* and *Lied der Nacht* were widely staged in the 1920s and were still in the repertory of some German opera houses in 1933. His *Overture to a Puppet Play* for orchestra became internationally popular under conductors such as Furtwängler, Keilberth, Szell, Weingartner, and Busch. Yet, from 1933, discharged from his post as Director of the Conservatoire in Mainz, he returned to Vienna, forced to abandon the operatic genre, and accordingly his works of that period reflect his displacement, in particular the Violin Sonata in D, which reflects his need to abandon large scale genres such as operas, in favour of more the practical and mobile chamber medium. One

---

3   A similar division into chronological categories characterizes the analysis by Lydia Goehr in her recent book *Elective Affinities* (New York: Columbia University Press, 2008). In her chapter 'The Musicality of Violence', Goehr writes about 'works of commemoration' and how 'Sometimes they are composed after and sometimes during an event of extreme violence' (171). Her essay considers possible analogies between the art works and the acts they aim to commemorate.

larger work stands as an exception, the *De Profundis* of 1937, a vocal solo-choral symphony in five movements dedicated 'to the memory of this time, its misery and its victims', whose Baroque texts (dealing with the 30 Years' War) reflect the composer's sense of the darkening horizon of the times: it was premiered only much later, in 1948 in Mainz. In 1938 he came to Britain, staying at first in London (within view of Kensington Gardens) in various boarding houses, after which, thanks to a chance encounter with Donald Francis Tovey, Professor of Music at Edinburgh, he moved with his family to Edinburgh. At first he had a post as Library cataloguer, during 1938, but eventually was to settle, as University Lecturer in Music, and become a leading figure in the musical life of the city.

Of the large migration in the 1930s of around 70,000 refugees from Hitler's Europe, some 27,000 shared the experience of internment, which famously produced such talented groups as the Amadeus Quartet (three of whom were interned on the Isle of Man).[4] From early 1940, Britain enacted a policy of internment to some 27,000 'enemy aliens', many of whom were ironically Jewish refugees from Nazi Germany. Hans Gál was one of the most significant composers to have been interned, alongside Karl Rankl (who became Director of Music at the Royal Opera House, Covent Garden)[5], Egon Wellesz (1885–1974) and Franz Reizenstein (1911–1968), a refugee from Nazi Germany who arrived in Britain in 1934.[6]

The initial process of internment for Gál began in May 1940 when together with other Edinburgh refugees, he was accommodated in a disused hospital for a few days and then transferred to a transit camp at Huyton near Liverpool. A month later, all these people were moved across the Irish Sea to Douglas, on the Isle of Man. Much has been written about the way a camp 'university' was established there, with lectures, study groups, and innumerable cultural events.[7] Gál, too, found the company stimulating, but the experience far from pleasant, especially since for several weeks, he had no idea of the fate of his eldest son Franz, who had been

---

4   Louise London, *Whitehall and the Jews 1933–1948* (Cambridge: Cambridge University Press, 2000), 12.

5   Rankl's internment experience is described in an interview by Paul Conway with Mrs Christine Rankl on 12 July 1999, published on Music Web at http://www.musicweb-international.com/rankl/index.htm.

6   In the case of Reizenstein, there is less obviously explicit reference to the experience of exile and internment in his output. Rather, it is more implicit in the stylistic hybridity of his musical language combining the contrapuntal extended tonal style of Hindemith, his teacher in 1930 at the Berlin Academy, with the more elegiac lyricism of Vaughan Williams and Constant Lambert with whom he studied soon after finding refuge in Britain.

7   See for instance, Daniel Snowman, *The Hitler Émigrés* (London: Chatto & Windus, 2002), 106–12; also essays in *Forced Journeys – Artists in Exile in Britain c.1933–45* (London: The London Jewish Museum of Art, 2009); Shulamith Behr and Marian Malet, *Arts in Exile in Britain 1933–1945; Politics and Cultural Identity* (Amsterdam: Rodopi, 2002); Jutta Vinzent, *Identity and Image: Refugee artists from Nazi Germany in Britain* (1933–1945) (Weimar: Verlag und Datenbank für Geisteswissenschaften, 2006).

interned at the same time, but separated from him. Within the constraints of internment, and perhaps because of them, Gál composed two works—the *Huyton Suite* (Op.92) for flute and two violins (the only instruments that were available in the camp) and a camp revue, *What a Life!*. As documented in his diary of the period *Music behind barbed wire*, a text originally written and published in German as *Musik hinter Stacheldraht. Tagebuchblaetter aus dem Sommer 1940*, which records daily life in the Huyton and Douglas internment camps in witty and often moving detail, the first two performances of the *Huyton Suite*, given on 30 and 31 July, were a resounding success.

In his diary Gál commented at length on the difficulties that arose from trying to rehearse the music.[8] But far more telling are his responses to the two performances. On 1 August, he commented on the 30 July performance:

> An experience like this performance is recompense for all kinds of hardship. I can hardly remember any chamber music piece of mine having such a direct impact and such an immediate effect as the *Huyton Suite* did. But then nowhere else can one find the audience for whom a piece was so tailor-made and dedicated as this was to my friends and fellow-sufferers. They see themselves in the mirror of this music, which reflects the feelings and life of all of us at that time; they feel that much more strongly in the supra-real, more general expression of music than they would feel it in a concrete utterance. The listener's own memory and imagination contribute creatively. All facial expressions are transfigured when the morning reveille sounds for the first time. The performance was unexpectedly good, it sounds like silver filigree in the small room.[9]

Nonetheless, owing to some interruptions during this performance, Gál reported greater satisfaction with the rendition of the *Huyton Suite* on the following day, which he regarded as the date when the work had its complete première:

---

8   For further details regarding the problems arising from rehearsing the *Huyton Suite* see the chapter 'The Abyss and the Berries' by Suzanne Snizek in the present book, 207–9.

9   Hans Gál, *Musik hinter Stacheldraht. Tagebuchblätter aus dem Sommer 1940* (Berne: Peter Lang, 2003) 95. The German original reads: 'Ein Erlebnis wie diese Aufführung entschädigt einen für allerhand Erlittenes. Ich kann mich kaum erinnern, dass je ein Stück Kammermusik von mir so unmittelbar gepackt und gewirkt hätte wie die 'Huyton-Suite' gewirkt hat. Aber man findet ja auch nirgends sonst das Publikum, dem ein Stück so unmittelbar zubestimmt und zugeeignet wäre, wie dieses meinen Freunden und Leidensgenossen. Sie sehen sich selbst im Spiegel dieser Musik, die unser damaliges Fühlen und Leben reflektiert; sie fühlen das in der überrealen, allgemeineren Ausdrucksweise der Musik viel stärker als sie es in einer konkreten Äußerung fühlen würden. Die Erinnerung, die eigene Phantasie des Hörers schafft mit. Alle Mienen sind verklärt wie zum ersten Mal der Morgenruf erklingt. Die Aufführung war unerwartet gut, in dem kleinen Raume klingt's wie Silbergran.'

The performance was even better and more secure than the first, the players are now properly on top if it. At the end there was never-ending cheering. It is hard to say how much of this effect was extra-musical. I would like to see the reaction of an unfamiliar, objective audience. But it is good, that much I know.[10]

Gál's remarks highlight a fundamental aesthetic issue: can the piece be fully understood merely as entertaining chamber music? My thesis is that the *Huyton Suite* locates itself specifically in the internment experience, through its title, its instrumentation, which reflects the available forces of flute and two violins, and specific extra-musical allusions in the flute part of the first and last of four movements to a 'morning reveille' fanfare. This quotation, first heard at the conclusion of the first movement (Example 1) was evidently much enjoyed, as Gál recorded how 'All facial expressions are transfigured when the morning reveille sounds for the first time.'[11]

The quotation of the reveille in the final movement is even bolder, clearly signposted as an interruption to the main texture, in which a sprightly flute is set over an ostinato string pattern. Suddenly the fanfare-rising fifths emerge over an intriguing texture of *sul ponticello* tremolando and triple-stopped pizzicato chords (Example 2).

The title of the last movement, a playful Italianisation 'Fanfaronata', highlights the work's essentially optimistic and happy quality, a characteristic that is also present in the camp revue *What a Life!*. However, in the third movement, 'Canzonetta', a theme and four variations, there is a more meditative mood reflected in the mixture of a minor mode in the first part of the theme (Example 3) and the major mode of the second part of the theme (Example 4), both of which undergo variation, thereby highlighting the double edge of Gál's wartime refugee experience.

The more elegiac passages of the first part of the theme and its variations express a degree of pain and loss both for his temporary separation from his family and in the displacement to his recently adopted country. Yet the more delicate, pastoral character of the second part also conveys his feelings of relief at being in England and celebrates the creative aspects of internment, experienced by other émigrés at Huyton and Douglas.

---

10 Gál, 95. The German original reads: 'Die Aufführung war noch besser und sicherer als die erste, die Spieler stehen nun erst richtig über der Sache. Zum Schluss war nicht enden wollender Jubel. Schwer zu sagen was an dieser Wirkung außermusikalisch ist. Ich würde das Stück nun gern von einem fremden objektiven Publikum hoeren. Aber gut ist es, soviel weiss ich schon.'

11 Gal, 95: 'Alle Mienen sind verklärt, wie zum ersten Mal der Morgenweckruf erklingt.'

Example 1 – Hans Gál, Huyton Suite Op. 92, I - Alla Marcia (Concluding Flute Quote of the Reveille) © by N. Simrock GmbH. Reproduced by kind permission of Boosey & Hawkes Music Publishers Ltd.

Example 2 – Hans Gál, Huyton Suite Op. 92, IV - 'Fanfaronata', bars. 44–55 © by N. Simrock GmbH. Reproduced by kind permission of Boosey & Hawkes Music Publishers Ltd.

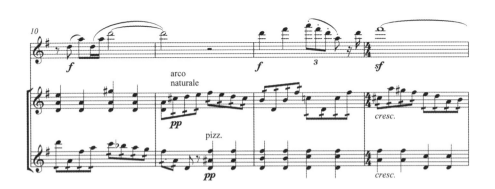

Example 3 – Hans Gál, Huyton Suite Op.92, III - Canzonetta, Theme, Part 1 © by N. Simrock GmbH. Reproduced by kind permission of Boosey & Hawkes Music Publishers Ltd.

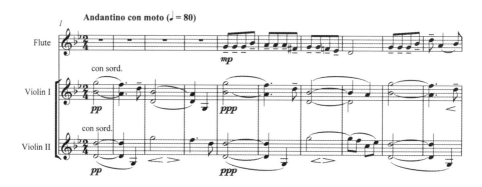

Example 4 – Hans Gál, Huyton Suite Op.92, III - Canzonetta, Theme, Pt. 2
(bars. 29–42) © by N. Simrock GmbH. Reproduced by kind permission of Boosey & Hawkes Music
Publishers Ltd.

Like Gál's *Huyton Suite*, Vilem Tauský's *Coventry* similarly arose from the midst of the war, but offers a very different experience: Tauský (1910–2004) had been a successful operetta conductor and composer in Prague in the 1930s, then fled the Germans in 1939 with a harrowing journey to France and then England, where he served as a bandmaster with the Czech Army in Exile. Tauský experienced the 1940 bombing of Coventry, and recalled how he was 'deeply moved by the whole experience [...] Within a few days, I had written my string quartet *Coventry*.'[12] The work is based on the Saint Wenceslas Chorale, a fourteenth-century Czech theme with connotations of nationalism and wartime resistance: apart from works like Suk's *Meditation* Op. 35, it was used for instance in the slow movement of the 3rd quartet by Pavel Haas, a work composed in 1938 three years before Terezín, and was also used by Martinů in his *Memorial to Lidice* (1943), a 'public musical' memorial in memory of the Nazi massacre of a village northwest of Prague in 1942 as reprisal for the assassination of Reinhard Heydrich.[13] *Coventry* thus expresses Tauský's sense of loyalty to his native country, but also shows the

---

12   Vilem Tausky, *Vilem Tausky tells his story* (London: Stainer and Bell, 1979), 82.

13   For more detailed discussion of the historical significance of citations of the Saint Wenceslas Chorale in Czech music see Michael Beckerman, 'In Search of Czechness in Music', *19th-Century Music*, Vol. 10/1 (Summer, 1986), 61–73.

start of his acculturation to British life, since it was premiered at Myra Hess's National Gallery Series. That process of acculturation is also evident in a set of *Variations on a Welsh Folk Song* composed in 1943, one of his still little-known and unpublished compositions.[14] Tauský reflected later on his transformation from exile to émigré: 'How glad I was to find refuge in England! But I could not have dreamed in my wildest moments that I should build the second half of my life here, and that it would become my home.'[15]

Tauský's wartime experiences were reflected musically mainly in his performances for the troops. In contrast, Egon Wellesz (1885–1974), who was a highly regarded composer and musicologist in Vienna, responded to his enforced emigration after the *Anschluß* in 1938 with a five year compositional silence. He had been one of the most interesting young students of Schoenberg, an expert in Byzantine music, and champion of the avant-garde. It is striking that it was only after settling in his newly adopted home in Oxford in 1943 that he found a new inspiration to compose, resulting in his 5th String Quartet. Significantly, the work's second movement was given the title 'In Memoriam', which he later explained as a farewell to his earlier life, and to the friends of his youth and young manhood. Yet it also marked the start of a new phase of creativity—leading to choral settings of Gerald Manley Hopkins (an Oxford poet), and the composition of nine symphonies.

Even more specific in its programmatic depiction of loss of *Heimat* and displacement is the 2nd String Quartet of 1936 by Berthold Goldschmidt (1903–1996), the composer and conductor who was born in Hamburg yet lived most of his life in Britain after 1935. One of the most promising composers of his generation, a student of Schreker in Berlin, and assistant to Kleiber at the Berlin world premiere of Berg's *Wozzeck*, Goldschmidt's music suffered a relatively cool reception in Britain, as has been extensively documented.[16] The 2nd Quartet is a case in point: although the first work he composed in England, it had to wait 17 years before its premiere in 1953.

The first movement represented, for Goldschmidt, his 'fearful joy at having escaped from the Nazis […] the scherzo […] represents an escape from danger, already past for oneself, but still threatening our relatives in Germany. […] The third movement, *Folia* is an elegy for what had already happened in Germany. I had lost two cousins in a concentration camp and just before that my sister had died "a natural death" under the neglectful "care" of a Nazi nurse.'[17] The title 'Folia' has a double edge: musically it refers to the Baroque structure based on a re-

---

14   Tauský's wartime works include: 1940, 2 Military Marches: *The Czechs are Marching, Call to Arms,* 1941, *Coventry: A Meditation for String Quartet,* 1942, Variations on a Welsh tune for piano, 1943, Music for documentary film about the Czech Army in England – *Interim Balance,* 1944, Czech Christmas Carols in English for Czech Red Cross. I am grateful to Graham Melville-Mason for informing me that the Tauský archive is currently housed at Cardiff University as part of the Dvořák Society Collection and Archive.

15   Tausky, 58.

16   See, for example, Paul Banks, 'The case of 'Beatrice Cenci', *Opera*, Vol. 39, (1988), 426–32.

17   Berthold Goldschmidt, 'Preface', String Quartet No. 2 (London: Boosey & Hawkes, 1991)

peating pattern, here a three-note motif that is reiterated occurs over 70 times; at the start it is presented by the viola, later taken over by the cello (Example 5). Yet the title is also intended to allude to the 'folly' of Nazism.

Example 5: Berthold Goldschmidt, String Quartet no. 2 (1936), III – 'Folia' (Opening bars showing the recurrent motif in viola and cello). © Reproduced by kind permission of Boosey & Hawkes Music Publishers Ltd.

Certainly the anxiety evident in the terms 'fearful joy' and 'escape from danger' points to a period of Goldschmidt's experience that is often overlooked. As is well documented, prior to 1933 Goldschmidt was considered 'one of the great hopes of German music.'[18] His opera *Der Gewaltige Hahnrei*, first performed with great acclaim in Mannheim in 1932, was set for a Berlin premiere in 1933 that never materialized. There followed a period between 1933 and 1935, when having been dismissed, along with so many Jewish musicians, from public life, Goldschmidt engaged in musical activities that emphasised his Jewish identity. Under the umbrella of the Jewish Cultural League, he conducted an orchestra of Jewish musicians, many of whom subsequently joined Huberman's Palestine Orchestra, and he composed several 'Jewish' works, most notably the masterly *Variations on a Palestine Shepherd's Theme* for piano of 1934 and a little-known musical theatre piece, *Das Makkabäerspiel*, for speaker and two pianos, to texts by Joachim Prinz, which also quotes a traditional Jewish tune. Published jointly by the Zionist Organisation for Germany and the Keren Kayemet LeYisrael, its treatment of the Hanukah story, the Maccabaean resistance against oppressive Hellenism, was clearly allegorical and conveyed a powerful contemporary message to the Jewish audiences. Music provided a means of escape from danger, for when Goldschmidt was summoned to the Gestapo in 1935, it was a discussion about music that moved the Gestapo Officer to let him go, advising him to leave Germany as soon as possible. Goldschmidt chose England, where he had some professional contacts and soon found a flat in northwest London, at 13 Belsize Crescent, where he was to live for the rest of his life.

If the expressive heart of the 2nd Quartet is the elegiac 'Folia', the finale is also an act of recollection and resistance. It reworks a theme used in Goldschmidt's 1933 Incidental Music to the Berlin State Opera's production of *Wilhelm Meister*, his last official commission in Germany, which had been performed with the composer's name suppressed: the self-quotation, in its demonstration of authorship, thus acts as a declaration of freedom in his new found refuge.

The musicologist Michael Struck has compared the 2nd Quartet with Shostakovich's 8th String Quartet of 1960, dedicated 'To the Memory of Victims of Fascism and War', highlighting its similar tension between mourning gestures and energy of the dance.[19] As well as shared expressive features, there is also a close correlation with Goldschmidt's 3rd Quartet composed over fifty years later in 1989. This work was commissioned for the inauguration of the Rendsburg Jewish Museum in 1989, which resulted from the German premiere of the 2nd Quartet in the Rendsburg Synagogue the previous year, to mark the 50th Anniversary of Kristallnacht.

---

18   See Hans Redlich, 'Berthold Goldschmidt', in *Musik in Geschichte und* Gegenwart Vol. 5 (Kassel/Basel: Baerenreiter, 1956), 487.

19   Michael Struck, 'Evidence from a fragmented musical history: Notes on Berthold Goldschmidt's Chamber Music', *Tempo*, 174 (1990), 2–10.

The 3rd Quartet dates from Goldschmidt's remarkable 'Indian summer' that saw a string of late masterworks, and is an example of the second type of musical memorial mentioned earlier, a work which recalls wartime experiences with the benefit of a larger perspective of time. Like Shostakovich's use of the motto DSCH (the first four musical letters of his name) in his 8th Quartet, which adds a layer of personal meaning beneath the public dedication, Goldschmidt's quartet also uses a motto with public and private symbolism, the musical letters of the Ministry of Culture of Schleswig Holstein, the commissioners, (E)S C H – H, combined with those of Goldschmidt's native city of Hamburg—the notes HBG—which incidentally, perhaps, also contains the composer's initials BG (see Fig.1).

Figure 1: Motifs based on Initials in Berthold Goldschmidt's String Quartet no. 3

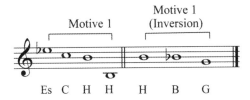

The motto first appears in the opening bars of the quartet, as shown below in Example 6, where the first violin presents Motive 1 in bars 1–3 with a rise from E-flat to C, and an octave descent from B to B. The cello repeats the motive in bars 4–5 .

Example 6 - Motifs based on Initials in the opening bars of Berthold Goldschmidt's String Quartet no. 3 ©Reproduced by kind permission of Boosey & Hawkes Music Publishers Ltd.

Yet the composer adds a more specific personal meaning through the use of quoted themes. He recalled that:

> [...] even in this latest work the Terror could not be forgotten or ignored. But how to represent it? Any quotation from a Nazi song would have sullied the music. But fate had come to my aid: a few years before, I had set Heine's poem *Belsatzar (Belshazzar)* for a cappella choir. At the first performance (in Austria in 1985), the fanatical march rhythm of the melody, associated with Belshazzar's blasphemous words 'Jehovah, I hold you forever in scorn – For I am the King of Babylon'!, was instantly recognized as an ironic allusion to the infamous past. Accordingly I incorporated the Belshazzar theme in the first section of the Third Quartet where it plays a menacing role up to the point where a traditional Jewish melody is contrapuntally combined with it and gains the upper hand. It is the melody for Chanukah, the Festival of Lights.[20]

Figure 2 – Goldschmidt: Theme from 'Belsatzar'

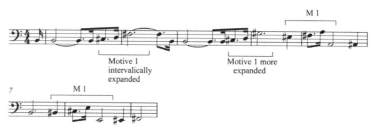

Belsatzar had, like the 3rd quartet, resulted from the belated premiere of a pre-war work, Goldschmidt's 1931 Weill-like setting of Erich Kästner's *Letzte Kapitel*, a satirical prophecy of doom, foretelling the destruction of the world in 2003. What is particularly remarkable is that the Nazi-style theme from *Belsatzar* already incorporated the quartet's motto. This mysterious musical occurrence clearly influenced the composer's decision to develop it long before the themes are brought into contrapuntal confrontation. In the confrontation, it is interesting to note how the programmatic drama is enacted through distancing the quoted themes from their surroundings: firstly both themes are clearly more 'tonal' than the prevailing chromatic idiom, both have a four-bar phrase structure which contrasts with the flowing phrasing of the rest of the material, and each is highlighted through salient timbre and register. Here the stark dotted march rhythm is finally neutralized by the smoother lyrical contour of the 'Hanuka' tune (Example 7).

---

20   Berthold Goldschmidt, 'Preface', String Quartet No. 3 (London: Boosey & Hawkes, 1989)

Example 7 – Berthold Goldschmidt, String Quartet no. 3 bars. 138–156 (Quotations of 'Hanuka' theme in viola and 'Belsatzar' theme in cello)
© Reproduced by kind permission of Boosey & Hawkes Music Publishers Ltd.

2

At a subtle level the 'Hanuka' tune, which derives from a central European folk song source that was transferred to a Lutheran chorale, expresses an optimistic vision of a synthesis of Jewish and European values. On a more personal level, it almost certainly alludes to his own past, particularly the difficult and dangerous period of the *Makkabäerspiel*. Yet as a late work, the quartet also embodies the positive aspects of acculturation: to the post-Expressionist style of his early works are brought the English lyricism of Goldschmidt's works of the 1940s and 50s, such as the much discussed opera *Beatrice Cenci* (which won the Festival of Britain Prize in 1951 but was never accorded its rightful production), refined through the concise economy of expression of his late flowering.

Another work that embodies as a whole the tripartite émigré experience of persecution, migration and acculturation is the Fifth String Quartet by Joseph Horovitz (b.1926). This is perhaps surprising since Horovitz, like Alexander Goehr (b.1932), is an émigré of a younger generation, and matured artistically not in pre-war Europe but in post-war Britain and France. Commissioned for the 60th Birthday of the Viennese art historian Sir Ernst Gombrich by his publisher, the Phaidon Press, founded in Vienna by the composer's father, Bela

Horovitz (1898–1955), it was premiered on 1 June 1969 by the Amadeus Quartet, three of them also Viennese émigrés.

In a programme note to the published score, Horovitz describes how the emotional content of his quartet was deeply influenced by the coincidence of the Viennese origin of composer, dedicatee, and three of the performers:

> We made England our home when Nazi jackboots strode the streets of Vienna, and the *Gemütlichkeit* on the surface cracked overnight from the pressure of the festering growth below. I was eleven then, and not until now had this experience consciously influenced my music.[21]

The advantage of the thirty year temporal perspective for Horovitz is that he can appreciate the positive elements of the lost world of his childhood: 'The vision of the Amadeus Quartet playing in this Gallery, for Ernst Gombrich's birthday, has now made me realise how much of what was good in Vienna has survived to flourish here and to benefit the whole world of art and culture.'[22]

'What was good in Vienna' is musically evoked in the main theme, derived (as in the Goldschmidt and Shostakovich quartets) from the musical initials of Gombrich's name, E–G. Horovitz inverts the interval and in adding characteristically Viennese appoggiaturas, the world of Mahler and Strauss seems not too far away (Example 8).

The 'Gombrich theme' generates the entire musical material, particularly influencing the bitonal harmony which contributes both to the conflict and resolution of the single movement design. Though everything is derived from this motto, there are two main thematic statements, with the first lyrical theme's accompaniment figure becoming a faster rhythmic motif that soon asserts itself as an opposition to the first theme. It becomes increasingly dissonant, intended to evoke the 'decadent chromaticism' of music in pre-war Vienna, and sets up a stark conflict, which is worked through in the main development section of the work, before a recapitulatory epilogue resolves tension and leads to a peaceful tonal stability in E major.

Memories of wartime are introduced specifically through two quotations, a Viennese popular song and the Nazi march. The song in Viennese dialect is *Mei Muatterl war a Weanerin* ('My mum was a Viennese'), the melody composed in 1908 by the prolific songsmith Ludwig Gruber (1874–1964). Remarkably, the composer only became aware of the tune after it had appeared logically out of the material, thus the compositional process itself sparked an awakening of childhood memory. As shown in Example 9, its lilting waltz theme is very Viennese in its appoggiaturas and contour, and when it first appears, it is as if it were already implied in the Gombrich theme.

---

21 Joseph Horovitz, 'Programme Note to String Quartet no.5', (London: Novello, 1969).

22 Horovitz, 'Programme Note'.

Example 8 – Joseph Horovitz, String Quartet no. 5 (Opening bars with the E-G Initial Motif) ©1969, Novello & Company Limited. Reproduced by kind permission of the publishers.

String Quartet 5 (Opening)

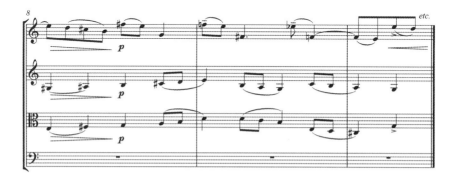

Example 9 – The theme of the Viennese song in Horovitz's Quartet no. 5 ©1969, Novello & Company Limited. Reproduced by kind permission of the publishers.

"Mei Muaterl War A Wearnarin"

The first deliberate quotation of the theme, at Figure 39 of the score, suggests a memory: it appears first in viola, then shared with violins and cello and doubled; the chromatic harmony adds to the sense of being half-remembered; then the tune emerges boldly into the foreground, the violin marked 'abandonato', accompanied with an aptly Viennese C major waltz texture. Yet as soon as the memory has become clear, it vanishes, a distorted echo by the cello marked 'grotesco' acting like a cinematic 'dissolve' (Example 10).

Example 10 – Joseph Horovitz, String Quartet no. 5, from 6 bars before Rehearsal Mark 32; Quotation of the Viennese popular song ©1969, Novello & Company Limited. Reproduced by kind permission of the publishers.

The ensuing texture is soon interrupted brutally by the return of the aggressive chromatic texture, with a sinister appearance of the Nazi *Horst Wessel Lied*, parodied through bitonal harmonies, in what the composer has called a 'grimace' (Example 11). The intrusion interrupts the peaceful Viennese song, just as the composer's Viennese life was brutally interrupted by the Nazis.

Example 11 – Joseph Horovitz, String Quartet no. 5, Rehearsal Mark 39 (allusion to the 'Horst Wessel' Lied) ©1969, Novello & Company Limited. Reproduced by kind permission of the publishers.

Horovitz's Fifth String Quartet stands apart from his main output of works which are coloured by his unique neo-classical jazz synthesis, yet it occupies a special place in that oeuvre: in 1972 the *Musical Times* critic Ernest Bradbury admired it as 'a work of its time, and who knows—also of the future'.[23] Its relevance for the future is shown by one of the younger Austrian composers, Hannes Raffaseder, who uses a theme from Horovitz's quartet in his own 2nd Quartet composed in 2001.[24] The Horovitz was recently released on CD by the young Carducci Quartet, one of several works for which the composer was awarded the 2008 Cobbett Prize for Chamber Music by the Worshipful Company of Musicians.[25]

CONCLUSION

To what extent do such intimate chamber works by Horovitz and Goldschmidt, and all the works discussed so far, represent as clearly defined a genre as the third category outlined at the start of this chapter, that of public commemorative pieces? In his liner notes to the 'Continental Britons' CD of Tauský's *Coventry,* Michael Haas asks the pertinent question as to why that piece is so little known in relation to the more popular *War Requiem* by Britten.[26] Clearly Tauský complements Britten, his personal elegy for the destruction of Coventry Cathedral balanced by the more public pacifist commemoration of the Cathedral's reconsecration in 1962.

One might speculate that public works rely less on personal experience: it is certainly worth noting that none of the British-Jewish composers of public wartime commemoration works are themselves émigrés, yet many are closely connected with émigrés. For instance, Benjamin Frankel composed his 1951 Violin Concerto, dedicated 'in memory of the 6 million' for the violinist Max Rostal, an émigré closely associated with émigré composers. Wilfred Josephs, whose 1963 *Requiem* is a setting of the Hebrew 'Kaddish', was a pupil of Max Deutsch in Paris, while Ronald Senator, whose *Holocaust Requiem* was premiered in Canterbury Cathedral in 1985, was a pupil of Egon Wellesz. It seems that émigré composers on the whole seem to have steered clear of such public commemorative works. One exception is Joseph Horovitz's *Ad Astra*, a 1990 RAF commission for the 50th Anniversary of the Battle of Britain. This, however, reflects his British rather than Austrian experience, his memory of the Blitz in London as a teenager. The work has clear echoes of Walton and Finzi, as at the dramatic climax, when a solo trumpet etches out a morse-code SOS rhythm, and clarinets swirl in ascending harmonies like a fighter-pilot spiralling towards the stars.

---

23   Ernest Bradbury, 'Joseph Horovitz: A Survey', *The Musical Times* (April 1970), 383–85.

24   For further details regarding Raffaseder's 2nd Quartet 'What Gap?', see
      http://www.raffaseder.com/werke/what_gap.html.

25   The 5th Quartet is recorded on Carducci Classics CSQ6482.

26   Michael Haas, 'Programme notes to Tauský's *Coventry*', *Continental Britons,* Nimbus NI5730–1.

Horovitz's celebration of Britishness in *Ad Astra* emphasises something about émigré composers as a whole: despite ex post facto honours and commissions from their native countries, as in the case of Goldschmidt, Reizenstein and Horovitz, they do not consider themselves as 'exiled' in the sense that they have not expressed a desire to return to the country of their birth. Rather, their music documents a process of adaptation and acculturation shared by tens of thousands of Jewish refugees from Nazism who came to Britain in the 1930s, and who absorbed the customs and aspirations of their host country whilst enriching it with their continental heritage.

If the autobiographical works under discussion represent merely a small piece in larger jigsaw of émigré music as a whole, it is nevertheless a significant piece. Precisely because of their intimate and personal nature, they may be considered as a particularly potent type of musical testimony to the past, as pertinent as large-scale musical commemorations, yet evoking different and sometimes complex aesthetic identities and attitudes. Above all, they represent works of musical memory whose intrinsic aesthetic qualities are enriched with unique historical significance.

Florian Scheding

'Problematic Tendencies'

Émigré Composers in London, 1933–1945

Wenn ich an London denke in der Nacht, dann bin ich um den Schlaf gebracht.
(Kurt Weill in a letter to Lotte Lenya, 17 July 1935)[1]

Today, our society is anything but stable, and a serious composer often feels that his music is not needed, that his aims in composing run contrary to the wishes of society. So he has the choice either of continuing to express what he wants to express with the danger of isolating himself more and more and ending in a vacuum—or of turning to the composition of music for his living, in which case the writing of serious music often becomes a hobby—a very unhealthy state of affairs. What the composer needs is […] to have a purpose to write for, to know that this work is wanted. (Mátyás Seiber, 1944)[2]

INTRODUCTION: ÉMIGRÉ VOICES

Any collection of essays, which claims to investigate the impact of Nazism on music and musical development, must consider music that remained outside the direct sphere of influence of the Nazis. Undoubtedly one of the most obvious and tangible ways in which the Nazis affected musical life outside Nazi Germany is through those musicians who they threatened and forced to leave Germany, Austria, and the Nazi-occupied territories. Migration of musicians between 1933 and 1945 was sizeable, and included a number of prominent composers that were at the forefront of musical developments of their time. Arriving in places virtually everywhere in the world as refugees, these musicians affected the musical lives of their adopted countries, some more so than others. At the same time, the musical circumstances and

---

1 Quoted in Stephen Hinton, 'Hindemith and Weill: Cases of "Inner" and "Other" Direction', in *Driven Into Paradise: The Musical Migration from Nazi Germany to the United States*, ed. Reinhold Brinkmann and Christoph Wolff (Berkeley: University of California Press, 1999), 267.
2 Mátyás Seiber, 'Mozart and Light Music', *The Listener* 31:805 (1944), 673.

cultural lives they migrated to influenced them, to varying degrees. Two conclusions emerge from this. Firstly, Nazism impacted upon the musical lives of countries such as the USA or Britain in an indirect way, by causing musicians to migrate there. Secondly, these migrations led to varying degrees of musical and cultural exchange between the host countries and the immigrants. This multi-directionality makes any attempt to generalise the effects of migration and displacement upon musical and cultural landscapes extremely difficult. It creates a complexity in which there are at least as many stories and as many interpretations as there are individuals concerned.

Of the 400 musicians from Austria and Germany that came to Britain during the Hitler years (a figure estimated by Erik Levi and endorsed by Jutta Raab Hansen[3]), I have chosen to focus on the activities of several refugee composers who came to London in the years following 1933. While mentioning other musicians when appropriate, I concentrate on those composers who had been reasonably successful prior to their migrations and who had composed serious music, however defined, before their displacements. Since very nearly all of the émigré composers who sought refuge in Britain first moved to London, it is probably fair to say that their participation in musical life in the British capital, which forms the basis for this chapter, can be considered more or less representative for their musical involvement in the country as a whole.

It can be extremely tempting for musicologists to analyse any given work by any given émigré composer in such a way as to detect in it unequivocal evidence of exile and displacement, particularly so since the stories of the émigrés are often colourful and tragic. Thus when assuming that a composer is desperate, or sad, we expect to find despair, or sadness, in their compositions. If, on the other hand, their music sounds cheerful, or happy, we solve this conundrum by suggesting that the work reflects defiance or irony. In fact, it is as possible to read displacement into every single work composed by every single émigré as it would be to deny its existence or relevance.

I refrain from participating in such a fallacy in this chapter, and do not offer any in-depth analyses of any of the émigrés' compositions. Instead, I investigate three basic questions, which, I believe, can be much more revealing. Firstly, how were the voices and works of the immigrant composers heard? It seems obvious that only voices that are heard can fully participate in a dialogue. The works of immigrant composers that were not performed, for

---

3   Erik Levi, 'The German Jewish contribution to musical life in Britain', in *Second Chance: Two Centuries of German–speaking Jews in the United Kingdom,* ed. Werner Mosse, Julius Carlebach, Gerhard Hirschfeld, Aubrey Newman, Arnold Paucker and Peter Pulzer (Tübingen: Mohr, 1991), 279; Jutta Raab Hansen, *NS-verfolgte Musiker in England. Spuren deutscher und österreichischer Flüchtlinge in der britischen Musikkultur* (Hamburg: von Bockel, 1996), 19.

example, can hardly have made an impact upon British musical life, however much or little they speak of migration or exile. Secondly, which institutions did the émigrés participate in or were admitted to, and in which capacities? The scale of institutional involvement and the sheer quantity of performances of their music can surely tell us something about the extent to which the immigrants managed to integrate into musical life in London. Thirdly, what factors contributed towards the relative silence of the avant-garde? As I will suggest in this chapter, a common feature of the work catalogues of numerous émigré composers is that they turned to lighter musical idioms after their migrations to England. Several pertinent musical institutions, too, displayed little support for the musical avant-garde, including those erected by the émigrés themselves.

THE MUSIC AND LIFE CONFERENCE, 1938

The occasion at which several prominent émigré composers made one of their first public appearances in Britain was a two-day conference, 'Music and Life', in May 1938. It was held in London's Queen's Hall, which was later destroyed in the blitz, in the course of the festival of the International Society for Contemporary Music (ISCM). The event was organised by the British Section of the ISCM, the London Contemporary Music Centre (LCMC), and aimed to discuss 'the problems of contemporary music,' as the programme leaflet states.[4] It is worth noting how the conference organisers allocated the panels with regards to the émigrés. With the exception of Ernst Hermann Meyer, head of the music section of the Free German League of Culture who presented a memorandum on contemporary musical research, all non-British speakers were put into the same session, the last of the conference's opening day on 28 May. Hanns Eisler spoke on the Twelve Note System, Franz Reizenstein lectured on Hindemith's New Theory, Mordecai Sandberg gave a paper on the Micro-tonal System, Alois Hába spoke on Non-thematic Composition, and Mátyás Seiber contributed a talk on Swing. Ironically, the session was entitled 'Problematic Tendencies in Contemporary Music.'

As the titles of their papers show, each of the contributors talked about a musical style or technique of which they could reasonably claim special expertise. Furthermore, all but one of them, Alois Hába, who was to endure the war in Prague, sought to build a new life in a country that was foreign to them. Like most other refugees, the approximately seventy composers that came to Britain between 1933 and 1945 were eager to find jobs. The émigré composers' appearances at the conference as well as their choices of topics must therefore be understood as self-promotions of their abilities. Yet, reception in the national press of the émigrés' partici-

---

4   I have consulted a programme leaflet held by the British Library (shelfmark X.800/33521).

pation was practically non-existent. Erik Chisholm, the sole British member of the session, was the panel's only representative mentioned in *The Times*, for example, even though the reviewer complained that Chisholm's paper on Folk Song in Contemporary Music 'managed to go round all the world but never mention English folk song.'[5] *The Musical Times* mentioned the émigrés, but ridiculed their contributions as implicitly pretentious, incompetent, and unintelligible—with the exception of Mátyás Seiber who, of course, did not lecture on an avant-garde topic:

> One session of the Congress was devoted to 'Problematic Tendencies (what a phrase!) in Contemporary Music.' Here were expounded the Twelve-Tone System; Hindemith's New Theory; the Micro-Tonal System (Dr. Sandberg, the expounder, played a harmonium whose keyboard must have measured four or five feet, and whose compass was precisely a fourth!); Non-Thematic Composition (Mr. Alois Haba's pet—its intention, so we were told, is to reflect the spirit of the new brotherhood of mankind), and so on. At the very end of this most exhausting session came Mr. Seiber on 'Jazz Music,' and it was refreshing to listen to someone who not only understood his subject thoroughly but was able to express himself as intelligibly and unpretentiously. That his subject had not the slightest relevance as a 'problematic tendency' was frankly admitted by Mr. Seiber: this in itself was a relief.[6]

These details are significant on two levels. Firstly, as the British section of the ISCM, the LCMC was an institution interested in the promotion of contemporary music and comparatively open to avant-garde styles and international collaboration. Yet, headlining the émigrés' topics as 'problematic tendencies' inevitably implies scepticism about the techniques and styles they were trying to advocate and, hence, reservations about the émigrés themselves. Secondly, the decision to assign all foreigners to the same conference session was tantamount to isolating them. The review in *The Times* confirms this reading. The exclusion of the immigrants shows that one of Britain's largest newspapers did not consider their appearances or aesthetic convictions worth mentioning. Moreover, the somewhat absurd complaint that English folk music was not covered in a conference dedicated to contemporary art music reveals nationalist and anti-foreign undertones.

Press coverage of the ISCM festival that followed a few weeks after the Music and Life conference, in June 1938, was likewise slim, even though critical response was mostly positive. Alan Frank, in *The Musical Times*, lauded the programme and quality of performances

5   'Music and Life Congress: Public Attitude to Modernism', *The Times*, 30 May 1938, 21.
6   Alan Frank, 'Music and Life, 1938', *Musical Times* 79 (1938), 461. The parentheses are in the original.

and found that the festival compared favourably with the previous one in Paris.[7] The correspondent of *The Times* shared this viewpoint, and, like Frank, considered a performance of Webern's *Das Augenlicht* a highlight—one of the few cases, incidentally, where a musical work that was not performed under the Nazis was forced into exile while its composer stayed behind. *The Manchester Guardian* also praised Webern's work 'for its thought, precision and clarity of style,' but singled it out as the exception to the modernist rule: 'One after another [...] composers exhibited poverty of thought, clumsiness of technique, deformity of style, and everything else that we commonly typify as amateurish. [...] The music was intelligible to the point of superficiality, and its prevailing mark was that very concealment of ordinariness under the cloak of vehemence of which we have in the past acquitted the leaders of the movement.'[8] While *The Manchester Guardian* thus assigned little aesthetic value to the avantgarde in general, *The Times* described progressive music as essentially alien and foreign in no uncertain terms, with London portrayed as 'the ancient City which they have come from all quarters of Europe to conquer with their modernity.'[9] Following the festival, in December 1938, the honorary secretary of the LCMC, E. Hart, felt compelled to assure the public in a letter to the *Musical Times* that the British submission of works to the next ISCM festival, held in 1939 in Warsaw and Krakow, would be almost free of foreign influences: 'Of the few works submitted by foreign composers living in this country, who have no section, only one work was chosen: Three pieces for oboe and piano by Franz Reizenstein.'[10]

EMPLOYMENT BANS

Few émigrés in 1933 predicted the eruption of the Second World War six years later; fewer still the Holocaust. Likewise, as Adorno admitted, 'the outbreak of the Third Reich took my political judgement by surprise.'[11] Yet in 1934, one year after the initial shock wave of German-Jewish emigration following Hitler's rise to power, it briefly looked as though the Nazi government might adopt a more 'legal' course, and several thousand Jews even returned to Germany.[12] Accordingly, refugee numbers went down between 1934 and 1937. Indeed, it was

7   Alan Frank, 'The ISCM London Festival', *Musical Times* 79 (1938), 537–38.
8   William McNaught, 'Modern Music: Festival at Queen's Hall', *The Manchester Guardian*, 18 June 1938, 19.
9   'Modern Music: Festival at Queen's Hall', *The Times*, 18 June 1938, 12.
10   E. Hart, 'I.S.C.M. Festival', *Musical Times* 79 (1938), 931.
11   Theodor W. Adorno, *Minima Moralia. Reflexionen aus dem beschädigten Leben* (Frankfurt am Main: Suhrkamp, 1951), 366
12   Marion Berghahn, *German–Jewish Refugees in England* (London and Basingstoke: Macmillan, 1984), 72.

a widespread hope amongst émigrés that Hitler's regime was going to be over sooner rather than later. Many British intellectuals shared such beliefs. Only weeks after the German Interior Minister, Wilhelm Frick, had announced the establishment of concentration camps on 8 March 1933, the British composer, Ethel Smyth, who had studied in Leipzig in 1877, expressed her conviction that Germany's 'lapse from civilization shown by the expulsion from Germany of Jewish musicians [...] is merely a passing phase of national madness [...] and one of which, ere long, all Germans will be ashamed.'[13] In the first years of the Nazi regime, many musicians and composers decided to keep a low profile and wait until the spook was over. Even those who had been dismissed from their academic and teaching posts due to the *Gesetz zur Wiederherstellung des Berufsbeamtentums* (Law for the Restitution of the Professional Civil Service), promulgated on 7 April 1933, that banned all 'non-Aryans' from official positions, were at first reluctant to leave Germany. Up until 1938, therefore, only a handful of refugees decided to move to Britain.

In March 1938, however, two months before the 'Music and Life' conference, Nazi Germany had annexed Austria, and the émigrés' hopes that the Third Reich would be short-lived had been eradicated. As the *Anschluß* created a new wave of refugees from Austria, refugee numbers skyrocketed and soon exceeded most estimates. According to Paul Tabori, 1939 saw over 80,000 exiles in Britain, 63,000 of them new arrivals.[14] Amidst this refugee crisis, the British government hoped that the migrants would not stay, and, in the meantime, there had to be assurances that they would not become a drain on public resources.[15] While the French Interior Minister Camille Chautemps encouraged his countrymen 'to give German refugees the same hospitality formerly offered in analogous circumstances to Italian, Spanish and Russian citizens,' the British administration was more cautious in its declaration. 'We do not [...] admit that there is a "right of asylum" but when we have to decide whether a particular political refugee is to be given admission to this country, we have to base our decision [...] on whether it is in the public interest that he be admitted.'[16]

---

13   Ethel Smyth, 'Germany To–Day', *The Times*, 27 April 1933, 8.

14   Paul Tabori, *The Anatomy of Exile* (London: Harrap, 1972), 235.

15   For an overview of the government's response to the refugee crisis see Colin Holmes, 'British Government Policy towards Wartime Refugees', in *Europe in Exile: European Exile Communities in Britain, 1940–1945*, ed. Martin Conway and José Gotovitch (New York and Oxford: Berghahn Books, 2001), 11–34.

16   Both statements are quoted in Stephanie Barron and Sabine Eckmann (ed.), *Exiles and Émigrés: The Flight of European Artists from Hitler.* Exh. cat. (Los Angeles: Los Angeles County Museum of Art; New York: Harry N. Abrams, 1997), 387.

In the early days of the Third Reich, reports that eminent artists and scientists were being dismissed for being Jewish were widely condemned in the British press and many academics invited their German-Jewish colleagues to come to Britain. For example, in 1933, a group of twenty prominent British scientists urged the government 'to make it clear that those whose intellects are to be accounted as among the finest in Germany to-day and who, simply because they happen to be Jews, are being dismissed from their posts, would find here safe refuge and opportunities for continued scientific activity.'[17] Yet, the situation was different for musicians. The economic crisis of the 1920s and the advent of the talkie in British cinemas had forced many instrumentalists out of their jobs. Foreign instrumentalists and singers, especially Austrians, Germans, and Italians, had excellent reputations in Britain, and fears now grew that the new arrivals, many of them well trained and with impressive CVs, would compete on the tight job market and take the few jobs there were for themselves. The Incorporated Society of Musicians (ISM) took up these fears and lobbied the government to ban foreign musicians from any form of musical employment. While a system was in place where the Home Office could provide exceptional work permits for refugees, these were extremely difficult to obtain, especially for lesser-known musicians. Except for a select few, Austrian and German émigrés in particular found it impossible to secure employment in British orchestras and ensembles.[18]

With the start of the war, it became even more difficult for the Austrians, Germans, and Italians amongst the émigré musicians to find jobs. As refugees, they were evidently not supporters of the fascist regimes in their homelands. Even so, absurdly, they were classified as 'enemy aliens' and thus not eligible to work, whether paid or unpaid. For the composers, the situation was particularly bad. They were not allowed to give lessons, nor was it legal for British institutions such as conservatories or universities to employ them. Likewise, 'enemy aliens' could not accept commissions for new compositions or have their works performed for a fee. Even without these rules in place, it is unlikely that an establishment such as the Royal College of Music, for example, would have offered a permanent teaching post to a foreigner, with George Dyson doubling as the college's director and the head of the ISM. Famous instrumentalists including Artur Schnabel and Emanuel Feuermann, as well as celebrated ensembles such as the Busch Quartet became so frustrated that they moved on to the USA and elsewhere. Unable to find paid work as musicians, many émigrés who remained in Britain took up menial labour. Leopold Spinner, a pupil of Paul Pisk and Anton Webern, for instance, worked as a

---

17 A.B. Appleton, Joseph Barcroft, F. W. Rogers Brambell, H. M. Carleton, F. A. E. Crew, W. A. Fell, Alan W. Greenwood, John Hammond, Julian S. Huxley, D. Keilin, F. H. A. Marshall, WM. C. Miller, Geo. H. F. Nuttall, Michael Pease, F. R. Petherbridge, Cresswell Shearer, Arthur Walton, J. T. Wilson, H. E. Woodman, and John R. Barker, 'Jews in Germany', *The Times*, 26 April 1933, 12.

18 Levi, 291.

lathe operator in a locomotive factory to make ends meet, and Hindemith pupil Franz Reizenstein spent the war as a railway clerk. Eventually, on 27 April 1938, the Foreign Office declared 'minor musicians and commercial artists of all kinds [...] as *prima facie* unsuitable'[19] for entry and, with Britain entering the war on 3 September 1939, the doors were closed to practically all refugees, with only small numbers managing to enter the country until the end of the war.

THE BBC AND THE BAN ON ALIEN COMPOSERS

In this environment the BBC was an exception and became a haven for many refugee musicians.[20] Mosco Carner, Berthold Goldschmidt, Hans Keller, Franz Reizenstein, Mátyás Seiber, and Leo Wurmser, for example, belonged to a group of émigrés that significantly influenced the BBC's programming and programmes during the war. Highly regarded as music experts, these émigrés took on casual jobs as session musicians and rehearsal conductors, authoring some programmes and were occasionally commissioned to make arrangements of certain pieces. Some, like Seiber, could be heard on air introducing musical programmes. The refugees' influence was maybe greatest in the Overseas Services, especially in the European programmes, propaganda stations that were, after all, aimed at the countries they had come from. Berthold Goldschmidt, for example, who struggled to find any employment at all after his migration in 1935, became the musical director of the German section in 1944.

Given the BBC's willingness to employ refugee musicians in spite of the administrative difficulties of having to obtain work permits every time any of them was recruited for any job, the composers amongst the émigrés hoped that their music might also be broadcast. Their works were practically non-existent in London's concert circuit, and it was extremely difficult for any foreigner to organise performances. The radio could provide the platform the émigré composers needed to become better known to a wider public and, hence, improve their chances of finding work and facilitate their integration.

The corporation's role was ambiguous, however. If the émigrés' abilities as musicologists, musicians, and conductors were well respected by the BBC, their status as composers was

---

19   Circular of the Foreign Office, 27. April 1938, PRO FO 372/3284/9, quoted in Bernard Wasserstein, 'Britische Regierungen und die deutsche Emigration von 1933–1945', in *Exil in Großbritannien: Zur Emigration aus dem Nationalsozialistischen Deutschland.*, ed. Gerhard Hirschfeld (Stuttgart: Klett-Cotta, 1983), 54.

20   Much material for this section stems from the BBC Written Archives Centre (WAC) in Reading Caversham, Berkshire, amongst them a file on Mátyás Seiber (RConti Matyas Seiber—Composer [1941–1962]), and a file on émigré composers generally (Rconti 27/3/5—Music General—Alien Composers—File 5: 1945).

significantly less so. The ban on alien composers elucidates particularly well the climate that migrant musicians experienced even in a principally friendly institution. In an open letter of 1940, for example, signatories Frederic Austin, Granville Bantock, Thomas Dunhill, Theodore Holland, John Ireland, Sidney Jones, Constant Lambert, Martin Shaw, Ethel Smyth, and Ralph Vaughan Williams pressurised the BBC to limit broadcast times of music by foreign composers. They complained, 'out of every twenty-two hours of serious music provided today eighteen hours are given over to the foreigner! It is inconceivable that any fair-minded listener will consider this to be an adequate recognition of native music.'[21] In July 1940, the BBC internally and confidentially blacklisted 73 Austrian-born and 239 German-born composers. The list was soon revised and numbers increased to 117 Austrians and 248 Germans. Prominent names included dead composers, such as Alban Berg, Gustav Mahler, and Hugo Wolf, none of whom could be described as precursors of the Nazis by any stretch of the imagination. A second group consisted of living composers who had not emigrated, such as Anton Webern and Karl Amadeus Hartmann. Only a handful of them had clear Nazi-affiliations, such as Franz Lehár, a favourite artist of Hitler's. Unfortunately, however, a further substantial group of names on the list was made up of émigré composers like Kurt Weill, Ernst Toch, Erich Wolfgang Korngold, Arnold Schoenberg, Felix Weingartner, Alexander Zemlinsky, Hugo Kauder, Egon Wellesz, Hanns Eisler, Paul Hindemith, Max Kowalski, Robert Müller-Hartmann, and Kurt Schröder. All in all, however, approximately a quarter of all banned composers were Nazi-refugees. Absurdly, some of them were even employed by the corporation, such as Berthold Goldschmidt.[22]

The BBC displayed a general reluctance to broadcast music composed by émigrés on the Home Service, even by those not blacklisted, and including composers actually working for the corporation. Music by Walter Goehr, Ernst Hermann Meyer, Franz Reizenstein, Arthur Willner, and Leo Wurmser, for example, was rejected for broadcast.[23] One particularly absurd case is that of Mátyás Seiber. Born Hungarian in Habsburg Budapest in 1905, he was not considered Austrian or German, and his name was not added to the list of banned alien composers. Even though Seiber only became a British citizen after the war, his 2nd String Quartet had been performed at the 1941 ISCM festival in New York as Britain's entry, co-representing the United Kingdom together with Benjamin Britten's *Les Illuminations*. As it was Britain's contribution, Seiber expected the BBC to broadcast the quartet. Yet, the BBC panel responsible for selecting

21 Frederic Austin et al, 'The BBC and British Composers', *The Author* 51:1 (1940), 10. See also Lewis Foreman, *From Parry to Britten: British Music in Letters 1900–1945* (Portland: Amadeus, 1987), 239.
22 See Raab Hansen, 197.
23 See ibid., 174–76.

music for broadcasts rejected the work.[24] In June 1943, the panel also rejected Seiber's Serenade for wind sextet for broadcast on the Home Service. Ironically, the European Service had included the same work in a programme just three months earlier, on 10 March. This case not only shows inconsistencies between the BBC's individual sections. It also exemplifies that economic considerations—recording new works may have been too expensive with the war imposing financial constraints—were not at the core of the rejection. Already recorded for the European Service, the Serenade could have been reused cost-effectively for the Home Service.

It is difficult to ascertain definite numbers of broadcasts of chamber music. Records were not kept systematically and programmes announced in the *Radio Times* often changed at the last minute. Yet, it seems certain that pieces such as Mátyás Seiber's Divertimento for clarinet and string quartet, which was broadcast on the Home Service on 24 September 1941, represent an exception. Files pertaining to orchestral music do exist, however. They reveal that, between 1933 and the end of 1945, a mere six orchestral compositions by émigré composers were accepted for broadcast. Two of them are orchestrations or arrangements of other works, while the other four can be categorised as light music: Ernst Toch's *Bunte Suite* (broadcast 8 January 1934; Toch migrated to the USA in the same year), Fritz Hart's *Fantasy: Cold Blows the Wind* (25 September 1936), Karol Rathaus's *Serenade* (30 October 1936) and suite *The Lion in Love* (13 May 1938), Hans Gál's orchestration of Schubert's *Divertissement* (8 November 1939), and Mátyás Seiber's arrangement of *Four Greek Songs* for soprano and string orchestra (1 February 1945).[25] Besides revealing the limited number of broadcasts of works by refugee composers, this list shows that, at the height of the war, no émigré compositions could be heard on the Home Service. Most pre-date 1939, and Gál's and Seiber's orchestrations skim the outer edges of the war. More significantly, the BBC did not broadcast one single serious work composed by a refugee on the Home Service during the Nazi regime.

INTERNMENT OF 'ENEMY ALIENS'

If their compositions were not broadcast or performed, at least the émigrés were free. On 24 October 1939, Parliamentary Under-Secretary of State for War, Viscount Cobham, declared in the House of Lords that the internment of foreigners 'is not likely to happen, as there are

---

24   See BBC Written Archives WAC Rcont1 Matyas Seiber—Composer [1941–1962]. The Second Quartet eventually received its British premiere eight years later, on 5 March 1949 in a London concert of the Amadeus Quartet that was organised by the LCMC.

25   The BBC also broadcast Wellesz's Piano Concerto in 1936, but strictly speaking this was two years before the composer had settled in England.

far fewer enemy aliens, especially of military age, in this country now than there were at the commencement of the last war, in spite of all the refugees. The figure I have been given as likely to be interned as enemy aliens is somewhere between 1,000 and 1,500, as against a figure of over 29,000 during the last war.'[26] By March 1940, one hundred and twenty tribunals had assessed the cases of 73,800 refugees and classified 64,200 of them as completely harmless, 55,460 of them explicitly described as 'refugees from Nazi oppression.'[27] Internment was advised in a mere six hundred cases, less than one per cent of the total of refugees.

Yet this was about to change. After the fall of France in June 1940, when Britain suddenly found itself as one of only a few European countries not invaded by the Wehrmacht, all foreigners, especially Austrians, Germans, and Italians, whether fascist or anti-fascist, became suspect. In summer 1940, while the BBC was blacklisting Austrian, German, and Italian composers, Churchill decided to 'collar the lot' and the government swiftly interned Austrians, Germans and Italians, including those classified as harmless refugees. This led to the absurd situation that real Nazi sympathisers, a few spies and even war criminals were interned in the same camps as Jewish émigrés. Apart from a few exceptions, historians have treated the internment of 'enemy aliens' by the British government as a mere footnote to the main narrative of Britain at war.[28] Yet Colin Holmes estimates that '22,000 Germans and Austrians finished up in camps, as did 4,300 Italians'[29] and Peter and Leni Gillman quote a total number of 27,200,[30] a figure eighteen times the maximum Cobham had declared in parliament in October 1939 and all but identical to the number of internees during World War One. Amongst the interned were the composers Franz Reizenstein and Karl Rankl, for example, the latter a pupil of Schoenberg and Webern, who had immigrated to Britain in 1939 and now found himself imprisoned amongst 15,000 other 'enemy aliens' on one of the three internment camps on the Isle of Man. Norbert Brainin, Siegmund Nissel, and Peter Schidlof, three quarters of the later Amadeus Quartet, met as internees. Soon, even more drastic measures were put into place. Thousands were forcibly deported to Canada and Australia, an operation during which about 175 German and almost 500 Italian refugees lost their lives when, on 2 July 1940, the Arandora Star on her way to Canada was bombarded and sunk by German U-boats.[31] The pianist and

---

26   Peter and Leni Gillman, *"Collar the Lot!" How Britain Internet and Expelled its Wartime Refugees* (London: Quartet Books, 1980), 8.

27   Gillman, 46.

28   The notable exceptions to this are the already cited book by Gillman, François Lafitte, *The Internment of Aliens* (London: Libris, 1988), and Richard Dove (ed.), *"Totally un–English"? Britain's Internment of "Enemy Aliens" in Two World Wars* (Amsterdam and New York: Rodopi, 2005).

29   Holmes, 20

30   Gillman, 173.

31   Mark Donnelly, *Britain in the Second World War* (New York: Routledge, 1999), 48.

musicologist, Peter Stadlen, for instance, was first interned in the camp in the Huyton district of Liverpool and then deported to Australia before he returned one and a half years later after Ralph Vaughan Williams had interceded on his behalf.

A few of the musicians amongst the interned have reported about their experiences. Hans Gál, for example, wrote a graphic account of his internment on the Isle of Man in his auto-biographic *Musik hinter Stacheldraht*.[32] In 1990, Peter Stadlen published an article recalling his internment and subsequent deportation. In contrast to Gál's account, Stadlen's casual and almost apologetic writing seems to be marked by self-censorship. While Stadlen highlights the experiences of other émigré musicians, he downplays his own hardship and paradoxically even agrees with his own internment, 'because above all else, I wanted Hitler to lose the war, and, after all, eventual spies might very possibly have posed as refugees.'[33] Stadlen's gratefulness towards Britain, the country that, after all, had saved his life, may explain this reluctance to condemn the political actions of his host's former government.

OPPORTUNITIES IN MORLEY COLLEGE AND THE ROYAL GALLERY CONCERTS

Another particular case that must be considered in this context is Morley College, and since it is such a striking exception in the contemporaneous environment, a brief sketch of Morley's wartime situation seems worthwhile. Founded in 1889 as an institution providing evening classes for working adults, Morley College had acquired some reputation for its music department, particularly with Gustav Holst's appointment as Director of Music from 1907 to 1924. After German bombs had destroyed the College's main building on 15 October 1940, student numbers dropped significantly, from 3,300 in 1939 to 2,000, which very nearly led to the college's extinction. The institution's current director of music, Arnold Foster, resigned, and Morley's orchestra, the South London Orchestra, disbanded. Amidst the crisis, the college's principal, Eva Hubback, appointed Michael Tippett as Music Director. It became his first task to rebuild the College's musical life. Despite the disappearance of the rehearsal accommodation, Tippett re-established the choir and various new instrumental ensembles were also founded, such as the Morley College String Players and the Morley College Orchestra. Due

---

32 Hans Gál, *Musik hinter Stacheldraht. Tagebuchblätter aus dem Sommer 1940* ed. Eva Fox-Gál (Bern: Lang, 2003). It should be noted that in the article on Hans Gál published in the *New Grove Dictionary of Music and Musicians*, neither this book nor the composer's internment as an enemy alien are mentioned.

33 Peter Stadlen, 'Österreichische Exilmusiker in England', in *Österreichische Musiker im Exil*, ed. Monica Wildauer (Kassel: Bärenreiter, 1990), 128.

to the blackout forced upon London during the blitz, numbers of concerts were reduced in the capital. At the same time, the austere war climate increased the need for cultural diversions. Tickets for the monthly concerts in Morley's small Holst Memorial Room therefore became increasingly sought after. Morley's several ensembles quickly acquired a considerable reputation and participated regularly in London's concert life as well as making recordings for the BBC—outside earnings that were a welcome support for the college's shaky finances.

In defiance of the ISM's pressure not to employ non-British citizens, Tippett invited numerous émigrés to fill vacant positions and join the music ensembles. As his biographer Ian Kemp puts it, 'Morley became strikingly cosmopolitan.'[34] Amongst the teaching staff were Walter Goehr, Mátyás Seiber, and Walter Bergmann, an expert in Baroque music and figured bass who taught recorder classes and conducted. Émigré musicians such as Norbert Brainin, Paul Blumenfeld, Peter Gellhorn, Maria Lidka, Siegmund Nissel, Suzanne Rozsa, Peter Schidlof, Jani Strasser, Ilse Wolf, and Leo Wurmser joined the college's orchestras or vocal ensembles or acted as soloists.

In addition to employing émigrés, Morley College concerts frequently included contemporary music, often programmed alongside pre-Classical works. In London's concert life that was dominated by Classical and Romantic music, such enterprising programming was an exception. Moreover, the concerts made no discernible distinction between contemporary British and foreign composers. Tippett tried out several of his new compositions in the Holst room, for example his Concerto for Double String Orchestra, Stravinsky's *Les Noces* was repeatedly performed in the College and *Dumbarton Oaks* received its British premiere there. Leo Wurmser's Clarinet Quintet was given, and Morley ensembles premiered Seiber's *Pastorale and Burlesque* for flute and string orchestra. The émigrés were well aware of Morley's exceptionality, an awareness that is maybe best summarised by Ilse Wolf: 'We all fled to Morley, even half-bombed-out, because it was a haven where we could feel happy.'[35]

The cosmopolitan atmosphere drew many prominent figures of contemporary British musical life to the College. Ensembles like the Amadeus Quartet, three of whose members played in the College's ensembles (Brainin, Nissel, and Schidlof), and composers such as Seiber first met Benjamin Britten and Peter Pears there, for example. The appointments of all these 'enemy aliens' did not go unnoticed, however. Tippett reports that Vaughan Williams sent a disapproving letter to Eva Hubback, 'but she stood firmly behind [Tippett] and the reputation of Morley's music grew apace.'[36]

Apart from exceptions such as Morley College, the émigré composers' involvement in London's musical circles was in most cases restricted to the odd lecture, arrangement duties,

34   Ian Kemp, *Michael Tippett: The Composer and his Music* (London: Eulenburg, 1984), 43.
35   Roger Lucas, 'Ilse Wolf: "a way of life"', *More* 1:2 (1975), 4.
36   Michael Tippett, *Those Twentieth Century Blues: An Autobiography* (London: Hutchinson, 1991), 115.

or the writing of programme notes.[37] Public performances of serious compositions can be traced only extremely rarely, even taking into account the circumstances of war that restricted London's concert life. One place where contemporary music by émigrés could very occasionally be heard was the National Gallery. With all concert halls closed due to the blackout during the blitz, the National Gallery Concerts were organised by Myra Hess, as a series of lunchtime concerts. They were continued throughout the war, until early 1946, in the main hall of the empty National Gallery in Trafalgar Square, the precious collection of paintings having been moved out to a quarry in Wales.[38]

Against the background of the labour restrictions, the National Gallery Concerts represented a relative haven for émigré musicians and, like the BBC and Morley College, must be seen as a clear exception. A friend of the Queen, Myra Hess was remarkably successful in securing them work permits, and, together with Adrian Boult and Ralph Vaughan Williams, formed the Musicians' Refugee Committee (MRC), a support network erected for that very purpose. The programme leaflets of the National Gallery concerts often feature émigré musicians, such as Maria Lidka, Ilona Kabos, and Louis Kentner. Yet, compared to the performers, the composers are underrepresented. Seiber's name, for example, occasionally appears on the National Gallery concert programmes. Nonetheless, his participation was almost entirely restricted to writing programme notes or giving introductory talks. Only five performances acknowledge Seiber as a composer. In two cases his name appeared as the arranger of folk songs for choir and once on 21 February 1941, where émigrés Louis Kentner and Ilona Kabos performed his transcription for two pianos of the *Popular Song* from Walton's *Façade*. Only two of Seiber's serious compositions were performed, both in the summer of 1943, the Serenade for Wind Sextet (LPO Wind Ensemble; 4 June) and the *Phantasy* for 'cello and piano (Edward Silvermann and Margaret Good; 19 July).

BRITISH ANTI-MODERNISM AND ÉMIGRÉ SNOBBISHNESS

For those Continental European émigré composers who had, in some way or another, associated themselves with the avant-garde, musical life in Britain was a complete shock. Despite the efforts of younger composers like William Walton and Benjamin Britten, Elgar's late-romantic pathos and the Celtic nationalism of Arnold Bax still largely epitomised British

---

37 Amongst other primary sources for London's concert life between 1933 and 1945, such as newspaper announcement and reviews, the most important source for the years following 1938 I have consulted is the substantial collection of programme leaflets compiled by Ernst Henschel, which is held by the British Library. Henschel arrived in London in 1938.

38 The collection made by Myra Hess of programmes, lists of performers, and works performed in the National Gallery Concerts is held by the British Library.

musical style at the time the waves of Nazi refugees became larger and rolled in more regularly in the mid- to late-1930s. Little had changed since London's Royal College of Music had refused Britten a grant to study with Berg in Vienna in the early 1930s. At the Music and Life Conference, for example, Vaughan Williams discredited the avant-garde as 'this wrong-note stuff', and Malcolm Sargent objected to new music 'expressing the "spirit of the contemporary age."'[39] For many émigrés, such attitudes constituted attacks. One year later, the Free German League of Culture, one of the largest émigré organizations, stated unequivocally: 'Today, nothing happens in a vacuum of "pure art" or "pure science."'[40] Compared to lighter music, the avant-garde was under particularly difficult circumstances, an attitude to which a plethora of contemporaneous articles and critiques in newspapers and periodicals testify. Amidst an atmosphere of anti-German hostility that bubbled away in British musical life from the First World War onwards, in 1934, one year after Hitler's takeover, Constant Lambert published his book *Music Ho!*, subtitled 'a study of music in decline,' a highly acclaimed and scathing attack on all musical things modernist. And Vaughan Williams' famous statement that the immigrants should refrain from constructing a 'little Europe' in Britain is tantamount to him urging foreign composers to abandon the avant-garde styles they brought with them from the Continent if they wished to integrate into British musical life.[41]

The anti-modernist stance is maybe best characterised by the assessment of the émigrés' legacy. Erik Levi, for example, argues that the greatest impact of the émigrés lay not in their avant-garde compositions but in their music for films.[42] Indeed, many composers turned to composing for films willy-nilly and for financial reasons, such as Walter Goehr, Hans May, Ernst Hermann Meyer, Mátyás Seiber, Mischa Spoliansky, and Josef Zmigrod. Some of them composed film and light music under aliases in the hope that their names as serious composers would not be tainted. Seiber often adopted the name Geo S. Mathis, while Zmigrod became Allan Gray. As for the BBC, the list of the banned 'alien' composers reveals a staggering number of avant-garde composers, practically all of whom were either Nazi refugees or dead. In fact, the war did not end the ban on 'alien' composers. An internal BBC note from 3 July 1945 announces revisions of the ban, but categorically states, 'it is not anticipated, however, that there will be a general release on works by German and Austrian composers.'[43] In addition, there existed a certain snobbishness amongst several émigré musicians who considered

39   Quoted in Frank, 461.
40   'Der FDKB: Was er kann, was er ist und was er will', *FDKB-Nachrichten*, 4 December 1939.
41   Ralph Vaughan Williams, 'Nationalism and Internationalism', *National Music and Other Essays.* 2nd ed. (Oxford and New York: Oxford University Press, 1987), 154–59.
42   Erik Levi,'Deutsche Musik und Musiker im englischer Exil 1933–1945', in *Musik in der Emigration 1933–1945: Verfolgung, Vertreibung, Rückwirkung*, ed. Horst Weber (Stuttgart: Metzler, 1994), 202–3.
43   BBC Written Archives: WAC Rcont1 27/3/5—Music General—Alien Composers—File 5: 1945.

the musical life of Britain provincial and inferior to that of Austria, Germany, and France. Brahms allegedly called Britain 'the land without music,' and even though it is doubtful that he ever did make such a statement, the attitude still resounded powerfully in the ears of many Continental European composers. The book by Oscar Schmitz, *Das Land ohne Musik: englische Gesellschaftsprobleme* [The Land without Music: Problems of English Society], published in 1914, would no doubt have been known to many of them.[44] The ideology of crass anti-modernism of British institutions such as the Royal College of Music, the employment bans imposed upon musicians and composers, and also the émigrés' own mind-set all contributed to the decision of many composers to leave Britain soon after their arrival. Most moved on to the USA, amongst them prominent figures such as Hanns Eisler, Erich Katz, Ernst Křenek, Karol Rathaus, and Ernst Toch. Like many of these, Kurt Weill had considered staying when he arrived in London in 1934. Yet, his opera *A Kingdom for a Cow* failed so dramatically on the London theatre scene in 1935 and was so heavily lambasted by the critics that he moved on to New York.[45] The same is true for progressive theorists like Adorno, who arrived as a university lecturer and was told by Oxford University that he had to do a doctorate there first if he wanted to be considered for a teaching post.[46] Some, most prominently Arnold Schoenberg, did not migrate to the United Kingdom at all, in spite of plans to do so—Britain's loss became America's gain.

Others, such as Hans Gál, Berthold Goldschmidt, Louis Kentner, Karl Rankl, Franz Reizenstein, Mátyás Seiber, Leopold Spinner, Peter Stadlen, and Egon Wellesz remained and eventually became naturalised British citizens. To my knowledge, only two of them managed to secure full-time posts at an academic institution in Britain in the years between 1933 and 1945. Arriving in England in 1938, Wellesz became a fellow of Lincoln College, Oxford, in 1939, and, after his internment on the Isle of Man, a university lecturer in 1943. Wellesz's academic affiliations may seem to imply that the pupil of Schoenberg and Adler and co-founder of the ISCM enjoyed great esteem in British musical circles. Yet, it was his scholarly expertise in Byzantine music rather than his compositions and insight into contemporary music that secured him the job. Indeed, after the war, in 1947, he was promoted as Reader in Byzantine Music. Hans Gál was appointed lecturer at Edinburgh University in 1945, but until relatively recently was chiefly remembered not for his compositions in a late-Romantic idiom but for

44   Oscar Schmitz's book was in fact translated into English by Hans Herzl under the title *The Land without Music* (London: Jarrolds, 1926).

45   Stephen Hinton, 'Großbritannien als Exilland: Der Fall Weill', in *Musik in der Emigration 1933–1945*, 213–27.

46   Evelyn Wilcock, 'Adorno in Oxford 1: Oxford University Musical Club', *Oxford Magazine* (Hilary Term) 1996, 11 and 'Adorno in Oxford 2: A Merton Circle', *Oxford Magazine* (Trinity Term) 1997, 10–12.

his scholarly writings on Viennese Classicism and the biographies of several Austro-German 19ᵗʰ-century figures such as Brahms, Wagner, and Schubert. Gál had achieved some considerable success prior to his migration, especially with his opera *Die heilige Ente*. In Britain, 'he remained active as a composer but never re-established his pre-war career and relatively little of his output is known,' as Conrad Wilson and Alexander R.C. Scott candidly write in the *New Grove*.[47]

FIRST CONCLUSION: THE PARALYSIS AND SILENCE OF AVANT-GARDE MUSIC

All this makes for overwhelmingly depressing reading. Arriving in Britain as highly trained and often highly acclaimed musicians, the émigrés could not work in their profession, the British public was disinterested in progressive music, and many of the refugees were imprisoned and deported. London's concert circuit and BBC programming reveal that there was practically no platform of any significance for avant-garde music in London's musical life. Exceptions like Morley College pale into insignificance when compared with the harshness of the BBC's policies regarding the migrants' compositions, for example. It is clear that the rejection of music that had in many cases been performed, published, and broadcast prior to their migrations had devastating effects on many composers. The loss of a cultural or societal context conducive to their music, together with the shock of exile, affected the creative output of most composers. For many, it resulted in a state of artistic paralysis and silence.

Prior to his migration, Berthold Goldschmidt had been decorated with the Mendelssohn State prize, his Piano Sonata op. 10 was heard at the 1929 ISCM festival, and his opera *Der gewaltige Hahnrei* received much critical acclaim before performances were cancelled due to the Nazi takeover. After his arrival in Britain in 1935, Goldschmidt's productivity declined drastically. When he restarted, after the war, he anonymously submitted his opera *Beatrice Cenci* for an opera competition organised by the Arts Council for the Festival of Britain. Alongside Goldschmidt's work, the jury shortlisted *Deidre of the Sorrows* by Austrian-born Karl Rankl and *A Tale of Two Cities* by Australian-born Arthur Benjamin. As Diana Ashman suggests these names 'must have caused some consternation for the Arts Council as none of the three was British born. Although the Scheme had specified that foreign composers resident in Britain could apply, the fact that all three were immigrants was potentially embarrassing to the Council, having promoted it under the auspices of the Festival of Britain as part of the celebra-

---

47   Conrad Wilson and Alexander R. C. Scott, 'Gál, Hans.' *Grove Music Online. Oxford Music Online.* Oxford University Press http://www.oxfordmusiconline.com/subscriber/article/grove/music/10508 (October 2009).

tions of British achievement and the British way of life.'[48] The Arts Council refrained from its original intentions to have the winning operas produced in London (at Covent Garden, Sadler's Wells, or by the Carl Rosa Company) and none of them enjoyed any exposure at the festival.[49] In the mid-1950s, Goldschmidt stopped composing again for twenty-five years, and is today maybe chiefly remembered for his co-completion, with Deryck Cooke, of Mahler's Tenth Symphony.

Egon Wellesz did not write any music from his migration in 1938 until 1943. Even when Wellesz re-started composing, his works represent a gradual approach towards the avant-garde idiom of the interwar years. A period dominated by four traditionalist Brucknerian symphonies (composed 1945, 1947, 1950 and 1952) follows the war, while symphonies five to nine (1956, 1965, 1968, 1970 and 1971) increasingly include atonal elements with strong reference points to the Schoenberg School, a style that, by that time, had gone out of fashion in Darmstadt and elsewhere. Mátyás Seiber's first years in Britain, too, were characterised by a significant decline in creative output. For ten years, Seiber did not compose any music that could be said to continue the line of his avant-garde compositions of the years in Frankfurt. Like Wellesz, Seiber's paralytic silence is followed by traditionalist works, film and light music on the one hand, and compositions in the idiom of the Schoenberg School on the other.

Leopold Spinner represents a contrasting case. He had been performed at ISCM festivals and decorated with several awards and prizes before the war. Spinner did not stop composing for any long period after his arrival in Britain in 1939 and, with the exception of his settings of Irish folk songs, never deviated from the dodecaphonic method. Yet, unwilling to make concessions and uncompromisingly modernist in his works, he has been totally ignored in his adopted country. In 1958 he succeeded Erwin Stein as editor of Boosey and Hawkes—it was his first permanent musical post in Britain nearly two decades after his immigration. The second edition of the *New Grove* even misquotes his name, embarrassingly including the middle name, Israel, which the Nazis forced upon every male Jew in their infamous 1938 Nuremberg laws.[50]

---

48 Diana Ashman, *Opera for All.* MMus dissertation (University of London, 2010), 30. See also Paul Banks, 'The Case of *Beatrice Cenci*', *Opera* 39:4 (1988), 426–32.

49 The same fate befell *Wat Tyler* by communist Alan Bush, which was chosen as a fourth winner some time later. In operatic terms, the Festival of Britain is today associated with Britten's *Billy Budd*, which was commissioned outside the opera competition and performed after the actual festival had ended.

50 Michael Graubart, 'Spinner, Leopold Israel', *The New Grove Dictionary of Music and Musicians.* 2nd Edition, vol 24, ed. Stanley Sadie (London: Macmillan, 2001), 187. Graubart acknowledges his error in *Grove*'s online edition, see Michael Graubart, 'Spinner, Leopold', *Grove Music Online. Oxford MusicOnline.*Oxford University Press. http://www.oxfordmusiconline.com/subscriber/article/grove/music/26427 (October 2009).

Does this narrative of British hostility and musical provincialism suffice to explain this conspicuous silence of the avant-garde? Can the fact that avant-garde music played a remarkably limited role in London's musical life between 1933 and 1945 solely be attributed to the difficulty of wartime conditions? Or is this narrative of British indifference too monolithic? How do the few émigré compositions fit into all this? Where did the avant-garde survive with which they arrived so richly equipped? An investigation of the émigrés' self-initiated musical activities in Britain between 1933 and 1945 can provide some insight in order to answer these questions.

THE FREE GERMAN LEAGUE OF CULTURE

Very soon after the refugees started arriving in Britain, and especially in 1938, with refugee numbers at their peak, they began to organise themselves and erected numerous support circles. One of these organisations was the *Freier Deutscher Kulturbund,* the Free German League of Culture (FGLC).[51] Formed by German émigrés in 1938 in London as a centre for émigré artists and intellectuals, its primary goal was to promote an image of German culture in opposition to Hitler, to portray a better Germany. The League acquired a beautiful house in Hampstead, in northwest London, and as entry to the League was not restricted to Germans, members of many Continental European diasporic communities visited the League or participated in its activities. London's Northwestern areas, particularly Belsize Park, Swiss Cottage, Hampstead, Kilburn, and Golders Green, were highly popular with European intellectuals. Many émigrés lived and moved in 'émigré neighbourhoods' in close proximity to other exiles, some of whom they knew from earlier days, others who they now met in London. A common joke at the time suggested that shouting 'Herr Doktor!' anywhere in Golders Green would make uncountable European intellectuals in exile appear in all surrounding windows and doors. An English butcher on Haverstock Hill had to adapt to a lot of old ladies suddenly looking for *Wiener Schnitzel,* novelist and former Jewish child refugee from Hitler, Eva Ibbotson, remembers.[52] Hungarian émigré György Mikes even wrote a satiric guide for foreigners entitled *How to be an Alien,* published first in 1946 by André Deutsch—another émigré from Budapest—that soon became a bestseller even among the British.

---

51   The majority of the papers of the *Freier Deutscher Kulturbund* (Free German League of Culture) I have consulted are held by the Akademie der Künste, Berlin, and the Deutsches Bundesarchiv (German Federal Archives), Berlin.

52   Eva Ibbotson, 'How the schnitzel came to London's leafy streets', *Camden New Journal,* 9 September 2004, www.camdennewjournal.co.uk (October 2009).

The history of the FGLC is scarcely researched. The papers of the League were transferred to East Berlin soon after the war, effectively putting them out of reach for Western researchers. Even in former East German scholarship, with the exception of an article by Ulla Hahn from 1977, only very little has been written on the League.[53] What few writings there are, such as Hahn's, are dominated by an aim to present the League through the socialist lens, as a cell of communist freedom fighters preparing in exile the socialist post-war society that was to be established in the German Democratic Republic. No particular emphasis is placed on the musical activities of the FGLC. In September 2010, over seventy years after its foundation, Charmian Brinson and Richard Dove published the first book-length study on the League, providing a welcome and comprehensive insight into the League's history based on an extensive wealth of archival material.[54]

In organisational terms, the FGLC had several sub-sections. Among them were divisions for literature and émigré authors, painters, and also musicians. Other exiled communities gathered in comparable organisations and had similar sections. In 1942, for example, Austrian refugees founded the Austrian Musicians Group, which later changed its name to the Anglo-Austrian Music Society (AAMS), an organisation that continues to play a part in London's cultural scene. At first sight, it would appear that these organisations were eager to provide platforms for the avant-garde compositions of their members. One of the first concerts including one of Mátyás Seiber's serious works outside the National Gallery Concert series, for example, was organised under the auspices of the Association of Free Hungarians in Great Britain and the London Hungarian Club and held in London's Queen Mary Hall on 18 December 1943. Entitled 'A Concert of Hungarian Music,' pianist Ilona Kabos, violinist Eda Kersey, clarinettist Frederick Thurston, and the Blech String Quartet performed Bartók's *Contrasts* for violin, clarinet and piano, Kodály's Second String Quartet, Leo Weiner's Second Violin Sonata op. 11, and Seiber's Divertimento for clarinet and string quartet, composed before his migration.

As for the FGLC, the League's music section (André Asriel, Ernst Hermann Meyer, Peter Stadlen, and Ingeborg Wall) from 1941 onwards organised Modern Chamber Music pro-

---

53   Ulla Hahn, 'Der Freie Deutsche Kulturbund in Großbritannien. Eine Skizze seiner Geschichte', in *Antifaschistische Literatur: Programme, Autoren, Werke* vol. 2, ed. Lutz Winckler (Kronberg / Taunus: Scriptor, 1997), 131–95.

54   Charmian Brinson and Richard Dove, *Politics by Other Means: The Free German League of Culture in London 1939–1946* (London: Vallentine Mitchell, 2010). The volume is a much–expanded version of a book chapter by the same authors, 'The Continuation of Politics by Other Means: The Freie Deutsche Kulturbund in London, 1939–1946', in *"I didn't want to float; I wanted to belong to something." Refugee Organizations in Britain 1933–1945,* ed. Anthony Grenville and Andrea Reiter (Amsterdam: Rodopi, 2008) (Yearbook of the Research Centre for German and Austrian Exile Studies 10), 1–25.

grammes. One of these concerts, on 25 March 1942, included (unidentified) works by the film composers Ludwig Brav, Berthold Goldschmidt, and Mátyás Seiber.[55] Given the numbers of émigré composers and musicians in Britain, many of them living in the neighbourhood of the FGLC's base, there would have been ample opportunities to stage further concerts like these. The next one, on 1 April 1942, featured works by André Asriel, and again by Brav and Seiber. Yet, in the papers of the Free German League of Culture, now mainly housed in the Akademie der Künste in Berlin, I have been able to find a mere five further concerts with programmes including contemporary compositions, a number also confirmed by Jutta Raab Hansen.[56] This makes a total of seven concerts—one in 1941, four in 1942, one in 1943, and one in 1944.

Hahn only touches upon the musical activities of the FGLC briefly and does not specify concerts of contemporary music, but my survey of the materials of the FGLC, such as correspondence between members of the League's music section, concert programmes, advertisements, and reviews, has left me with the distinct impression that, strikingly, even the support circles erected by the émigrés themselves seem to have paid little attention to what was, after all, one of Hitler's prime targets in the field of music. Assessment by Brinson and Dove of the role of avant-garde music in the League remains vague and even makes for almost contradictory reading at times. On the one hand, the authors claim that 'from the beginning, the FGLC took seriously its role in offering the composers in its ranks the opportunity to perform their works' and write of 'a desire on the part of the Free Germans to perform contemporary music.' On the other, they also state 'around 90 per cent of the works performed [...] were taken from the Baroque, Classical or Romantic repertoires [...] a selection [that] points to a rather less than adventurous programming policy, to say the least.'[57]

The League's music section to all evidence did not have an outspoken interest in providing a platform for 'degenerate' music and was much keener to organise cabarets, for example. Five new cabaret productions were staged in 1942 alone, and the League even acquired a new building to house cabaret performances. In addition to the dozens of cabaret and folk-song events, there were many hundreds of concerts dedicated to Schubert songs, Mozart string quartets, and Beethoven piano sonatas. Even during the internment crisis of 1940 and 1941, when numerous of its musicians were imprisoned on the Isle of Man and elsewhere, the League managed to initiate about forty different musical events per year.[58] In comparison, the seven concerts featuring a handful of works by Asriel, Brav, Seiber, Goldschmidt, and

55   See the announcement in *Freie Deutsche Kultur* 1:3, (1942).
56   Raab Hansen, 286.
57   Brinson and Dove, 94–6.
58   These figures are taken from Brinson and Dove, 95.

others, pale into insignificance. Conversely, the literature section was much more engaged in promoting contemporary writing. In spite of a small market and the substantial efforts it took to keep operations afloat financially, the League published three newspapers and either published under its own auspices or supported the publication of numerous books by writers such as Jan Petersen and Max Zimmering.[59]

The reasons for this are surely manifold, but I think that two points are important in this context. Firstly, because of its supposed links to the political left, it was possibly deemed that avant-garde music could alienate the more conservative forces of British society instead of motivating them to assist the fight against Hitler. Albeit in an American rather than a British newspaper, a review from the *New York Times* supports this reading. The programme reviewed was the ISCM concert in the New York Public Library on 21 May 1941, which included Anton Webern's String Quartet, the First Piano Sonata by Viktor Ullmann, Paul Dessau's *Les Voix de Paul Verlaine à Anatole France*, 7 Piano Pieces by Artur Schnabel, and Mátyás Seiber's Second String Quartet. Olin Downes, the paper's music critic, openly associated avant-garde music with Hitler's rise to power by posing the rhetorical question in which his article culminates: 'Is it any wonder that the culture from which [these works] emanate is even now going up in flames?'[60]

Secondly, as a spearhead of progressive thinking, avant-garde music was ill-equipped as a vehicle for nostalgia and homesickness for the émigrés themselves. The Hungarian émigré societies, the Society of Free Hungarians in Great Britain, the Free Hungarian House, and the Hungarian Club in London, for example, put considerable efforts into the London Pódium, which staged performances of three cabaret programmes in 1943 and 1944 in front of an audience totalling nearly a thousand Hungarian émigrés.[61] One of them, *Balaton*, with music by Mátyás Seiber and lyrics by György Mikes, was recorded by the BBC and broadcast on the Hungarian Service. Most songs were co-productions by Seiber and Mikes, with song titles such as *Nekum csak a drága, öreg Budapest kell* (I only need the good, old Budapest) and composed in an accessible musical style. As Adorno put it, 'in the memory of emigration, every German venison roast tastes as if it was freshly felled by the *Freischuetz*'.[62]

---

59   Jan Petersen, *Weg durch die Nacht: Erzählungen*, and Max Zimmering, *Der Keim des Neuen: Gedichte* were both published in 1944 by the League.

60   Olin Downes, 'Chamber Program Heard at Library', *The New York Times*, 22 May 1941, 24.

61   London Pódium, *Pont Ugye Mint Az Angolok… A Londoni Pódium Kiskönyve* (London, 1945). See also Florian Scheding, '"I Only Need the Good, Old Budapest": Hungarian Cabaret in Wartime London' in *Twentieth-century Music and Politics: Essays in Memory of Neil Edmunds*, ed. Pauline Fairclough. (Farnham: Ashgate, 2012), 211–30.

62   Adorno, 78.

THE SOCIETY FOR THE PROMOTION OF NEW MUSIC

Amidst all of this, a handful of composers got together to support the performance, acceptance, and recognition of avant-garde music. In 1943, two émigrés, Francis Chagrin and Mátyás Seiber, co-founded the Committee (later renamed Society) for the Promotion of New Music (spnm). Part of the LCMC, the spnm cannot be compared to organisations helping émigrés and refugees, such as the AAMS, the MRC, or the FGLC. In contrast to these organisations, it did not deal with social matters of foreign musicians, such as obtaining work permits. Instead, the spnm's main aim was to promote public performances and, generally, stimulate the interest in, and acceptance of, contemporary music.

Even though it was founded on 22 January 1943 as a primarily British organisation, the spnm's scope was fundamentally cosmopolitan and internationalist—or, at least, non-nationalist. Its founding statutes specify the organisation's aim to 'get in touch with *all* composers [...] who are living in this country.'[63] The words 'British,' 'Britain' or any other terms referring to nationality or nationhood, are avoided. Even though Chagrin, who acted as secretary-organiser, and Seiber were the only non-British nationals in a Committee of twenty-one members, they exerted some considerable influence, as did Mosco Carner and Walter Goehr who joined the association soon after its foundation. Besides Seiber and Chagrin, the list of the spnm's founding members reads like a who-is-who of contemporaneous British musical life: Ralph Vaughan Williams, who once referred to the Committee as 'Society for the Prevention of Cruelty to New Music'[64] and Arthur Bliss were honorary presidents, other founding members were William Alwyn, Barbara Banner, Lennox Berkeley, Benjamin Britten, Edric Cundell, Roy Douglas, Howard Ferguson, Arnold Goldsborough, Sidney Harrison, John Ireland, Leonard Isaacs, Gordon Jacob, Constant Lambert, Muir Mathieson, Sidney Northcote, Clarence Raybould, Thomas Russell, Michael Tippett, and William Walton. Moreover, concert programmes reveal a relatively high proportion of émigré musicians and composers. Seiber mentions cellist Sela Trau, violinist Max Rostal, and pianists Ilona Kabos and Franz Osborn, amongst others, as well as Berthold Goldschmidt, Louis Kentner, Erich Katz, Franz Reizenstein, Vilém Tausky and himself.[65]

---

63   My emphasis; quoted in Mátyás Seiber, 'The Committee for the Promotion of New Music', in *Music of Our Time*, ed. Ralph Hill and Max Hinrichsen (London: Hinrichsen, 1944), 181.

64   Ursula Vaughan Williams, *R.V.W.: a Biography of Ralph Vaughan Williams* (London: Oxford University Press, 1964), 257.

65   Seiber, 182.

Every composer was invited to submit compositions, which were, if approved by five juries and, upon the recommendation of the Committee, performed in fortnightly concerts held initially in the Polytechnic's Fyvie Hall in London. Following the performances and in the hope of establishing closer links between the composers and their public, members of the audience were invited 'to express freely their impressions and to offer constructive criticism.'[66] The Committee then recommended the selected pieces to concert-giving organisations and record companies. A list of nine works suggested for recording to Decca in 1944, which includes émigré Franz Reizenstein's *Prologue, Variations and Finale* for solo violin and Seiber's *Phantasy* for cello and piano, as well as a look at the works selected for performance by the Committee, bears witness to the spnm's overall support for progressive and avant-garde compositions, without any visible distinctions drawn between British and non-British composers. Indeed one should note that in 1945 Decca accepted the spnm's recommendation and released a recording of Seiber's *Phantasy* for cello and piano shortly after the war. This practice contrasts rather sharply with the BBC music panel's selections, for example, concerning both style and the issue of nationality, even though the selection processes of both institutions were comparable on paper. In his article on the spnm, Seiber expressed his wish that 'all composers should come to know of the Committee's work and thus realise that their colleagues are prepared and anxious to help them in their struggle for recognition. This knowledge, it is hoped, will create a greater feeling of fraternity amongst composers and the consciousness that together they have a part to play in society.'[67]

SECOND CONCLUSION: IS THERE A PATTERN?

A conclusion of this chapter cannot fail to observe that there was hardly any avant-garde music in Britain in the years from 1933 to 1945. Fuelled by xenophobia on the one hand and anti-modernism on the other, British musical life into which the émigré composers and musicians arrived represented neither the time nor the place for the avant-garde to blossom. Faced with this environment, restricted by employment bans, interned on the Isle of Man, and deported to Australia or Canada, many composers simply stopped writing avant-garde music during the time discussed here, or mellowed their style considerably from challenging avant-garde idioms to more digestible music for films and cabarets. Crucially, however, this is not simply Britain's responsibility, but the émigrés' too. The support circles they erected, such as the FGLC, displayed little efforts to support progressive music. Only towards the end of the war did matters change a little, with institutions such as Morley College and the spnm seeking

---

66   Ibid., 183.
67   Ibid.

to provide platforms for new music. After the end of the war, and particularly from the 1950s onwards, things changed, and the picture loses some of its bleakness. In any case, the musicians who were forced by Hitler to leave the continent and who migrated to Britain engaged in a plethora of activities and thus enriched British musical life. Some of the émigré composers impacted more upon British musical life than others; some became successful teachers of a future generation of composers, others didn't; some developed new interests and excelled in them (or didn't), others never changed their style much, yet others stopped composing for a while, or forever. Whether there is a clear pattern in all this is a different matter. Maybe the way in which the émigrés integrated into British society institutionally, for example, can help to reveal acculturation processes as well as begin to untangle the multi-directional complexity I have already mentioned in the introduction to this chapter. On the other hand, maybe there does not need to be a pattern. After all, cultural richness and diversity are one of the hallmarks of the Weimar Republic, from where many of these composers came, and music historians tend to regard this complexity as a virtue. Maybe we can make similar assessments for the bewildering array of activities of the émigré musicians in Britain.

Francisco Parralejo Masa

Nazism, Anti-Semitism and Music in the Second Republic Spain (1931–1936)

'Spain has ceased to be Catholic.' This simple assertion, uttered by the leftist leader Manuel Azaña in 1931, constitutes still today one of the most accurate and concise definitions of the Spanish Second Republic (1931–1936)—the first modern democratic system in Spanish history. Born amid popular fervour in 1931, and overthrown by a reprehensible military coup five years later, the Republic ushered in a period of political and social renewal that was almost unprecedented in the history of modern Spain. Republican leaders pursued not only large-scale economic and social reforms, but also sought to eliminate all those cultural and ideological elements that had constituted the main component of the nation's identity for several generations. With that goal they spread an aggressive, secular and leftist national creed, which was placed in direct opposition to the most widespread and deeply rooted feature in the national identity: Catholicism.[1]

Nevertheless, in a country that was primarily Catholic, these political decisions were regarded in many quarters as a fundamental attack against one of the most strongly identifiable pillars of the nation. Not surprisingly, there was strong opposition to this policy, and voices hostile to the new government branded their approach not only as anti-Catholic but also (and primarily) as anti-Spanish. In order to reinforce this claim, many publications accused the regime of pursuing connections with powerful external enemies. Among these, one of the most relevant was Juan Tusquets's *Orígenes de la revolución española* (Origins of the Spanish Revolution) first published in early 1932 in which the new government was described as the Spanish representative of an international conspiracy made up of Jews and Masons.[2] Several

---

1   Bibliography on the Second Republic is enormously broad. Probably the most complete study published up to date in English is still Stanley Payne, *Spain's first democracy: The second republic 1931–1936* (Madison: University of Wisconsin Press, 1993).

2   Juan Tusquets, *Orígenes de la revolución española* (Barcelona: Editorial Vilamala, 1932). On Tusquets, see Paul Preston, 'Una contribución catalana al mito del contubernio judeo-masónico-bolchevique', *Hispania Nova*, 7 (2007), online on http://hispanianova.rediris.es; and Jordi Canal, 'Las campañas antisectarios de Juan Tusquets (1927–1939): Una aproximación a los orígenes del contubernio judeo-

months later, other books, including Léon de Poncins's *The secret forces of revolution*, Ford's *The international Jew*, and the first of at least nine editions of *The protocol of the Elders of Zion*, reinforced Tusquets's claim.[3] Further publications appeared during this period, all emphasising the lack of a true Spanish character in the regime and its link with the international Jewish-Masonic-Bolshevik conspiracy.[4]

In any case, the continuous presence of the Jewish component in all these imaginary conspiracies was hardly comprehensible, since Spain had practically no Jewish presence for four centuries. Yet as Álvarez Chillida has argued, this stance was understandable:

in the first place because of the sinister image of Jews that had existed in popular imagery: even though there were no Jews in Spain, everybody knew who they were. The Catholic right wing, exploited this fear linking the regime with Jews as demonic and Christ killers. A second reason for this position relates to the fact that after centuries of genuine identity, "Jewish" was regarded by many as opposite to "Spanish", above all by National-Catholics who defended nationalism based on a Catholic-Spanish essence. Republicans, nationalists and workers' supporters were real enemies whose character was still more dangerous for both God and Spain by their link or subordination to unreal Jews.[5]

masónico-comunista en España', in *La masonería en la España del siglo XX*, ed. José Antonio Ferrer Benimelli. (Toledo: Universidad de Castilla-La Mancha, 1996), 1193–1214.

3   Léon de Poncins, *Las fuerzas secretas de la Revolución. F. M. Judaísmo* (Madrid: Fax, 1932); Henry Ford, *El judío internacional: un problema del mundo* (Barcelona: Costa, 1932). For a brief introduction on *The Protocols*, see Norman Cohn, *Warrant for genocide. The Myth of Jewish World Conspiracy and the Protocols of the Elders of Zion* (London: Serif, 1967). On the dissemination of *The Protocols* in Spain, see José Luis Rodríguez Jiménez, 'Los protocolos de los sabios de Sión en España', *Raíces*, (Spring 1999), 27–40.

4   Among the most notable publications are the following: Sergio de Chessin, *La tormenta que viene de Oriente* (Barcelona: Poblet, 1931); Felipe Robles Dégano, *La conspiración judía contra España* (Ávila: Imprenta de Emilio Martín, 1932); Emilio Mola Vidal, *Memorias de mi paso por la Dirección General de Seguridad* (Madrid: Bergua, 1933); and Mauricio Karl [Julián Mauricio Carla Villa], *Asesinos de España: marxismo, anarquismo, masonería* (Madrid: Bergua, 1935). For modern commentaries on this issue, see José Antonio Ferrer Benimelli, *El contubernio judeo-masónico-comunista: del satanismo al escándalo de la P-2* (Madrid: Istmo, 1982); Gonzalo Álvarez Chillida, 'La eclosión del antisemitismo español: de la II República al Holocausto', in *El antisemitismo en España,* ed. Gonzalo Álvarez Chillida and Ricardo Izquierdo Benito (Cuenca: Ediciones de la Universidad de Castilla-La Mancha, 2007), 181–206; José Antonio Ferrer Benimeli, 'La prensa fascista y el contubernio judeo-masónico-comunista', in *Masonería y periodismo en la España contemporánea,* ed. José Antonio Ferrer Benimeli (Zaragoza: Prensas Universitarias de Zaragoza, 1993), 209–30.

5   Gonzalo Álvarez Chillida, *El antisemitismo en España. La imagen del judío (1808–2002)* (Madrid: Marcial Pons, 2002), 349.

Therefore, references to Jews as intangible atavistic enemies functioned as a very efficient mechanism for the mobilization of conservative groups whose goals were to overthrow the new democratic system. Propagation of chimerical assertions about Jews was a means of settling down a collective identity, which underwent several questionings and constant ups and downs.[6] And it also functioned as a hugely effective discursive resource in order to bring together all rival forces, despite their big differences, into one battle front. In this context, the arrival of Nazism in Germany in 1933 could not help but stimulate long-standing Spanish anti-Semitism and provide the most reactionary groups with a new model of antidemocratic action. It is therefore not surprising that the German National Socialist government made big propagandistic efforts in this respect after it seized power, and that Hitler was the first foreign leader who helped the Francoist uprising after the outbreak of the Civil War.[7]

In this chapter, my aim is to weigh up the impact of Nazism and anti-Semitism on musical criticism during the short democratic experience embodied in Spain by the Second Republic. To that end, the writings of two recognized critics, whose political tendencies are completely at odds with each other, will be compared: Víctor Ruiz Albéniz (1885–1954), ultraconservative critic who became one of the greatest defenders of Francoist cause, and Adolfo Salazar, 'progressive' critic *par excellence*, an emblem of Republican government, who was forced into a long-term exile from his native country after the Civil War. It should be emphasised, however, that despite my intention to provide as thorough an analysis as possible of the impact of Nazism and different anti-Semitic ideologies on musical criticism, this is work in progress and the conclusions that follow are necessarily provisional.

THE COLONIAL TRACE

Víctor Ruiz Albéniz's career as journalist started in 1909, when he worked as a doctor in the

---

6   As Gavin I. Langmuir argues: 'Chimerical assertions are propositions that grammatically attribute with certitude to an out-group and all its members characteristics that have never been empirically observed […] The initial or originating function of chimerical assertions would seem to be to express the awareness of individual members of the in group of a menace within themselves, their awareness at some psychic level that there are threatening cracks in their personality between their imagination or impulses and the social values they have internalized, their feeling that they are not comfortably integrated either with their society or within themselves. Chimerical assertions […] function to relieve the resulting tension – the anger, fear, or guilt – by expressing its existence openly in a socially acceptable form, by presenting the interior conflict as a social problem, a struggle between the in-group and its acknowledged enemies'. Langmuir, *Toward a definition of antisemitism* (Berkeley, Los Angeles, Oxford: University of California Press, 1990), 326–40. Cited quotations: 328 & 338.

7   Ángel Viñas, *Franco, Hitler y el estallido de la Guerra Civil. Antecedentes y consecuencias* (Madrid: Alianza Ensayo, 2001), 335–402.

Spanish mines in Beni Bu Ifrur, North Africa. Under the pseudonym of El Tebib Arrumi (the Christian doctor), he had tirelessly defended the Spanish colonialist process by adopting a modern view regarding collaboration with local powers.[8] Yet despite the fact that his political thinking was orientated at the beginning towards a modern democratic liberalism, his ideas were transformed as time went by into a strict and traditionalistic nationalism—a probable consequence of his close contact with colonial military circles.[9]

The most relevant element in this ideological change came from the traditionalistic and grandiose rhetoric of the historian, Marcelino Menéndez Pelayo. Menéndez Pelayo was undoubtedly the most influential historian of nineteenth–century Spain, someone who defended the idea that the deepest essence of the nation was unmistakably linked to the Catholic Church. Thus, any other attempt at carrying out another political or social organisation of the country was necessarily condemned to be temporary and accidental. Cosmopolitan people (or dissidents) could not possibly be regarded as 'true Spaniards', because, in his own words, 'nationality is a fluctuating value which is subordinated to religion. Therefore, those who don't practice it are not pure Spaniards; they may be born in Spain but they don't belong to the nation.'[10]

This precise yet exclusive duality was a constant force in the political thinking of some conservative Spanish groups, which, as Balfour and Quiroga state, would end up interpreting 'the [whole] history of Spain as a struggle between orthodox patriots and heterodox traitors, between pure followers of 'national' Catholic traditions and those contaminated by heretical foreign ideas.'[11] Such feelings were in fact intensified in colonial military circles, for which this

---

8   Ruiz Albéniz's career in Africa is analyzed in Filipe Ribeiro de Meneses, 'Popularizing Africanism: The Career of Víctor Ruiz Albéniz, *El Tebib Arrumi*', in *Journal of Iberian and Latin American Studies*, vol. 11/1 (April 2005), 39–63. Ruiz Albéniz's wide knowledge of problems in the Spanish colonization process is further defended in a paper given at the Argel Rural Colonization Congress in 1930, published as *Colonización española en Marruecos: 'Rapport' presentado al Congreso de Colonización Rural de Argel*. (Madrid: Imprenta Saez Hermanos, 1930). The historian Sebastian Balfour described him as 'a notable Arabist and a proponent, along with the mining companies, of a neo-colonialist strategy of not interfering with the existing power balance in the Rif'. Sebastian Balfour, *Deadly embrace: Morocco and the road to the Spanish Civil War* (Oxford: Oxford University Press, 2002), 17.

9   Ruiz Albéniz's first steps towards liberalism are mentioned in Mari Cruz Seoane and María Dolores Saiz, *Historia del periodismo en España. 3. El siglo XX: 1898–1936* (Madrid: Alianza Editorial, 1996), 94 & 257. His initial liberal choice of politics next to Christian democracy can be observed in his continuous defence of children's rights. See Patricio de Blas Zabaleta and Eva De Blas Martín-Merás, *Julián Besteiro. Nadar contra corrient* (Madrid: Algaba, 2002), 176.

10   Marcelino Menéndez Pelayo, *Historia de los heterodoxos españoles* (1880/82). Available online at http://www.cervantesvirtual.com/servlet/SirveObras/01361608688915504422802/index.htm.

11   Sebastian Balfour and Alejandro Quiroga, *The reinvention of Spain. Nation and identity since Democracy* (Oxford: Oxford University Press, 2007), 21.

division was more severe because of the strict distinction typical of warring factions between friends and enemies and patriots and traitors.

Such militarist and close-minded visions of the nation become evident in Ruíz Albéniz's work after 1924, when he joined the extreme rightist paper *Informaciones,* whose editor-in-chief was, significantly, another colonial war veteran, Augusto Vivero. In 1925 the newspaper became a property of the conservative millionaire Juan March, and from that point on, a re-actionary antidemocratic editorial line was consolidated reaching its zenith in 1931, when the Second Republic seized power.[12]

In this historical moment, *Informaciones* stood out as one of the most right-wing publica-tions up to the point that it ended up becoming the major link between groups that took part in the coup shortly before Civil War. Its sympathy for Nazism was evident from the very out-set and in 1934, through the auspices of the German ambassador in Madrid, it agreed to be-come a covert agent of Nazi propaganda in exchange for a monthly remuneration fluctuating between 3,000 and 4,000 pesetas. From that moment on, aggressively anti-Semitic articles appeared, authored by some of the most bigoted and close-minded columnists of the period. Juan Pujol, director of the newspaper, contributed greatly to this process with his anti-Jewish novel *El hoyo en la arena* (The Hole in the Sand).[13]

Ruiz Albéniz's contributions to the newspaper included daily articles espousing his own political opinions, writings about the colonial situation, and musical criticism from 1931.[14] In 1934, as a result of the newspaper's special arrangement with the German government, he published several articles under the title *Under the swastika (Academic travel in today's Germany).*[15] In them he provided a documentary chronicle of his travels throughout Ger-many, offering an almost Arcadian description of the country and its rulers. Nevertheless, if we look carefully at the material expounded in these articles, we will realize that despite his

---

12   The relationship between Ruiz Albéniz and March was very close, up to the point that the critic col-laborated intensely in the millionaire's escape from prison in 1934. Josep Pla, *La segunda república española. Una crónica 1931–1936* (Barcelona: Destino, 2006), 747.

13   For more information on the role of newspapers as a link between conservative groups, see José María Gil Robles, *No fue posible la paz* (Barcelona: Ariel, 1968), 408. Discussion of the accommodation with the Nazi regime can be found in Viñas, 185–87, anti-Semitism of the newspapers, in Seonae and Saiz, 426–27 and Álvarez Chillida, 311–14. On Juan Pujol, see *Ibid.,* 295–96.

14   Huertas Vázquez situates Ruiz Albéniz as the newspaper's director a few months before the coup. Nev-ertheless, we have found no more sources which corroborate this information. See Eduardo L. Huer-tas Vázquez: 'Víctor Ruiz Albéniz "Chispero"', prologue to Víctor Ruiz Albéniz, *Aquel Madrid…! (1900–1914)* (Madrid: Ediciones La Librería, 2002), xii.

15   Víctor: Ruiz Albéniz 'Bajo la cruz gamada (Viaje de estudio por la Alemania de hoy)', *Informaciones,* 19 September 1934, 21 September 1934, 22 September 1934, 25 September 1934, 27 September 1934, 29 September 1934, 2 October 1934, 4 October 1934.

unquestioned exaltation of the Nazis, his own distinctively biased political ideology was far removed from National Socialist principles.   Furthermore, Ruiz Albéniz ignores systematically the messianic and purely modernist elements of Nazism (following the conceptualization established by Roger Griffin[16]) and describes the regime as eminently traditionalist. According to him, the social cohesion and rapid economic progress experienced in Germany after 1933 were not the result of a political revolution, but the unambiguous consequence of respect for ancient national traditions. In other words, German resurgence was possible thanks to its citizens' patriotism and their explicit and strict rejection of all non-national traditions.

This way of approaching the national element as a monolithic traditionalist entity is clearly mirrored in his musical criticism, especially in his particular understanding of the exact nature of Spanish music.   In this respect, Ruiz Albéniz unequivocally endorses a nationalist ideology of the traditional kind (that is to say, one based exclusively on folklore and using Isaac Albéniz as the model[17]) as opposed to a false internationalism in which there are no differences between styles or tendencies.

A good illustration of his position can be gleaned from his attitude to the music of Manuel de Falla. Ruiz Albéniz considered the French period works of the Andalusian composer as a magnificent reflection of the purest 'Spanish music essence.' However, his final works, especially his Harpsichord Concerto, were not accepted into the national canon because of their relationship with European Neoclassicism, a movement that he regarded as foreign and therefore incompatible with any type of Spanishness. This argument with regard to the Harpsichord Concerto was emphatically stated in an article published in 1934:

> I must energetically protest at the fallacy that appeared in programme notes of the concert. According to them, Falla's work is profoundly related to Castilian music. Yet to claim that the Concerto we're judging has something Castilian in it is a true blasphemy.[18]

Paradoxically, the Castilian dimensions of this work, as Carol Hess has suggested, are based on the presence and sublimation of several music references essentially linked with the Spanish Catholic tradition.[19] Nevertheless, according to Ruiz Albéniz's exclusive rhetoric, the pres-

---

16   Roger Griffin, *Modernism and Fascism. The sense of a new beginning under Mussolini and Hitler* (London: Palgrave Macmillan, 2004).

17   Ruiz Albéniz was Isaac Albéniz's nephew and his personal doctor during composer's last days. See Walter Aaron Clark, *Isaac Albéniz. Retrato de un romántico* (Madrid: Turner, 2002), 291.

18   Acorde, [Víctor Ruiz Albéniz], 'En el auditorium. Strawinsky [sic], Schoemberg [sic] y Falla', *Informaciones,* 21 June 1934.

19   'Clearly in the Concerto, Falla had done much more than merely abandon *andalucismo* in favour of a modernist idiom. Rather, he had allied that very idiom with prevailing constructions of Spanish Ca-

ence of the smallest non-Spanish element is enough to keep the work out of the national canon, regardless of the composer's intentions or possible intellectual connections.[20]

At the same time as this aesthetical discourse was taking place, Ruiz Albéniz established clear analogies in the political and musical areas, especially in relation to the National Music Board and Lyric Theatres, a newly established Republican government organisation for music management. Although one acknowledges that the Board's interventions were extremely biased[21], it must also be remembered that Ruiz Albéniz's criticism attempted from the very beginning to discredit its task by a discourse that disregarded its 'national' condition precisely because of its progressive ideas. Thus, he stated about a *zarzuela* (comic opera) by Basque composer Pablo Sorozábal:

> We live in fear that the dishonest work of National Music Board will end up by twisting the rules of Spanish classic *zarzuela* in order to offer us another type of music, which is bound to be quality music, but cannot join the glorious and beloved *zarzuela* which people demand in national auditoriums.[22]

Ruiz Albéniz's attacks against the Board concentrated essentially on two of its members: President Óscar Esplá and secretary and *alma mater*, Adolfo Salazar. In his vision, Ruiz Albéniz considered it a huge problem that the musical destinies of the country relied on people who were not regarded as 'national'. As he said in an article published in April 1934:

tholicism'. Carol A. Hess, *Manuel de Falla and Modernism in Spain* (Chicago and London: University of Chicago Press, 2001), 245.

20　The same contrast between 'cosmopolitism' and 'Spanishness' is fiercely stated by Ruiz Albéniz in many other articles during this period. See, for example, 'Último concierto de la Filarmónica', *Informaciones*, 30 October 1931 (on Manuel Palau); 'En el Español. Orquesta Filarmónica', *Informaciones*, 24 April 1932, and 'Concierto de la Filarmónica en honor del maestro Arbós', *Informaciones*, 22 December 1933 (on Salvador Bacarisse); and 'La Orquesta sinfónica', *Informaciones*, 30 March 1934 (on several young composers).

21　See Francisco Parralejo Masa, 'Essor et déclin des nouveaux idéaux : presse, politique et musique en Espagne (1918–1936)', in *Représentations médiatiques de l'homme politique (XVIIIe – XXIe siècle)* (Versailles: Université de Versailles Saint-Quentin-en-Yvelines, 2010); Beatriz Martínez del Fresno, *Julio Gómez. Una época de la música española* (Madrid: ICCMU, 1999), 317–22; and Christiane Heine, 'Bacarisse Chinoria, Salvador', in *Diccionario de la música española e Iberoamericana*, vol. II, ed. Emilio Casares Rodicio (Madrid: Sociedad General de Autores y Editores, 1999–2002), 4–24.

22　Acorde [Víctor Ruiz Albéniz], 'Correo de teatros. Anoche se estrenó "Katiuska" en Rialto', *Informaciones*, 12 May 1932.

Spanish authors […] are not equivalent to 'Spanish music'. The work of Esplá, Halffter, Bacarisse, Del Campo, Salazar, Bautista, Pittaluga, etc., etc., may be written by Spanish authors, but it is not of pure lineage and nationalist orientation.[23]

Therefore, as we have seen, Ruiz Albéniz's first aim was to defend a nationalist conservative discourse and oppose the political methods of the new regime. Yet, as has been already mentioned, his ideas were also not especially compatible with Nazism. For instance, no references praising the revolution in social structure carried out by the Hitler regime can be found in any of his writings. Neither does he mention the messianic arrival of the 'new man', typical of fascism,[24] nor intellectual censorship and racial politics. Furthermore, despite the close connections between his newspaper and Nazism, as well as the intense anti-Semitic activity carried out by extreme right-wing publications, no references attacking Jews can be found in his entire work.

Once again, the reason for this attitude may relate to his colonial experience. Jews did not constitute an identifiable group in Spain, but they did in North Africa, where Ruiz Albéniz spent a great part of his life. In fact, in the course of the colonization process, many Sephardic Jews (Jews who had been expelled from Spain in 1492 and still preserved their ancestors' language and customs) explicitly supported Spanish troops. This fact ensured that a significant number of Africanist officers ended up defending the Hispanic identity of the Jews that settled down there or, at least, helped to maintain a respectful attitude towards them.[25]

For these reasons, it is perhaps not surprising that in Ruiz Albéniz's criticism, Jewish interpreters or composers were always linked with their original nationality. The critic disdained the kind of racial distinctions that other newspapers mentioned frequently. Besides, all the great Jewish interpreters that appeared in Spain during the period were warmly praised, and racial stereotypes were avoided in the case of assessing performers such as Ania Dorfmann, Jascha Heifetz, Artur Rubinstein, Harold Bauer, Wanda Landowska, Alexander Brailowsky, Mischa Elman and Yehudi Menuhin.

---

23   Acorde [Víctor Ruiz Albéniz], 'En el Español. Festivales de música y danza', *Informaciones,* 30 April 1934.

24   Jean Clair, *Les années 1930. La fabrique de "l'Homme Nouveau"* (Paris: Gallimard, 2008).

25   The most significant example in this respect is Francisco Franco whose attitude towards Jews during Second World War was, at least, ambiguous. See the different approaches to this issue by Gema A. Junco, 'Spain under Franco (1938–1975)', in *Antisemitism. A Historical Encyclopedia of prejudice and persecution,* ed. Richard S. Levy (Santa Barbara:, ABC-CLIO, 2005), 674–75; and Andrée Bachoud, 'Franco y los judíos: filosefardismo y antisemitismo', in *El olivo y la espada,* ed. Pere Joan i Tous and Heike Nottebaum (Tübingen: Niemeyer, 2003) 379–90. About the relationship between the Sephardic communities and the Spanish nationalism, see Eva Touboul Tardieu, *Séphardisme et hispanité: l'Espagne à la recherche de son passé (1920–1936)* (Paris: Presses de l'Université de Paris-Sorbonne, 2009).

This clear distinction made by Ruiz Albéniz between his writings and the newspaper's editorial line takes us back once more to the complex function of Nazism in Ruiz Albéniz's ideological organisation chart. As we have already seen, his political thinking tended rather towards an exacerbated traditionalism typical of Spanish colonialist circles rather than to the racist messianic National Socialist 'new Germany'. Nevertheless, this Germany embodied an eloquent example of a society that had been militarized and homogenized by power, and it could be viewed as an ideal model for solving the Spanish social and economic crisis.

Likewise, National Socialism ended up being no more than a dialectic subterfuge, a rhetorical tool for the huge campaign that advocated the building of a new society based not on fascist principles, but precisely on a non-modern and strictly traditionalist regime, according to ancient Spanish conservatism.[26]

THE COMPLEX ROOTS OF SPANISH PROGRESSIVE ANTI-SEMITISM

Paradoxically, the only music critic who developed a somewhat consistent anti-Semitic outlook did not work for any reactionary newspaper, but precisely for the publication that most fittingly stood for modernity and cosmopolitism in the new regime, *El Sol*. In this case, we are referring to Adolfo Salazar, a paradigm of a liberal and internationalist critic, who was secretary and theoretician of the republican National Music Board and represented politically the opposite side of the coin to Ruiz Albéniz's ideas.

One of the best examples of Salazar's position was reflected in an article about the situation of the Jews in Germany published in *El Sol* in April 1933:

> What does it mean being a Jew in Germany? […] Unless a person makes his religion evident […], it cannot be assessed if he has or has not Hebrew blood in his veins. […] What is really involved here is [not the expulsion of the Jews but] the expulsion from Germany of all those who are not blonde, hundred per cent Teutonic and, above all, 'Aryan'. In other words, the big neutral, edge-headed, sitting ducks, Teutonic mass does not welcome in its files the excrescences produced by Jewish spiritual sharpness. […] Let's not defend the Jews, whose social vices have been described by Pío Baroja in a recent article. And let's not attack them either. It would be ridiculous if Spaniards attacked the Jews, given that one of their essential abilities is their adaptability, above all since the times of Isabella the Catholic […] They changed the clothes of the synagogue for those of the Catholic Church, but even so they never quite managed to take the tonsure. […]

---

26   The non-fascist dimension of the Spanish conservatism has been pointed out by many authors. For a concise and brilliant introduction, see François Furet, *Le passé d'une illusion. Essai sur l'idée communiste au XXe siècle* (Paris: Robert Laffont, 1995), 407–31.

Regarding Spain, this question would be just a curiosity if it wasn't for a tricky consequence; namely, the future invasion of Jewish musicians who are already thinking (and
wondering) if it is possible to make themselves a 'position' here. We presume that the
rich and talented Jews will emigrate to the USA, and we shall only gain the poor ones.
Thanks to the general snobbery, and through exemplary preparation of recommendations,
intrigue, skilful handling of interests of various natures, party politics (rightist as well as
leftist and ultra-leftist) and the rest of the repertoire, they will take root easily and in a very
short time [in Spain].[27]

From reading this article, we can draw three fundamental conclusions. Firstly, Nazism is described as an aggressive mass movement whose main feature is its intellectual mediocrity and
its hatred for highly educated people. Jews are considered an intellectual elite and not an
identifiable 'race'. Thus, hatred for Jews is by no means a racial issue, but the result of the rise
to power of uneducated and aggressive masses.

Following the Spanish philosopher José Ortega y Gasset and many other European intellectuals of his time, Salazar conceived society as an organic entity hierarchically divided into
elites and masses. The former are defined by their superior intellectual skills and, therefore,
are considered to be the natural rulers of society. The latter are defined by their intellectual
mediocrity and their inability to control their passions. Therefore, they are considered to be
an obedient working class. Consequently, Salazar distrusted democracy and any kind of mass
movement (either socialists or traditionalists), since both pose an unacceptable subversion of
the natural hierarchies that should guide every society.[28] It is no coincidence therefore that in
his writings, the masses are described as 'fickle and inconsistent' or 'common and tasteless.'[29]
Furthermore, 'true art' is defined by opposition to '*vox populi's* stupid mumbling.'[30]

Among us, the selected minority is almost the only thing that counts. The rest of the
population has no pulse, only amorphous modes of reaction to the artistic phenomenon.
Therefore, this [the artistic phenomenon] is doomed to isolation; to die, eventually.[31]

27   Adolfo Salazar, 'Un programa alemán en la Sinfónica. Los alemanes de Hitler y los músicos judíos', *El
      Sol,* 13 April 1933.
28   An analysis of Salazar's ideological background by the author appears in Francisco Parralejo Masa
      'Jóvenes y selectos: Salazar y Ortega en el entorno europeo de su generación (1914–1936)', in *Los señores
      de la crítica Periodismo musical e ideología del modernismo en Madrid (1900–1950),* ed. Teresa Cascudo
      and María Palacios (Seville: Doble J., 2011), 57–95.
29   Adolfo Salazar, 'La música española en tiempos de Goya', *Revista de Occidente* (November 1928),
      334–77 (quotation 341).
30   Adolfo Salazar, *La música actual en Europa y sus problemas* (Madrid: José Mª Yagües, 1935), 14.
31   Adolfo Salazar, 'Cómo va el pulso del mundo', *El Sol,* 4 December 1926.

For Salazar, the masses do not have the capacity to govern themselves. They cannot control their passions and have no self-criticism. For this reason, the government of the masses is always exclusionary, irrational and arbitrary. And the main victims of this kind of government will always be the intellectual elites, the 'selected minority'. Indeed, with regard to this point, there is no difference between Nazism, communism, or populism: all of them are based on the same reversed hierarchy.

Salazar assumes that Jews, despite their 'faults', constituted a fundamental part of European elites. He states this idea repeatedly; for instance, in many of his approaches to the nineteenth century, or by defending illustrious Jews, like Heine.[32] For this reason, the exclusion of Jews will be necessarily present in all mass movements: it is not a racial issue, but an intellectual one.

Also as a result of this reasoning, a massive immigration of 'affluent' Jews, that is, Jews with a fine educational background, would be positive for Spain despite the risk of 'racial contamination'. However, it would not be acceptable in the case of those impoverished Jews from the East who lived in miserable conditions and had enthusiastically joined revolutionary leftist movements. Accepting them would be equivalent to reinforcing the masses' wish for subversion. To this point, the division between rich and poor Jews becomes a projection of the social division between elites and masses: the former, constructive and enriching, and the latter, pernicious and destructive.

A second conclusion resulting from Salazar's argument is that despite their 'social vices', Spaniards cannot criticize the Jews because they constitute a hidden (but fundamental) part of Spanish society. However, they can never be fully integrated in Spain. In order to understand this assertion, it is necessary to remember a bit of history concerning the Jews in Spain. In 1492, Queen Isabella of Castile ruled that all non-Christian Spaniards should convert to Christianity or leave the country. Many Jews chose to emigrate but a considerable number preferred to be baptized and remained in Spain. Although originally, conversion to Christianity did not imply any loss of rights, from this moment onwards the concept of 'blood purity' became an obsession for the Spanish administration. Jewish lineages were investigated and separated from public activity through the 'Statutes of purity of blood' and the mere suspicion of any Jewish ancestor became a cause of social exclusion.[33]

Furthermore, despite the complete elimination of Judaism from Spanish public life, the image of the Jew as a sinister character remained prevalent, particularly in popular culture. Jews were often considered to be instigators of any dangerous action, whether an act of vio-

---

32   Adolfo Salazar, *El siglo romántico* (Madrid: J. M. Yagües, 1936).
33   See Christiane Stallaert, *Ni una gota de sangre impura: la España inquisitorial y la Alemania nazi cara a cara* (Barcelona: Galaxia Gutenberg, 2006).

lence or misbehaviour. For this reason we find negative references to Jews not only in conservative writings, but also in many popular or left-wing texts. In fact, the same semi-demoniac image of the Jews developed by the ultra-conservative groups can also be found in some leftist discourses, especially amongst those produced by the most visceral anti-clericalist writers. Some of them, like Pío Baroja, Juan Machimbarrena or Segismundo Pey Ordeix (as well as Vicente Blasco Ibáñez, who died in 1928), developed a harsh anti-Semitic discourse in which 'infiltrated Jews' were made responsible, among other things, for every atrocity committed by the Catholic Church.[34] This attitude is particularly germane to Salazar's already quoted remark that 'they [the Jews] changed the clothes of the synagogue for those of the Catholic Church, but even so they never quite managed to take the tonsure.' Indeed, it is hardly coincidental that in 1933 Salazar also made the following statement:

> Servants make the worst masters, and the harshest of the anti-Semites are the own shameful Israelites. Many of the cruelties that have taken place in Spanish inquisition were attributed to converted Jews.[35]

It is particularly noteworthy that Salazar mentioned the name of Baroja, whose visceral anti-Semitism was well-known in Spain. In fact, the quoted article was published in the newspaper *Ahora* only a few days before Salazar's, and it would be later included in an anthology provocatively entitled *Communists, Jews and other people of the worst kind*.[36]

Nevertheless, Baroja's anti-Semitism had little to do with the harsh Christian anti-Semitism advocated during this period by right-wing tendencies. On the contrary, his anti-Semitism was the projection of a deeply anti-Christian ideal.[37] In his novels, Jews appear as repulsive and hypocritical human beings, sexually perverted and lacking any kind of crea-

---

34 See Pío Baroja, *Comunistas, judíos y demás ralea* (Valladolid: Editorial Reconquista, 1938); Segismundo Pey Ordeix, *Patología nacional. Jesuitas y judíos ante la República* (Barcelona: Maucci, 1932); Juan Machimbarrena, *El oro. El socialismo. Los judíos* (San Sebastián: Nueva Editorial, 1932). On left wing anti-Semitism in Spain see Manfred Böcker, *Antisemitismus ohne Juden. Die Zweite Republik, die antirepublikanische Rechte und die Juden. Spanien 1931 bis 1936.* (Bern: Peter Lang, 2000), 314–15; Álvarez Chillida, 207–13 and 308–10; and Josep Massoti Muntaner, 'Pey-Ordeix, Segimon', in *Gran enciclopedia catalana*, vol. 11 (Barcelona: Cap del departament de Paisos Catalans, Max Cahner, 1978) (www.enciclopedia.cat).

35 Adolfo Salazar, 'Hitler–Parsifal o el wagnerismo, religión de Estado', *El Sol,* 20 September 1933.

36 Pío Barojo, 'Los judíos', *Ahora,* 9 April 1933. See also Barojo, *Comunistas, judíos y demás ralea.*

37 See Böcker, 71–75; Jacques Petrus Thérèse de Bruyne, *Antisemitisme bij Pío Baroja.* (Groningen, VRB, 1967); Álvarez Chillida, 291–94; and José–Carlos Mainer, 'Los judíos en la literatura española de la primera mitad del siglo XX: notas sobre un tema', in *Judíos en la literatura española*, ed. Jacob M. Hassan and Ricardo Izouierdo Benito (Cuenca: Ediciones de la Universidad de Castilla-la Mancha, 2001), 375–402.

tivity. However, the most hateful thing about them, according to Baroja, was their almost complete responsibility for two of the most damnable tendencies of society: egalitarianism (either democratic or socialist) and Christianity, whose fanaticism was regarded as originally Semitic.

Many ideas taken from Barojian thinking pervade Salazar's writings, like his hatred for democracy or the insistence on the Jewish component of the Catholic Church. However, the most influential of all was the view that regarded Jews as incapable of true creativity despite the fact that they were gifted as artisans and had the capacity to assimilate a good amount of information. Thus, the lack of originality that Salazar takes for granted in Mendelssohn is described as 'a clear response to the concept of Israelite art.'[38] Referring to Max Reger, he states: 'I don't know if Reger was a Jew or not. He might be, according to his lack of personality or his inability to create new means of expression.'[39] And he attributes Meyerbeer's unskilled and untalented opportunism to 'his sharp Israelite instinct.'[40] Besides, he emphasizes the connection between Judaism and wealth accumulation, pointing out the prosperous situation affecting both the Mendelssohn and Meyerbeer families.

The third and final conclusion to draw from Salazar's writings is the emphasis he places on what he regards as the crucial opposition between Jewishness and Spanishness. This is an idea that was again assimilated from Baroja, for whom 'the "Jewish" was regarded primarily as an intellectually alien principle', as Böcker states.[41] And this affirmation leads us to a different type of anti-Semitism, one of a nationalist kind. In fact, although Baroja's anti-Christian anti-Semitism remains almost an exception in the cultural scene of the time, this nationalist anti-Semitism was frequently encountered in nineteenth-century Spanish literature, which had often focused on the picture of the Jew as 'foreign' or an 'invader'.[42]

Such a position is reiterated in Salazar's writings too. Not surprisingly, the Madrilenian critic appropriated a long historiographical tradition, which insisted upon the exclusive character of Spanish music in relation to the rest of European musical developments. This belief derived originally from the ideas of Felipe Pedrell, the Catalan composer and theoretician. As Juan José Carreras has pointed out:

> Spanish nationalism distinguished itself by its obsessive rejection of foreign influences, a fact demonstrated by the strict distinction between what is alien and what is one's own.

---

38   Adolfo Salazar, 'Mendelssohn', in *El siglo*, 205–19 (quotation 218).
39   Adolfo Salazar, 'Goldberg y Neumark, en la Sociedad Filarmónica', *El Sol*, 30 January, 1935.
40   Adolfo Salazar, 'La ópera romántica en Francia y en Italia', in Salazar, 261–88 (quotation 274).
41   Böcker, 3.
42   Norbert Rehrmann, *Das schwierige Erbe von Sefarad. Juden und Mauren in der spanischen Literatur. Von der Romantik bis zur Mitte des 20. Jahrunderts* (Frankfurt, Vervuert, 2002).

This dichotomy is articulated in a binary discourse which balances among the 'self' and the 'other', the 'national' and the 'foreign'.[43]

Although Salazar was strongly influenced by this nationalist and essentialist historiographical tendency, his anti-Semitism concept had not yet been explicitly formulated within this tradition. In fact, these ideas undoubtedly derived from outside Spain and most obviously from the other side of the Pyrenees.

Salazar's connection with French culture had been very intense since his youth. He kept close contact with extreme nationalist Parisian circles and was a member of the nationalist *Société Française de Musicologie*.[44] Likewise, Salazar had actively taken part since the years of the Great War in spreading the idea of a 'Latin community', in other words a nationalist rhetoric that claimed both countries (France and Spain) were cultural allies opposed to German nationalism.[45] This idea of a 'Latin community' was particularly attractive to Salazar, firstly because it enabled there to be some acknowledgement of the role of Spanish music in the international sphere, and secondly because it enabled the renewal of Spanish musical tendencies through its acquaintance with other European traditions. However, this 'Latin community' ideal, warmly received by Spanish progressive circles, was in France linked mainly to the Catholic right wing and to Charles Maurras's group, *Action Française*. In the same way, some of its greater defenders in the musical area were well-known anti-Semites, for example Henri Collet.[46]

Collet's presence proved to be very significant in this respect since he was an acknowledged Hispanist whose publications aroused considerable attention in Spain.[47] In his writings, he subscribed to the Hispanic isolationist theory, reinforcing the notion of 'the extremely specific nature of Spanish musical temperament'[48], and reminding his readers of the alien nature of

---

43 Juan José Carreras, 'Hijos de Pedrell. La historiografía musical española y sus orígenes nacionalistas (1780–1980)', *Saggiatore Musicale,* VIII (2001), n. 1, 131–69. From the same author, see 'Introducción', in Mariano Soriano Fuertes *Historia de la música desde la venida de los fenicios hasta el año de 1850* (Madrid: Ed. Facsímil, ICCMU, 2007), v–xxiii.

44 Despite being a constant feature in different biographies of Salazar, he was not in fact a founding member of the Société. See Sara Iglesias, ' «Le devoir est partout» – Reflets de la guerre dans la fondation de la Société française de musicologie en 1917', in *La Grande Guerre des musiciens,* ed. Stéphane Audouin–Rouzeau, Esteban Buch and Myriam Chimènes (Paris: Symétrie, 2009), 203–14. I thank Sara Iglesias for letting me read her article before it was published.

45 Hess, 161–98.

46 Samuel Llano, *El hispanismo y la cultura musical de París, 1898–1931.* Doctoral thesis (Universidad Complutense de Madrid, 2006), 71–91. I thank Samuel Llano for his help with this information.

47 Especially Collet's books *Le Mysticisme musical espagnol au XVIè siècle* (Paris: Max Eschig, 1913) and *L'Essor de la musique espagnole au XXe siècle* (Paris: Max Eschig, 1929).

48 Barcelona *SIM,* 15 April 1911, in Llano, 104. On the longevity of topics coined by Collet in Spanish

the Jewish element with regard to the Spanish race, and the incapability of Jews to be able to effect true assimilation with this culture.[49] Furthermore, Collet's definition of French nationalism, which claimed a modern nationalism that was related to the idea of 'classicism' and to historical sources that had been 'cleansed' of foreign influences, was to prove highly influential for Salazar[50], as was also the case with the theories of another distinguished French rightist thinker, Jean Cocteau. The circle of influences is obvious, given the significant place occupied by Salazar in Collet's Spanish modernity view[51], and the number of Cocteau's quotations in Salazar's writings, especially in *Música y músicos de hoy* (1928).[52]

Thus, we can observe here a strange transmutation: ideals, which in the ultranationalist France defined a conservative identity, functioned in the denationalized Spain as reflections of a 'progressive' ideology. It is no wonder then that many approaches made by openly republican intellectuals like Salazar, were subsequently exploited by the triumphant national-Catholicism that arose in the Francoist dictatorship.[53]

In any case, one should note that Salazar's disapproval of the German government increased during the following years mostly because of the racist aggressiveness demonstrated by the Nazis, a fact which Salazar clearly regarded as the origin of Europe's destruction. In this way, he bravely defended the undervalued Jewish composer Arnold Schoenberg after his initial difficulties with the Nazi regime.[54]

Finally, and as a necessary corrective, it must be emphasized that Salazar moderated many of his views after becoming aware of the horrors of the Holocaust. From that moment, he removed race allusions and almost eliminated any prejudice or attack against Jews in his writings.

CONCLUSION

The 1930s was a period of deep social and political crisis. Many certainties were being challenged and a new society—a mass society—was arising. The nineteenth century, paraphrasing

musical historiografía, see Emilio Ros-Fábregas, 'Historiografía de la música en las catedrales españolas: Nacionalismo y positivismo en la investigación musicológica', in *Codex* XXI, 1 (1998), 68–135.

49   Henri Collet, 'El porvenir de la música española', *Gaceta Musical*, 1 (Mayo 1928), 18–19.

50   Collet's influence on Salazar, especially his description of *Les Six* published in 1920 ('Un livre de Rimsky et un livre de Cocteau – Les cinq Russes, les six Français et Erik Satie', *Comoedia*, 16 January 1920 & 23 January 1920) can be observed especially in Salazar's book *Modesto Mussorgsky y su "Boris Godunof". Boceto histórico-crítico* (Madrid: J. Amado, 1925).

51   Collet, *L'Essor*, 151–52.

52   Adolfo Salazar, *Música y músicos de hoy* (Madrid: Editorial Mundo Latino, 1928), especially 78 & 343.

53   Ismael Saz, *España contra España: los nacionalismos franquistas* (Madrid:, Marcial Pons, 2003).

54   Adolfo Salazar, 'Los sesenta años de Schoenberg.- Cómo vemos a los otros y cómo ellos nos ven', *El Sol*, 16 February 1935.

Michael Walter, had come to an end.[55] In Spain, as in many other countries, a large discussion over the meaning of nation was taking place, especially after the establishment of the first democratic system in the modern sense of this term: the Second Republic. In Spain, as in the rest of Europe, Nazism and anti-Semitism had a profound impact upon the large intellectual struggle that was taking place in political circles, especially as discursive tools against the democratic system.

Needless to say, musical criticism participated in these discussions. The two critics, cited here, proved to be major figures both in the musical and political fields. They were placed on apparently opposing sides and each had a different approach to the concept of national identity. On the one hand, there was the view of Ruiz Albéniz, which presented an enormously restrictive idea of the Spanish as an isolated entity, essentially Catholic, militarist and traditionalist, an idea justified by negation of the national condition to all those who were unable to accept or obey it. On the other hand, there was the position of Adolfo Salazar—an elitist whose vision based on a restrictive nationalism focused on the ideas of 'race' and 'historical purity' and projected itself abroad by means of an international language.

Nazism was used by Ruiz Albéniz as an accessible example of a traditionalist, hierarchical, patriotic, and militaristic system. Ruiz Albéniz deliberately avoids mentioning anti-Christian racist ideas, which would have scarcely been accepted by his followers or himself. Salazar's rejection of National Socialism did not reflect an open democratic ideal, but rather a deeply elitist principle focused on a differentiation between 'selected minorities' and the 'masses', a distinction subverted destructively by Nazis. His rejection of Jews would also be part of a nationalist restrictive ideology based on the French model represented by Collet in France and Baroja in Spain.

It turns out that both discourses are not as different as one might have expected. They proved to be mutually exclusive, just like almost all discourses in 1930s Spain. Nevertheless, there exists a fundamental divergence between both: Salazar's ideology excluded totalitarian tendencies, condemned explicitly Nazi racism (despite his openly anti-Semitic stance) and defended democracy as a political system that was the lesser of two evils. Nothing like this is encountered in Ruiz Albéniz's writings.

After a terrible war in which he did not participate, Salazar went into exile. Ruiz Albéniz, on the other hand, held several positions during the forty years dictatorship born after a war he had exalted, encouraged, and legitimised (even before it took place). Therefore, and despite their potential similarities, both positions unfortunately cannot really be judged on the same moral plane.

---

55   Michael Walter, 'Music of seriousness and commitment: the 1930s and beyond', in *The Cambridge History of Twentieth–Century music*, ed. Nicholas Cook and Anthony Pople (Cambridge: Cambridge University Press 2004), 286–306.

Gemma Pérez-Zalduondo

The musical policies of the Third Reich in relation to the first years of Francoism (1938–1943)[1]

Without the Third Reich's support of the army, there can be little doubt that General Franco could not have seized power in Spain, driving out the legitimate government of the Second Republic and causing the Civil War that devastated the country between 1936 and 1939. This support arose as a result of the increased Nazi propaganda campaign in Spain, a country that the regime considered strategic to the enforcement of its expansionist policies. Even though Germany eventually came to distrust the weak presence of the Spanish Falange, the authoritarian party within Franco's first regular Government, and the consequent influence of the monarchical and clerical factions brought about by the coup, the two countries worked closely together. For instance, a Hispanic-German Cultural Agreement was signed in 1939.[2] Relations were particularly fruitful in certain cultural areas such as film and music. On the German side, the main objective behind such exchanges was the implementation of Nazi ideological propaganda in Spain, a process that was achieved in several ways.

Firstly, the presence of renowned German opera companies, artists and directors, in addition to the instrumental training imparted by Germans in Spain, was highly significant, not least for enhancing the vitality of Spanish musical life between 1939 and 1943.[3] This factor is particularly noteworthy when compared to the following decade, for it was only in the early 1950s that Spain began to emerge out of its long-standing international isolation. No less

[1] This work is related to the Research Project 'Música, ideología y política en la cultura artística durante el franquismo (1938-1975)', funded by the Ministerio de Ciencia e Innovación (MICINN-HAR2010-17968).

[2] For information on German cultural policy in Spain, see: Jésus De la Hera Martínez, *La política cultural de Alemania en España en el periodo de entreguerras* (Madrid: High Council of Scientific Research, 2002).

[3] For information on Hispanic-German musical relations during these years, see Gemma Pérez-Zalduondo, 'La música en los intercambios culturales de España con Alemania (1938–1942)', in Gemma Pérez-Zalduondo and María Isabel Cabrera García, *Cruces de caminos: intercambios musicales y artísticos en la Europa de la primera mitad del Siglo XX* (Granada: Editorial Universidad de Granada, Ministerio de Ciencia e Innovación, Université François-Rabelais de Tours (Equipe de Recherche & d'Accueil de Doctorants *Lieux et enjeux des modernités musicales)* 2010), 407–50.

important was the presence in Spain of some of the main German ambassadors in musical affairs, as well as that of Nazi musical icons, who either visited Spain regularly, as did the Berlin Philharmonic Orchestra, or were mentioned repeatedly in the Spanish press as part of Nazi propaganda, as in the case of the conductor, Wilhelm Furtwängler.[4] It should be noted too that whereas some concerts by German artists were still organised by private organizations during this period, the most highly publicised performances were the responsibility of the cultural institutions of the new Spanish state, in collaboration with their German counterparts.

Secondly, music was a particularly effective vehicle of Nazi propaganda which affected the ideas postulated by Falangist musicians and critics. Many indeed wrote extremely enthusiastically about the achievements of Nazism with regard to musical policies and expressed particular admiration for the Nazi creation of a highly effective system of symbols connecting the Aryan nation, ideology, race and music.

Thirdly, from 1941, Spanish music festivals were organized in the German city of Bad-Elster, in order to evoke pride among Spaniards by appraising them, through the official press, of the widespread appreciation of Spanish culture in Germany, a country whose importance within the history of music was repeatedly highlighted. The aforementioned Falangist critics dedicated many pages to bolstering the achievements of Spanish composers, and elevating their own experiences in assisting the great Wagnerian commemorations. The most active and influential of them, the Falangist priest Federico Sopeña would author a memoir of such events, published in 1942, coinciding with the moment when Nazi music propaganda reached even greater heights due to the number of concerts featuring German musicians in Spain as well as Spanish musicians in Germany, and by their frequent mention in the Spanish press.[5]

Nevertheless, apart from the most obvious manifestations of German-Spanish musical exchange, there are other subtle yet important aspects of Nazi cultural influence during the period spanning the first years of Francoism that warrant further exploration. In this respect, four issues deserve special emphasis: 1) the articulation of musical responsibilities within the scope of the Falange, the authoritarian Spanish party; 2) the symbolic value attached to anthems; 3) censorship of musical activity and 4) the rejection of Afro-American music.

---

4   Federico Sopeña, 'La Orquesta Filarmónica de Berlín', *Vértice*, 56 (May 1942), 19–20; 'La semana musical hispano-alemana, a través de la prensa del Reich', *Ritmo*, 159 (October 1942), 6.

5   Federico Sopeña, *Dos años de música en Europa: Mozart – Bayreuth – Strawinsky* (Madrid: Espasa-Calpe, 1942).

THE ESTABLISHMENT OF MUSICAL LIFE WITHIN THE SCOPE OF THE FALANGE:

The growth of the Spanish Falange during the first months of the Civil War was impressive. Its radical rhetoric and paramilitary structure, in addition to the discredit attached to those conservative organizations that had accepted the legitimacy of the Republic, were responsible for its popularity. After the death of its founder, Jose Antonio Primo de Rivera, Franco handled the Falange as an instrument for politically mobilizing the civilian population, a mass movement that aided them in identifying with their Fascist and Nazi allies.[6] Through a decree passed on 19 April 1937, the party merged with other political bodies; as a result, the Traditionalist Spanish Falange and the JONS (Falange Española Tradicionalista y de las Juntas de Ofensiva Nacional-Sindicalista or Spanish Traditionalist Phalanx of the Assemblies of National-Syndicalist Offensive) (F.E.T. y de las J.O.N.S.) became the only existing political body, and the Falangists occupied the most important positions within the administration and the party. On 30 January 1938, when Franco constituted his first government, they took over the responsibility for the union of social ministries. The Falange developed a complex organization that lasted until the end of Franco's regime, although its power and influence were reduced after 1943, following the turn of events in the World War. According to many historians,[7] apart from the political gestures made by Franco's government to fulfil the pact made with the Axis nations during the Spanish hostilities, Nazi and Fascist ideas influenced the policies implemented by the Falange. A good example occurred in March 1938 when the Fuero del Trabajo or Labour Charter was passed, a kind of 'false constitution' based on the *Carta del lavoro* of Italian Fascism.[8]

---

6   Julián Casanova, *República y Guerra Civil* (*Historia de España*, vol. 8, ed. Josep Fontana y Ramón Villares) (Barcelona: Crítica/Marcial Pons, 2007), 349–50.

7   Coincidentally, numerous studies on Francoism stress the importance of the relationship with Germany from the Civil War until 1943, the period which was labelled by the historian Stanley Payne as a 'Germanic phase', see Stanley G. Payne, *El régimen de Franco* (Madrid: Alianza Editorial, 1987), 281–322. Also, strategic and ideological affinities, such as the 'complicity' between the new Spanish state and fascist regimes has been emphasised. (Borja de Riquer, *La dictadura de Franco (Historia es España*, vol. 9…, 2010), 16). But at the same time, diverse monographs have highlighted influences or concrete models adopted from totalitarianisms; for the system of censure in cinematography and newsreel production, see Benito Bermejo Sánchez, 'La Vicesecretaría de Educación Popular (1941–1945): un "ministerio" de la propaganda en manos de Falange', *Espacio, Tiempo y Forma, S.V., Historia Contemporánea*, 4 (1991), 83, the control of the press, see Eduardo Ruiz Bautista, *Los señores del libro: propagandistas, censores y bibliotecarios en el primer franquismo* (Gijón (Asturias): Ediciones TREA, 2005), 88, and the organization of 'The Winter Help' in 1937, see Carme Molinero, *La captación de las masas. Política social y propaganda en el régimen franquista* (Madrid: Cátedra, 2005), 26, etc.

8   Casanova, 359.

The militant Falangists were given the responsibility for encouraging cultural life during the Civil War. Although research on musical activity during the Spanish conflict is still in its early stages, the first data that is particularly striking concerns the dynamism exhibited by certain Falangist musicians. For example, the pianist José Cubiles took over the Betica Orchestra, created many years before by Manuel de Falla, to stage concerts organized by sections of the party from 1938 in different Spanish cities.[9] Likewise, the Falange administered instrumental and vocal training, directed by musicians with an extensive pre-war career, which although presented as new ventures, actually replaced other similar programmes from the Republican period. For instance, the Symphonic Orchestra of Granada of the F.E.T. of the J.O.N.S. was organized under the composer and musician Ángel Barrios;[10] the Orfeon of the same city 'assigned to the Provincial Propanganda Service and sponsored by the F.E.T. of the J.O.N.S.', is shown to be under the direction of Valentín Ruiz Aznar, the chapel master of the cathedral of Granada.[11] A process of political and state institutionalization of musical life in Spain is evident, at least from 1938, a characteristic shared by other totalitarian regimes. In addition, during the same period, concerts were organized by German citizens in Spain,[12] and others where German musicians collaborated with Spanish musicians.[13] During the Civil War, music therefore started to form a part of the burgeoning relations between both countries.

With regard to the repertoire featured at these events, it should be noted that works by Spanish musicians linked to the Republic were not represented. Nevertheless, the Betica Orchestra's programmes in the pre-war period included contemporary French works, and, at least until February 1938, also Mendelssohn,[14] except on those occasions when the organizers were German or the performers were German musicians.

---

9   See the handouts of the following concerts: 29 March 1938 in the Cinema del Soldado of Seville organized by the Feminine Section of Culture of F.E.T. and the J.O.N.S; 10 and 11 May in the Teatro Cervantes of Malaga organized by the Provincial Delegation of Press and Propaganda of the F.E.T. and the J.O.N.S.

10 Programme of the first concert of the Symphonic Orchestra of the Falange of Granada, held in the Municipal Building on 25 July 1938, 'feast of Saint John Apostle'.

11 Programme-invitation for the concert 'inauguration of the Orfeon', held on 25 September 1938.

12 Programme of the concert organized by the German Colony of Seville, held at the Andalucía Palace on 23 April 1939 of the Betica Chamber Orchestra, conducted by Manuel Navarro.

13 The same Betica Orchestra, conducted by José Cubiles with the German singer Charlotte Dahmen, visited numerous Spanish cities from August 1938. See *Orquesta Bética de Cámara 1921. Orquesta Bética Filarmónica 1962–1987. Memoria de los últimos 25 años* (Seville: S. E, 1987), 13.

14 Concert programme of the Betica Chamber Orchestra, conducted by José Cubiles, on 20 February 1938 in the Teatro de la Exposición of Seville, organized by the Provincial Delegation of Press and Propaganda of the Falange.

On the other hand, the press repeatedly touted German musical policy as an ideal, as was the case, for example, in an article published in April 1939 by the guitarist Regino Sáinz de la Maza. In surveying developments in German music during the early part of the twentieth century, he pointed out that:

> the last consequences of Wagnerian romanticism, sound symbolism appeared to have been exhausted. Creative potential is replaced by a cultural spiritualism. Work requires the support of theory. Thus arose highly diverse tendencies: Academicism, Impressionism, Atonalism, Polytonalism, Expressionism, Anti-romanticism, pure music, abstract music and many others. Germany became the battlefield where these tendencies warred with each other, thereby offering proof of the insecurity and the loss during this period of change. Music was hotly debated, in an attempt to resolve the several problems that threatened to sterilize it by speculations. The internal mechanism of creation was reversed. However the advent of the new regime rescued German music from this dead end, putting a halt to all these experiences. Hitler's Germany has corrected the course of music and orientated it once more towards its glorious traditions. The nation that has given the world the most distinguished figures of music representing the profoundly musical spirit of its soul, could not be lost in theories which carried within themselves the seed of decomposition. This need of salvation had already been felt and expounded by Richard Eichenauer in 1932. In his book *Musik und Rasse*, he defends the future of European Music from the dangers that threaten to destroy it. His theory is that European Music, based on the harmonic and polyphonic score, is a Nordic invention, and this tradition has solely been preserved by its creators, the Nordic races. Germany today offers us a glimpse of a nation prepared to guide the destinies of art, realizing its cultural and spiritual value, and the moral influence that it exercises.[15]

This text demonstrates the admiration felt by the Falange for the Nazis, a fact which does not change at least until the later turn of events in the World War. Furthermore, such admiration strongly suggests that German musical policy served as a reference point for the Spanish totalitarian party's policy during this period. Besides, the writers of texts, many of whom were similar to the one mentioned above, were often the Falangist musicians and critics who were not only responsible for the administration of Spanish musical activity, but also were often invited to musical events in Germany.

After the end of the Civil War, in 1941 a new structure was stipulated for the party, consisting of four departments, all of which were given responsibilities on musical matters. These

---

15   Regino Sáinz de la Maza, 'Pasado y presente de la música alemana', *Vértice* (April 1939) (special edition dedicated to Germany).

included the Department of Popular Education, which was responsible for education, propaganda, cinema, theatre, radio broadcasts and censorship[16] and the Department of Services, which was responsible for those aspects of musical activity related to information, law and research. However, for present purposes, our focus will be directed to the other two Departments. The first to be discussed here is the General Department, which headed the Feminine Section and the Youth Front. The Feminine Section was given charge of the political and social training of the Spanish woman,[17] which it carried out, among other issues, through disciplines related to instruction on household matters imparted in educational and work centres. Folklore as a link to 'tradition' and the 'land', served as a vehicle for diffusing ideology, and as a differentiating element of education between the two sexes.

The Feminine Section's activity in the field of music, especially in the collection and practice of folklore, was intense and involved all Spanish women. It was sustained over a long period of time, particularly given that it was the last Falangist institution to disappear after Franco's death. It was put in charge of the Choirs and Dances, organized since 1942 in all regions of Spain. Competitions between these groups, held once every year, were widely publicized in the press. They also fulfilled an outstandingly important role as cultural ambassadors in other countries, often where Spanish politicians were not invited.

Documentary evidence reveals that officials of the Feminine Section travelled to Axis nations on at least sixteen occasions between 1938 and 1942. Thirteen of these visits were to Germany, and the rest to Italy, Portugal and Austria.[18] On the other hand, the musicologist Beatriz Martínez del Fresno states that the reason for these prolonged visits to Germany was primarily to study the structure and functioning of German home economics schools and to participate in the 'Strength through Joy' celebrations.[19] There were also reciprocal arrangements with visits of 'German comrades' to Spain.[20]

---

16   The *Law of 20 May 1941* created the Department and decreed that all services of press and propaganda would come under its jurisdiction.

17   *Decree of 28 December 1939* (Office of the Head of State) (BOE 29 December).

18   Kathleen Richmond, *Las mujeres en el fascismo español. La Sección Femenina de la Falange, 1934–1959.* (Madrid: Alianza, 2004), 69–70. Also see Beatriz Martínez del Fresno, 'La danza in Spagna durante il Franchismo', in *Sara Acquarone. Una coreografa in Italia*, ed. Alessandro Pontremoli (Turin: UTET 2009), 54–89.

19   The relations between the Feminine Section and the Axis nations during the Civil War and World War II as well as the position occupied by folklore and folk dances in them, have been studied by Beatriz Martínez del Fresno in: 'La Sección Femenina de Falange y sus relaciones con los *Países amigos*. Música, danza y política exterior durante la Guerra Civil y el primer franquismo (1937–1943)', in *Cruces de caminos*, 357–406.

20   See the letter dated 1 December 1942 sent by the Chief of the Cinematographic Department of the National Delegation of Propaganda to the Director of Rera Laboratories requesting copies of documentaries on these visits (AGA, *Cultura* (03)48 Caja 21/45).

The Youth Front was established in 1940 to 'ensure the training and discipline of the Fatherland in the Catholic, Spanish and military spirit of F.E.T. and the J.O.N.S.'[21] Participation was obligatory for all students, which explicitly included all those studying at music conservatoires, and the subjects they were taught included pre-military, political, physical and sports education. Moreover, after 1944, the Front was assigned the responsibility of carrying out 'an extensive labour of political and social education', as well as propaganda among the working–class youth. In their camps, colonies, hostels, courses and academies, the anthems, religious and popular songs played an important role both as a medium of education and for propagating ideology. The organization edited compilations of these repertories,[22] and photographs and texts published in Falangist magazines testify to the importance of music in their activities,[23] which were primarily centred on the collective practices that were also characteristic of musical education under the Nazis.[24] As a matter of fact, the Advisory Committee of Culture and Art was responsible for promoting 'the creation of bands, choirs, street music groups, etc.',[25] along with organizing 'musical competitions' such as 'the Caudillo's Trophy'.[26]

One of the Youth Front's most significant celebrations was the Song Day, to commemorate the end of the Civil War. The text of this event is an example of the fiery public rhetoric of that period, as well as the glorification of the Civil War, now identified with the Crusades:

> In the explosion of jubilee with which Spain marked the declaration of Victory, it was also our youth that sang the meaning of the Crusade, the glory of the Fallen and the return of the victorious banners, with the purest joy.[27]

The rules also stipulated that the festivities would celebrate 'the national values of which folk songs remind us, that are a synthesis of the sentiments and unity of the Spanish people'. This

---

21 *Law of 6 December 1940* (Office of the Head of State) (BOE, December).

22 The first was *Canciones para Marchas y Campamentos*, edited by the Youth Front in 1942. It contains the text of 106 songs, of which 31 are marches and anthems and the rest, folk songs.

23 This aspect is especially evident in the publications of the Falange, such as the magazine *Vértice* and the daily newspaper *Arriba*.

24 For an introduction to the topic of musical education in the Third Reich, see Noèmi Lefebvre, 'La enseñanza musical en el Tercer Reich: la perversión de un modelo', in *Catálogo de la Exposición La música y el Tercer Reich. De Bayreuth a Terezin* (Barcelona: Fundació Caixa Catalunya y Cité de la Musique de París, 2007), 128–35.

25 *Order of 29 April 1944* (Secretary General of Movement) (BOE, 31 May).

26 *Order of 20 February 1942* (National Delegation of the Youth Front) (BOE, 30 March).

27 *Instruction of 20 February 1942* (National Delegation of the Youth Front) (BOE, 30 March). For more data on the campaign for the Song Day see Rafael Abella, *Crónica de la posguerra 1939–1955* (Barcelona: Ediciones B.S., 2008), 274–75.

identification between song and sentiment has strong historical foundations having been formulated during the nineteenth century, whilst the call to unity and the utilization of music
and art to inculcate the values of collectivity is characteristic of totalitarian ideologies.[28] What
is new is the integration of music into a political education that favoured warrior values for
young men and which perpetuated the values of pre-industrial societies for women.

The second Department that warrants detailed consideration here was one concerned
with Social Work. It was in charge of the National Delegations of Syndicates, which brought
together the workers, including those in music.[29] It also controlled musical issues through
some of its sub-departments, such as the Union Work of Education and Recreation. In 1942,
the list of activities arranged by this organization in Barcelona included: 45 concerts of the
Symphony Orchestra, 8 of the Symphony Band, 26 appearances of the Military Band in as
many parades and 18 concerts organized with the collaboration of national and foreign artists. Besides, in the city theatres and in the provinces, the 'producers' were able to witness 'the
best works of musical comedies and *zarzuelas*'.[30] This data corroborates what has already been
noted on the grouping of musical formations within the scope of the Falange, of which some
existed before the war. Federico Sopeña refers to this fact when he explains that Education
and Recreation promoted the creation of orchestras or cooperated in the maintenance of others, 'generally smaller and conforming to the classical orchestra format'. He gives the example
of the Orchestra of Madrid, among others, which 'cooperates with the cultural works of the
State, performing in factories, workshops and other similar workplaces.'[31]

The Union Work of Education and Recreation was also given the responsibility of educat-
ing working-class youth under the age of 21, in collaboration with the Youth Front, in factories and workshops, on public holidays and vacations, through musical activities, especially
choral groups. The Feminine Section guided the working class and peasant women placed in
the Agrarian Union Groups, also under this Department. The musicologist Beatriz Martínez
del Fresno has demonstrated the existing similarities between the musical activities of these

28 For the concept of unity in music and art in the first phase of Franco's regime, see María Isabel Ca-
    brera García and Gemma Pérez-Zalduondo, 'La unidad: concepto referencial para las artes y la música
    en el primer franquismo', *Cuadernos de Arte de la Universidad de Granada*, 35 (2004), 183–96.

29 The musicologist Beatriz Martínez del Fresno analyzed the publications of the National Syndicate of
    Performance, which included music professionals, their purging and classification along with their
    work regulation in: 'Realidades y máscaras en la música de la posguerra', in *Actas del Congreso Dos déca-
    das de cultura artística en el Franquismo (1936–1956)* Vol. II, ed. Ignacio Henares, María Isabel Cabrera
    García, Gemma Pérez Zalduondo and José Castillo (Granada: Universidad de Granada, 2001), 31–82.

30 Antonio Trape Pi, 'Un año de fecunda actuación sindical', *Vértice*, 53/54 (February/March, 1942), 82.

31 Federico Sopeña, Gerardo Diego and Joaquín Rodrigo, *Diez años de música en España* (Madrid: Espa-
    sa-Calpe, 1949), 108.

institutions and those of other totalitarian regimes. For example, the activities of the Union Work of Education and Recreation, which include the aforementioned Choirs and Dances, were inspired by the *Opera Nazionale Dopolavoro* of Fascist Italy, and also by Nazi organizations such as *Kraft durch Freude* (Strength through Joy).[32] In other words, Nazi and Fascist organizations served as models for those created by the Falange in Spain, and its members had opportunities to gain first-hand knowledge on their organization and functioning.

The year 1942 witnessed the creation of the two institutions solely responsible for music—the Commissariat for Music and the Council for Music—both working under the auspices of the Ministry of National Education, which itself was directed by a Catholic royalist. The Falange would be represented in these institutions by the Secretary of the Commissariat, Federico Sopeña, and Council members such as Antonio Tovar, who had been in charge of the publicity and propaganda of the F.E.T. The Commissariat's prime responsibility was to monitor professional music training imparted in the conservatories, in addition to the organization of the National Orchestra of Spain, for whose members, compulsory affiliation to the Spanish Syndicate of Performance was a requirement. In my opinion, the division of responsibilities with regard to musical activity derives primarily from the role in education and propaganda conferred on it by the Falange, an idea derived again from Nazism.[33] This sharing of responsibilities between different institutions and organizations seems to contradict the strategy followed by the politicians of the Second Spanish Republic (1931–1936), who delegated all charges on music to a sole institution, the National Junta of Music and Lyrical Theatre.[34]

ANTHEMS AS SYMBOLS AND REPRESENTATION OF IDEOLOGY

As the war progressed, the new state adopted the paraphernalia, symbols and gestures of mass totalitarian manifestations. The press published numerous articles that proposed the style of Nazi Germany as a model. An important text is that by Federico Urrutia, published in a special edition of the Falangist magazine *Vértice* dedicated entirely to Germany:

> The life of the population has an external appearance, characteristic of each member that constitutes it and models it before history. As is popularly said «the face is the mirror of the soul», we may also affirm that the State liturgy, as well as the cultural and artistic mani-

---

32   Martínez del Fresno, 'Realidades', 57.
33   See the discussion of musical life in the Third Reich, considered to be propaganda, in Erik Levi, *Music in the Third Reich* (London: Macmilllan, 1994), 25–27.
34   *Decree of 21 July 1931* (*Gaceta de Madrid*, 22 July).

festations of a population, is the true reflection of its civic life and of the philosophical «I»
of its destiny.

In accordance with this criterion, Germany therefore must surely be the most organized
human family that has been able to endow its collective life with an aesthetic splendour.
The creators of National Socialism have realized their role as demigods and mythological
life has once again risen with all the force of its rituals, the integral value of the symbols,
the exact meaning of the song, and the mythical theory of blind and captive forces, converted to colours, geometry, art and violence.

Only thus is the Cyclopean magnitude of the «Nazi» liturgy conceived
[…]

The stadium and the highway for the muscle, the snowy peaks for the song, the forest for
meditation, clarinets and flags for the arrogant cry, parades for rhythm and symphony of
steel in a spectacular display of discipline for the burning equation of each day.[35]

This diatribe also dedicates a paragraph to education in the Third Reich:

In camps for children, the drum and the dagger give them a military gesture which will
remain with them for the rest of their lives; in the luminous fields of sport, women acquire
their vigour and their beaming smiles with the graceful movements of dance and armed
with the bow and the arrow; the soldier prepares in peace time for war in an atmosphere of
epic songs that reminds him of his warrior pride, and the civilian man is incorporated into
the State's emotive harmony with the gesture of the raised banners.[36]

Frequent emphasis was placed on the similarities between totalitarian regimes drawing comparison between Spanish achievements and those of their German counterparts. As an anonymous editor of the daily newspaper *Arriba* declared about the kinds of civil and military rites:
'Spain already has a State that takes care of these values and the dignity and decorum of the
masses; as Goebbels will one day discover.'[37]

The celebrations of Franco's victory and the symbols and rituals that constituted the image
of the regime until its end adopted the 'aesthetic of the masses' that was called for since 1937:

The new political principles of two European states that have long been fighting against
social disintegration and the pernicious influences of Russia, have brought to light a new

---

35   Federico Urrutia, 'La liturgia "nazi"', *Vértice* (April 1939).
36   Ibid.
37   'Goebbels y algunas definiciones del nuevo estilo', *Arriba*, 1 June 1939.

art that is a clear result of their political consciousness and of their ardent veneration of idealism and order.

[...]

Let us learn from Germany and Italy who have created this new aesthetic and sincerely feel this eagerness to demonstrate their unity in a bright and enthusiastic manner. Their military formations, trained athletes, disciplined youth, women gymnasts, their flags, their perfect monuments evoke an Empire and their great cities open their triumphal avenues, their great squares and stadiums make it possible to congregate masses of millions, that can move and sway at the call of one commanding voice.[38]

The acclamation of Nazi rhythms, architecture and aesthetics and the reference to Greek classicism are accompanied by a multitude of photos of contemporary German celebrations.

Simultaneously, there were rites and religious demonstrations of a medieval nature supposedly derived from glorious Spanish traditions that harmonized with the Falangists. It should not be surprising, therefore, that it was a Jesuit musicologist, the father Nemesio Otaño, who authored an important work, published in the *Ritmo* magazine of music of which he was also the editor, on the recovery, analysis and dissemination of historical military repertoire and the creation of works belonging to this genre that were destined to be symbols of the new times, of the authentic race and the true Spain imposed by the victors. There were constant references to totalitarian regimes, especially Germany, on this point:

Military music, especially in marches, is such a highly valued psychological element, that—we may state without exaggeration—a great part of the informative warrior spirit of a people depends on it. I refer, specifically, to the German nation.[39]

The German factor was of significant importance for Francoism, which may be evaluated from another angle by observing certain initiatives of Spanish institutions: in 1941, a compilation of official anthems, including anthems of the Falange and of the different divisions of the armed forces, was scheduled to be published. The files stored in the General Archives, located in Alcalá de Henares, from where these documents have been taken, contain all the handwritten scores, some harmonisations and the authorizations of the music, composers and authors for their publication. Although plans for publication never materialised, it is particularly important to note that the file includes the *Horst Wessel Lied,* the Anthem of German National Socialism, and the *Giovinezza,* the official Fascist Anthem, both of which were to be incorporated in the

---

38   'Estética de las muchedumbres', *Vértice*, 3 (June 1937).
39   Nemesio Otaño, 'El Himno Nacional y la música militar', *Ritmo*, 138 (September 1940), 3.

planned collection. Nevertheless, there is a significant difference: while a new text was formu-lated for the National Socialist Anthem with slogans and messages referring to the Falange, Franco and Catholicism, a free translation of the original Italian anthem is incorporated. In other words, although both were to be included in the collection, the first appropriates the mu-sic and adds to it the ideological messages of Francoism, while the second is merely translated.[40]

The contrasting approaches to the anthems illustrate the different level of military assis-tances given to Franco during the Civil War, the varying admiration felt by the Falange for other regimes allied to it, and in my opinion, the different levels of efficiency of the propa-ganda machinery of Fascism and Nazism in Spain.

Stories and chronicles of these years offer an idea of the pro-German fervour prevalent in Franco's Spain: when the historian Rafael Abella explains how the German boats disembarked in different cities during the Spanish conflict, he points out that 'they were applauded in marches, in football matches or in the inevitable concerts held by their music bands.'[41]

In any case, the desire to incorporate Spain among the achievements of the totalitarian countries was distinctive and although the country did not actively participate in World War II, its friendship and affinity with other friendly regimes was evident, as was its search for models to elaborate the rites and symbols required by the new Spanish regime.

Germany's interest in deepening its friendship with Spain became apparent when soon after, in January and February 1942, the Hispanic-German Music Festival held in Madrid and Bilbao boasted the presence of the General Intendant of Music of the Ministry of Propaganda of the Reich, Heinz Drewes.

CENSORSHIP OF MUSICAL ACTIVITY WITHIN THE SCOPE OF THE FALANGE

For the Falange, as for Nazism, both art and music had to function as an adjunct to the State. This idea materialized in the form of institutions that constituted a parallel govern-

---

40 The Spanish text of the German anthem is:
   'Blue shirt and red beret / blue phalanx and *requetés* in company / united we went when Franco / raised the flag for one faith.
   For honour, Fatherland, and justice / we fight today in the dawn / and if death comes and embraces us / Long live Spain! We shall say in falling.
   The youth are ready for war / Soldiers they wish to be/ and to make Spain One, Great and Free / / with the sacred Empire of the Cross.
   Arise, brother Spaniards! / A soldier of Franco the Saviour am I / Spain has risen upon this earth / and firmly marches to the beat of the drum'. AGA, *Cultura* (03)48 Caja 21/45.
41 Rafael Abella, *La vida cotidiana durante la Guerra Civil* (Barcelona: Planeta, 1975), 215.

ment within the Party. In this way, the highly powerful Department of Education, created in 1941, formed a music section within its Department of Oral Propaganda in 1942, which was renamed the Department of Oral Propaganda and Music Education, a term that highlighted the symbiotic relationship between musical activity and propaganda.

The Department was represented by a Delegate in each provincial capital who issued weekly reports informing the central office in Madrid of all musical and theatrical events, conferences, and so on, which had taken place in their respective cities. Each delegate also notified the Spanish capital on any matters requested, for example, concerning information on any individual able to carry out propaganda duties, lists of cultural or philharmonic associations, orchestras, publishing houses or record companies. Their function, in short, was to inform as well as exercise censorship.

Enquiries on important propaganda events were especially meticulous. For example, the report on the concert by the Berlin Chamber Orchestra, conducted by Hans von Benda and held in Granada in November 1942, contains very detailed information on the decorations and appearance of the hall, with carpets, garlands, tapestry, German and Spanish flags, etc. Moreover, articles on this event published in newspapers, which measured its impact in terms of publicity, are also included.[42]

The procedures that were followed to approve the staging of a concert by the pianist Ricardo Viñes and its radio broadcast are examples of the complicated bureaucratic machinery resulting from censorship. The respective file contains fourteen different documents, which include a request for reports on the socio-political conduct of the performer and the consequent certificate issued by the Chief of the Section of Information:

> After having consulted the records in the Archives of this Section of Information, consisting of personalities that sympathize with the Government of the Republic, we conclude that there is no information referring to the socio-political conduct of Mr. Ricardo Viñes.[43]

Once the doubts as to the possible leftist leanings of the musician were cleared, the National Representative of Propaganda accepts the payment to the artist of 1500 pesetas, and a new report, remitted to the Vice-Secretary of Popular Education provides further background regarding the figure of Viñes, highlights his merits and debut performances in Europe 'of the best works of our composers', cites Debussy and Ravel who dedicated their compositions to him,

---

42   'Weekly part of number four activities, corresponding to the week from the 23 to the 29 November, 1942'. (AGA, *Cultura* (03)48 Caja 21/118).

43   The report is dated 1 June 1942 (AGA, *Cultura* (03)48 Caja 21/103).

and finally advises that a concert be organized where he 'may perform as a soloist'.[44] So-called 'social-political investigations on musicians who worked with the left-wing' were also issued from the provinces and sent to Madrid. In other words, a purge on whoever was suspected of indifference to the Regime was put into place. For example, on the 9 September 1942, the Head of the Department of Oral Propaganda and Music Education asked the Provincial Representative of Girona to provide 'a detailed account of all the composers, instrumentalists and musicians in general who had politically collaborated with the left-wing, clearly specifying what this collaboration consisted of, and on what date it was given.'[45] It is important to remember that a purge had already been set in motion in 1942, which extended to music professionals and government officials, and was particularly strict with regard to teachers, and inevitably included the teaching staff in music conservatories.

We have been able to study documents in which the Vice-Secretary demanded efficiency in the vigilance of the educational and moral nature of cultural events from the delegates, especially with regard to magazines on music or musical comedies. Often, the National Secretary reprimanded the provincial delegate, as was the case with the delegate of Girona in December 1942:

> I hope, that from now on, you will inform me, albeit briefly, of the musical activity of this province, even though no concert or conference on musical subjects are organized by this Delegation, and I also warn you that you are in charge of both censorship and control of those concerts held in cafes, bars, etc., and of ensuring that no performances of forbidden works are carried out.[46]

1942 was the year in which Nazi propaganda achieved its most intensive impact on Spanish musical life, the decisive moment of the Axis nations' expansion in the world, when all aspects of musical activity began to be censored by the Falange. From May, the National Representative of Propaganda signed orders[47] intended to censor concerts[48], conferences on musical

---

44   Ibid.
45   9 September 1942 (AGA, Cultura (03)48, 21/118).
46   31 December 1942 (AGA, *Cultura* (03)48 Caja 21/118).
47   All included in AGA, *Cultura* (03)48 Caja 21/102.
48   'Considering that it is necessary to maintain the dignity of public musical acts held in Spain, that in any case, must meet the high standards set by our musical prestige, this Delegation proposes that future concerts be brought beforehand under its control, for authorization. It is therefore necessary that all Musical Societies— cultural and philharmonic—the Organized Orchestras—the Symphonic and Philharmonic Orchestras of Madrid, Barcelona, etc.—that perform periodically, the registered concert agencies—the Casa Daniel, Caballero, etc.—and the Spanish Theatre of Madrid, the Liceo of Barce-

matters, musical publications[49], music in the press[50] and gramophone recordings[51]. In short, the censorship of any activity relating to music and musicians was made compulsory, and this process was set in motion more than five years after the musical policy of Franco's regime commenced in 1938, at a time when, as was mentioned before, the course of the World War made it appear as if the advance of the totalitarian regimes was unstoppable.

THE REJECTION OF AFRO-AMERICAN MUSIC

The parallels between Nazi and Falangist totalitarian ideologies would, in theory, explain the similarities between certain aspects of their musical policies. Yet Spain's continuous references to Germany also suggest that the country was, to a certain extent, also considered as a model in other areas. Such allusions to Nazi musical policy were, as we have seen in previous sections, quite frequent in the Spanish press since 1939, but we may also find them in 1942, in the internal documentation of the Department of Popular Education, which, in this last year, published a circular stipulating censorship of any adaptation of classical repertoire into danceable rhythms. The text reads as follows:

> Having abused inconsiderably and without the slightest respect, the adaptation of im-
> mortal works of art, true masterpieces of musical literature, to danceable rhythms, and this
> arbitrary irresponsibility being highly damaging to the adequate formation of our people's

---

lona, etc.—that frequently organize concerts, submit to this Delegation, a quarterly plan detailing the number and variety of recitals that are to be staged during these three months, as well as the specialty, names and nationalities of the participating artistes.'

49 'Considering that one of the most important missions of this Section is the regularization, control and direction of musical publications, directing their efforts to the principal purpose of dignifying musical production, all Spanish publishers must submit to this Section from the established date, three copies of all works that they intend to publish, for their previous perusal by the censors and authorization'.

50 'After confirming that lyrical contests and musicals organized for advertising purposes do not fulfill the minimum requisites of artistic dignity, and therefore are detrimental to our musical culture, this Section deems it necessary to insist on the advisability of regulating such events, be they public or radio broadcasts'.

51 'Bearing in mind that for the complete direction of Spanish musical activities—one of the principal aims of this delegation—all such activities should be regulated and controlled, it is absolutely impera-tive that a strict vigilance be maintained—as censorship—on the national production of records. This can only be achieved if all Spanish production houses are required to send to this Delegation, for cen-sorship purposes, a complete list of records to be supplied, with the name of the author or authors of the composition and the main musician or musicians. Also, when registering compositions that have not yet been published, three originals of the work must be submitted for review'.

musical taste – one of the aims that this Department must follow up – and which we believe to be essential, – just as has been done in Germany –a n order must be enacted that
strictly forbids these unspeakable threats.

This order must include the immediate confiscation of discs and scores of this type of
music that have already been registered and printed; its radio broadcast and performance
in bars, cafes, dances or any other public establishment must be banned, and the total
prohibition of any recording and publishing that damages the musical prestige of Spain.[52]

The protests against the adaptations referred to in the text had been growing in intensity after
the end of the Civil War. For example, the composer Joaquín Turina, head of the Commissariat
of Music (Ministry of National Education) since 1942 and the highest official for musical affairs,
had already stated his opinion on the matter. In 1941 he alluded to the 'discredit of jazz, to the
triviality of variety shows', to the frivolity and low standards of 'street music played in dances,
bars and party salons', but also ironically justified these practices because, according to him, they
responded to the necessity of 'obtaining daily sustenance', which made them 'respectable' and
even pleasant. Nevertheless, he censured the adaptation of classical works to 'frivolous' rhythms.[53]

Protests were also raised against the radio broadcasts of jazz. In the *Ritmo*, Francisco Padín
criticized this style as a 'degrading music, artistically and morally—we have used the exact
words of the illustrious editor of the *Ritmo*—of modern 'jazz' and its by-products', in the words
of Father Otaño. The basis for criticism was the artistic and moral superiority of historical
works and of Spanish folklore over danceable rhythms and jazz, which were regarded as 'stri-
dent and unpleasant', but another argument had to be added: the search for a Spanish musical
identity with a concrete history and repertoire. It was a 'crusade for culture and Spanishness':

And we have expanded upon this commentary because Music –better written in small
letters- music of 'jazz, exotic and sensual, as is heard on the radio, in variety shows and
even in operettas and revues which dub them as performances, deceiving the innocent
and unsophisticated, without taking into consideration the repertoire played by bands in
dance salons, is now unbearable, and it offends our ears with savage, black rhythms, when
one may extract and vulgarize all that may be extracted from the copious and abundant
never-ending source of Spanish folklore. And even if that were not the case, it would still
be Spanish, and that is enough.[54]

---

52   Letter written by Torres López, Acting National Counselor of the National Representative of Propagan-
      da to the Vice-Secretary of Popular Education dated 21 May 1942. AGA, *Cultura* (03)48 Caja 21/102.
53   Joaquín Turina, 'El asesinato de la Música', *Ritmo*, 144 (April 1941).
54   Francisco Padin, 'A propósito de una campaña a favor de la Música española', *Ritmo*, 147 (July–Au-
      gust 1941), 7.

Such demands finally obtained a response from the Department of Popular Education in the form of the above-mentioned regulation, parallel to another passed by the National Syndicate of Performance[55] to which an editorial in the *Ritmo*, presumably written by Father Otaño, refers:

> The alarming proportions acquired by the invasion of Negroid music, with its profane interpretations of great ideas, gems of musical craftsmanship, constituted a serious threat to Western culture and civilization, which demanded forceful resistance to a barrier, a unanimous and formidable opposition, capable of smashing, of cancelling the destructive effects of artistic purity that Negroid music, with its instruments and interpretations, represented. The National Syndicate of Performance has opposed this avalanche of depraved performances of bands that practice a frivolous art, passing a regulation that completely prohibits the desecrating versions of works that should have no versions, no interpretations, other than the original, conceived by the great and immortal composers, which deserve private and public respect.[56]

The writer of this text hails the regulations, which 'will punish unscrupulous musicians, as well as render them unfit to exercise their profession' that carry out such adaptations and establishes his opinions pointing out that:

> If coarse language wounds cultured ears and weakens the morale of the people, the same occurs with music at the service of human passions, and it needs persecution and punishment, until coarse musical language, by sound and rhythm pornographic, is completely eradicated from our environment, where we must breathe only pure air.[57]

He ends with an exhortation to everybody to contribute 'to the yearned-for artistic purge', for which 'one has only to be vigilant and report all unlawful musical activity'.[58]

As we can observe, this process of nationalization of Spanish music defends at the same time the 'Western civilization' where works by Jews are excluded by other authors, as an anonymous author quoted by López-Chávarri points out: 'End the fox-trots once and for all. They are part of the arsenal of Jewish souls set in motion to degrade the chosen races, and it

---

55   'Órdenes de este Sindicato Nacional: Grupo de Música', *Boletín del Sindicato Nacional del Espectáculo*, 5 (Agosto 1942), 17, in: Martínez del Fresno, 'Realidades', 79.
56   'El Sindicato Nacional del Espectáculo y sus recientes disposiciones', *Ritmo*, 159 (October 1942), 3.
57   Ibid.
58   Ibid.

is pure idiocy to continue dulling our senses with them'.[59] This identification of black, barbarian and Jewish souls possesses certain racist connotations that are easily identifiable with Nazism.[60]

A surprising example of how far this rejection of 'Negro' rhythms went is the story of the scandal created by the performance in April 1942 of *Tres postales madrileñas*, an orchestral work written in 1931 by one of the most popular post-war musicians, José Muñoz Molleda.[61]

The contradictions and the problems that the censorship of these 'Negro', or simply, 'foreign' rhythms provoked in practice, as in Germany, can also be observed within the complicated issue of music that was broadcast for soldiers. In 1941 and 1942 Spanish National Radio recorded two festivals on gramophone records, which included voices of the mothers of 'voluntary' soldiers of the *División Azul*, or Blue Division, the Spanish military contribution to the German Army during the Second World War. These records, which were sent to Berlin, contained the entire show, including its music. In the report sent to the National Representative of Propaganda on 28 December 1941, the Director of the National Radio defends his position on the musical section, and, once again, the decision is justified by using an example of the German manner:

> It is possible that the musical aspect of this show is not lacking in criticism, though it could be reproached as having an excess of Cuban music and dance. Firstly, I must say that my personal opinion toward the use of this type of orchestra is completely favourable. We are calling out to soldiers, who mostly come to know the name of these orchestras through music records, on the radio, or in public establishments, etc., both of them, – Rogelio Barba and Manolo Bell –world famous. I have even heard the latter at the Berlin Scala in the middle of a war.[62]

In this case the problem was confined to the Cuban rhythms, which were, from a moral point of view, seen as problematic. Moreover, further on in the letter, the Director of the National Radio points out his dissatisfaction with the official alternative to this type of light music, folklore:

---

59   San Sebastian, 7 March 1938, in Eduardo López Chavarri, 'Sigue la "matanza" de los grandes maestros', *Ritmo*, 153 (February–March, 1942), 4.

60   A few months before, in November 1941, just prior to the organization of the musical censorship to which we have referred, Falange announced the campaign to 'eliminate crypto-leftists, former masons, and those guilty of activities that were considered 'immoral' or simply 'incompatible with the party'. See Payne, 303.

61   The chronicler defends the musician, if and when 'he does not get carried away by styles and strange tendencies.' See: 'Información musical',*Ritmo*, 154 (April 1942), 11.

62   Report from the Director of National Radio, 28 December 1941.

Of course, my wish would have been to find a good orchestra of popular Spanish music but, apart from the unfortunate orchestras of '*pulso y pua*' of Education and Recreation and the Regional Centres, there is nothing at all useable. We must not forget that this has been our biggest success, as we have had two very expensive musical groups performing even at eleven o'clock in the morning and who fill the theatre every night.[63]

He concludes, 'Either way, on this point as well as on all others, I await your superior judgement and advice.'[64]

The contradiction, on one hand, between the National Catholicism that advocated a return to tradition—and the use of folklore with regard to music—as moral salvation for the new Spain, and on the other, the reality of a country recently arisen from a bloody Civil War, divided between the victorious and the defeated that found itself submerged in an economy struggling to survive, was always present. Even the Department of Education forestalled the protests of the clergy and their colleagues against the moral content of the broadcast musical comedies, saying that they were only 'trivialities, but not highly scandalous trivialities', and that 'the specialists lacked unanimity' on the morality criteria.[65] As we can see, even though there were considerable differences between the situations in both Spain and Germany in 1942, there also existed important parallels between the two.

To summarize: common elements can be identified between 1938 and 1943 in the criteria that was followed for the establishment of musical responsibilities in the German and Spanish totalitarian party apparatus, especially with regard to the concept of music as propaganda. It is also possible to point out certain similar strategies in the policies developed by both parties, such as the nationalization of musical activity. It may also be considered that these elements and strategies are characteristic of power wielding in totalitarian states, in particular the rejection of the avant-garde, the concept of unity, the symbolical function of music in their rites and its role as the representation and transmission of ideologies, are shared features in the discourses on art and music.

The manifest admiration of the Falangists for the German regime in the area of music, and the efficiency of Nazi propaganda where music played a major role, has been emphasised. Data that demonstrates the existence of a profound knowledge of Nazi musical policies by musicians, and Falangist critics was evident, not least through their presence in the Germany on official missions dealing with music and the abundant propaganda that was carried out

---

63   Ibid.
64   Ibid.
65   Letter written by the Chief of the Section of Cinematography and Theatre to the Chief of the Section of General Affairs of Propaganda, dated 16 October 1942 (AGA, *Cultura* (03)48 Caja 21/46).

in Spain, hailing the Third Reich's initiatives and proposing them as a model, as if it were an order. Finally, the dates of the texts and that of the quoted regulations coincide with the most intensive moment of Hispanic-German musical relations and with the culminating point of the expansion of the Axis nations—spring and summer of 1942—which leads us to assume that the fascination felt by the government and the Falange for the successes of the totalitarian regimes and the desire to join their ranks influenced, or at least served as an affirmation or reference point for decision-making on the functioning and control of musical activity in Spain. It is therefore all the more ironic that from 1943 onwards, with the turn of events in World War II and despite continuing musical exchanges between Germany and Spain, all references to the Third Reich were officially prohibited and consequently the impact of Nazi musical propaganda was considerably diminished.

Eva Moreda-Rodríguez

Hispanic-German Music Festivals during the Second World War

Between July 1941 and August 1942, Germany and Spain jointly celebrated three music festivals. Two of them (July 1941 and August 1942) took place in the Saxonian village of Bad Elster; the other one (January 1942) was held for the most part in Madrid, with a final concert in Bilbao, in the Basque Country. The series of festivals was organized by governmental departments responsible for music (the Ministry of Propaganda in Germany, the Comisaría de Música in Spain), with the support of other organizations such as the Asociación Hispano-Germana (Hispanic-German Association), and their participants included a number of well-known names from the musical scene of both countries, such as conductors Herbert Albert and Karl Böhm, pianist Winfried Wolf (on the German side), composers Joaquín Turina and Joaquín Rodrigo, guitarist Regino Sáinz de la Maza, pianist and conductor Ataúlfo Argenta at the beginning of his career, and cellist Gaspar Cassadó (on the Spanish side).

In spite of the remarkable material and human resources dedicated to the organization of these festivals, it is evident that neither of the countries was in a particularly suitable frame of mind at that moment for cultural exchanges of this nature—Germany was, of course, fighting the Second World War, whereas Spain was recovering from almost three years of civil war (1936–1939) which had resulted in an authoritarian regime led by General Francisco Franco. Understandably, in such a convoluted international context, the meaning of the Hispanic-German music festivals, as they were usually referred to by the Spanish press (*festivales de música hispanoalemanes*), went beyond the musical or the artistic and acquired a remarkable political and diplomatic role, mainly in promoting diplomatic relations between Spain and the Axis, and in enhancing pro-German enthusiasm among the Spanish population. It is the aim of this chapter to clarify, in the first place, the nature of such a role by analysing the historical context in which these events took place and the events and symbols that surrounded them.

A second section of this chapter will focus on the reception of the festivals on the Spanish side, mainly in musical criticism and in the musical press, assessing the centrality of the concept of a canon in this reception—a reception which is highly illustrative of how Francoism intended to present itself and its music in a conflicted world, and to relate with other musical traditions which were perceived to be more advanced. Indeed, Spanish critics seemed to regard the festivals as an occasion to become acquainted with the German canon (understood in its more traditional formulation from Beethoven to Richard Strauss) in its purest form, whereas they regarded contemporary German composition (examples of which were also presented at the festivals) with suspicion, as though they deemed it unable to enter the canon. At the same time, the canon also seemed to be central feature of the way in which the Spanish delegation presented itself at the festival, trying to offer programmes that highlighted the values and principles on the basis of which Francoist musicology had constructed Spanish music history.

Spanish musical life in the immediate post-Civil War years (that is, from the end of the conflict in 1939 to the late 1940s, when the regime started a timid process of liberalization) has received little specific attention from scholars, and the importance of musical exchanges with the Axis countries has often been reduced to vague references stressing propagandistic aims,[1] or even ignored completely; none of the chapters of the most recent comprehensive volume about Spanish music of the 1940s[2] assesses the role of international exchanges in the musical life of Spain during this era. Indeed, one should note that exchanges with Italy have been more widely studied[3] than exchanges with Germany, even though the latter were more frequent and arguably more significant than the former. Through the study of three concrete musical events, this chapter intends to build a foundation for further study into the musical exchanges of the Franco regime with the Axis countries as a way of constructing and reconstructing the regime's musical life and self-image.

THE FESTIVALS IN CONTEXT

In order to understand the importance of the German-Hispanic music festivals, it is crucial to take into account the particular historical moment in which they took place, which not surprisingly coincides with the span of time of greater pro-Axis enthusiasm of the Franco regime. The relations between Francoist Spain and the Axis were by no means uniform during the

---

1   *Música española entre dos guerras*, ed. Javier Suárez Pajares (Granada: Publicaciones del Archivo Manuel de Falla, 2002), 13.
2   *Joaquín Rodrigo y la música española de los años cuarenta* , ed. Javier Suárez Pajares, (Valladolid: Glares, 2005).
3   Gemma Pérez Zalduondo, 'Alfredo Casella e la musica italiana in Spagna (1915–1945)', *Chigiana,* 44 (2003), 379–97; Gemma Pérez Zalduondo, 'Música y músicos italianos en España (1931–1943)', *Speculum Musicae,* 10 (2004), 65–94; Eva Moreda–Rodríguez 'Italian Musicians in Francoist Spain. The Perspective of Music Critics', *Music and Politics,* 2 (2008). http://www.music.ucsb.edu/projects/musicandpolitics/archive/2008-1/moreda.html.

Second World War years, and parallels can be drawn between their evolution and the strug-gles for power among the different factions which supported General Franco. The following paragraph will try to provide an outline of Franco's foreign policy during the Second World War—an outline that will be, necessarily, very basic but which will be crucial to understand-ing the context in which the three Hispanic-German festivals and other musical events were organized.

A first phase of pro-Axis enthusiasm can be traced from the start of the Second World War, in September 1939 (just four months after the end of the Spanish Civil War), until the summer of 1942. During this period, the victorious manoeuvres of Germany on France even encouraged Franco to consider the possibility of entering the war on the Axis side on at least two occasions (a first round of negotiations with Germany about Spain's future role in the war took place in the last months of 1940, and in the summer 1941 the Russian campaign lifted Franco's enthusiasm again). Internally, this phase was marked by the political hegemony of the Falange—an organization of strong fascist tendencies within the Franco regime, which had been founded back in 1933 by José Antonio Primo de Rivera—within the Spanish govern-ment. Falangists guaranteed a corpus of theoretical elaborations (often based in primitive racial theory or distorted historical perspectives) that aimed to justify a Spanish-German-Italian alli-ance. After the summer 1942, the increasingly difficult situation of Germany and the decline in influence of the Falange within the Franco government led to a more reserved policy towards the Axis powers. Finally, from approximately August 1944, the main aim of Spanish foreign policy was to convince the Allies that Spain had never meant to do them any harm, and that the Franco regime hardly shared any ideological affinities with Nazism and the Fascio.

Musical exchanges between Spain and Germany, and Spain and Italy followed, to a re-markable extent, the tendencies in the mutual relations of the three countries. Exchanges happened with greater frequency before the summer of 1942, and the most significant events (such as the three Hispanic-German music festivals or the visit of composer Alfredo Casella to Spain) also took place before this date. Afterwards, they started to become scarcer and somehow less significant, being limited to visits of soloists and some ensembles that were not integrated in the context of a broader festival. However, scarcer as they were, it is significant that they continued well beyond the phase of stronger political bounds between the Franco government and the two big fascist regimes. Indeed, the fact that musical relations with Ger-many and Italy were maintained until a rather late phase of the war (fall 1944) suggests that their interruption was due to the critical military situation of the Axis in the face of the Allies rather than to a desire on either side to end diplomatic and cultural relations, even after the possibility of Spain entering the war had vanished.

The three festivals, and the programme of musical events in which they were integrated from 1939 to 1944, must not be considered separately, but rather within the context of the propagandistic aims of the regimes of Germany, Italy and Spain: for all three, the spread of the national culture abroad—or rather of their particular conception of national culture—constituted one of the main points of their political programme. For the Institutes of German and Italian culture, concerts were only a subset of a much broader schedule of events, which included lectures on a variety of subjects (from science to art, with an emphasis on those topics that could support the superiority of Italian or German culture or the historical inevitability of their expansion abroad), language tuition (supported by foreign language broadcasts at the Spanish national radio), art and press exhibitions or poetry readings. Spanish newspapers of the time seemed to be particularly keen on reporting the success achieved by performances of the *Siglo de Oro* playwrights[4] in Germany. Sports events, to various degrees of professionalism,[5] were also used to reinforce the political and economic links between Spain and the Axis countries during the Second World War years.

The impact of the musical exchanges on the ideas of music critics and of musicians at large, which will be discussed in the following section, cannot be understood as separate from the previous tradition of international cultural relations of the country. Indeed, the existential and identity concerns of the Generation of '98[6] at the end of the nineteenth century, had engaged the intellectual sectors of Spain in defining the identity and essence of the country during the next decade. In this process of redefinition, however, foreign influences were not neglected: on the contrary, some intellectuals (the so-called *europeístas*) actively sought for models that could help in reviving the cultural life and identity of marginalized Spain. France was the model preferred by some of the most relevant philosophers of the first two decades of the twentieth century, such as Ramiro de Maeztu and José Ortega y Gasset,[7] whereas

---

4   Namely Pedro Calderón de la Barca and Lope de Vega. An example of such performances was the staging of Calderón's *La vida es sueño* in Berlin's Staatliches Spielhaus in March 1943 (*Informaciones*, 5/3/43). The fact that Spanish classical theatre blossomed during the 16th and 17th centuries was largely used by the Franco regime to emphasize the historical importance of the Spanish empire and its hegemony both culturally and politically.

5   Indeed, the different kinds of musical exchanges also tried to involve an audience as large as possible, from art music *connoisseurs* or *bel canto* lovers, to regular people who enjoyed folk and military music events in the open air.

6   The Generation of '98 was a group of Spanish poets, novelists, essayists and philosophers active in the first decades of the twentieth century in Spain. Their name is a reference to the Spanish-American war which took place in 1898, causing the loss of the last Spanish colonies and provoking a deep moral, social and political crisis in the Spanish population. They aimed to individualize the national essence of Spain by researching its history and traditions, but at the same time attempted to adapt to Spain the main philosophical trends of European Irrationalism.

7   Emilio Casares Rodicio, 'Manuel de Falla y los músicos de la Generación del 27', in *Manuel de Falla tra la Spagna e l'Europa: Atti del Convegno Internazionale di Studi (Venezia, 15–17 Maggio 1987)*, ed. Paolo Pinamonti (Firenze: Olschki, 1989), 49–63.

another faction, of which one of the most prominent representatives was composer Conrado del Campo, decided to approach Berlin and Vienna rather than Paris.[8] The outbreak of the Second World War tipped the balance decidedly in favour of the Germanic tradition.

THE ORIGINS AND MEANINGS OF THE HISPANIC-GERMAN MUSIC FESTIVALS

Sympathies between Nazi Germany and Francoist supporters can be traced even before the Civil War started: in 1936, musicologist Higinio Anglés, who would then be a prominent figure in Francoist musicology, engaged actively in granting a strong German representation in the conference of the International Musicological Society held in Barcelona, fearing that without this intervention the conference would be very well attended, 'by Jews who no longer live in Germany.' Potter reports that 'he ultimately demonstrated so much pro-German support at the conference in the face of perceived anti-German sentiments that the German consul in Barcelona personally thanked him.'[9] During the Spanish Civil War, musical exchanges with Germany were already in place: cellist Gaspar Cassadó, for example, performed in several German cities and violinist Juan Manén did the same in Berlin at the end of 1936. Right after the end of the struggle, in December 1939, Germany sent conductor Franz Konwitschny to conduct an opera season at Barcelona's Teatre del Liceu, and Herbert von Karajan was invited to conduct the Orquesta Filarmónica de Madrid in May 1940; other German soloists also performed in Spain in the following months. By February 1941, influential critic Federico Sopeña (who was also a member of the Comisaría de Música[10]), on the occasion of a second visit of Konwitschny, suggested in the newspaper *Arriba* that a Hispanic-German music festival should be organized:

> I have already talked about the extraordinary task of musical exchange which we could undertake with Germany. Not only could artists from both countries face the respective

---

8   Jorge de Persia, 'Falla, Ortega y la renovación musical', *Revista de Occidente,* 156 (1994), 102–16. .

9   Pamela M. Potter, *Most German of the Arts: Musicology and Society from the Weimar Republic to the End of Hitler's Reich* (New Haven: Yale University Press, 1998), 83.

10   Literally, 'Commission of Music.' The Comisaría de Música was founded by the regime in 1939. At first, it was jointly managed by composer Joaquín Turina, pianist José Cubiles and musicologist Nemesio Otaño, but formally Turina was its first commissar. During its first years of existence, the main aim of the Comisaría was to create and manage the Agrupación Musical de Música de Cámara (National Chamber Ensemble) and, specially, the Orquesta Nacional (National Orchestra). Turina was replaced after his death by Antonio de las Heras.

audiences: the most important thing is personal communication among musicians [...].
We have to multiply the opportunities for mutual learning.[11]

The Asociación Hispano-Germana (Spanish-German Society), whose main stakeholders in
Spain were Falangists such as Salvador Merino and Pilar Primo de Rivera,[12] on the other
hand, had also been encouraging musical collaboration among both countries since August
1940, when composer, musicologist and broadcaster Richard Klatowsky was sent to settle in
Madrid in August 1940, with the task of selecting Spanish music that could be broadcast on
the German radio.[13] In the following years, Klatowsky would be a crucial collaborator with
the Comisaría de Música and the Ministry of Propaganda in organizing the three Hispanic-
German music festivals.

In such circumstances, it is clear that the festivals bore a special significance within the
context of cultural and musical exchanges undertaken by both regimes. Indeed, the festivals
were the first time that the governments of both countries (through the Comisaría de Música
and the German Ministry for Foreign Affairs) directly collaborated in putting together week-
long events engaging some of their most remarkable figures and surrounded by clear political symbols. Authorities of both countries responsible for the cultural and musical life were
present at the festivals, such as Heinz Drewes, referred to by the Spanish press as Generalin-
tendant of the Third Reichsmusikkammer (he was in fact Goebbels's music representative in
the Ministry of Propaganda, heading the music department in that ministry), or composer
Joaquín Turina, who was head of the Comisaría de Música at the time, and other civil and
religious authorities, up to national ministers, were present as well. The embassies that other
countries kept in Spain were also invited to attend the celebrations, and, on the occasion of
the second festival, representatives from the Vatican City, Germany, Portugal, France, Chile,
Peru, Japan, Finland, Romania, Ireland, Switzerland, Sweden, Denmark, Hungary, Guate-
mala, Croatia, Turkey, Bolivia, Slovakia and Manchukuo joined the audiences.

Another way in which the festivals were charged with political content was to complement
them with other events, such as trips, of an obvious symbolical significance. The German
delegation that visited Spain in January 1942 made also short official trips to Toledo and to
El Escorial, two small cities near Madrid. Both places played an important role in Francoist
mythology: in Toledo, the Francoist troops had heroically resisted the siege of the Republican
army during the days of the Civil War; in El Escorial, the German delegation visited the tomb
of José Antonio Primo de Rivera—the founder of Spanish Fascism in the early 1930s, who was

11   Federico Sopeña, 'El festival de música alemana', *Arriba*, 11 February, 1941.
12   Wayne H. Bowen, 'Pilar Primo de Rivera and the Axis Temptation', *The Historian*, 67 (2005), 66.
13   'Grata visita. Richard Klatovsky', *Ritmo*, 136 (1940), 13.

the object of a peculiar personality cult all throughout the regime. The programme included also visits to places, which, in the eyes of the dictatorship, embodied the essence of Spain and were often presented as typically Spanish, such as an Andalusian *fiesta* in Seville or the plains of La Mancha (the land of Cervantes' Don Quixote): the trip of the German delegates all around Spain was chronicled by Joaquín Turina in *Dígame*.[14] Similarly, when the Spanish delegation went to Bad Elster in 1941, they also visited Bayreuth—a place of obvious ideological resonances for the Nazi regime—and Zwickau, the birthplace of composer Robert Schumann.

FESTIVALS AND THE CANON (I): GERMANY

Beyond the political significance explicitly attributed to the three festivals by their organizers, which has been analysed in the previous section, the musical press also contributed to reinforce and further their impact on the general population by forging particular readings of these exchanges. The Spanish side, which will be the focus of my analysis, is particularly interesting, as it reflects the problematic relationship of Spanish musical criticism with the notion of canon and reveals remarkable contradictions caused by the way Spaniards saw Germany (as the canon-builder *par excellence* during the 18th and especially the 19th centuries) and the way they saw themselves (as a nation whose music, after the splendour of the 16th and 17th centuries, had entered a decadence and become peripheral afterwards), according to the conception of Spanish music history predominant in Francoist musicology.

To guide my analysis, I will use the definition of canon provided by Lydia Goehr: a process initiated in the early nineteenth century with Beethoven, which assumed a 'terrorist character' towards the end of the century, with the boom of nationalist ideologies in Germany, when 'the elected works came to be identified with music's essence, truth, and sole future.'[15] Goehr describes canonization as a process in which 'a living culture can become a dead tradition,' and this, ironically, implies that 'having at least found its history, Germany was no longer living or making one.'[16] Spain, on the other hand, was not the only example of imposition, for political propaganda uses, of the German canon as universal. Referring to the context of Vichy France, Manuela Schwartz has pointed out that, after all, German repertoire already dominated musical programmes before the war, and so the French audiences (and, similarly, the Spanish ones) would not have identified it as propaganda in an aggressive, menacing way, enhancing thus its effectiveness and subtlety.[17]

---

14   Joaquín Turina, 'El festival de música hispanoalemán', *Dígame*, 3 February 1942.

15   Lydia Goehr, 'In the Shadow of the Canon', *The Musical Quarterly*, 86 (2002), 314.

16   Goehr, 316.

17   Manuela Schwartz, 'La musique, outil majeur de la propaganda culturelle des Nazis', in *La vie musicale sous Vichy*, ed. Myriam Chimènes (Brussels: Complexe, 2001), 105.

For music critics covering the three Hispanic-German music festivals, this meant the blind acceptance and the glorification of the German canon as the peak of musical achievement. The canon was, indeed, perceived in Spain as a fossilized set of works and composers, and it was implicit in the discourse of the critics that what Germany could now offer to the world (and, specifically, to Spain) musically was new renditions of already established works. Reformulations of this idea are to be found in most of the reviews of Spanish critics covering the festivals: the main function of the events was not only to foster friendship and collaboration between musicians and composers of both countries, but also to present the German canon in all of its splendour. Joaquín Rodrigo, who at the time was also music critic for the newspaper *Pueblo* and wrote for other various publications, outlined that the first task of the series of international music festivals with Spanish participation should be the preparation of model versions of works of the international repertoire, particularly of those countries involved in the festival,[18] and Regino Sáinz de la Maza, guitarist and music critic of the newspaper *ABC*, stated that the main purpose of musical exchanges should be the presentation in Spain of canonical German composers according to the purest performance criteria of the German tradition.[19] Sopeña, on the other hand, praised German musicians for playing works that were part of the German canon, but had remained almost unknown in Spain thus far, such as Brahms's symphonies.[20] This explains the immutable enthusiasm of Spanish critics towards the performances by German soloists and orchestras, which were always the object of great expectations.

However, contemporary German composition was, in that regard, a sort of non-canon, as if to suggest that the tradition of German symphonism had been terminated somewhere at the beginning of the twentieth century. Richard Strauss was generally acknowledged as the last symphonic giant, being probably the only living German composer whose reception was invariably positive. During the second festival, works by contemporary German composers Max Trapp, Ottmar Gerster, Theodor Berger and Josef Ingenbrand were played, but their reception was far more cautious and cool than that of their performing counterparts, which invariably collected the unconditional approval of Spanish critics. The most negative review was probably that of Joaquín Rodrigo. On the basis of the works to which he had listened by the abovementioned German composers, he described contemporary German music as characterized by 'an absence of philosophical worries, tendency to a self-contained music, without indulging in an exaggerated objectivism or a pretended dehumanization.'[21] Particularly, he

18   Joaquín Rodrigo, 'Al margen del festival de música hispanoalemán', *Escorial*, 17 (1942), 423.
19   Regino Sáinz de la Maza, 'Música', *ABC*, 12 February 1941.
20   Federico Sopeña, 'Primer concierto hispanoalemán', *Arriba*, 27 January 1942.
21   Rodrigo, 424.

considered Gerster and Ingenbrand 'of little interest,' especially the latter, whose *Bolero* 'justifies any kind of suspicions about his talents.' Even Max Trapp, whom he considered the worthiest of the four, is reported to employ modes in a way 'which is bound to be temporary and unsuitable for fruitful derivations,' and he described Trapp and his colleague Berger as merely imitators of Hindemith, but 'with less attitude and less mastery.'[22] As negative as his review was, Rodrigo, however, stated clearly that he wished to be cautious in his judgement because what he had heard at the festival had not been enough for him to assess the techniques of these four composers in detail and in an objective manner.

For *Radio Nacional*, the official newsletter of the Spanish national radio station, Rodrigo softened his criticism, but still he did not go further in his praise than to describe Gerster's compositions as 'healthy provincial music'—a somewhat back-handed compliment. He also judged Trapp as no more than 'interesting' but lacking in 'critical rigour' in his selection of melodic material.[23] Sopeña, on the other hand, only made a generally cautious judgement on Trapp's work (he placed it in the trend of 'return to the broader audiences', which, in his opinion, characterized certain other strands of contemporary music, particularly by composers such as Hindemith) but then stepped back by saying that, having listened to just one work by this composer, he did not wish to give a definitive opinion. [24]

The review of Conrado del Campo (also a composer) for *El Alcázar* is slightly more enthusiastic. Although he classified Ingenbrand's *Bolero* as 'whimsical and slightly monotonous,' he wrote positive remarks on Trapp and Ingenbrand, but his comments were almost exclusively directed towards the technical mastery of the composers,[25] which is understandable given Del Campo's admiration and knowledge of contemporary German music, to the point that the Spanish press often labelled him a Spanish Strauss. The coolness and reserve of the most prominent Spanish critics towards modern German composition only found an exception in *Informaciones*, one of the main supporters of the Axis among the Spanish media (both before and after the start of the Second World War, often featuring passionate defences of Nazi politics): on the occasion of the third Hispanic-German festival, the journal's critic Antonio de las Heras described Otto Wartisch as 'a powerful Atlas' and saw in Berger the spirit of eighteenth-century German composers.[26]

---

22 Rodrigo, 425.
23 Joaquín Rodrigo, 'Los festivals de música hispano-alemanes', *Radio Nacional*, (1942).
24 Federico Sopeña, 'Musica', *Arriba*, 30 January 1942.
25 Conrado del Campo, 'Primer festival hispano-alemán', *El Alcázar*, 27 January 1942 & 30 January 1942.
26 Antonio de las Heras, 'La semana musical hispano-germana', *Informaciones*, 22 July 1942.

FESTIVALS AND THE CANON (II): SPANIARDS ON THEMSELVES

The perspective officially promoted by the Franco regime as to the history of Spanish music, following on the inaugural perspectives of Spanish musicology as formulated by Felipe Pedrell at the beginning of the 20th century, largely implied that some of the periods that contributed more composers and works to the Germanic canon—the eighteenth and most of the nineteenth century—were in Spain hardly more than a long decadence in which the Spanish musical essence nearly succumbed to Italian influence. Spain, thus, was not included in the international canon and had no canon of its own. This meant that the exaltation of the Germanic canon in the festivals could potentially create an imbalance in the way that bilateral musical exchanges were perceived, suggesting in some way a hardly assumed inferiority complex on the part of Spain.

Approval from Germany, repeatedly described as the most musical nation in the world,[27] could definitively validate the inclusion of Spain in the canon. Such approval could be intrinsically bound to political concomitance. Thus, the joint music festivals of both nations were linked to their equivalent political destiny, as expressed by Sopeña on 3 August 1941 in a typically inflamed style on the occasion of the first Hispanic-German music festival:

> The fact that the most musical of nations, Germany, organizes in the middle of the war a series of concerts dedicated to Spanish music is not only a proof of vitality – it bears as well the symbol of the special unity of these two nations, whose sons are fighting together again against the universal enemy: Communism. [...] Tomorrow, our shared triumph in the trenches which protect the best essences of both nations will initiate a new artistic communion.[28]

Every Spanish musical success in Germany or before a German audience was thus anxiously saluted as an act of validation.[29] In 1941, after attending the first Bad Elster festival, Federico

---

27 For example, Del Campo in *El Alcázar* (27 January 1942) expressed his 'admiration and amazement' at the high standards of German musical life, even in a time of war.

28 Federico Sopeña, 'El festival de música hispanoalemán', *Arriba*, 3 August 1941.

29 See for example Federico Sopeña, 'Primer concierto hispanoalemán', *Arriba*, 27 January 1942 ('We are already in the most transcendental days of our musical life') and 'Crónica de Bad Elster', *Arriba*, 29 July 1942 (German critics are reported to have shown 'astonishment and enthusiasm' after having listened to Spanish music); Joaquín Rodrigo, 'Gran semana musical hispanoalemana', *Pueblo*, 22 January 1942 or Antonio de las Heras, 'La semana musical hispano-germana', *Informaciones*, 28 July 1942: 'To triumph here [in Germany] in the chamber music genre means to receive approval in the 'world at large'.

Sopeña in his review for *Arriba* on 3 August 1941 described a Germany invaded by Spanish music as a result of the visit of the Spanish delegation:

> The consequences of this festival have to be immediate and constant. The concert programmes, the radio broadcasts, the music reviews are, as we are told, the desperation of editors, because they are full of Spanish names. This is a glory for us.[30]

On the Spanish side this implied, as well, the perceived need to create a 'mini-canon' which could go hand in hand with the German one. Ideal performers had to be singled out: Sáinz de la Maza, José Cubiles, Ataúlfo Argenta, Gaspar Cassadó, Lola Rodríguez Aragón, all of them participants at one or several Hispanic-German festivals, were extensively celebrated at the time as the best Spanish performers (it must be considered that the Civil War had also caused an exodus of international-standard performers, such as cellist Pau Casals, who otherwise would have undoubtedly constituted a valuable addition to the prestige of the festivals), and they used to give concerts several times per month in Madrid and other Spanish cities. But others had to be created from scratch, not only for the festivals but for other exchange contexts as well: namely, a national orchestra (the Orquesta Nacional[31]) and a chamber ensemble (the Agrupación Nacional de Música de Cámara,[32] also known as Quinteto Nacional), both put together and managed by the Comisaría in the early 1940s. The international function of the Agrupación Nacional de Música de Cámara was highlighted by Sopeña only a few months after its foundation, proclaiming that it had already 'taken successfully the triumphal

---

30 Sopeña means that the editors struggled because they had to double-check innumerable Spanish names which were strange to them. The context suggests that this is a rhetorical exaggeration rather than an actual fact.

31 Although there were already two working orchestras in Madrid (the Orquesta Sinfónica and the Orquesta Filarmónica), the Comisaría assumed the task of creating a national orchestra, unlike in Germany, where Goebbels revitalized existing orchestras for similar purposes. The process of creation took a full three years, since Turina's first attempts in 1939 and the *oposiciones* (examinations) through which the members of the orchestra were made civil servants. However, most of the members of the Orquesta Nacional were also members of the Sinfónica or the Filarmónica.

32 The Agrupación Nacional de Música de Cámara was a chamber ensemble of five members (the classical string quartet plus a pianist), which could be split into different variants to perform different works. Unlike the Orquesta, whose creation was problematic and took a number of years, the Agrupación can be considered the most tangible achievement of the Commission of Music. An interesting fact is that in September 1940, Federico Sopeña presented the Agrupación in the Falangist newspaper *Arriba* as 'a great triumph of the Falange', arguing that the ensemble had been developed by the Delegación Provincial de Educación Nacional, controlled by the Falange at the time. It is significant of the struggles that different factions of the Franco government during the post-Civil War years engaged in attempts to 'score goals' against each other.

name of Spain beyond our frontiers.'[33] The Orquesta Nacional's task, on the other hand, was described as 'to grant a thorough knowledge of European music' in Spain,[34] and its success abroad was almost invariably labelled in hyperbolic terms as extraordinary or apotheosis. Critics described incredible scenes of enthusiasm among the public, which was said to have complimented the orchestra with cries of *¡Arriba España!*[35], as reported by Sopeña of a German audience in Bad Elster in 1941.[36]

With regard to repertory, there is no evidence that the Comisaría commissioned works to be premiered in Germany or other foreign countries, but some reviews suggest that the regime had a clear idea of which kind of compositions were deemed acceptable enough to be performed abroad, and that newly premiered works were carefully listened to with a view to convert them into an export product whenever possible—in other words, to present them as representations of the features that a Spanish canon should have. On the occasion of the premiere of Guridi's *Diez melodías vascas* in December 1941, Sopeña wrote for *Arriba:* 'We now have two obligations: repeat it[37] [this work] and let it be heard by European audiences, for its orchestral language excludes every regional[38] particularity'.[39] The work was indeed presented in Bad Elster the following year, and on the occasion of a further performance in Madrid in January 1943 Sopeña labelled it as 'a precious European divulgation of our regional colours,' recalling the pleasure and the surprise it caused among the German audience, for it did not match the commonplaces usually associated with Spanish music, but at the same time it was imbued with a 'typically Spanish flair'.[40] Sopeña describes a similar situation again in an article published in *Arriba* about Falla's Harpsichord Concerto. Sopeña recalls that a German critic who attended the Bad Elster festival in 1941 was desperate when failing to clearly recognise any Spanish dance in Falla's Harpsichord Concerto, and yet he identified the work as unequivocally Spanish.[41] According to the critics, what made Spanish music particular and un-

---

33   Federico Sopeña, 'El Quinteto Nacional', *Arriba*, 21 November 1940.

34   Federico Sopeña, 'La Orquesta Nacional con Freitas Branco', *Arriba*, 26 March 1942.

35   Literally, 'up with Spain'. This cry was promoted by the Falange and then, officially, by the Franco regime, as opposed to the Republicans' *¡Viva España!*

36   Federico Sopeña, 'El festival de música hispanoalemán', *Arriba*, 3 August 1941.

37   Hard as it was to have a work premiered in the post-Civil War years, it was even more difficult to have it played a second time. Rodrigo notes it repeatedly in his articles for *Pueblo* during these years.

38   The Spanish term here is *castizo*, which has a somewhat pejorative meaning.

39   Federico Sopeña, 'La Orquesta Sinfónica con Jordá', *Arriba*, 23 December 1941.

40   Federico Sopeña, 'Tres músicos de 1943', *Arriba,* 3 January 1943.

41   Federico Sopeña, 'El concierto de Falla', *Arriba*, 26 July 1944. Interestingly, the fact that the Harpsichord Concerto was dedicated to and first performed by the Jewish harpsichordist Wanda Landowska was omitted in the reviews of the festivals (and indeed it is hardly referred to in Spanish music criticism of the 1940s).

mistakeable was an undefined 'essence', 'spirit' or 'soul', which was rarely defined in musical terms but which was to be found in the music of all the composers celebrated by the Franco regime, from Tomás Luis de Victoria to Falla or Rodrigo.

An example of the Spanish canon that was deemed suitable for presentation abroad is the programme of the Spanish delegation for the third Hispanic-German festival, held in summer 1942 in Bad Elster. The symphonic nature of the event excluded the Spanish music of the sixteenth and seventeenth centuries, and so the programme included the string quartets of Juan Crisóstomo Arriaga (who was often called a 'Spanish Mozart' due to his talent and his premature death in 1826 at only 20 years of age), works by the two composers who were celebrated as having brought a new golden age to Spanish music and given it an international dimension in the early 20th century (Isaac Albéniz's *Triana* and Enrique Granados's *Goyescas*), an example of high-profile zarzuela (José María Usandizaga's *Las Golondrinas*), one of the most folklore-based of Falla's works (the piano concerto *Noches en los Jardines de España*), samples of the composers of the Generación de los Maestros (Conrado del Campo's *Divina Comedia*, Jesús Guridi's *Diez Melodías Vascas*, and Joaquín Turina's piano trios), and new music of the younger generations (Ernesto Halffter's *Rapsodia Portuguesa* and *Sonatina*, and Joaquín Rodrigo's *El Lirio Azul*), albeit in its less audacious, more traditional version. The discourse of critics and musicologists about modernism, traditional music and the history of Spanish music interlocked to shape a programme that is highly significant of the ways in which Spanish critics and musicians viewed their own background.

CONCLUSION

Two important aspects regarding the impact and effectiveness of the three Hispanic-German festivals among its contemporaries require further discussion. Firstly, it is clear that attendance at the concerts was restricted to a minority of the Spanish population, geographically and socially speaking, but still the impact of the festivals was able to reach beyond this narrow scope with the help of the press, which was thus a critical tool in transforming such events into propaganda by combining a glamorous vision of them, potentially attractive to the non-specialist reader, and ideas of essential unity, concomitance and mutual help between the Axis countries and Spain. Secondly, these exchanges and the political content behind them influenced the perception of Spanish music critics towards foreign musical traditions as well as that of their own, constructing a circular relationship in which the contact with foreign criticism and musicology instilled new ideas in Spanish critics—ideas that they started to apply to the Spanish as well as the foreign canon. The supposedly national traits of every work, composer and performer were thoroughly highlighted to accommodate to an extremely essentialist conception of the history of music, which was seen as fragmented in national schools. The circle was then closed in that these new conceptions were used to judge the musical exchanges which continued taking place until 1944.

BIBLIOGRAPHY OR REVIEWS IN THE SPANISH PRESS WHICH CHRONICLE HISPANIC/NAZI MUSIC RELATIONS

Anonymous 1940. 'Grata visita. Richard Klatovsky', *Ritmo*, 136: 13

_____. 'En el Staatliches Spielhaus de Berlín se representó "La vida es sueño"', *Informaciones*, 5 March 1942

De las Heras, Antonio. 'La semana musical hispano-germana', *Informaciones,* 22 July 1942

_____. 'La semana musical hispano-germana', *Informaciones,* 28 July 1942

Del Campo, Conrado. 'Primer festival hispano-alemán', *El Alcázar*, 27 January 1942

_____. 'Primer festival hispano-alemán', *El Alcázar*, 30 January 1942

Rodrigo, Joaquín. 1942a. 'Al margen del festival de música hispanoalemán', *Escorial*, 17: 423-6

_____. 1942b. 'Los festivales de música hispano-alemanes', *Radio Nacional*, 170: 12

_____. 'Gran semana musical hispanoalemana', *Pueblo*, 22 January 1942

Sáinz de la Maza, Regino. 'Música', *ABC*, 12 February 1941

Sopeña, Federico. 'El Quinteto Nacional', *Arriba*, 21 November, 1940

_____. 'El festival de música alemana', *Arriba*, 11 February, 1941

_____. 'El festival de música hispanoalemán', *Arriba*, 3 August, 1941

_____. 'La Orquesta Sinfónica con Jordá', *Arriba*, 23 December 1941

_____. 'Primer concierto hispanoalemán', *Arriba*, 27 January, 1942

_____. 'Música', *Arriba*, 30 January, 1942

_____. 'La Orquesta Nacional con Freitas Branco', *Arriba*, 26 March 1942

_____. 'Crónica de Bad Elster', *Arriba*, 29 July, 1942

_____. 'Tres músicos de 1943', *Arriba*, 3 January 1943

_____. 'El concierto de Falla', *Arriba*, 26 July 1944

Turina, Joaquín, 'El festival de música hispanoalemán', *Digame*, 3 February 1942.

Emile Wennekes

'Some of the Jewish musicians are back at their desks'

A case study in the remigration of European musicians after World War II[1]

In early February 1945, incarcerated Dutch violinist Samuel Swaap received a release note which contained the following message:

> You are placed on the February 5th transport to Switzerland. In order to ensure that things are in order, you are requested to go to the meeting point at Langestrasse 3 with your baggage, today: Sunday the 4 February 1945, from 7.00 pm until 11.00 pm. Only hand luggage and one suitcase are allowed, because the journey will take place in an express train and no hand luggage carrier has been made available for you.[2]

This little note addressed to the former concertmaster of the Hague Philharmonic ('Het Residentie Orkest') meant the end of protracted hardships in the so-called 'beautified' concentration camp of Theresienstadt (Terezín). Together with approximately 1200 other Jews, Swaap was sent on a transport to Switzerland in February 1945, as part of an exchange programme that was the outcome of a series of cloak-and-dagger stories and secret police games, in which personalities like Heinrich Himmler, the former Swiss president Jean-Mary Musy and the Jewish activist Recha Sternbuch each played a part. Even the Union of Orthodox Rabbis of the United States and Canada and the American Jewish Joint Distribution Committee in Switzerland were involved in a string of events that illustrate the grotesque side of Nazi

---

1   This chapter is derived from a collage of papers presented at conferences in Wolfenbüttel, London and San Francisco (AMS). Parts of this information can also be found at:: http://orelfoundation.org/ index.php/journal/journalArticle/034some_jewish_colleagues_are_back_at_their_desks034/ and in: Emile Wennekes, 'Neu anfangen, neue Anfänge: Musikalische Remigration in den Niederlanden', in Tagungsband „Wo anknüpfen?" Internationale musikwissenschaftliche Tagung zu Exil und Rückkehr an Musikhochschulen. 16.–18.12.2005, Bundesakademie Wolfenbüttel, ed. Dörte Schmidt and Matthias Pasdzierny. (Forthcoming). I am grateful to Johan Giskes (Amsterdam City Archive), Frits Zwart (Nederlands Muziek Instituut) and Cynthia Wilson (wwclassics) for their collaboration and support. All translations form Dutch and German sources are by the author.
2   The Hague: Nederlands Muziek Instituut (NMI), Archive 169, Swaap, 1.5.1

power.[3] Among Swaap's acquaintances in this exchange were a handful of befriended Jewish musicians of Dutch nationality, amongst them—to name just a few fellow sufferers—the former solo-harpist of the Concertgebouw Orchestra, Rosa Spier and Samuel Tromp, former associate leader of the second violin group of the same orchestra.

Switzerland must have been heaven in comparison with Theresienstadt. Yet it turned out to be a long stay, taking weeks, even months, before this group was allowed to leave the deportee camp on the outskirts of Montreux. Only as late as August 1945 were the musicians actually repatriated into the Netherlands itself. In some cases, it took less than a few days; in others, it was some weeks before they could reclaim their places in their respective orchestras and the music high schools or conservatories where they used to play and teach in the pre-Nazi period.

The group of Terezín survivors is a typical example of a category of Dutch-Jewish musicians that were destined to survive National Socialist atrocities. Coming back to their home country after the war, they were confronted with new difficulties, hardly less existential, not least for the orchestral musicians in trying to regain their places at their desks. Attempting to classify this specific group in the broader perspective of 'remigration' as Nazi-survivors, these individuals also wanted to 'remigrate', as it were, to their former professional positions.

The theme of remigration of musicians has, until now, hardly ever been the subject of detailed academic scrutiny. Indeed, notwithstanding a few exceptions, there is as yet precious little interest in the specific theme of remigration particularly after end of World War Two.[4]

---

3   Although many of the motives behind this transportation remain unclear, the main driving force may well have been a desire on the part of some major Nazi officials, such as Himmler and Seyß-Inquart, to save their own skins at a stage in which the Third Reich was on the verge of collapse. As is well known, Himmler, behind Hitler's back, had already started negotiations with the Allied Forces about releasing concentration camp prisoners. One plan was to cut a deal with the prisoners of the 'Model Camp' at Theresienstadt, see Manfred Flügge, *Rettung ohne Retter. Oder: Ein Zug aus Theresienstadt* (Munich: Deutscher Taschenbuch Verlag, 2004); Joseph Friedenson and David Kranzler, *Heroine of Rescue: The incredible story of Recha Sternbuch who saved thousands from the Holocaust* (Brooklyn, NY: Mesorah Publications, 2009).

4   Apart from the literature referred to in this article, specific mention should be made of the ninth volume of *Exilforschung. Ein internationales Jahrbuch*, ed. Claus–Dieter Krohn, Erwin Rotermund, Lutz Winckler and Wulf Koepke, which focused on the theme 'Exile und Remigration' (Munich: edition text + kritik, 1991). However, this volume does not contain any articles specifically orientated towards music. A later volume (no. 26) in the same series contains two articles of more direct relevance to remigration and music, see Therese Muxeneder, 'Ethik des Bewahrens. Exil und Rückkehr des Schönberg-Nachlasses', in *Exilforschung: Ein internationales Jahrbuch*, ed. Claus-Dieter Krohn (Munich: edition text + kritik, 2008), 44–66, and Matthias Pasdzierny, '"Der Ozean, der mich seit jener Zeit von dem Geburtslande trennte, hat wieder zwei Ufer [...]". Der Künstlerfonds des Süddeutschen Rundfunk und das deutsch-jüdische Musikexil', in *Exilforschung: Ein internationales Jahrbuch*, ed. Claus-Dieter Krohn (Munich: edition text + kritik, 2008), 195–231.

In this particular instance, remigration is defined as the moving back from one place or locality to the one from which the person in question originates, or to the one in which he or she established an existence. Especially in cases where the previous migration was not in all aspects voluntarily and for instance politically motivated, this general notion could be given a second dimension by including not only the return to one's homeland, but also to one's home and to the *locus professionis*—in this chapter, the positions in the orchestra which the musicians were forced to leave.

The conclusion drawn in 2005 by German musicologist Dörte Schmidt was that 'remigration is a political theme also in the history of the arts.'[5] Yet in international terms, remigration cannot be regarded as a mass phenomenon. In fact, the number of musicians deported from Germany during the war has been estimated at 4000.[6] Of these, a mere five to ten per cent returned to their countries of birth. To what extent many of them managed to reclaim their former positions, however, remains for the moment purely a matter of speculation. Thus far, remigration has only functioned as a 'coda' to the theme of exile in individual biographies or in research relevant to the historical development of certain institutions (conservatories, orchestras, et al). But considering remigration, a coda does not do justice to the specificity of the subject. Within the complexity of remigration, it is not so much the pursuer that is the motor of the events, as is the case with the issue of exile. Remigration deals with the consequences the pursued draw from the pursuit,[7] posing crucial questions in the order of 'can I return home?', 'do I want to return?', and if so: 'under which conditions?' A systematic, theoretical framework of remigration must still be developed. Some preliminary conclusions indicate however that there are substantial differences between different countries. To limit the comparison between Germany and the Netherlands, one could tentatively conclude that the number of exiles in the latter was substantially less than in the former. Then there is the crucial psychological difference inherent in the fact that it was not fellow countrymen who forced—in one way or the other—the involved to leave the country, but an occupier. Ergo: the one question as to whether one should return to the nation that was responsible for all the atrocities was then only partly relevant since the occupier had already been defeated. Nevertheless, the large moral question itself retained some relevance in the sense that fellow Dutchmen did (or had to) acquiesce to all the terror; some of them even benefited from the absence of the refugees or deportees.

---

5   Dörte Schmidt, 'Über die Voraussetzungen unserer Musikkultur. Die Aktualität der Remigration als Gegenstand der Musikgeschichtsschreibung', in *Mann kehrt nie zurück, man geht immer nur fort. Remigration und Musikkultur*, ed. Maren Köster and Dörte Schmidt (Munich: edition text + kritik, 2005), 9.

6   Maren Koster, 'Musik-Remigration nach 1945. Kontuoren eines neuen Forschungsfelds', Köster & Schmidt, 20.

7   Schmidt, 'Voraussetzungen', Köster & Schmidt, 12.

Specific to the German/Austrian situation, Maren Köster has identified nine, albeit somewhat hybrid and overlapping categories in the remigration of musicians:

1) remigration immediately after the war's end, 2) belated remigration in the 1950s, 3) remigration of musicians that only temporarily lived (or could/wanted to live) in Germany or Austria, 4) remigration in old age, 5) remigration of a specific category of musicians that had remained in the Soviet Union, 6) remigration by those who were forced to leave their new homeland (the most obvious example being Hanns Eisler), 7) alternative migration to Switzerland, 8) 'remigration of ideas' (i.e. not an actual remigration for different reasons, yet involving those that retained a strong relationship with their homeland), and finally 9) musicians persecuted by the Nazis who had never actually gone into exile.[8]

Only two of these categories are—to some extent—relevant to the Dutch situation. The Dutch-Jewish musicians described here all belong to Köster's first category; they all returned in the 'Phase of the Immediate Remigration', that is to say within the first months after war's end. And all of them lived during their absence with Holland very much in their hearts. But since none of the musicians voluntarily went into exile, Köster's ninth category is actually the most appropriate, particularly as all the protagonists in this chapter were camp survivors.

It is not my intention to present exhaustive biographical data of the specific persons featured here, but the adventures of these musicians do signify representative cases, since the impact of remigration cannot be described without concrete personal information. This chapter furthermore deals explicitly with orchestral musicians that are relatively unknown to a larger audience, rather than with composers or renowned soloists. In comparison to the scholarly attention that until now was paid to the exiles, remigration is less a story of the well-known elite, rather a story of the relatively unknown. This survey focuses on a group of Jewish musicians that coincidentally (or not?) shared the same experience to a large extent in the course of events. But in returning home, they were confronted with different circumstances from which they drew different conclusions.

One could point out that there are more categories than this type of Jewish musician alone. A second could be found, for example, in the group that went into hiding, thus managing to survive German oppression without exile. A third category of remigrated survivors were musicians of non-Jewish origin that had survived condemnation to Nazi labour camps. A fourth category consists of those that went voluntarily into exile in order to survive or escape the National Socialist regime.

All these categories had their own specific problems. Although evidently different from all the others, a final fifth category can be identified: the group of non-Jewish musicians that remained in their positions—sometimes even enhancing them in the absence of their former

---

8   Köster, 21–25.

Jewish colleagues—during the German occupation. The musicians of this category were convicted and fired in the first weeks after the end of the war by the layman tribunals. Once they served their time, some of them tried to once more apply for their former jobs.

Before focusing on the question of the specific circumstances that faced the Jewish concentration camp survivors as they tried to regain their pre-war employment, it is necessary to provide some general historical background. The Nazi occupation of the Netherlands commenced with the invasion of German military forces on 10 May, 1940. After the devastating bombardment of Rotterdam four days later, the Dutch army surrendered. At first, much remained as before: after only a short intermission, concert life and radio programmes continued as before. But as early as the autumn of 1940, the varnish of Nazi correctness and tolerance wore thin. Censorship was proclaimed and performances of music by Jewish composers were banned. The Dutch government was drastically reorganised with considerable ramifications for cultural life. In October, all musicians were obliged to submit a declaration of their 'Aryan' origin. Five months later in March 1941, all Jewish musicians were banned from music high schools and orchestras. Thereafter, Jewish participation in jazz and entertainment ensembles was officially prohibited; this was one of the consequences resulting from the foundation on 25 November 1941 of a Dutch counterpart of the German Kulturkammer ('Kultuurkamer'), which had a separate department for Music. After its inception, being active in public concert life was only possible as a member of the so-called 'Muziekgilde', a guild hermetically closed to all Jews.

Life became very harsh for those currently unemployed musicians. Only occasionally were financial arrangements made between individual musicians and the orchestras that were forced to fire them. The symphonic orchestra of Arnhem ('Arnhemse Orkestvereniging', later the 'Gelders Orkest') for instance offered them three month's salary as compensation, citing contractual obligations. Not much later, the orchestra offered to pay out their pension claims, which generally amounted to one year's salary. However, the Nazified Ministry of Culture did not sanction that these remittances could be paid at the expense of the orchestra's budget, so private funding was required.

After their dishonourable discharge, for a total of 73 seemingly lucky musicians of Jewish descent, an alternative was proffered through the creation of the Amsterdam-based Jewish Symphony Orchestra, conducted by Albert van Raalte.[9] For eight months—from November 1941 until July 1942—this orchestra offered a deceptive prospect for the future, somewhat comparable with the Jewish Cultural League in Nazi Germany. The musicians in question had

9   Pauline Micheels, 'Het Nederlandse muziekleven tijdens de Duitse bezetting', in *Een muziekgeschiedenis der Nederlanden*, ed. Louis-Peter Grijp et al. (Amsterdam: Amsterdam University Press, 2001), 636–43.

at least a real position, they gave concerts (a total of 25 performances, with exclusively Jewish composers on the programmes), and they had an attentive (but also exclusively Jewish) audience. Yet the moment deportations started—in the summer of 1942—the Jewish orchestra was forced to end its activities. What happened next is well known: a substantial number of the Jewish musicians from Holland were brutally killed in the years to come in the gas chambers of Auschwitz and Sobibor. Nevertheless, fifty per cent of the Dutch-Jewish orchestral musicians survived, substantially more than in many other professions.

In April 1941, 57 so-called 'volljüdische' musicians had been employed in the eight Dutch symphony orchestras of the time, a figure of more than eleven per cent.[10] About half of them—29—amazingly survived the war. Fourteen of these were members of the Concertgebouw Orchestra, five of them played with The Hague Philharmonic and four with the Rotterdam Philharmonic Orchestra. The remaining six were employed by local symphony orchestras, in Utrecht, Arnhem and Groningen. Yet the 'Aryanisation' of musical life in the Netherlands did not provoke any serious opposition. Although Nazi intimidation and terror thwarted any potential unrest, non-Jewish musicians also occasionally even benefited from Nazi cultural politics in terms of enhancing their careers and offering them financial stability. The National Socialist rulers strictly controlled musical life, but in return, more funding than ever before was applied to this art form, which in reality produced a considerable rise in the wages for Kultuurkamer-musicians. Some of these Nazi regulations were even adopted by the post-war Dutch government. For example, the first post-war Cultural Budget in 1946 shows entries and figures explicitly based on those initiated by the Nazis.[11] The subsidies for orchestras—and thus their musician's salaries—were raised ten times in comparison to the pre-war period, a significant residue of the German occupation.[12]

This contextual information enables us to return to the fate of the above-mentioned group of musicians circling around Europe, from one concentration camp to the next transit camp. One of them was Rosa Spier (1891–1967), who from 1932 had been the first harpist of the Amsterdam Concertgebouw Orchestra, and a teacher at the leading music high schools of Amsterdam and The Hague, the city where she was born and raised.

Spier began her musical education at the Royal Conservatory in The Hague and later continued to study with Otto Müller of the Berlin Philharmonic. After she was sacked following

10   Pauline Micheels, *Muziek in de schaduw van het derde Rijk* (Zutphen: De Walburg Pers, 1993), 164.

11   Wouter Paap, 'Afscheid van Minister G. Van der Leeuw', *Mensch en Melodie* (1) 1946, 234.

12   The total for Music in the national budget of 1939 was f 242,842.00, of which ƒ132,500.00 was reserved for orchestras. In 1941 the budget exclusively for orchestras was f 412,500.00. See Peter Lurvink, 'De Nederlandse componisten in de muziekpolitiek tijdens de bezetting', *Oorlogsdocumentatie '40–'45: Tweede Jaarboek van het Rijksinsitutuut voor Oorlogsdocumentatie* (Zutphen: De Walburg Pers, 1990), 106.

the Aryanisation of the Concertgebouw Orchestra in 1941, she joined the previously mentioned Jewish Symphony Orchestra. Obviously she expected that this orchestra would survive the German atrocities, since she stipulated that should she get a good offer from abroad, her contract could be annulled.[13] This proved to be in vain. She went into hiding immediately after the orchestra was dismantled in mid-1942. But she was soon betrayed by Nazi collaborators and was deported first to Westerbork. After this she ended up in Theresienstadt, from where she was sent, as has already been mentioned, to Switzerland. Although it was quite a relief to be moved to a neutral country, the regime at the Swiss camp was still very rigid. Nevertheless, Rosa Spier was repeatedly allowed to take the train to residential Montreux to play the harp in a villa where Ms. Viotta-Prager, the widow of the former director of the Royal Conservatory of The Hague, had settled.

In May 1945 Rosa Spier wrote from Switzerland to Amsterdam that she looked forward to playing again in the Concertgebouw Orchestra. In August of that year, she finally could return home, that is to say, to the city that used to be her hometown. In reality, post-war Amsterdam for Rosa Spier meant a 'huge deception', as she later wrote in her as yet still unpublished memoirs.[14] In the first instance, a better future seemed on the horizon for Rosa Spier. Directly after her return, she was indeed allowed to reclaim her former position in the orchestra. Yet as soon as 1 October 1945, she resigned and accepted a position in the newly established radio orchestra.[15] In this job she would earn a higher salary, but a remark in the minutes of the orchestra's Board Meeting indicates that Spier especially hoped to get more possibilities to perform as a soloist in her new working environment.[16] However, matters are never as neutral as formulated in such minutes. In her memoirs, she wrote the following about her life in post-war Amsterdam:

> The return to my homeland in August 1945 made me [....] experience deep disappointments, which forced me to accept a job at the radio. With this move I showed a willpower as yet unequalled, and I am still immensely grateful that I then had the strength and the courage despite my bad physical state.[17]

---

13 Piet Heuwekemeijer, *Van Rosa Spier tot Rosa Spier Huis. Vijftig jaar symfonieorkest. De autobiografie van Piet Heuwekemeijer* (Amsterdam: Uitgeverij de Appelbloesem Pers, 2000), 46.

14 Rosa Spier, *Mijn Levenservaringen* (Unpublished manuscript). The Hague: NMI, Archive 120 A 11, Box 715.

15 Amsterdam: City Archive (ACA), (i.e. former) Gemeente Archief Amsterdam, Archive Concertgebouw Orchestra, 1089, Minutes Board, 28 February 1945.

16 Amsterdam: ACA, Archive Concertgebouw Orchestra, 1724 B, Former members L-Z.

17 Spier.

She claimed that her frequently solo participation with the radio orchestra was highly curative. Whether the fact that Albert van Raalte—under whom she already had performed during her time with the Jewish Symphony Orchestra—was named as chief conductor of the new radio orchestra also played a role in her decision to change positions, is speculative. A remarkable detail in Spier's correspondence is the fact that she applied to join a tour to Scandinavia with the Concertgebouw Orchestra almost two years later: 'Payment doesn't play any role', she wrote to the orchestra's board. She was clearly not anticipating a permanent return to her old job. But, 'this travel would work as a balm for the wound which my last travel abroad—in a cattle truck—has created […], a very painful memory which is still highly alive.'[18] Her application was rejected.

What exactly happened in those first two months, when Spier again performed with the Concertgebouw Orchestra, remains a mystery. Even her memoirs do not give a clearer idea concerning her disappointments, nor do Board minutes or her correspondence. Could it be that she was upset that her former student Phia Berghout had replaced her as first harpist even though officially Berghout was named as first harpist only after Spier resigned?[19] The whole episode is shrouded in a thick mist.

Rosa Spier was but one of a whole group of Jewish musicians in the Concertgebouw Orchestra that were confronted with the 'Aryanisation' of musical life. Almost twenty percent—16 of 88—of the orchestra's musicians were forced to resign.[20] A floor-plan of a pre-war *St. Matthew Passion* performance under chief-conductor Willem Mengelberg cynically illustrates the course of events. In this plan, the seating of the orchestra in this specific work is sketched, including the names of the musicians. The floor-plan was obviously used year after year, also in 1942. Although all the Jewish musicians were fired by that time, their names are still in the plan as silent witnesses to what was going on.[21]

Among the sacked musicians were the second and the third concert master, the first viola player, a second cellist, the substitute first bassoonist and the first trombone player—musi-

18   Undated letter, probably from Feb. 19, 1947. Amsterdam: ACA, Archive Concertgebouw Orchestra, 1724 B, Former members L–Z.

19   See Mimi Rijpstra-Verbeek, *Harpe diem. Phia Berghout's Arpeggio* ('s-Gravenhage/Rotterdam: Nijgh & Van Ditmar 1974), 41–42.

20   Truus de Leur, *Eduard van Beinum 1900-1959. Musicus tussen musici. Een biografie* (Bussum/Amsterdam: Thoth, 2004), 179.

21   Bottom left: first violinist B. Meyer; bottom right: concertmaster J. Hekster. Frontstage left: concertmaster L. Rudelsheim. First circle from left to right: second violinists S. de Boer, S. Tromp, S. Snijder [Schneider], L.Pens, S. Fürt[h], J. Koen. Second circle: viola player J. Muller, cellist S. Brill. Third circle: bass player S. Gomperts. See Henriette Straub, 'Een raadselachtig opus. De *Matthäus*-traditie van het Concertgebouworkest tot en met 1958', in *De Matthäus-Passion. 100 Jaar passietraditie van het Koninklijk Concertgebouworkest*, ed. C.M. Schmidt et al. (Bussum & Amsterdam: Thoth, 1999), 55.

cians we will come across later in relation to their reparations. The concert master Zoltán Székely, who was appointed in 1940, only stayed for a short time; the authorities discovered that, despite his declaration of Aryan origin, he was of Jewish descent. All aforementioned vacancies were filled during the years 1941–42.

The position of the substitute leader of the second violin group also needed a replacement. After the dismissal of the Jewish orchestra member Samuel Tromp, Piet Heuwekemeijer was named in his place. What, however, became of Samuel Tromp?

At the age of 19, Groningen-born Samuel Tromp (1902–1987) moved to Amsterdam, where he applied for a job as a bank employee while studying the violin at the capital's conservatory. He continued his study with Lucien Capet in Paris and with Oskar Back in Amsterdam. Tromp joined the Concertgebouw Orchestra in the season of 1928–29, in the position of second violinist. As a result of the 'Aryanisation' policy during the Nazi Occupation, he was fired in June 1941, after which he became a member of the Jewish Symphony Orchestra. A few months later deportation was inevitable; via the transit locations Barneveld and Westerbork, he ended up—as 'Verdienstjude'—in Theresienstadt. Not only Tromp, but all the musicians of this chapter were part of the so-called 'Barneveld Group', a privileged list of 'wirtschaftliche wertvolle Juden' or 'Prominentjuden' of Dutch origin named after their gathering place in the tiny town of Barneveld. The musicians within this group either already enjoyed some fame, like Spier and Swaap, or—as was the case of the Jewish members of Concertgebouw Orchestra—became part of the list (probably) through the direct intervention of conductor Willem Mengelberg.[22] They were deported as a group to 'the polizeiliches Durchgangslager' Westerbork, where they also enjoyed some (minor) privileges, and from there to Theresienstadt, still mainly members of a separate group of prisoners.

Following his release in Switzerland, Tromp finally returned to Amsterdam where the orchestra welcomed him back on 11 September 1945. He did not return to his old position however, but was now named tutti player in the first violin group[23] since his former position had been officially given to Piet Heuwekemeijer. Did this seemingly uncomfortable situation cause any conflicts or hard feelings? It doesn't look like it, if we study the surviving archive materials. Apparently it was the newly named chief conductor who proposed this compromise. Eduard van Beinum had replaced Willem Mengelberg when he himself was banned due to his reprehensible attitude of collaborating with the Nazis. Van Beinum suggested that Heuwekemeijer could remain in his present position, whereas Tromp would achieve a sort of

---

22   Boris De Munnick, *Uitverkoren in uitzondering? Het verhaal van de Joodse 'Barneveld-groep' 1942–1945* (Barneveld: BDU, 1992), 15.

23   *Waar bemoei je je mee? 75 Jaar belangenstrijd van de Vereniging 'Het Concertgebouworchest'*, ed. Johan Giskes et al. (Zutphen: De Walburg Pers, 1991), 85.

promotion by moving to the first violin group, but as a tutti player with reduced responsibilities. As compensation, Tromp would receive a monthly bonus in order to make his salary
comparable to his former leading position.[24] Studying the relevant correspondence, this specific job rotation indeed seems to have taken place without rancour and in a friendly atmosphere. In 1946 Tromp was even named Secretary of the so called Association ('Vereniging')
of the Concertgebouw Orchestra. In later years Tromp was twice elected President of this
highly influential peer pressure group of the orchestra's musicians. In this position, he had to
collaborate closely with Heuwekemeijer who became managing director of the orchestra in
the 1950s.

The Association's minutes dated 16 May 1945—shortly after the liberation of Holland—
mention the preparations for the first post-war concerts. They state that all musicians could
only temporarily take their places: 'the definite placing can only be decided when all colleagues are again present.'[25] Tromp had not as yet returned to the Netherlands. Most likely,
he must have written to the Association only shortly afterwards, because on 23 June, the
Secretary and President jointly responded to Tromp in Switzerland: 'It is very remarkable
that someone after a long time of suffering and at the prospect of some improvement in his
personal situation firstly expresses the hope that all his friends will be spared the things he has
experienced. Your heartfelt interest in the well-being of your colleagues is proof that the warm
feelings of solidarity within the orchestra could not be destroyed by the humanly disgrace-
ful experiences of the war.' The letter ends with the words: 'some of the Jewish colleagues are
back at their desks; they received a warm welcome.[26] The ones still missing are the colleagues
from Switzerland. With pleasure we are looking forward to your safe homecoming in our
good Amsterdam.'[27]

One need not doubt the sincerity of these board members of the Association; even during
the occupation the influential organisation always acted socially and with fraternity. As soon
as 1944 post-war plans were being made, a first point on the list of actions was the return of
Jewish colleagues to their former posts. In the second place, however, somewhat contradictory
to this, it was noted that orchestra members hired during the occupation should retain their
new found positions. These two conditions could have potentially caused conflicts between
the hired and the fired, but they didn't—at least the official orchestra's minutes don't suggest
that such problems existed. The strategy relevant to the job rotation of Samuel Tromp seems

---

24   Heuwekemeijer, 46–47; 58–59.
25   Amsterdam: ACA, Archive Concertgebouw Orchestra, 1021, Without number, Minutes of the 16 May
     1945 Meeting, 10.
26   At the first concert in October, the Jewish colleagues were welcomed once again. Amsterdam GAA:
     Archive Concertgebouw Orchestra, 1021, Minutes Board.
27   Amsterdam: ACA, Archive Concertgebouw Orchestra, 1021, Outgoing letter, 23 June 1945.

exemplary. Moreover, new vacancies were created in the midst of the catharsis or post-war purification of Dutch society; Nazi sympathizers were dismissed on the spot.

In comparison to the situation in some other countries, it appears that the possibilities for Jewish instrumentalists to return to their former posts in the orchestras of the Netherlands were indeed quite good. The cases of Tromp and Spier at the Concertgebouw Orchestra seem to be comparable with the situation pertaining to other Dutch symphony orchestras. Yet not all musicians wanted to regain their places; individuals used their return in some cases for a brand new start. In a way this is true for Rosa Spier as well. While some had grave misgivings about the whole process, others did not or could not react to the explicit invitation to return to the orchestra, as was the case for example with former second concert master Leon Rudelsheim. In July 1945 it appeared that he had accepted another job and possibly even went abroad.[28]

Yet while remigration to one's homeland is one matter, the return to one's pre-war desk in an orchestra is another. This leads one to ask the question as to what was the actual position of the now re-hired musicians in a broader sense. We must not forget that those that returned were often in a terrible physical condition and state of mind, without means of existence, sometimes even without a roof over their heads. In general, they had lost all their belongings in the chain of events, which for a lot of musicians also meant that they were deprived of their instruments. Rosa Spier was rather fortunate in this respect: she more or less coincidently got her own harp back, after it was recovered from the bottom of a house boat.[29] Furthermore, Sam Tromp managed to rescue his violin and smuggle it back to the Netherlands.[30] But many others were far less lucky. Sometimes it was even questioned whether certain musicians had ever owned as valuable an instrument as they later claimed. Moreover, insurance premiums had not been paid in years. No one—state nor city, insurance company nor orchestra—accepted any financial responsibility or liability for the losses that were incurred as a result of the changing political situation.

In other words, although these musicians were indeed still alive, the downside for them was that many were ill and bankrupt. As early as the summer of 1945, the Board of the Concertgebouw Orchestra discussed what the official date of re-hiring of the returned musicians (and those expected to return) should be: should it be the day they actually appeared at their desks again? Or should the organisation perhaps adhere to a more symbolic date? After ample consideration, the second option was chosen: all musicians fired during the Nazi occupation

---

28 Amsterdam: ACA, Archive Concertgebouw Orchestra, 1724 B, Former members L–Z.
29 Ad van Liempt, *Hitler's Bounty Hunters. The Betrayal of the Jews* (Oxford & New York: Berg, 2005), 78.
30 Aaron Tromp, *Memories of a Potatot Thief: The Extermination of a Dutch Jewish Family 1940–1945,* (s.l.: Marom Israeli Culture, 2013), 111–14.

were re-hired as of 8 May 1945, in fact three days after the capitulation of German forces in Holland and the same day that the Third Reich finally collapsed.[31]

Another difficult matter was the question of the compensation for missed wages. It took years, in some individual cases even decades, before this complex matter could be settled to some sort of satisfaction for all concerned parties In close relation to missed wages stands the aforementioned matter of pre-paid pension claims: at their dismissal halfway into 1941, the Jewish musicians were given a remittance on their future pension. Now, officially, the whole sum had to be refunded to the orchestra which caused insurmountable problems for those involved. A quote from a female musician from the Symphony Orchestra of Arnhem presents the problem in an extremely succinct manner:

> [...] in order to once again get a pension assurance, we—the fired—had to pay back the whole pension payment. For me (and I think for most of us) this is impossible! [...] I know, there's been enormous suffering on all sides, but without bringing 'us' (the Jews) too much up out of this Slough of Despondency, I believe, I may argue that we have suffered the most in terms of our financial situation. Our belongings are gone, our future unclear. Of course, survivors are aware on a daily basis of the miracle of not having been gassed; this is not a matter of complaining in the slightest. But an existence without financial means and with only vague prospects unfortunately causes this future to appear very distressing.[32]

In the first post-war year, there was already much discussion as to who should be made responsible for handing out financial compensation. The government took a great deal of time to create a law of compensation which in the end turned out to only be applicable to civil servants. Since orchestras were regarded as private companies, the government effectively turned its back on the musicians involved, considering them to be in private employment. But this issue was further exacerbated by the fact that orchestras had limited savings from which to draw funds. Two and a half years after the liberation of Holland, none of the Jewish musicians in question had been given any compensation payments whatsoever. Confronted with this situation, the Board of the Concertgebouw Orchestra established a fund in which they deposited a quarter of monies as owed. It was not until halfway through 1949, however, that an official settlement was finally reached. In the end, the outstanding wages were paid over a period of four to five years. Nonetheless, the total amount paid in compensation was first reduced by the salaries earned in the Jewish Symphony Orchestra and other income.

---

31   The Rotterdam Philharmonic decided to hire their musicians as of 7 May, 1945.
32   Quoted in Micheels, 342–43.

The calculations of compensation for those missed wages vary from more than 15,000 Guilders for second concert master Leon Rudelsheim, to approximately 13,500 Guilders for first trombone player Haagman, as well as for solo harpist Rosa Spier. Of the sixteen Jewish musicians that were members of the orchestra until forced Arayanisation, three were gassed, together with their families. Their compensations were divided among the survivors, of which eleven joined forces in a lobby group. Of the remaining two musicians, Rudelsheim did not return to the orchestra and Spier rejoined the orchestra for only a short period of time. The latter, nevertheless, obviously did benefit from the judicial efforts of her former colleagues.

Other orchestras in the Netherlands, like the Rotterdam Philharmonic, studied the agreements made in Amsterdam,[33] and signed comparable compensation contracts. Notwithstanding these examples, there were also orchestras that failed to offer any compensation at all. The orchestra of the city of Groningen, for example, did not reach a settlement with their musicians, something which until late in the 1970s was still the source of great frustration for those involved.[34]

The Residency Orchestra of The Hague finally signed an agreement with their formerly dismissed Jewish musicians on 24 July 1950, five years after the end of the war. The person who had to be compensated most was concert master Samuel Swaap: he had lost nearly 17,000 Guilders in wages. This sum was reduced by 700 Guilders due to his participation in the Jewish Symphony Orchestra, of which he had also been the concert master.

As has already been mentioned, Samuel Swaap (1889–1971) also belonged to the Theresienstadt Group. He was one of the most gifted students of Carl Flesch at the Amsterdam Conservatory, made his debut as soloist with the Concertgebouw Orchestra at the age of sixteen, of which he became first violinist in 1909, holding that position until 1913. After this period he had a short career in Finland, only to return to his home country due to the outbreak of the World War I. In 1914 he was named concert master of the orchestra of The Hague. Just like other Jewish musicians, he was fired in 1941 and subsequently joined the Jewish Symphony Orchestra. In 1944 he was deported via Westerbork to Theresienstadt, finally returning via Switzerland to The Hague and regaining his former position. Like Rosa Spier, he was befriended by the widow of Henri Viotta, the former director of the Royal Conservatory, whom he also visited in Montreux to play duets.

A single letter from Switzerland was sufficient for him to return to his music desk. 'Of course you can regain your former position of first concert master the moment you arrive', responded the Board of the orchestra.[35] When his contract for compensation was finally signed,

---

33   Amsterdam: ACA, Archive Concertgebouw Orchestra, 1699, April 1949.
34   Micheels, 346.
35   The Hague: NMI, Archive 169, Swaap, 1.5.1.4, Letter from Groen to Swaap, 9 June 1945.

Swaap had already retired, although he was still often seen and heard in public, now as a conductor. The other Jewish members of the orchestra of The Hague with less prominent positions were nevertheless promised compensations of on an average 6,000 Guilders.[36] The striking detail in these Hague contracts, however, was that the orchestra closed a deal with the musicians to pay only half of the salary actually missed, and this over a period of five years. A higher sum was financially impossible for the orchestra's management to underwrite. It was only able to put a mere 3,000 Guilders aside each year for this kind of compensation.

Clearly, local circumstances differed substantially. The musicians of the Concertgebouw Orchestra were better off than their colleagues in The Hague, and far better off than their colleagues in the North of Holland (including Groningen). This was the case during and after the war. The fact that fourteen—almost half of the total amount of surviving orchestral musicians—were members of the Concertgebouw Orchestra can be explained by the great prestige the orchestra and its conductor Mengelberg enjoyed with the Nazis, augmented by the great effort the Board took time and time again to get the orchestra's musicians privileged positions in the concentration camps.

The Amsterdam orchestra was not only regarded as the leader in terms of the quality of its performances and its international reputation, but it also set the standard for the post-war financial compensation of Jewish musicians. It nevertheless took years—too many years for those involved—until Amsterdam's settlements were reached. And in the end, these settlements were largely symbolic. Compensation for the physical and mental suffering experienced by the Jewish musicians was of course impossible. Their feeling of being expelled by colleagues, so-called friends, as well as ignored by their own government was a burden they had to bear for the rest of their brutally destroyed lives.

Yet they courageously went on and had to pick up the pieces of their lives where they had left off, perhaps having no other choice. It is no use pointing accusing fingers in one direction or the other. For instance, to condemn orchestral management for its failures seems far too easy. But it is our moral duty to shed some scholarly light on this so quickly forgotten fate of the surviving Jewish musicians as they returned to their desks after the 'great' war was over. The 'smaller' war for compensation took far longer to end.

---

36   The Hague: NMI, Archive 169, Swaap, 1.5.1.2.

The Contributors

Kristof Boucquet studied both history and musicology at the University of Leuven (Belgium) and received a doctorate degree in musicology, with a dissertation on the tonal songs of Arnold Schoenberg (2007). In addition to the music and theory of Schoenberg and his pupils (Berg, Webern, Ullmann), his main research topics include the history and analysis of twentieth-century music, music historiography and music aesthetics (especially Theodor W. Adorno). He has published on these topics in journals such as *Musik & Ästhetik* ('Adorno liest Benjamin: Sprache und Mimesis in Adornos *Theorie der musikalischen Reproduktion*', 2010), *Dutch Journal of Music Theory* ('Adorno's Theory of Musical Reproduction', 2009) and *Revue belge de musicologie* ('Schenker and Schoenberg Revisited', 2005). As a postdoctoral research fellow in the Musicology Department of the University of Leuven, he is currently working on a project concerning the interaction of music history with analysis in twentieth-century music.

Juliane Brand is an independent scholar and developmental editor. She was awarded a PhD in musicology in 1991 from Yale University and has most recently provided content for the scholarly website www.karlweigl.org. Her books and published articles include 'The Dispersion of Hitler's Exiles: European Musicians as Agents of Cultural Transformation', *Rediscovering Suppressed Musical Treasures of the Twentieth Century,* http://orelfoundation.org/, *Briefwechsel Arnold Schönberg–Alban Berg*. Ed. with Christopher Hailey and Andreas Meyer. Briefwechsel der Wiener Schule 3. (Mainz: Schott, 2006), *Alban Berg: Master of the Smallest Link,* translated and edited with Christopher Hailey (Cambridge: Cambridge University Press, 1991), *The Berg-Schoenberg Correspondence* translated and edited with Christopher Hailey and Donald Harris (New York: W. W. Norton, 1987) and *Rudi Stephan*. Komponisten in Bayern–Dokumente musikalischen Schaffens im zwanzigsten Jahrhundert 2. (Tutzing: Hans Schneider, 1983).

Magnar Breivik is a professor of musicology at the Norwegian University of Science and Technology - NTNU, Trondheim. His particular field of interest is twentieth-century music and aesthetics, with an emphasis on the interrelationships between music and the visual arts, musical theatre, film music, music in the Weimar Republic, and music in exile. In addition to various studies on the music of Kurt Weill, he has published articles on such composers as Gustav Mahler, Arnold Schoenberg, Alban Berg, Paul Hindemith, and Ernst Krenek. His most recent book is *Musical Functionalism: The Musical Thoughts of Arnold Schoenberg and Paul Hindemith,* (Hillsdale, NY: Pendragon Press, 2011).

Albrecht Dümling is a musicologist and music critic based in Berlin. He studied music, musicology, journalism and German literature in Essen, Vienna and Berlin where he worked under Carl Dahlhaus. After writing his doctoral dissertation focusing on the relationship between Arnold Schönberg and Stefan George, he has written several books including *Laßt euch nicht verführen: Brecht und die Musik* (Munich: Kindler, 1985), *Die verweigerte Heimat: Léon Jessel – der Komponist des "Schwarzwaldmädel"* (Düsseldorf: DKV, 1993) and *Die verschwundenen Musiker: jüdische Flüchtlinge in Australien* (Vienna: Böhlau, 2011). After twenty years as music critic for the Berlin newspaper *Der Tagesspiegel* and the *Frankfurter Allgemeine Zeitung*, he is currently a regular contributor to the *Neue Musik-Zeitung* and several radio programmes. As a co-founder of the International Hanns Eisler Society, he was instrumental in creating the new Gesamtausgabe (HEGA), the complete edition of the musical and literary works of the composer. In 1988 he created the exhibition 'Entartete Musik. A critical reconstruction' (Düsseldorf 1938/1988)', which travelled to more than 60 places world-wide. Since 1990 he is chairman of „musica reanimata", a Society for the Promotion of Composers persecuted by the Nazis, which in 2006 was awarded with the German Critics' Prize. He is editor of the book series 'Verdrängte Musik' (Pfau-Verlag, Saarbrücken), board member of the Gotthard Schierse Stiftung, member of the Advisory Board of the International Centre for Suppressed Music and of the research project 'Lexikon verfolgter Musiker und Musikerinnen der NS-Zeit'. For his activities for the rediscovery of persecuted musicians he was awarded the European Cultural Prize KAIROS of the Alfred Toepfer Foundation Hamburg in 2007.

Melina Gehring completed both her master's degree in Musicology and her Ph.D. in American Studies at the University of Hamburg, Germany. She also holds an M.Phil. in International Relations from the University of Cambridge, UK. She has published in Musicology as well as in American Studies, and has taught courses in the latter at the University of Hamburg and the University of Rostock. Her book on Alfred Einstein was published in 2007 by von Bockel Verlag in Hamburg. In her Ph.D. project, she studied the labyrinth myth in contemporary American fiction. Her non-academic alter-ego has worked as a music critic in Hamburg and as a desk officer at the German Federal Foreign Office in Berlin. She is currently living in the United States and teaches at Dartmouth College.

Lily E. Hirsch was awarded a PhD from Duke University in 2006 and was most recently Assistant Professor of Music at Cleveland State University. She has published the books *A Jewish Orchestra in Nazi Germany: Musical Politics and the Berlin Jewish Culture League* (Ann Arbor: University of Michigan Press, 2010) and *Music in American Crime Prevention and Punishment* (Ann Arbor: University of Michigan Press, 2012). A frequent contributor to *Musical Quarterly, Philomusica*, the *Journal of Popular Music Studies, American Music* and *Popular Music &*

Society, she wrote the chapter 'Segregating Sound: Robert Schumann and the Third Reich' in *Rethinking Schumann*, ed. Roe-Min Kok and Laura Tunbridge (Oxford: Oxford University Press, 2011). Her current work is a volume focused on Jewish music in Germany after the Holocaust which she is co-editing with Tina Frühauf.

Erik Levi is professor of music and director of performance at Royal Holloway, University of London. He studied music at the Universities of Cambridge and York and in Berlin. He is author of the books *Music in the Third Reich* (Basingstoke: Macmillan, 1994) and *Mozart and the Nazis* (New Haven: Yale University Press, 2010), and co-edited with Florian Scheding *Music and Displacement* (Lanham: Scarecrow, 2010). A frequent broadcaster on the BBC, he has written extensively on music during the 1930s for various journals and is a critic for the *BBC Music Magazine*.

Malcolm Miller studied at the Universities of Cambridge and Sussex, receiving his PhD from King's College London. From 2010 to 2013 he was Associate Fellow at the Institute of Musical Research at the University of London and is an Associate Lecturer for the Open University. He has contributed articles on nineteenth- and twentieth-century music to various publications including *Musical Opinion, Tempo, Musical Times* and *The* Strad and is editor of *Arietta*, the journal of the Beethoven Piano Society of Europe.

Eva Moreda Rodriguez is the Lord Kelvin Adam Smith Research Fellow in Music at the University of Glasgow. She specializes in the political and cultural history of Spanish music in the twentieth century; her articles have appeared in *Twentieth Century Music, Bulletin of Hispanic Studies, Music and Politics*, and *Hispanic Research Journal*, among others. She has received grants and an award from the Lucille Graham Trust, the Music and Letters Trust, and Indiana University. Her current research project is concerned with the rehabilitation of exiled composers (Roberto Gerhard, Julián Bautista, Rodolfo Halffter, Jesús Bal y Gay, among others) in Francoist Spain from the 1950s onwards. Before joining the University of Glasgow, she completed her PhD at Royal Holloway, University of London and held research and teaching posts at the Royal Academy of Music and the Open University.

Katarzyna Naliwajek-Mazurek is a member of the faculty of the Institute of Musicology at the University of Warsaw. Her current research activity is focused upon the interrelationship between music and war at the turn of 1940s. A prolific author, she is the recipient of a number of prestigious prizes including the Feicht Award of the Musicologists' Section of the Polish Composers' Union in 2009 for her doctoral dissertation on music and aesthetics in the work of Constantin Regamey and the Hosenfeld/Szpilman Gedenkpreis presented at Lüneburg

University in January 2011 for her multimedia exhibition Music in Occupied Poland 1939–1945 presented several times in different language versions in France, Germany and Poland.

Francisco Parralejo Masa has written about the relationship between music and politics in different Spanish publications, including *Revista de Musicología* and *Audioclásica,* and has published articles on this subject in edited books in Spain, the United Kingdom and France. In 2005 he won a doctoral scholarship from the Junta de Castilla y León (Spain) and from 2006 to 2009 he taught at the University of Salamanca. During this time he undertook research visits to the University of Cambridge and the École des Hautes Études en Sciences Sociales (Paris). He is now finishing his PhD on music and politics in twentieth-century Spain and holds a chair in History of Music at the Professional Conservatory of Music 'Joaquín Villatoro' in Jerez de la Frontera (Spain).

James Parsons is Professor of Music History at Missouri State University, in Springfield, Missouri. He has lectured throughout the United States, the United Kingdom, Germany, Hungary, and the Czech Republic, and has published on the music of Mozart, Johann Friedrich Reichardt, Beethoven, Schubert, Hanns Eisler, and Ernst Krenek for *Austrian Studies, Beethoven Forum, Early Music, Eighteenth-Century Music,* the *Journal of the American Musicological Society, Music Analysis, Music & Letters,* and *Telos.* Support for his research has come from the National Endowment for the Humanities, the Fulbright Commission, and the German Academic Exchange (DAAD). In 2004 he edited *The Cambridge Companion to the Lied* for Cambridge University Press, a volume to which he also contributed two essays, one on the eighteenth-century Lied, the second on German song during the twentieth century.

Gemma Pérez Zalduondo holds a PhD in Art History (Musicology) and is a Professor at the University of Granada and principal researcher for the Spanish Ministry of Science and Innovation project *Music, ideology and politics in artistic culture during Francoism (1938–1975).* Her most recent scholarly work deals with the relation between music and ideology, politics, and power in Spain during the first decades of Francoism (1938–1958): transformational processes of musical discourse inherited from the nineteenth century during and after the Spanish Civil War, as well as its connections with the rest of Europe (*Una nueva música para el "Nuevo Estado": música, ideología y política en el primer franquismo.* (Seville: Libargo, 2013). She has also explored the role of music as propaganda within the framework of totalitarian regimes, and more specifically, in the cultural exchange between Spain, Italy, and Germany during World War II and has worked on different aspects of music in Spain during the first third of the twentieth century, such as the associationist phenomenon, identity discourse and musical critique in the context of the artistic culture of that time. Among her major publications is the interdisciplinary book *Cruces de caminos: intercambios musicales y artísticos en la Europa de la primera mitad del siglo XX* (Granada/Tours: Editorial Universidad de Granada, Ministry of Science and Innovation, and Université François-Rabelais de Tours, 2010). Her current research project is focused on music in Andalusia during the Civil War as well as policies enacted upon "popular" music that influenced Spanish music in in the 1950s which will appear in the forthcoming publication *Music and Francoism*, edited with Germán Gan Quesada, to be issued by Brepols.

Florian Scheding is Lecturer in Music at the University of Bristol, having previously occupied a similar post at the University of Southampton. A cultural historian of music, his main interest of research is music and migration, especially the displacement of European musics and musicians caused by the extreme political upheavals and catastrophes that characterise the Twentieth Century. He posits that an approach to music and music history through the lens of migration can challenge and enrich socio-cultural understandings of music as well as conceptions of music historiography. He has published on the music of migrant composers during World War II such as Mátyás Seiber and István Anhalt, music by émigrés for film, cabaret of diasporic communities, and historiographies of exile studies, amongst other topics. A collection of essays, *Music and Displacement: Diasporas, Mobilities and Dislocations in Europe and Beyond*, co-edited with Erik Levi, was published in spring 2010 by Scarecrow Press in the Europea series edited by Martin Stokes and Philip V. Bohlman.

Suzanne Snizek is currently Visiting Assistant Professor in Music at the University of Victoria, in British Columbia, Canada, where she teaches flute, chamber music, and a musicology course called 'Issues in Suppressed Music.' As a scholar, she has contributed chapters to the edited volumes *La Captivite de Guerre au XXe Siecle: Des Archives, Des Histoires, Des Memoires* (Paris: Armand Colin, 2012) and *Cultural Heritage and Prisoners of War: Creativity behind Barbed Wire* (New York: Routledge, 2012) as well as to various web and magazine articles. She is also an internationally active flautist, teacher, clinician and adjudicator.

Joshua S. Walden is Andrew W. Mellon Postdoctoral Fellow at Johns Hopkins University and The Peabody Institute. After receiving his PhD with Distinction from Columbia University, he held a Junior Research Fellowship at Merton College, University of Oxford, and an Edison Fellowship from the British Library Sound Archive. He is the editor of *Representation in Western Music* (Cambridge University Press, 2013) and *The Cambridge Companion to Jewish Music* (in progress for Cambridge University Press). His articles appear or are forthcoming in *Journal of the American Musicological Society, Journal of the Society for American Music, Journal of the Royal Musical Society, Musical Quarterly, Journal of Mod-*

ern Jewish Studies, and elsewhere. He has been awarded research grants from the American Musicological Society, the YIVO Institute for Jewish Research, and the British Academy.

Emile Wennekes is chair professor of Post-1800 Music History and former Head of School, Media and Culture Studies at Utrecht University, the Netherlands. He has published on diverse subjects including Amsterdam's Crystal Palace, Bernard Haitink, Bach and Mahler reception, and contemporary music in the Netherlands; some books are available in translation (six European languages and Chinese). He previously worked as a journalist for the Dutch dailies *NRC Handelsblad* and *de Volkskrant*, and was artistic advisor and orchestral programmer before intensifying his academic career. His current research focuses on three themes. Within the university, as well as under the auspices of the International Musicological Society (for which he chairs the Study Group Music and Media (MaM)), he focuses on 'Mediatizing Music'. A second topic concerns the measurement of stages of absorption while listening to music, and last, but not least, he researches the theme of the 'Remigration of Jewish Musicians'.

Ben Winters is Lecturer in Music at The Open University, UK. He read music at Christ Church, University of Oxford and returned to Christ Church in 2002 to read for a DPhil in musicology which he completed in 2006 with the aid of a University Graduate Studentship, a Halstead Scholarship, and a Wingate Fellowship. From 2006 to 2008, he was University Research Fellow in Musicology at City University, London; and from 2008 to 2009 he was an Early Career Research Associate at the Institute of Musical Research, University of London. He is the author of *Erich Wolfgang Korngold's* The Adventures of Robin Hood*: A Film Score Guide* (Lanham: Scarecrow Press, 2007) and *Music, Performance, and the Realities of Film: Shared Concert Experiences in Screen Fiction* (forthcoming, Routledge). He has published widely on Korngold and film music and his articles have appeared in *Music & Letters*, the *Journal of the Royal Musical Association*, *Cambridge Opera Journal*, *Brio*, *Music, Sound, and the Moving Image*, and *Interdisciplinary Humanities*. Recent publications include an edited issue of *Music, Sound, and the Moving Image* devoted to 'Music and Narrative in Film', and chapters in the following collections: *Music in the Western: Notes from the Frontier*, edited by Kathryn Kalinak (London: Routledge, 2011); *Music, Sound, and Filmmakers: Sonic Style in Cinema*, edited by James Wierzbicki (London: Routledge, 2012); and *Magic, Myth and Monsters: Music, Sound and Fantasy Cinema*, edited by Janet K. Halfyard (Sheffield: Equinox Press, 2012).

Index

böhlau

HARTMUT KRONES (HG.)

**HANNS EISLER – EIN KOMPONIST
OHNE HEIMAT?**

SCHRIFTEN DES WISSENSCHAFTSZENTRUMS
ARNOLD SCHÖNBERG, BAND 6

Hanns Eisler, (u. a.) Komponist der DDR-Nationalhymne, 1898 in Leipzig
geboren und 1962 in Berlin gestorben, war weder Leipziger noch Berliner,
sondern Wiener. Eisler, der zweijährig nach Wien zog und dort u. a. bei
Arnold Schönberg studierte, ging 1925 nach Berlin, emigrierte 1933 über
Wien und viele andere Stationen in die USA, wurde dort 1948 ausgewiesen,
erhielt dann in Wien keine Anstellung und übersiedelte schließlich 1949 nach
Ostberlin. Dort konnte er zwar Fuß fassen, fühlte sich aber nie „zu Hause".
Die Beiträge aus der Feder führender Eisler-Forscher befassen sich sowohl
mit diesen biografischen Umständen als auch mit Kompositionen, die Eislers
Sehnsucht nach einer „Heimat" dokumentieren.

2012. 486 S. ZAHLR. S/W-ABB., TAB. UND NOTENBSP. GB. 170 X 240 MM
ISBN 978-3-205-77503-4

BÖHLAU VERLAG, WIESINGERSTRASSE I, A-IOIO WIEN, T:+43 I 330 24 27-0
INFO@BOEHLAU-VERLAG.COM, WWW.BOEHLAU-VERLAG.COM | WIEN KÖLN WEIMAR

AMAURY DU CLOSEL

ERSTICKTE STIMMEN

„ENTARTETE MUSIK" IM DRITTEN REICH

Im Mai 1938 wurde in Düsseldorf unter der Ägide der nationalsozialistischen Kulturverantwortlichen eine Ausstellung mit dem Titel „Entartete Musik" eröffnet. Diffamiert wurden darin der „Musikbolschewismus", die atonale Musik, der Jazz und natürlich die Musik jüdischer Komponisten. Viele jener Künstler, die im Namen der Säuberung des deutschen Musiklebens damals auf den Index gesetzt wurden, haben – durch Deportation oder in der Anonymität des Exils verschwunden – ihren gebührenden Platz im heutigen Musikschaffen noch nicht wiedererlangt. Das große Verdienst von Amaury du Closels Buch besteht darin, dass es sich nicht nur auf die bekannten Namen wie Schönberg, Weill, Zemlinsky oder Schreker beschränkt, sondern das Leben und Wirken von rund 200 Komponisten rekonstruiert, die heute fast vergessen sind. Nach Erläuterung des ideologischen Konzeptes „Entartete Musik" beschreibt der Autor jene Institutionen und Gesetze, die die systematische Auslöschung der „unerwünschten" Elemente in der deutschen Musikwelt überhaupt erst ermöglichten. Im letzten Teil des Buches werden die Schicksale und Biografien der Komponisten im Exil in Frankreich, Großbritannien, der Schweiz, in den USA und Südamerika sowie in Japan dargestellt.

2010. 506 S. GB. 170 X 240 MM. | ISBN 978-3-205-78292-6

BÖHLAU VERLAG, WIESINGERSTRASSE I, A-IOIO WIEN, T:+43 I 330 24 27-0
INFO@BOEHLAU-VERLAG.COM, WWW.BOEHLAU-VERLAG.COM | WIEN KÖLN WEIMAR

ULRICH DRÜNER, GEORG GÜNTHER

MUSIK UND „DRITTES REICH"

FALLBEISPIELE 1910 BIS 1960 ZU
HERKUNFT, HÖHEPUNKT UND
NACHWIRKUNGEN DES
NATIONALSOZIALISMUS IN DER MUSIK

In der Musik beginnt das „Dritte Reich" nicht erst 1933 und endet nicht wirklich 1945. Dies ist die Einsicht, wenn man die Musik der Zeit von 1900 bis 1960 studiert. Der Band ist aus einem Antiquariatsprojekt von etwa 700 Dokumenten entstanden und begnügt sich nicht, wie bisher üblich, die musikalischen Makrostrukturen des „Dritten Reichs" anhand von 30 bis 40 Titeln zu illustrieren. Vielmehr wird in breiter dokumentarischer Fülle den Fragen nachgegangen, aus welchen Traditionen Musik und Musikwissenschaft der Nazis kamen, worin ihre ideologisch-ästhetische „Eigenart" besteht und wie sie nach 1945 weiter wirken. Ferner werden die „Entartete Musik" und die auf ihre Autoren gerichtete „Eliminierungs-Literatur" sowie die Musik in Exil und Emigration dargestellt. Viele Dokumente zeigen in erschütternder Direktheit, mit welchen Problemen die Musiker jener Zeit konfrontiert waren.

2012. 390 S. 45 S/W-ABB. GB. 170 X 240 MM | ISBN 978-3-205-78616-0

This is an admirable book based on meticulous research and immense knowledge.
[...] It has to be essential reading for all those interested in the subject.
                                        Journal of Contemporary European Studies

BÖHLAU VERLAG, WIESINGERSTRASSE 1, A-1010 WIEN, T:+43 1 330 24 27-0
INFO@BOEHLAU-VERLAG.COM, WWW.BOEHLAU-VERLAG.COM | WIEN KÖLN WEIMAR

böhlau

FRITZ TRÜMPI

POLITISIERTE ORCHESTER

DIE WIENER PHILHARMONIKER UND
DAS BERLINER PHILHARMONISCHE
ORCHESTER IM NATIONALSOZIALISMUS

Vor der Folie eines Vergleiches zwischen den Wiener und Berliner Philharmonikern im »Dritten Reich« liefert Fritz Trümpi eine detailreiche Studie über nationalsozialistische Musikpolitik. Die Politisierung der beiden Konkurrenzorchester, welche überdies den Städtewettbewerb zwischen Wien und Berlin repräsentierten, diente beiderseits der nationalsozialistischen Herrschaftssicherung, war in ihrer Ausführung aber von signifikanten Unterschieden geprägt. Ausgehend von einem vergleichenden Aufriss der Frühgeschichte der beiden Orchester untersucht der Autor Kontinuitäten und Brüche im Musikbetrieb nach der Machtübertragung an die Nationalsozialisten und dem »Anschluss« Österreichs an NS-Deutschland. Dazu greift Trümpi auf ebenso brisante wie vielfältige Archivmaterialien zurück, die hier zum Teil erstmals der Öffentlichkeit präsentiert werden.

2011. 357 S. 5 TAB., 17 GRAF. UND 9 S/W-ABB. BR. 170 X 240 MM.
ISBN 978-3-205-78657-3

»[...] Ein Buch, das in Berlin und Wien für Aufsehen sorgt [...] und einen spannenden Einblick in die nationalsozialistische Musikpolitik [eröffnet].«
        Aargauer Zeitung

BÖHLAU VERLAG, WIESINGERSTRASSE 1, A-1010 WIEN, T: +43 1 330 24 27-0
VERTRIEB@BOEHLAU.AT, WWW.BOEHLAU-VERLAG.COM

ALBRECHT DÜMLING

DIE VERSCHWUNDENEN MUSIKER

JÜDISCHE FLÜCHTLINGE
IN AUSTRALIEN

Als nach 1933 viele Musiker vom NS-Regime aus Deutschland und Österreich vertrieben wurden, führte die Flucht manche bis ins ferne Australien.
Hier mussten sie sich eine neue Existenz aufbauen. Während es einigen we-
nigen gelang, die Musikkultur ihrer neuen Heimat entscheidend mit zu prä-
gen, wurden andere als „feindliche Ausländer" interniert und oft zum Wech-
sel des Berufs gedrängt. So verschwanden sie auf doppelte Weise und fielen
nicht selten dem Vergessen anheim.

Das Buch ist das Ergebnis einer jahrelangen Spurensuche in Archiven. Es lebt
aber ebenso von den Erkenntnissen aus zahllosen Gesprächen mit Über-
lebenden und Zeitzeugen. Damit gelingt es Albrecht Dümling, ein neues,
bisher kaum beachtetes Kapitel der Kulturgeschichte des Exils aufzuschlagen.
Das Buch legt Zeugnis ab vom persönlichen Mut der verschwundenen
Musiker und von ihrem Überlebenswillen und Pioniergeist vor dem Hinter-
grund der rassischen, politischen oder religiösen Verfolgung durch das Dritte
Reich.

2011. 444 S. 43 S/W-ABB. 2 KT. IN RÜCKENT. GB. 170 X 240 MM.
ISBN 978-3-412-20666-6

BÖHLAU VERLAG, URSULAPLATZ I, D-50668 KÖLN, T:+49 221 913 90-0
INFO@BOEHLAU-VERLAG.COM, WWW.BOEHLAU-VERLAG.COM | WIEN KÖLN WEIMAR

EXIL.ARTE-SCHRIFTEN
HERAUSGEGEBEN VON GEROLD GRUBER

böhlau

BAND 1

BRENDAN G. CARROLL

ERICH WOLFGANG KORNGOLD

DAS LETZTE WUNDERKIND

2012. 480 S. 53 S/W-ABB. GB. 170 X 240 MM
ISBN 978-3-205-77716-8

Schon früh wurde Korngold als Wunderkind gefeiert und international erfolgreich. In Hollywood gelang ihm die Etablierung eines neuen musikalischen Genres, der Filmmusik à la Korngold, welche bis heute als Maßstab gilt.

BAND 2

PETER WEGELE

**DER FILMKOMPONIST MAX STEINER
(1888–1971)**

2012. 300 S. 18 S/W-ABB. UND 88 NOTENBSP. GB.
170 X 240 MM
ISBN 978-3-205-78801-0

Max Steiner, der Mann, der die sinfonische Filmmusik im sogenannten Goldenen Zeitalter Hollywoods etabliert hat, ist für viele Zeitgenossen unbekannt. Dieses Buch ist die erste Monografie über diesen Filmmusikpionier.

BÖHLAU VERLAG, WIESINGERSTRASSE I, A-IOIO WIEN, T:+43 I 330 24 27-0
INFO@BOEHLAU-VERLAG.COM, WWW.BOEHLAU-VERLAG.COM | WIEN KÖLN WEIMAR